Robert Patterson

Fables of Infidelity and Facts of Faith

Robert Patterson

Fables of Infidelity and Facts of Faith

ISBN/EAN: 9783744793308

Printed in Europe, USA, Canada, Australia, Japan

Cover: Foto ©Thomas Meinert / pixelio.de

More available books at **www.hansebooks.com**

FABLES OF INFIDELITY

AND

FACTS OF FAITH.

A SERIES OF TRACTS

ON THE ABSURDITY OF

ATHEISM, PANTHEISM, AND RATIONALISM.

BY

ROBERT PATTERSON.

———•———

CINCINNATI:
AMERICAN REFORM TRACT AND BOOK SOCIETY.
1860.

PREFACE TO THE THIRD EDITION.

This is not so much a volume upon the Evidences of Christianity, as an examination of the Evidences of Infidelity. When the infidel tells us that Christianity is false, and asks us to reject it, he is bound of course to provide us with something better and truer instead; under penalty of being considered a knave trying to swindle us out of our birthright, and laughed at as a fool, for imagining that he could persuade mankind to live and die without religion. Suppose he had proved to the world's satisfaction that all religion is a hoax, and all men professing it are liars?—how does that comfort me in my hour of sorrow? Scoffing will not sustain a man in his solitude, when he has nobody to scoff at; and disbelief is only a bottomless tub, which will not float me across the dark river. If infidels intend to convert the world, they must give us some positive system of truth which we can believe, and venerate, and trust.

A glimmering idea of this necessity seems lately to have dawned upon some of them. It is quite possible that they have also felt the want of something for their own souls to believe; for an infidel has a soul, a poor, hungry, starved soul, just like other men. At any rate, having grown tired of pelting the Church with the dirt-balls of Voltaire and Paine, they begin to acknowledge that it is, after all, an institution; and that the Bible is an influential book, both popular and useful in its way. Mankind, it seems, will have a Church and a Bible of some sort; why not go to work and make a Church and Bible of their own? Accordingly they have gone to work, and in a very short time, have prepared a variety of ungodly religions, so various that the worldly-minded man who can not be suited with one to his taste, must be very hard to please. Discordant and contradictory in their positive statements, they are agreed only in negatives; denying the God of the Bible, the resurrection of the dead, and judgment to come. Nevertheless each discoverer or constructor presents his system to the world with great confidence, large claims to superior benevolence, vast pretensions to learning and science, and no little cant about duty and piety. Wonderful to tell, some of them are very fond of clothing their ungodliness in the language of Scripture.

No pains are spared to secure the wide-spread of these notions. Prominent infidels are invited to deliver courses of scientific lectures, in which the science is made the medium of conveying the infidelity. Scientific books, novels, magazines, daily newspapers, and common school books, are all enlisted in the work. The disciples of infidelity are numerous and zealous. It would be hard to find a factory, boarding-house, steamboat or hotel, where twelve persons are employed, without an infidel; and harder still to find an infidel who will not use his influence to poison his associates.

These systems are well adapted to the depraved tastes of the age. The business man, whose whole soul is set on money-making and spending, is right glad to meet the Secularist, who will prove to him on scientific principles, that a man is much profited by gaining the whole world, even at the risk of his soul, if he has such a thing. The young and ill-instructed professor of Christianity, whose longings for forbidden joys are strong, has a natural kindliness toward Rationalism, which befogs the serene light of God's holy law, and gives the directing power to his own inner liking. The sentimental young lady, who would recoil from the grossness of the Deist, is attracted by the poetry of Pantheism. Infidelity has had, in consequence, a degree of success very little suspected by simple-minded pastors and parents, and which is often discovered too late for remedy.

These tracts are written to expose the *folly* of some of these novel systems of infidelity—leaving others to show their wickedness. It may surprise some who would glory in being esteemed fiends, to learn that they are only fools. If they should be awakened now to a sense of the absurdities which they cherish as philosophy, it might save them from awaking another day to the shame and everlasting contempt of the universe.

I have not taken up all the cavils of infidelity. Their name is Legion. Nor have I troubled my readers with any which they are not likely to hear. Leaving the sleeping dogs to lie, I have noticed only such as I have known to bark and bite in my own vicinity, and know to be prevalent here in the west. They are stated as nearly as possible in the words in which I have heard them in public debate, or in private conversation with gentlemen of infidel principles. I have made no references to books or writers on that side, save to such as I am assured were the sources of their sentiments. In such cases I have named and quoted the authors. Where no such quotations are noticed it will be understood that I am responsible for the fairness with which I have represented the opinions which are examined. It is not my design to fight men of straw. One entire Lecture—that on Prophesy—was rewritten, because, as originally delivered, it did not fully and fairly represent the present position of infidels on that subject.

Every historical or scientific fact adduced in support of the arguments here used is confirmed by reference to the proper authority. But it has not been deemed needful to crowd the pages with references to the works of Butler, Buchanan, Paley, Leland, and the other great Christian apologists, from whom the greater part of what is valuable in these tracts has been drawn. The Christian scholar does not need such references; and to those for whose benefit I write, their names carry no authority, and their arguments are generally quite unknown. One great object of my labor will be gained if I shall succeed in awaking the spirit of inquiry among my readers, to such an extent as to lead them to a prayerful and patient perusal of several of the works named on the next page. They have heard only one side of the question, and will be surprised at their own ignorance of matters which they ought to have known.

Books on the evidences are not generally circulated. Ministers perhaps have some volumes in their libraries; but in a hundred houses, it would be hard to find half a dozen containing as many as would give an inquiring youth a fair view of the historical evidences of the truth of the gospel. Nor where they are to be found are they generally read. Being deemed heavy reading, the magazine or the newspaper is preferred. Ministers do not in general devote enough of their time to such sound teaching as will stop the mouths of gainsayers. I have been assured by skeptical gentlemen, who in the early part of their lives had attended church regularly for twenty-two years, that during all that time they had never heard a single discourse on the evidences. Moreover the protean forms of infidelity are so various, and many of its present positions so novel, that books or discourses prepared only twenty years ago, miss the mark; and rather expose to the charge of misrepresentation, than produce conviction. New books on infidelity are needed.

When these tracts were first published, it was not designed to make a book. Treating of different and discordant systems of irreligion, whose only common bond is opposition to the gospel, they are necessarily somewhat unconnected. The design was to make each tract as complete in itself as space permitted, and to secure a broadcast distribution of each among its own appropriate class of readers. This plan the writer still prefers. Hundreds will read a tract, who will not lift a volume. Forty or fifty penny tracts may be circulated for the price of one volume. But a very general desire having been expressed to have them collected into a volume, and the first edition in that form having been speedily exhausted, they are now presented in an improved dress, with the addition of a tract on the relations of Faith and Science. Fully conscious of many imperfections, yet firmly persuaded of the power of the truth which it exhibits, the writer commits this volume to Him whose Word does not return to him void.

CHICAGO, *December* 22, 1858.

Names of a few of the Standard Works on the Evidences of the Being and Perfections of God, and of the Truth and Authority of the Scriptures,

To be had of any respectable bookseller, or in public libraries.

Modern Atheism, by James Buchanan, L.L. D.
Typical Forms and Special Ends in Creation, by James McCosh, L.L. D., and George Dickie, M. D.
Religion and Geology, Edward Hitchcock, L.L. D.
The Architecture of the Heavens, J. P. Nichol, L.L. D.
The Christian Philosopher, Thomas Dick, L.L. D.
Natural Theology, William Paley, D. D.
The Analogy of Religion, Natural and Revealed, to the Constitution and Course of Nature, Joseph Butler, D. C. L.
The Bridgewater Treatises, Whewell, Chalmers, Kidd, &c.
The Comprehensive Commentary, William Jenks, D. D.
The Cause and Cure of Infidelity, Rev. David Nelson.
A View of the Evidences of Christianity, William Paley, D. D.
The Eclipse of Faith, ascribed to Henry Rogers.
The Restoration of Belief, ascribed to Isaac Taylor.
Lectures on the Evidences of Christianity, University of Virginia.
The Divine Authority of the Old and New Testaments Asserted, J. Leland, D. D.
An Apology for the Bible, in a series of letters to Thomas Paine, R. Watson.
A View of the Internal Evidence of the Christian Religion, S. Jenyns.
A Letter to G. West, Esq., on the Conversion of St. Paul, Lord Lyttleton.
Observations on the History and Evidence of the Resurrection of Jesus Christ, Gilbert West, Esq.
Difficulties of Infidelity, Faber.
Dissertations on the Prophecies, Thos. Newton, D. D.
An Introduction to the Critical Study of the Scriptures, T. H. Horne, Vol. 1.
The Evidences of Christianity, Charles Petit McIlvaine, D.D.

It is not supposed that any one person can read all these, but the reader is earnestly recommended to read several, that he may see the great variety of proofs which confirm Christianity, and which it is impossible for any single writer to exhibit.

CONTENTS.

No. 22. *I Don't Believe in Religion.*
Page.
Unbelief a Misfortune, ... 13
No harm in Opinions, ... 16
Unbelief rebels against God, ... 18
An Enemy to Civilization, Liberty and Humanity, ... 22

No. 23. *Did the World Make Itself?*
Eternity of Matter and Development Theory, ... 25
Marks of a Designer in the Structure of the Eye, ... 31
The Eye Maker sees, over a wide Field, far, and perfectly, .. 38
God's Eye upon you, ... 40

No. 24. *Is God Everybody and Everybody God?*
Pantheism, an antiquated Hindoo Notion, ... 41
A System of Deception and Hypocrisy, ... 66
Grossly immoral, ... 49
Virtual Atheism, ... 52

No. 25. *Have We any Need of The Bible?*
Civilization and the Bible, ... 57
Revelation impossible—Myths, ... 95
Revelation useless—the Inner Light, ... 63
Heathen and Infidels ignorant of God and Heaven, ... 72
Infidel and Heathen Morality—Plato's, Voltaire's, Paine's, . 76

No. 26. *Who Wrote the New Testament?*
The Bible not just like any other Book, ... 85
Two modes of Investigation, ... 86
Did the Council of Nice make the Bible? 89
The Mythical Theory—Evidence of Celsus 90
The Fragment Hypothesis—Bank Signature Book 92
The New Testament could not be corrupted, ... 99

No. 27. *Is the Gospel Fact or Fable?*
Historical Evidence—cotemporary, and epistolary,......... 97
Letters of Pliny, Peter, and John..............................102
Prove the existence, worship, holiness, and sufferings of the early Churches,..104

No. 28. *Can We Believe Christ and his Apostles?*
Gospel unique—Must take or refuse it as a Whole.......113
Testimony to its Truth circumstantial,.......................118
Witnesses numerous and independent,.......................120
Confirmed by their Sufferings and Death,....................123

No. 29. *Prophecy.*
Napoleon's—Apollo's—Obscurity,..............................129
Any Philosopher may predict Downfall of Empires,.......135
An awful Truth—if it be true,..................................136
Bible Predictions not the Indications of Experience,......137
Applications of *Moral*, not of *Natural* Law,.................139
Predict very improbable Overturns of Nations,.............141
Predict very improbable *Preservations*,......................149
Grand Distinction of God's Prophecy,........................155

No. 30. *Moses and the Prophets.*
What is Meant by Calling God the Author of the Bible?.161
Different Views of Inspiration—Every Book Inspired?....164
Connection of the Bible History and Morality,..............172
Rationalistic Explanation of the Miracles,...................173
Political Importance of the Sacred Books,...................174
The Testimony of Christ..175
Objections.—The Lost Books of Scripture,...................179
       The Law Abolished by the Gospel,............180
       The Imperfect Morality of Judaism,..........181
       The Imprecations of the Old Testament,.....182

No. 31. *Infidelity Among the Stars.*
Scientific Objections to the Bible,..............................189
    The Infinity and Self-Existence of the Universe,...193
Buffon's Cosmogony—Explosion of a Planet,.............219
The Nebular Hypothesis—La Place's Theory,............207
The Possibility of any Theory of Creation,................214

No. 32. *Daylight Before Sunrise.*

Infidel Objections to Genesis, ... 217
   The Hindoo and Egyptian Chronologies, ... 218
   The Bible wrong about the Age of the Earth, ... 228
   The Bible tells us that the Firmanent is solid, ... 232
   Light before the Sun, ... 238

No. 33. *Telescopic Views of Scripture.*

The Source of the Water of the Deluge, ... 253
The Stars fighting against Sisera, ... 255
The Circuit of the Sun—Grand Motion of the Stars, ... 264
Abraham's Seed as the Stars of the Sky for Multitude, ... 274
Future Glories of the Abode of the Redeemed, ... 280

No. 34. *Science, or Faith.*

Must Faith disappear before the Certainties of Science? ... 285
   Uncertainties of Science, ... 286
   Mathematics, ... 286
   Astronomy, ... 288
   Geology, ... 293
Your Science all founded upon Faith, ... 300
Faith Sufficient for this Life, ... 303
We need a Knowledge of which Science is ignorant, ... 304
All our dearest interests in the Region of Faith, ... 305
Religion the most experimental of the Sciences, ... 306
Religious Experience better attested than Science, ... 311
Religion the only Science which can make you happy, ... 313

No. 22.

I DON'T BELIEVE IN RELIGION.

"I don't believe in religion." So a great many people say, and a greater number think. When one of this class is urged to love Christ, to pray to God, to read the Bible, to keep the Sabbath holy, to worship God in his family, and bring them to Church, or any other plainly commanded duty which he dislikes, he will coolly reply, "I am not a member of the Church; I don't believe in religion." As if he supposed that the authority of God's law depended on his pleasure, or the truth of religion upon his belief of it.

Some of these unbelievers will lament their unbelief as a misfortune which somehow or other has befallen them. They would like to enjoy that high religious feeling which Christians possess, but really they are unable to believe the dogmas of religion. And as their opinions are the inevitable result of their education and circumstances, if they should happen to be wrong, they can not help it, but must just rely upon the infinite mercy of God to preserve them from the consequences of error, and do not see why they may not please God as well as the rest of the world, most of whom do not give themselves very much trouble about religion.

But this convenient creed is short at both ends. For the teaching of the Bible is that the rest of the world does not please God at all, but is crowding down the broad road to destruction; and the particular business of the Holy Spirit is to convince the world of this sin of unbelief. And if unbelief of the truth be a misfortune, and the mercy of God has not prevented it from falling upon them, it may happen that it will not prevent a further misfortune of the belief of a lie from falling upon them, for misfortunes never come single. If a blind man shall undertake to walk a crooked road, sincerely believing it to be straight, neither God's mercy nor his sincerity shall prevent him from falling into the ditch. So if a wordly-minded man shall persist in the belief that ungodliness is just as pleasing to God as piety, and contemptuously despise mercy and salvation through Christ, and sincerely believe that he is better off in the devil's service than in God's worship,

13

I see no good reason why God's mercy, which allowed all these unfortunate delusions to come upon him, may not as well allow them to remain upon him—and as he has had the misfortune to live in his sins because of his unbelief, why he may not have the misfortune to die in his sins, because of his unbelief—and, as God's mercy did not prevent him from despising the service of God in this world, why it may not well enough consist with allowing him to remain of the same opinion in the next world; aye, and to continue of the same opinion throughout eternity—and as his opinion led him to serve the devil on earth, notwithstanding God's mercy, why the same opinion may not lead him to continue in the devil's service in hell, notwithstanding God's mercy; for surely God's mercy is not bound to drag people to heaven, whether they will or no. If unbelief, then, be a misfortune merely, it is certainly a great one, the cause and beginning of many others, a fire that will surely burn the house it has caught on, a sickness that will be the death of the sufferer. The man who will not believe God's truth, must of necessity believe the devil's lie—for there is no third theory—and so live in error, and die in error, and find himself as far astray from truth and happiness in the next world as he was when he left this. And so unbelief and perdition are as firmly chained together by common sense, as they are by Holy Scripture, which says, "*He that believeth not shall be damned.*"

But still you may urge that, "It is very hard that God should damn a man for his opinions, seeing he cannot help them—that belief or unbelief is wholly involuntary. We believe where we have sufficient evidence; and where we do not see sufficient evidence, we can not believe if we would. If I see any thing with my own eyes, I cannot help believing it. If I have had experience of any feeling, I can not help believing its reality. If any scientific problem is mathematically proved to me, I can not help believing it. But religion gives no such proof to me; therefore I can not believe it. Its doctrines are beyond my comprehension. The miracles recorded in Scripture are contrary to all my experience, and the duties it requires are utterly beyond my power to perform. How can I believe such a mass of mysteries, or live up to such a standard of piety?"

The truth or falsehood of the Gospel does not depend on your likes or dislikes, nor the authority of God's law on your notions of your ability to keep it. God nowhere commands you to understand the mysteries of religion any more than the mysteries of nature. You never allege that you can not believe that the sunshine is warm and bright because you can not explain how it is so. Nor is the evidence on which you are called to believe the truths of religion the evidences of your senses; for you believe in God I hope, yet you never saw him: nor yet the evidence of your own experience; for you believe you will die, though neither you nor any one living ever experienced death. You have no more need for mathematical demonstration of the authenticity of the Bible, before you believe it and frame your life by it, than of the authenticity of the Constitution of the United States, or of the laws of Ohio, of which, nevertheless, you have not the slightest doubt, and frame your life accordingly.

And now, as to your not being able to help your unbelief, we will inquire a little into that. A person believes according to the evidence he sees of the truth of any statement, or according to the confidence he has in the integrity of the person who makes it. His view of the evidence depends upon the attention he gives to it. There may be sufficient evidence for the truth of religion, but the man who does not attend to it will not see it. The astronomer knows very well that the earth moves round the sun, because he has studied the evidence of that truth; while the savage who has not, or the school-boy who will not, obstinately asserts that the sun moves round the earth. This they very sincerely believe, because of their ignorance; and while they are ignorant they can not help believing as they do; but surely no one will say that they can not help their erroneous belief, unless he can show that they can not help their ignorance. The things revealed in the Bible are not self-evident truths—had they been so we had needed no Bible: he who would believe them must attend to the evidences of their truth which God has furnished. If any one, either from dislike of these truths themselves, or of the duties to which they lead, will refuse or neglect to consider these evidences, it is very certain that he will not believe them, and still more certain that he should not affirm that he can not help his unbelief. So when you say you can not believe the Bible in general, or some of its particular truths, that may be very true, because you keep yourself in ignorance of the evidence; but while you keep yourself ignorant, it is false to say you can not help your unbelief. You can certainly read the Bible through, from beginning to end. That is the very least examination that any book, worth reading at all, can receive. You know that it would be only a lie to your own conscience to say, "I can not help my unbelief of this book, which I have never read." Now I put it to your own conscience, Have you read the Bible through, yea or not? If not, your unbelief is wilful. You can help it, but you will not.

When I speak of reading the Bible, I do not mean such a cursory and forced perusal as a lazy school-boy gives his arithmetic, reading the words and figures because he is told to do so, but never giving any serious study to learn their meaning, nor applying to his teacher for aid in his difficulties; but, after yawning over a page or two, throwing down the book with disgust, and saying he can not believe such nonsense. Just so some persons read the Bible, either because they are told to do so by their parents, or because their consciences say they should; but they fill their hearts and minds with other matters, and when their sleepy attention is by chance roused enough to see a difficulty, they never grapple with it; and, though God has promised his Holy Spirit as a teacher to those who ask him, they never thought it worth while to try whether he was in earnest or not. Now, let the conscience of every such person answer, Is it your fault or God's that you are thus impious? Until, then, you repent of your impiety, and earnestly pray for the Holy Spirit to teach you the truth, and pray in vain, it is utterly false for you to say that you can not help your unbelief. Your religion or irreligion is just as much a matter of your own choice as the trade you practice or neglect, at your pleasure.

But still it is urged: "Granting that we do choose our belief, what great harm can there be in doubting certain mysterious dogmas, or denying certain religious doctrines? There must certainly be room for harmless differences about religion, as well as about other things. My belief or unbelief can do no injury to God, who is far removed beyond the reach of my opinions. And if my opinions do no injury to my neighbors, I see no reason why I should perish eternally on account of them, even though they should prove to be erroneous, and I might have known better."

If,—aye, that is just the point, that *if.* Let us inquire whether unbelief of God's word, and contempt for God's law, be injurious treatment of Him or not; and whether a life of ungodliness and irreligion be a harmless example to set before your neighbors; and whether God could, with safety to the universe, allow such people as you to think and do as they please with impunity.

The character of the person whom you refuse to believe has certainly something to do with this matter, though you seem not to have thought of that at all. There are thousands of persons in this world who have no special claim upon your attention, and yet the honor due to all men as fellow-beings demands that when one of them addresses you, you listen to his communication. It is not until a person has earned the character of a public liar and cheat that you refuse him a hearing, and turn him out of doors. By your wilful unbelief and neglect of religion you treat God with more contempt than you would show to any passing stranger, and turn Him out to receive the like disrespect from others. If an intimate friend addressed a letter to you, and you returned it unanswered, unperused, unopened, every person who knew that, would at once conclude that this friend had deceived and injured you, and that you took this method of closing your intercourse with him, to prevent him from deceiving and injuring you again. God has been a good friend to you; yet you will neither read his letter nor believe his communication. Is that kindly to your friend? When the Secretary of Congress sends authenticated copies of the laws of the United States to the governors and people of the various States, if some of them should refuse to read them, and say they did not mean to pay any attention to them, because they did not believe in such things, would you think that this was simply a queer opinion of these people, but one that had no great harm in it? Would you think them good loyal American citizens, albeit they would neither acknowledge the Constitution, obey the laws, or submit to the judges? Would you not say that their rejection of the documents argued their disloyalty to the Government that sent them, that their disobedience proved their treason, and that their rebellion called for all the forces of the nation to suppress and punish it? God is your Governor. He has sent you a communication, but you will not receive it. It contains his laws, but you will not read them. You live in the daily violation of them, and say to your fellow-man you hope it is no harm, that your opinions on religion differ from God's, and surely there can be no great harm in one's opinions. When you answer to God for your sins, will you dare to say that you transgressed his law because you did not believe it—that indeed you never read it—that you did not think such a matter worthy of the least attention—that you did not believe in religion?

The Lord Jesus Christ is certainly worthy of better treatment than you give him. If you could prove him to be a liar and an impostor, if you could show that his teachings were impure and unholy, and that the record of his mighty works was all a fable, then your unbelief would be blameless. There is no middle ground for you to take. Jesus is either what he said he was—the Son of God, the Savior of sinners; and his Gospel is what he declares it is—God's message for your soul's salvation; or he is not what he professed to be, and so is a liar and an impostor, and as such to be despised by all honest men. This is what every unbeliever says by his conduct, namely, that Jesus is not worthy of belief. Now let me press this upon the conscience of every half-way unbeliever who may read this tract: Are you prepared to prove Jesus Christ to be an impostor and a cheat? Will you go to the judgment seat of God with the evidence in your hands that he is a liar, and his Gospel an imposture? It makes no difference what the form of your unbelief may be, whether you are a scoffing libertine or a decent church-goer—whether you have sense enough to see the consequence of unbelief, and honesty enough to avow it—or whether you try to cloak the unbelief of your heart by an oily-tongued civility—the language of every person who does not profess a hearty faith in Christ, and become a member of his Church, is most plainly and unmistakeably this:

"I do not believe Jesus Christ to be the Son of God."

"I do not believe that God sent him into the world."

"I do not believe that he taught the truth."

"I do not believe that he wrought miracles."

"I do not believe that he died to save sinners."

"I do not believe in forgiveness through his blood."

"I do not believe that he rose from the dead."

"I do not believe that he ascended up into heaven."

"I do not believe that he governs the world."

"I do not believe that he will come again to judge me and all the world at the last day."

"But I believe that—

"The Bible is a fable."

"That such a person as the Jesus it describes never lived."

"That the Apostles were vile lying impostors," and,

"That all Christians are either knaves or fools."

Can you imagine that it is an affair of no consequence that you thus vilify Christ and his Gospel, and put him to open shame?

The Holy Spirit bears witness to the truth of God's message, and of Christ's mission. He has attested the truth of the gospel by many most wonderful works; among others by teaching the first preachers to proclaim it in languages they never learned from man, else it had never come to your ears. Multitudes of those who saw these miracles were convinced so fully of the divinity of the gospel, that they suffered death rather than disown it. The Holy Spirit has given you stronger evidence of the truth of the facts of the gospel history, of the life and death, and resurrection of the Lord Jesus, than you ever had of any other history whatever. You have no such abundance of conclusive proof that such a man as George Washington lived and fought his country's battles, or that the Continental Congress declared the Independence of these United States, as you have that Jesus Christ rose from the dead, and that his Apostles preached the gospel and planted churches to preserve and proclaim it over the world. You have only one national holiday in the year to commemorate the Declaration of Independence, while every week has a "Lord's Day," to celebrate the resurrection of your Lord, and every church bell rings out in your hearing, "Christ is risen, Christ is risen." If you suppose it an easy matter to get people persuaded to give up their usual employments, and celebrate commemorations of things which never happened, you can try the experiment. Suppose you persuade the people of Kentucky, black and white, bond and free, to observe the 4th of August every year as a holy day, and to go to church and give thanks to God for the dissolution of the Union, or for some other event which never happened, and which, if they can help it, never will. You would, doubtless, be sent to the nearest lunatic asylum before you had proceeded far on such an errand. Now, do you think Christ and his Apostles were such madmen, or that the hundreds of thousands who believed them were fools? Or, that at some later period, the world was peopled with a race of idiots, and suddenly, in Italy and England, in Syria and Switzerland, in France and Persia, in Germany and Africa, a number of knowing men invented the gospel story, and got them to believe it, and persuaded them to employ a day in every week in hearing and commemorating events in which they were no ways interested, and which, in fact, never happened? How do you account for the observance of the Lord's Day, and of the Lord's Supper, and the existence of the Church of Christ? By your saying, "I don't believe in religion," you would make out these things to be all delusions of Satan. Are the struggles of your own conscience from the same source? Is it a light thing to strive with the Spirit of God, and quench the light within you, and feed your own soul with a miserable lie, which for very shame you dare not put into words, and tell to your neighbors?

Do you really believe that it is in no way offensive to God, that you treat his message with such contempt as you would not show to the meanest of your neighbors—that you receive his Son as a lying impostor—that you treat the writings inspired by the Holy Ghost as forgeries, and His ordinances as fooleries, and drown His voice in your own soul as a delusion? Is it a small sin to despise the Father, to reject the Son, and do despite to the Spirit of Grace? Or do you suppose He is only jesting who says, "*Vengeance is mine I will repay, saith the Lord.*"

And now let us inquire whether your unbelief be not as injurious to your neighbors as it is offensive to God, and hurtful to your own soul. Your opinions, it is true, will hurt nobody so long as you keep them to yourself. But you do not. Every action of your ungodly life proclaims them. Your neighbors all know that you do not serve God, that you do not love Christ, that you do not belong to his Church, and you tell them, "I don't believe in religion." So, by precept and example, you do your best to make them all of the same opinions, and teach them to imitate your practices. If irreligion and ungodliness be good for you, it is equally good for them. It is not your fault that all the world is not of your way of thinking and acting, for, if they would be guided by you, they would every one say as you say, "I don't believe in religion." God judges you according to your heart and intention, and according to the tendency of your conduct, though he does not let you do all the evil you would; just as you judge the villain to be an incendiary, and worthy of the penitentiary, who sets fire to your house, though you see it, and put it out before it is burned down.

Let us see now what would be the consequences of your unbelief to your neighbors, if God did not prevent them. Your forefathers were naked savages, with a piece of raw hide thrown over their shoulders, who lived in wattled huts, and ate roasted acorns, and burned their own children in sacrifice to devils. If you have a coat to your back to-day, or a loaf of bread in your cupboard, if you have a market to go to, or a road to reach it; if you have a school for your children, or children to send to it, you owe all these blessings to that religion which you say you don't believe. Yet you would do what you could to stop its progress, and allow the savage and the heathen to live on in misery, and butcher each other, as they ever have done, and say, "O, my opinions do no harm to my neighbors." Are you not worse than a savage?

You are an American—a friend of liberty. For six thousand years tyrants have trampled upon the liberties of mankind. Pharaohs and Nebuchadnezzars, Emperors of Rome and Emperors of Russia, the Sea Kings of Europe and the Khans of Tartary, Kings of France and Emperors of Germany, one race of tyrants after another, with bloody sword or legal chain, has hewn down the rights of men, and manacled their God-given liberties in every land where the religion of Christ has not reigned. The world's history does not show a single exception. The only notion of true liberty you have, you learned from the Bible. The manliness to speak for it, and fight for it, and die for it, which bequeathed your birth-right of liberty, your Puritan fathers gathered from religion. Religion, Christ's religion, which makes men free indeed, is the only safeguard of liberty. There is no liberty at this moment save in those lands where the religion of Christ prevails. Look over the map of the world. Have the people of China liberty? Are the people of Russia free? Have the butchering, kidnapping tribes of Africa freedom. Is Mohammedan despotism liberty? Is South American anarchy liberty? Would you submit to the police of France, or take a lodging in the dungeons of Italy? Would you exchange the Constitution for the Austrian concordat, or the ballot-box for three revolutions in the year? England and America, the lands of liberty, are the lands of religion; but you "don't believe in religion." A whole nation once did not. They voted that there was no God, that death was an eternal sleep, that reason was the only ruler, that the Sabbath and the worship of God should cease. Then, having removed the law of God, the only foundation on which the law of man can rest, they commenced butchering each other, until the streets of Paris ran ankle deep with blood, and the remnant rushed into the arms of absolute military despotism as a refuge from atheistic anarchy. And this, unbeliever, is what you would bring your country to, if you could. Let every one adopt your opinions, and we would have all the horrors of the French Revolution, and of Napoleon's decrees, and conscriptions and proscriptions, before seven years. How dare you say your unbelief does no harm to your neighbor, when it undermines the citadel of your country's liberties?

Your neighbors have consciences and souls. They know they have offended God. The guilt of unforgiven sin is a grievous load upon the heart of a sorrow-stricken, dying man. He knows, he feels in every fibre of his soul, that losses and disappointments, that sorrows and pains, that agony of mind and sickness of body, which ever follow the transgression of God's laws, are marks of God's displeasure. His common sense tells him that these things befall sinners too uniformly to happen by chance, and that the God who sends them has some reason for thus visiting sin. He knows, he feels, that if God continues to deal with sinners after death as he has done before it, the sinner will have sorrow. Then this death which approaches! Almighty God smiting every sinner with the sword of death, making earth one vast grave-yard, and tne human race, shrieking and flying from the fearful foe, compelled to become its tenants! What does it mean? And conscience says, and Scripture says, and he knows it to be true, *"The wages of sin is death."* O to be freed from this sin! O to be delivered from this punishment of a sore wounded conscience, of the pangs of guilt, of the present dread, and dreadful prospect of deserved torment! He has no power to repair the past, little ability to amend the brief future. What shall he do to be saved? In this extremity the gospel comes to his ears, the only religion on earth which even professes to offer free forgiveness of sins. He hears repentance and remission of sins proclaimed in Jesus' name. He is told, *"Believe on the Lord Jesus Christ and thou shalt be saved and thy house."* He inclines to believe the joyful sound, to accept pardon and peace in Jesus. But you stand at his side, and with a contemptuous smile you inform him, "I don't believe in religion."

Inhuman wretch! Were you able to prove religion false, surely in such a world of sorrow, and with such a certainty of a coming world of woe as its falsehood would render inevitable, it were horrid cruelty to snatch from the parched lips of the dying sinner the only draught of peace which earth affords. But how awful your conduct, seeing that you can not prove it false, nay, that in your own soul you more than suspect it true! You dash in pieces the chalice which contains the blood of Christ—you laugh to scorn the voice of mercy to a dying world—you chase peace from earth and hope of heaven from men.

Unbeliever! This is the hellish malignity of your sin. You turn your face to the way of ruin—you murder the only religion that can deliver men from sin and hell—you close the gates of heaven, put the torch to God's building of mercy, open the bottomless pit of woe, and plunge every sinner of earth into everlasting perdition! How long, think you, will God tolerate such an enemy of God and man?

Fly, fly to Christ for pardon of your awful guilt. Bless God that there is forgiveness even for such as you. And say to every one of your acquaintances to whom you have declared your unbelief, *"It is a faithful saying, and worthy of all acceptation, that Christ Jesus came into the world to save sinners, of whom I am chief."*

"God so loved the world that he gave his only begotten Son, that whosoever believeth in Him should not perish, but have everlasting life. For God sent not his Son into the world to condemn the world, but that the world, through Him, might be saved. He that believeth on Him is not condemned; but he that believeth not is condemned already, because he hath not believed in the name of the only begotten Son of God. And this is the condemnation, that light is come into the world, and men loved darkness rather than light, because their deeds were evil. For every one that doeth evil hateth the light, neither cometh to the light, lest his deeds should be reproved. But he that doeth truth cometh to the light, that his deeds may be made manifest that they are wrought in God.

"He that cometh from heaven is above all, and what he hath seen

and heard that he testifieth, and no man receiveth his testimony. He that hath received his testimony hath set to his seal that God is true. For he whom God hath sent speaketh the words of God, for God giveth not the Spirit by measure unto him. The Father loveth the Son, and hath given all things into his hand. He that believeth on the Son hath everlasting life; and he that believeth not the Son shall not see life, but the wrath of God abideth on him."—JOHN, chap. 3.

No. 23.

DID THE WORLD MAKE ITSELF.

Understand, ye brutish among the people;
And, ye fools, when will ye be wise?
He that planted the ear, shall he not hear?
He that formed the eye, shall he not see?
He that chastiseth the heathen, shall he be not correct?
He that teacheth man knowledge, shall he not know?—PSALM 94: 8, 9.

Has the Creator of the world common sense? Did he know what he was about in making it? Had he any object in view in forming it? Does he know what is going on in it? Does he care whether it answers any purpose or not? Strange questions you will say; yet we need to ask a stranger question: Had the world a creator, or did it make itself? There are persons who say it did, and with brazen-faced impudence declare that the Bible sets out with a lie when it says, that "In the beginning God created the heavens and the earth." Whereas, say they, "We know that matter is eternal, and the world is wholly composed of matter; therefore, the heavens and the earth are eternal—never had a beginning nor a creator."

But, however fully the Atheist and the Pantheist may know that matter is eternal, we do not know any such thing, and must be allowed to ask, *How do you know?* As you are not eternal, we cannot take it on your word.

The only reason which any body ever ventured for this amazing assertion is this, that "all philosophers agree that matter is indestructible by its very nature; that it can never cease to exist. You may boil water into steam, but it is all there in the steam; or burn coal into gas, ashes and tar, but it is all in the gas, ashes, and tar; you may change the outward form as much as you please, but you cannot destroy the substance of any thing. Wherefore, as matter is indestructible, it must be eternal."

Profound reasoning! Here is a brick fresh from the kiln, which will last for a thousand years to come; therefore, it has existed for a thousand years past!

The foundation of the argument is as rotten as the superstructure. It is not agreed among all philosophers that matter is, by its own nature, indestructible, for the very satisfactory reason that none of them can tell what matter in its own nature is.* All that

---

* It will be seen that the proof of the being of God here presented, rests upon the *impossibility* of self-existent *design* in matter.

25

they can undertake to say is, that they have observed certain properties of matter, and, among these, that "it is indestructible by any operations to which it can be subjected in the ordinary course of circumstances observed at the surface of the globe."* The very utmost which any man can assert in this matter is a negative, a want of knowledge or a want of power. He can say, "Human power cannot destroy matter;" and, if he pleases, he may reason thence that human power did not create it. But to assert that matter is eternal because man cannot destroy it, is as if a child should try to beat the cylinder of a steam engine to pieces, and, failing in the attempt, should say "I am sure this cylinder existed from eternity, because I am unable to destroy it."

But we are not done with the absurdities of the eternity of matter. We say to our would-be philosophers, When you tell us that matter is eternal, how does that account for the formation of this world? What is this matter you speak of? This world consists not of a philosophical abstraction called matter, nor yet of one substance known by that name, but of a great variety of material substances, oxygen, hydrogen, carbon, sulphur, iron, aluminum, and some fifty-one others already discovered.† Now, which of these is the eternal matter you speak of? Is it iron, or sulphur, or clay, or oxygen? If it is any one of them, where did the others come from? Did a mass of iron, becoming discontented with its gravity, suddenly metamorphose itself into a cloud of gas or a pail of water? Or are they all eternal? Have we fifty-seven eternal beings? Are they all eternal in their present combinations? or is it only the single elements that are eternal? You see that your hypothesis—that matter is eternal—gives me no light on the formation of this world, which is not a shapeless mass of a philosophical abstraction called matter, but a regular and beautiful building, composed of a great variety of matters. Was it so from eternity? No man who was ever in a quarry or a gravel pit will say so, much less one who has the least smattering of chemistry or geology. Do you assert the eternity of the fifty-seven single substances, either separate, or combined in some other way than we now find them in the rocks and rivers and atmosphere of the earth? Then how came they to get together at all, and particularly how did they put themselves in their present shapes?

---

* Reid's Chemistry, Chap. II, § 37, Chambers' Educational Course.
† Johnson's Turner's Chemistry, § 341.

Each of them is a piece of matter of which *inertia* is a primary and inseparable property. "Matter *of itself,* can not begin to move, or assume a quiescent state after being put in motion."* Will you tell us that the fifty-seven primary elements danced about till the air and sea and earth somehow jumbled themselves together into the present shape of this glorious and beautiful world, with all its regularity of day and night, and summer and winter, with all its beautiful flowers and lofty trees, with all its variety of birds and beasts, and fishes? To bring the matter down to the level of the intellect of the most stupid Pantheist, tell us, in plain English, *Did the paving-stones make themselves?*

Absurd as it seems to every man of common sense, there are persons claiming to be philosophers who not only assert that they did, but will tell you how they did it. One class of them think they have found it out by supposing every thing in the universe reduced to very fine powder, consisting of very small grains, which they call atoms; or, if that is not fine enough, into gas, of which it is supposed the particles are too fine to be perceived; and then by different arrangements of these atoms, according to the laws of attraction and electricity, the various elements of the world were made, and arranged in its present form.

Suppose we grant this uncouth supposition, that the world millions of ages ago existed as a cloud of atoms, does that bring us any nearer the object of getting rid of a creator than before? The atoms must be material if a material world is to be made from them; and they must be extended; each one of them must have length, breadth and thickness. The Pantheist, then, has only multiplied his difficulties a million times, by pounding up the world into atoms, which are only little bits of the paving stones he intends to make out of them. Each bit of the paving stone, no matter how small you break it, remains just as incapable of making itself, or moving itself, as was the whole stone composed of all these bits. So we are landed back again at the sublime question, *Did the paving stones make themselves?*

Others will tell you that millions of years ago the world existed as a vast cloud of fire mist, which, after a long time, cooled down into granite, and the granite, by dint of earthquakes, got broken up on the surface, and washed with rain into clay and soil, whence

---

* Reid's Chemistry; Chambers' Educational Course, p. 14, ? 37.

plants sprung up of their own accord, and the plants gradually grew into animals of various kinds, and some of the animals grew into monkeys, and finally the monkeys into men. The fire mist they stoutly affirm to have existed from eternity. They do not allege that they remember that, (and yet as they themselves are, as they say, composed body and soul of this eternal fire mist, they ought to remember,) but only that there are certain comets which occasionally come within fifty or sixty millions of miles of this earth, which they suppose may be composed of the fire mist which they *suppose* this world is made of. A solid basis, truly, on which to build a world! A cloud in the sky fifty millions of miles away, may possibly be fire mist, may possibly cool down and condense into a solid globe; therefore, this fire mist is eternal, and had no need of a creator; and our world, and all other worlds may possibly have been like it; therefore, they also never were created by Almighty God. Such is the Atheists' and Pantheists' ground of faith. The thinnest vapor, or the merest supposition, will suffice to build his eternal salvation upon; provided only it contradicts the Bible, and gets rid of God. We cannot avoid asking with as much gravity as we can command, Where did the mist come from? Did the mist make itself? Where did the fire come from? Did it kindle of its own accord? Who put the fire and the mist together? Was it red hot enough from all eternity to melt granite? Then why is it any cooler now? How could an eternal red heat cool down? If it existed as a red hot fire mist from eternity, until our Pantheists began to observe it beginning to cool, why should it ever begin to cool at all, and why begin to cool just then? Fill it as full of electricity, magnetism and odyle, as you please; do these afford any *reason* for its very extraordinary conduct? The utmost they do is to show you *how* such a change took place, but they can neither tell you *where* the original matter came from, nor *why* its form was changed. Change is an effect, and every effect requires a cause. There could be no cause outside of the fire mist; for they say there was nothing else in the universe. Then the cause must be in the mist itself. Had it a mind, and a will, and a perception of propriety? Did the mist become sensible of the lightness of its behavior, and the fire resolve to cool off a little, and both consult together on the propriety of dropping their erratic blazing through infinite space, and resolve to settle down into orderly, well-behaved suns and planets? In the division of the property, what became of the mind? Did it go to the sun, or to the moon, or to the pole star, or to this earth? Or, was it clipped up into little pieces and divided among the stars in proportion to their respective magnitudes; so that the sun may have, say the hundredth part of an idea, and the moon a faint perception of it? Did the fire mist's mind die under this cruel clipping and dissecting process; or is it of the nature of a polypus, each piece alive and growing up to perfection in its own way? Has each of the planets and fixed stars a great "soul of the world" as well as this earth, and are they looking down intelligently and compassionately on this little globe of ours? Had we not better build altars to all the host of heaven and return to the religion of our acorn-fed ancestors, who burned their children alive, in honor of the sun, on Sun-days?

An aqueous solution of the difficulty of getting rid of Almighty God, is frequently proposed. It is known that certain chemical solutions, when mixed together, deposit a sediment, or precipitate, as chemists call it. And it is supposed that the universe was all once in a state of solution, in primeval oceans, and that the mingling of the waters of these oceans caused them to deposit the various salts and earths which form the worlds in the form of mud, which afterward hardened into rock, or vegetated into trees and men. Thus, it is clearly demonstrated that there is no need for the Creator if—if—if—we only had somebody to make these primeval oceans——and somebody to mix them together!*

The development theory of the production of the human race from the mud, through the mushroom, the snail, the tortoise, the greyhound, the monkey, and the man, which is now such a favorite with Atheists and Pantheists, if it were fully proved to be a fact, would only increase the difficulty of getting rid of God. For either the primeval mud had all the germs of the future plants and monkeys, and men's bodies, and souls, in itself, originally, or it had not. If it had not, where did it get them? If it had all the life and intelligence in the universe in itself, it was a very extraordinary kind of god. We shall call it the *mud-god*. Our Pantheists, then, believe in a god of muddy body and intelligent mind. But,

---

* It might be supposed that such a theory is too palpably absurd to be believed by any save the inmates of a lunatic asylum, had not the writer and hundreds of the citizens of Cincinnati, seen a lecturer perform the ordinary experiment of producing colored precipitates by mixing colorless solutions, as a demonstration of the self-acting powers of matter. Common sense, being a gift of God, is righteously withdrawn from those who deny him.

if they deny intelligence to the mud, then we are back to our original difficulty, with a large appendix, viz: *The paving stones made themselves first, and all Pantheists and Atheists afterward.*

But the whole theory of development is utterly false in its first principles. From the beginning of the world to the present day, no man has ever observed an instance of spontaneous generation. There is no law of nature, whether electric, magnetic, odylic, or any other, which can produce a living plant or animal save from the germ or seed of some previous plant or animal of the same species. Nor has a single instance of the transmutation of species ever been proved. Every beast, bird, fish, insect and plant, brings forth after its kind, and has done so since its creation. No law of Natural Philosophy is more firmly established than this, *That there is no spontaneous generation nor transmutation of species.* From Cuvier down, all practical naturalists maintain this law. It is true there is a regular gradation of the various orders of animal and vegetable life, rising like the steps of a staircase, one above the other; but gradation is no more caused by transmutation than a staircase is made by an ambitious lower step changing itself into all the upper ones.

To refer the origin of the world to the laws of nature is no less absurd. Law, as Johnson defines it, is a rule of action. It necessarily requires an acting agent, an object designed in the action, means to attain it, and authoritative prescription of those means by a lawgiver. Are the laws of nature, laws given by some supposed intelligent being, worshipped by the heathen of old and the Pantheists of modern times under that name? Or do they signify the orderly and regular sequence of cause and effect, which is so manifest in the course of all events? If, as Pantheists say, the latter, this is the very thing we want them to account for. How came the world to be under law without a lawgiver? Where there is law, there must be design. Chance is utterly inconsistent with the idea of law. Where there is design, there must, of necessity, be a designer. Matter in any shape, stones or lightnings, mud or magnets, cannot think, contrive, design, give law to itself or any thing else, much less bring itself into existence. There is no conceivable way of accounting for this orderly world we live in but one or other of these two: Either an intelligent being created the world, or—*The paving stones made themselves.*

Leaving these brutish among the people—who assert the latter—to the enjoyment of their folly, let us ascertain what we can know of the great Creator of the heavens and the earth. God refers the Atheists and Pantheists of the Psalmist's days to their own bodies for proof of his intelligence, to their own minds for proofs of his personality, and to their own observation of the judgments of his providence against evil doers for proofs of his moral government. Our text ascribes to him perception and intelligence: *He that planted the ear, shall he not hear? He that formed the eye, shall he not see?* It does not say, He has an eye, or an ear, but he has that knowledge we acquire by those organs. And the argument is from the designed organ to the designing maker of it, and is perfectly irresistible. A blind god could not make a seeing man. Let us look for a little at a few of the many marks of design in this organ to which God thus refers us.

We shall first observe the mechanical skill displayed in the formation of the eye, and then the optical arrangements, or rather a few of them, for there are more than eight hundred distinct contrivances already observed by anatomists in the dead eye, while the great contrivance of all, the power of seeing, is utterly beyond their ken. I hold in my hand a box made of several pieces of wood glued together, and covered on the outside with leather. Inside it is lined with cotton, and the cotton has a lining of fine white silk. You at once observe that it is intended to protect some delicate and precious article of jewelry, and that the maker of this box must have been acquainted with the strength of wood, the toughness of leather, the adhesiveness of glue, the softness and elasticity of cotton, the tenacity of silk, and the mode of spinning and weaving it, the form of the jewel to be placed in it, and the dangers against which this box would protect it—ten entirely distinct branches of knowledge, which every child who should pick up such a box in the street would unhesitatingly ascribe to its maker. Now, the box in which the eye is placed, is composed of seven bones glued together internally, and covered with skin on the outside, lined with the softest fat, enveloped in a tissue compared with which the finest silk is only canvas, and the cavity is shaped so as exactly to fit the eye, while the brow projects over like the roof of a verandah, to keep off falling dust and rain from injuring it while the lid is open; and the eyebrows, like a thatch sloping outward, conduct the sweat of the brow, by which man earns his bread, away around the outer cover, that it may not enter the eye and destroy the sight. If it were preposterous nonsense to say that electricity, or magnetism, or odyle, contrived and made a little bracelet box, or spectacle case, how much more absurd to ascribe the making of the cavity of the eye to any such cause.

Let us next look at the shape of the eye. You observe it is nearly round in its section across, and rather oval in its other direction, and the cavity it lies in is shaped exactly to fit it. Now there are eyes in the world angular and triangular, and even square; and, as you may readily suppose, the creatures which have them cannot move them; to compensate for which inconvenience, some of them, as the common fly, have several hundred. But, unless our heads were as large as sugar hogsheads, we could not be so furnished, and we must either have movable eyes, or see only in one direction. Accordingly, the contriver of the eye has hung it with a hinge. Now there are various kinds of hinges, moving in one direction, and the maker of the eye might have made a hinge on which the eye would move up and down, or he might have given us a hinge that would bend right and left, in which case we should have been able merely to squint a little in two directions. But to enable one to see in every direction, there is only one kind of hinge that would answer the purpose—the ball and socket joint—and the Former of the eye has hung it with such a hinge, retaining it in its place partly by the projection of the bones of the face, and partly by the muscles and the optic nerve, which is about as thick as a candlewick, and as tough as leather. Most of you have seen a ship, and know the way in which the yards are moved, and turned, and squared by ropes and pulleys. The rigging of the eye, though not so large, is fully as curious. There is a tackle, called a muscle, to pull it down when you want to look down; another tackle to pull it up when you have done; one to pull to the right, and another to the left; there is one fastened to the eyeball in two places, and geared through a pulley which will make it move in any direction, as when we roll our eyes; and the sixth, fastened to the under side of the eye, keeps it steady when we do not need to move it. Then the eyelids are each provided with appropriate gearing, and need to have it durable too, for it is used thirty thousand times a day, in fact every time we wink. If God had neglected to place these little cords to pull up the eyelash, we should all have been in the condition of the unfortunate gentleman described by Dr. Nieuwentyt, who was obliged to pull up his eyelashes with his fingers whenever he wanted to see. There is, too,

DID THE WORLD MAKE ITSELF.

another admirable piece of forethought and skill displayed by the Former of the eye, in providing a liquid to wash it, and a sponge to wipe it with, and a waste pipe, about the size of a quill, through the bone of the nose, to carry off the tears which have been used in washing and moistening the eye. Now what absurdity to say that a law of nature, say gravity, or electricity, or magnetism, has such knowledge of the principles of mechanics as the eye proclaims its Former to have—that it could make a choice among multitudes of shapes of eyes and kinds of joints, and this choice the very best for our convenience; and that having known and chosen, it could have manufactured the various parts of this complicated machine. Such a machine requires an intelligent manufacturer; and yet we have only as yet been looking at the dead eye, paying no regard to sight at all. Even a blind man's eye proves an intelligent creator.

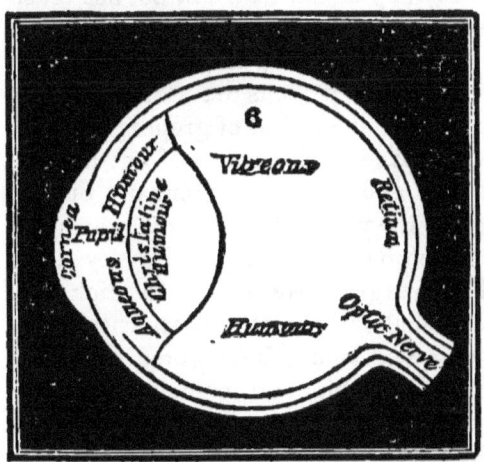

Let us now turn our thoughts to the instrument of sight. The optic nerve is the part of the eye which conveys visions to the mind. Suppose, instead of being where you observe it, at the back part of the eye, it had been brought out to the front, and that reflections from objects had fallen directly upon it. It is obvious that it would have been exposed to injury from every floating particle of dust, and you would always have felt such a sensation as is caused by a burn or scald when the skin peels off and leaves the ends of the nerves exposed to the air. The tender points of the fibres of the optic nerve, too, would soon become blunted and broken, and the eye, of course, useless. How, then, is the nerve to be protected, and yet the sight not obstructed. If it were covered with skin, as the other nerves are, you could not see through it. For thousands of years after men had eyes and used them, they knew no substance at once hard and transparent, which could answer the double purpose of protection and vision. And, to this day, they know none hard enough for protection, clear enough for vision, and elastic enough to resume its form after a blow. But men did the best they could, and put a round piece of brittle but transparent glass in a ring of tougher metal for the protection of the hands of a watch; and he who first invented the watch crystal thought he had made a discovery. Now observe in the eye; that forward part is the watch glass; the cornea, made of a substance at once hard, transparent, and elastic—which man has never been able to imitate—set into the sclerotica, that white, muscular coat which constitutes the white of your eye, acts as a frame for the cornea, and answers another important purpose, as we shall presently see.

But, supposing the end of the nerve protected by the glass, we might have had it brought up to the glass without any interposing lenses or humors, as, in fact, is nearly the case with some crustacea. We cannot well imagine all the inconveniences of such an eye to us. If we could see distinctly at all, we could not see much farther or wider than the breadth of the end of the nerve at once. Our sight would then be very like that faculty of perceiving colors by the points of the fingers, which some persons are said to possess. In that case, seeing would only be a nicer kind of groping, and our eyes would be more conveniently fixed on the points of our fingers; or, as with many insects, on the ends of long antennæ. Such a form of eye is precisely suited to the wants of an animal which has not an idea beyond its food, which has no business with any object too large for its mouth, and whose great concern is to stick to a rock and catch whatever animalculæ the water floats within the grasp of its feelers. But for a being whose intercourse should be with all the works of God, and whose chief end in such intercourse should be to behold the Creator reflected in his works, it was manifestly necessary to have a wider and larger range of vision; and, therefore, a different form of eye. Both these objects, breadth of field combined with length of range, are obtained by placing the optic nerve at the back of the eye, and interposing several lenses, through which objects are observed. By this arrangement a visual angle is secured, and all objects lying within it are distinctly visible at the same time. This faculty of perceiving several objects at the same time is a special property of sight which tends greatly to enlarge our conceptions of the knowledge of Him who gave it.. A man who never saw can have no idea of it. He cannot taste two separate tastes at once; nor smell two distinct smells at once; nor feel more than one object with each hand at once; and if he hears several sounds at the same time, they either flow into each other, making a harmony, or confuse him with their discord. Yet we are all conscious that we see a vast variety of distinct and separate objects at one glance of our eyes. I think it is manifest that the Former of such an eye not only intended its owner to observe such a vast variety of objects, but from the capacity of his own sight to infer the vastly wider range of vision of Him who gave it.

Besides the breadth of the field of vision, we also require length of range for the purpose of life. The thousand inconveniences which the short-sighted man so painfully feels are obvious to all. Yet it may tend to reconcile such to their lot to know that thousands of the liveliest and merriest of God's creatures cannot see an inch before them. Small birds and insects, which feed on very minute insects, need eyes like microscopes to find them; while the eagle and the fish-hawk, which soar up till they are almost out of sight, can distinctly see the hare or the herring a mile below them, and so must have eyes like telescopes. We, too, need to observe minute objects very closely, as when we read fine print, or when a lady threads a fine needle at microscope range; but, if confined to that range, we could not see our friends across the room, or find our way to the next street. Again, in traveling we need to see objects miles away, and at night we see the stars millions of miles away; but then, if confined to the long range, we should be strangers at home, and never get within a mile of any acquaintance. Now, how to combine these two powers, of seeing near objects and distant ones with the same eye, is the problem which the maker of the eye had to solve. Let us look how man tried to solve it. A magnifying lens will collect the rays from any distant object, and convey them to a point called the focus. Then suppose we put this glass in the tube of an opera-glass, or pocket spy-glass, and look through the eye-hole and the concave lens, properly adjusted, in front of it, we shall see the image of the object considerably magnified. But suppose the object draws very near, we see nothing distinctly; for the rays reflected from it, which were nearly parallel while it was at a distance, are no longer so when it comes near, but scatter in all directions, and those which fall on the lens are collected at a point much nearer to the lens than before, and the eye-glass must be pushed forward to that focus. Accordingly, you know that the spy-glass is made to slide back and forward, and the telescope has a screw to lengthen or shorten the tube according to the distance of the objects observed. Another way of meeting the case would be by taking out the lens and putting in one of less magnifying power, a flatter lens, for the nearer object. Now, at first sight, it would seem a very inconvenient thing to have eyes drawing out and in several inches like spy-glasses, and still more inconvenient to have twenty or thirty pairs of eyes, and to need to take out our eyes and put in a new set twenty times a day. The ingenuity of man has been at work hundreds of years to discover some other method of adapting an optical instrument to long and short range, but without success. Now, the Former of the eye knew the properties of light and the properties of lenses before the first eye was made; he knew the mode of adjusting them for any distance, from the thousands of millions of miles between the eye and the star, to the half inch distance of the mote in the sunbeam; and he has not only availed himself of both the principles which opticians discovered, but has executed his work with an infinite perfection which bungling men may admire, but can never imitate. The sclerotic coat of the eye, and the choroid which lies next it, are full of muscles which, by their contraction, both press back the crystalline lens nearer the retina, and also flatten it; the vitreous humor, in which the crystalline lens lies, a fine, transparent humor, about as thick as the white of an egg, giving way behind it, and also slightly altering its form and power of refraction to suit the case. Thus, that which the astronomer, or the microscopist, performs by a tedious process, and then very imperfectly, we perform perfectly, easily, instantly, and almost involuntarily, with that perfect compound microscope and telescope invented by the Former of the human eye. Surely, in giving us an instrument so admirably fitted for observing the lofty grandeur of the heavens and the lowlier beauties of the earth, he meant to allure us to the discovery of the perfections of the great Designer and Former of all these wondrous works.

But there is another contrivance in the eye, adapted to lead us further to the consideration of the extent of the knowledge of its power. We are placed in a world of variable lights, of day and night, and of all the variations between light and darkness. We cannot see in the full blaze of light, nor yet in utter darkness. Had the eye been formed to bear only the noon-day glare, we had been half blind in the afternoon, and wholly so in the evening. If the eye were formed so as to see at night, we had been helpless as owls in the day. But the variations of light in the atmosphere may be in some measure compensated, as we know, by regulating the quantity admitted to our houses—shutting up the windows. When we wish to regulate the admission of light to our rooms, we have recourse to various clumsy contrivances; paper blinds, perpetually tearing, sunblind rollers that will not roll, venetian blinds continually in need of mending, awnings blowing away with every storm, or shutters, which shut up and leave us in entire darkness. A self-acting window which shall expand with the opening of light in the mornings and evenings, and close up of its own accord as the light increases toward noon, has never been manufactured by man. But the Former of the eye took note of the necessities and conveniences of the case, and besides giving a pair of shutters to close up when we go to sleep, he has given the most admirable sunblinds ever invented. The nerve of the eye at the back of its chamber can not see without light, and its light comes through the little round window called the pupil, or black of the eye—which is simply a hole in the iris, or colored part. Now this iris is formed of two sets of muscles: one set of elastic rings, which, when left to themselves, contract the opening; and another set at right angles to them, like the spokes of a wheel, pulling the inner edge of the iris in all directions to the outside. In fact it is not so much a sunblind, as a self-acting window, opening and closing the aperture according to our need of light, and doing this so instantaneously that we are not sensible of the process.

It is self evident that the Maker of such an eye was acquainted with the properties of light and the alternations of night and day, as well as with the mechanical contrivances for adjusting the eye to these variable circumstances. He has given us an eye capable of seeking knowledge among partial darkness; and of availing itself for this purpose of imperfect light—an apt symbol of our mental constitution and moral situation in a world where good and evil, light and darkness, mix and alternate.

Perhaps some one is ready to ask, what is the use of so many lenses in the eye? It seems as if the crystalline lens and the optic nerve were sufficient for the purpose of sight, with the cornea simply to protect them. What is the use of the aqueous humor and the vitreous humor?

Light, when refracted through a lens, becomes separated into its component colors—red, yellow, green, blue, and violet; and the greater the magnifying power of the lens, and the brighter the object viewed, the greater the dispersion of the rays. So that if the crystalline lens of the eye alone were used, we should see every white object bluish in the middle, and yellowish and reddish at the edges; or, in vulgar language, we should see starlight.

This difficulty perplexed Sir Isaac Newton all his life, and he never discovered the mode of making a refracting telescope which would obviate it. But M. Dolland, an optician, reflecting that the very same difficulty must have presented itself to the Maker of the eye, determined to ascertain how he had obviated it. He found that the Maker of the eye had a knowledge of the fact that different substances have different powers of refracting or bending the rays of light which pass through them, and that liquids have generally a different power of refraction from solids. For instance, if you put a straight stick in water, the part under water will seem bent at a considerable angle, while if you put the stick through a little hole in a pane of glass it will not seem near so much bent. He further discovered that oil of cassia had a different power of refraction from water, and the white of an egg still a different power. He discovered also that the first lens of the eye, the aqueous humor, is very like water—that the crystalline lens is a firm jelly—and that the vitreous humor is about the consistence of the white of an egg. The combination of these three lenses of different powers of refraction, secures the correction of their separate errors. He could not make telescope lenses of jelly, nor water; therefore, he could not make a perfect achromatic telescope, but he learned the lesson of mutual compensations of difficulties which the Maker of the eye teaches the reflecting anatomist, and procuring flint and crown glass of different degrees of refraction, he arranged them in the achromatic lens so as nearly to remedy the defect.

I think you will at once admit that Dolland's attempt to remedy the evils of confused sight in the telescope, indicated a desire to obtain a precise and correct view of objects; and that his success in constructing an instrument nearly perfect for the use of astronomers, gave evidence that he himself had a clear idea of that perfect and accurate vision which he thus attempted to bestow on them. Shall we then imagine any inaccuracy in the sight of Him, who not only desired, but executed, and bestowed on us an instrument so perfectly adapted to the imperfections of this lower world, and whose very imperfections are the materials from which He produces clear and perfect vision? No! in God's eye there are no chromatic refractions of passion, or prejudice, or party feeling, or self-love. He sees by no reflected or refracted light. O Father of Light! with whom is no variableness, or shadow of turning, open our eyes to behold thee clearly!

Our text thus leads us to a knowledge of God's character, from the structure of the bodies he has given us. He that formed my eye sees. Though my feeble vision is by no means a standard or limit for his omniscience, yet I may conclude that every perfection of the power of sight He has given me, existed previously in Him. Has he endowed me, a poor puny mortal, the permanent tenant of only two yards of earth, with an eye capable of ranging over earth's broad plains and lofty mountains—of traversing her beauteous lakes and lovely rivers—of scanning her crowded cities, and inspecting all their curious productions—and specially delighting to investigate the bodily forms of men, and their mental characters displayed on the printed page? Has He given me the principle of curiosity, without which such an endowment were useless? Then most undoubtedly He has Himself both the desire to observe all the works of his hands, and the power to gratify that desire. The Former of the eye must of necessity be the great Observer.

Wheresoever an eye is found of His handy-work, and wheresoever sight is preserved by His skill, let the owner of such an instrument know that if he can see, God can, and as surely as he sees, God does.

If it is possible for us to behold many objects distinctly at once, it is not impossible for God to behold more. If He has given us an eye to look from earth to heaven, then His eye sees from heaven to earth. If I can see accurately, God's inspection is much more impartial. And if He has given me the power of adjusting my imperfect vision to the varying lights and shades of this changing scene, let me not dream for a moment that He is destitute of a corresponding power of investigating difficulties, and penetrating darknesses, and bringing to light hidden works and secret things. God is light. In Him is no darkness at all. Neither is there any creature that is not manifest in His sight, but all things are naked and opened to the eyes of Him with whom I have to do. He has seen all my past life—my faults, my follies, and my crimes.

When I thought myself in darkness and privacy, God's eye was upon me there. In the turmoil of business God's eye was upon me. In the crowd of my ungodly companions God's eye was upon me. In the darkness and solitude of night God's eye was upon me. And God's eye is on me now, and will follow me from this house, and will watch me and observe all my actions, on—on,—on—while God lives, and wheresoever God's creation extends.

"O God, thou hast searched and known me;
Thou knowest my down-sitting and mine up-rising;
Thou understandest my thoughts afar off.
Thou compassest my path and my lying down,
And art acquainted with all my ways.
For there is not a word in my tongue,
But, lo! O Lord, thou knowest it altogether.
Thou hast beset me behind and before, and laid thine hand upon me.
Such knowledge is too wonderful for me!
It is high, I cannot attain unto it.
Whither shall I go from thy spirit?
And whither shall I flee from thy presence?
If I ascend up into heaven, thou art there,
If I make my bed in hell, behold, thou art there!
If I take the wings of the morning,
And dwell in the uttermost parts of the sea,
Even there shall thy hand lead me,
And thy right hand shall hold me.
If I say, 'surely the darkness shall cover me,'
Even the night shall be light about me;
Yea the darkness hideth not from thee,
But the night shineth as the day;
The darkness and the light are both alike to thee."

No. 24.

IS GOD EVERY BODY, AND EVERY BODY GOD.

Pantheism is that perversion of reason and language which denies God's personality, and calls some imaginary soul of the world, or the world itself, by his name. While Pantheists are fully agreed upon the propriety of getting rid of a God who could note their conduct, and call them to account for it hereafter, and who would claim to exercise any authority over them here, they are by no means agreed, either in India, Germany, or America, as to what they shall call by his name. Public opinion necessitates them to say they believe in a God, but almost every one has his own private opinion as to what it is. We shall speak of it as we hear it pronounced from the lips of its prophets, here, as well as in the writings of its expounders, in Europe and Asia. Some of them declare, that it is some absolutely unknown cause of all the phenomena of the universe, and others, that it is the universe itself. A large class speak of it as the great soul of the world, while the more materialistic regard it as the world itself, body and soul; the soul being the source of all the imponderable forces, such as gravitation, heat, light, electricity, magnetism, galvanism, vegetable and animal life, and especially the mesmeric influence, of which many of them regard intellect as a modification; and the body being the sum of all the ponderable substances, such as air, water, earth, minerals, vegetables, and bodies of animals and men. This creed is popularly expressed in the sentence so often heard, "God is every thing, and every thing is God." But this vast generalization of all things into the higher unity—this exalting of monkeys, men, snails, and paving stones to the same level of divinity—by no means meets the views of the more unphilosophical and aspiring gods and goddesses, for the very reason that it is so impartial. To deify a man and his cat by the same process, is not much of a distinction to the former; and of what advantage is it to be made a god, if he does not thereby obtain some distinction? This levelling apotheosis is generally confined to the German Pantheists, of whom there are multitudes in this city. Their more ambitious American brethren ascribe the contented humility which accepts it, to the continual influence of the fumes of tobacco and lager beer. Man—the soul of man—is the great divinity of our American Pantheists. "The doctrine of the soul—first *soul*, and second *soul*, and evermore *soul*"*—is the doctrine which is to regenerate the world. God, in their view, is nothing till he attains self consciousness in man. "The universal does not attract us till housed in the individual. Who heeds the waste abyss of possibility? Standing on the bare ground, my head bathed by the blithe air, and uplifted into infinite space, all mere egotism vanishes. The currents of the universe being circulate through me, I am part or particle of God." "I stand here to say, 'Let us worship the mighty and transcendent soul.'"* "God attains to self consciousness only in the human soul." "Honor yourself." "Reverence your own individuality." "The soul of man is the highest intelligence in the universe." Such are the dogmas which, under the name of Positive Philosophy, are poured forth oracularly, unsupported by reason or argument, by the prophets of the new dispensation—the last and highest achievement of the human intellect.

It is very unfortunate, however, for the honor of the prophets of the nineteenth century, that this profound discovery was invented and illustrated, patented and peddled, by the Hindoos, among the people of India, two thousand years before the divinity had struggled into self consciousness in the mighty and transcendent souls of Schelling, Hegel, and Strauss—of Atkinson, Parker, or Emerson. We mean to show in this lecture, that it is an *Antiquated, Hypocritical, Demoralizing Atheism.*

1. *Pantheism is an Antiquated Heresy.*—It has rotted and putrified among the worshippers of cats and monkeys, and holy bulls, and bits of sticks and stones, on the banks of the Ganges, for more than two thousand years; yet it is now hooked up, out of its dunghill, and hawked about among Christian people, as a prime new discovery of modern philosophy, for getting rid of Almighty God. As the Hindoo Shasters are undoubtedly the sources from which French, German, and American philosophers have borrowed their dogmas, without leave or acknowledgment; and as is generally the case with depredators, they have not had time to take the whole system, we shall gratify and edify the public by a view of this sublime theology, as exhibited in the writings of the Positive Philosophers of India.

---

* Emerson.

"When existing in the temporary imperfect state of *Sagun*, Brahm (the Pantheist deity) wills to manifest the universe. For this purpose he puts forth his omnipotent energy, which is variously styled in the different systems now under review. He puts forth his energy for what? For the effecting of a creation out of nothing? "No," says one of the Shasters, but to *"produce from his own divine substance a multiform universe."* By the spontaneous exertion of this energy he sends forth, from his own divine substance, a countless host of essences, like innumerable sparks issuing from the blazing fire, or myriads of rays from the resplendent sun. These detached portions of Brahm—these separated divine essences—soon become individuated systems, destined, in time, to occupy different forms prepared for their reception; whether these be fixed or movable, animate or inanimate, forms of gods or men, forms of animal, vegetable, or mineral existences."

"Having been separated from Brahm in his imperfect state of *Sagun*, they carry along with them a share of those principles, qualities, and attributes that characterize that state, though predominating in very different degrees and proportions: either according to their respective capacities, or the retributive awards of an eternal ordination. Amongst others it is specially noted, that as Brahm at that time had awakened into a consciousness of his own existence, there does inhere in each separated soul a notion, or a conviction, of its own *distinct*, independent, individual existence. Laboring under this delusive notion, or conviction, the soul has lost the knowledge of its own proper nature—its divine origin, and ultimate destiny. It ignorantly regards itself as an inferior entity, instead of knowing itself to be what it truly is: a consubstantial; though it may be an infinitesimally minute portion of the great whole, a universal spirit.

"Each individual soul being thus a portion of Brahm, even as a spark is of fire, it is again and again declared that the relation between them is not that of master and servant, ruler and ruled, but that of whole and part! The soul is pronounced to be eternal *a parte ante;* in itself it has had no beginning or birth, though its separate individuality originated in time. It is eternal *a parte post;* it will have no end—no death; though its separate individuality will terminate in time. Its manifestation in time is not a creation; it is an effluence from the eternal fount of spirit. Its disappearance from the stage of time is not an extinction of essence—a reduction to nonentity; it is only a refluence into its original source. As an emanation from the supreme, eternal spirit, it is from everlasting to everlasting. Neither can it be said to be of finite dimensions; on the contrary, says the sacred oracle, "being identified with the Supreme Brahm, it participates in his infinity."

"After having enumerated all the elementary principles, atoms, and qualities successively evolved from Brahm, one of the sacred writings states, that though each of these had distinct powers, yet they existed separate and disunited, without order or harmonious adaptation of parts; that until they were duly combined together, it was impossible to produce this universe, or animated beings; and that therefore it was requisite to adopt other means than fortuitous chance for giving them an appropriate combination, and symmetrical arrangement. The Supreme, accordingly, produced an egg, in which the elementary principles might be deposited, and nurtured into maturity." "All the primary atoms, qualities, and principles—the seeds of future worlds—that had been evolved from the substance of Brahm, were now collected together, and deposited in the newly produced egg. And into it, along with them, entered the self-existent himself, under the assumed form of Brahma; and then he sat vivifying, expanding, and combining the elements, a whole year of the creation, or four thousand three hundred millions of solar years! During this amazing period, the wondrous egg floated like a bubble on the abyss of primeval waters, increasing in size, and blazing refulgent as a thousand suns. At length the Supreme, who dwelt therein, burst the shell of the stupendous egg, and issued forth under a new form, with a thousand heads, a thousand eyes, and a thousand arms. Along with him there issued forth another form, huge and measureless. What could that be? All the elementary principles having now been matured, and disposed into an endless variety of orderly collocations, and combined into one harmonious whole, they darted into visible manifestation under the form of the present glorious universe! A universe now finished, and ready made, with its entire apparatus, of earth, sun, moon, and stars. What, then, is this multiform universe? It is but a harmoniously arranged expansion of primordial principles and qualities. And whence are these? Educed or evolved from the divine substance of Brahm.

Hence it is that the universe is so constantly spoken of, even by mythologists, as a manifested form of Brahm himself, the supreme, invisible spirit. Hence, too, under the notion that it is the manifestation of a being who may assume every variety of corporeal form, is the universe often personified, or described as if its different parts were only the different members of a person, of prodigious magnitude, in human form. It is declared that the hairs of his body are the trees of the forest; of his head, the clouds; of his beard, the lightning. His breath is the circling atmosphere; his voice, the thunder; his eyes, the sun and moon; his veins, the rivers; his nails, the rocks; his bones, the lofty mountains!"*

"The substantial fabrics of all worlds having now been framed and fitted up as the destined abodes of different orders of being, celestial, terrestrial, and infernal, the question next arises, How or by whom were produced the various organized forms which these orders of being were designed to animate? Though hosts of subtle essences or souls flowed forth from Brahm, all of these remain inactive till united to some form of materialism. From this necessity the gods themselves are not exempted. While the souls of men, and other inferior spirits, must be encased in tabernacles fashioned out of the grosser elements, the souls of the gods, and all other superior spirits, must be made to inhabit material forms, composed of one or other of the infinitely attenuated and invisible rudimental atoms that spring direct from the principle of consciousness."

"Interminable as are the incoherencies, inconsistencies, and extravagancies of the Hindoo sacred writings, on no subject, perhaps, is the multiplicity of varying accounts and discrepancies more astonishing than on the present. Volumes could not suffice to retail them all. Brahma's first attempts at the production of the forms of animated beings, were as eminently unsuccessful as they were various. At one time he is said to have performed a long and severe course of ascetic devotions, to enable him to accomplish his wish; but in vain; at another, inflamed by anger and passion at his repeated failures, he sat down and wept; and from the streaming tear-drops sprang into being, as his first boon, a progeny of ghosts and goblins, of an aspect so loathsome and dreadful, that he was ready to faint away. At one time, after profound medita-

---

* Duff's India, pp. 99—114.

tion, different beings spring forth: one from his thumb, another from his breath, a third from his ear, a fourth from his side. But enough of such monstrous legends."*

There, now, reader, you have the original of the Development Theory, with vestiges of creation enough to make half a dozen new infidel cosmogonies, besides the genuine original of Pantheism, from its native soil. Our western Pantheists will doubtless reverence their venerable progenitors; and, should the remainder of the family find their way here in a year or two, via Germany, the public will be better prepared to give a fitting reception to such distinguished visitors, including their suite of divine bulls and holy monkeys—their lustrations of cow dung, extatic hook swingings, burning of widows, and drowning of children, and other Positive Philosophies, from the banks of the Ganges. What an outrage on decency for such men to call themselves philosophers and christians!

2. *Pantheism is a system of deception and hypocrisy.*—Has any man a right to pervert the English language, by fixing new meanings to words, entirely different from and contrary to those in common use? If he knows the meaning of the words he uses, and uses them to convey a contrary meaning, he is a deceiver. The name God, used as a proper name, in the English tongue, means "the Supreme Being; Jehovah; the Eternal and Infinite Spirit, the Creator and Sovereign of the Universe." † If, then, a man says he believes in God, but when forced to explain what he means by that name, says he means steam, heat, electricity, galvanism, magnetism, mesmeric force, odyle, animal life, the soul of man, or the sum of all the intelligencies in the universe, he is a deceiver, and vain talker, abusing language to conceal his impiety. Pantheism is simply Jesuitical Atheism. Willing to dethrone Jehovah, but unable and unwilling to place any other being in his stead, as Creator and Ruler of the universe, yet conscious that mankind will never embrace open Atheism, Pantheists profess to believe in God, only that they may steal his name to cloak their Atheism. We, in common with all who believe in God, demand, that, as their divinity is, by their own confession, essentially different from God, they shall use a different word to describe it. Let them call it Brahm, as their brethren in India do, or any other name not

---

* Duff's India, p. 119.   † Webster's Dictionary.

appropriated to any existing being in heaven or earth, or under the earth; and let them cease to profane religion, and insult common sense, by affixing the holy name of the Supreme to their thousand-headed monster.

But the very perfection of Jesuitism is reached, when Pantheists profess their high respect for the Christian religion. They do not generally speak of it as a superstition, though some of the vulgar sort do; nor do they decry its mysteries, as Deists are in the habit of doing; nor, as Socinians, and Unitarians, and Rationalists, attempt to reduce it to a mere code of morals. They grant it to be the highest development of humanity yet reached by the majority of the human race. The brute, the savage, the polytheistic idolator, the star worshipper, the monotheist, the Christian, are all, in their scheme, so many successive developments of humanity in its upward progress. There is only one step higher than Christianity, and that is Pantheism. Well knowing that Christianity is diametrically opposed to their falsehoods, and that the Bible, every where, teaches that the progress of man has ever been down from a state of holiness to idolatry and barbarism, they have yet the hardihood to profess respect for it, as a system of concealed Pantheism, and to clothe their abominations in Scripture language. They speak, for instance, of the "beauty of holiness in the mind, that has surmounted every idea of a personal God;" and of "God dwelling in us, and his love perfected in us," when they believe that he dwells as really in every creature: in that hog, for instance. Then they will readily acknowledge that the Bible is inspired. They *can accept*—that is the phrase—they can accept the book which denounces death upon those fools who, "professing themselves to be wise, change the truth of God into a lie, and worship and serve the creature more than the Creator," as merely a mystic revelation of the Pantheism which leaves man to "erect every thing into a God, provided it is none: sun, moon, stars, a cat, a monkey, an onion, uncouth idols, sculptured marble; nay, a shapeless trunk, which the devout impatience of the idolator does not stay to fashion into the likeness of a man, but gives it its apotheosis at once." Oh, yes; they accept the Bible as inspired—a God-inspired book—inasmuch as *every* product of the human mind is a development of Deity. The Bible, then, when we have the matter fully explained, is quite on a level with Gulliver's Travels, or Emerson's Address to a Senior Class of Divinity.

There is nothing, however, in this vast system of monstrosities, which fills the soul of a Christian with such loathing and detestation, as to hear Pantheists profess their veneration for the Lord Jesus, and claim him as a teacher of Pantheism. If there is one object which they detest with all their hearts, it is the Judge of the quick and dead, and the vengeance which he shall take upon them that know not God, and obey not the Gospel. Any allusion to the judgment seat of Christ fills them with fury, and causes them to pour forth awful blasphemies. They know that the Lord Jesus repeatedly declared himself the judge of the living and the dead—that "the hour is coming in which all that are in their graves shall hear his voice, and shall come forth: they that have done good, unto the resurrection of life, and they that have done evil, unto the resurrection of damnation;" and that the very last sentence of his public discourses is, "And these (the wicked) shall go away into everlasting punishment; but the righteous into life eternal." When they drop the mask for a moment, they can accuse apostles and disciples with "dwelling with noxious exaggeration about the *person* of Christ."* Christ, as revealed in the Gospel, they hate with a perfect hatred. But when it becomes necessary to address Christians, and beguile them into the deceitfulness of Pantheism, the tune is changed. Christ becomes the model man—"one conceived in conditions favorable to the highest perfectibility of the individual consciousness; and so possessed of powers of generalization far in advance of the age in which he lived. They can listen to and honor one of the best expounders of God and nature in the Man of Nazareth."† The vilest falsehoods of Pantheism are ascribed to Jesus, that those who, ignorant of his doctrine, yet respect his name, may be seduced to receive them. Of him who declared, "Out of the heart of man proceed evil thoughts, murders, adulteries, thefts, false witness, blasphemies," they have the hardihood to declare, "He saw with open eyes the mystery of the soul; alone, in all history, he estimated the greatness of man." Calculating upon that ignorance of the teaching of Christ which is so general among their audiences, they dare to represent the only begotten Son of God as teaching

---

* Emerson's Address to a Senior Class in Divinity.

† Hennell's Christian Theism, which shows how Theists of every nation—Christian, Jew, Mahommedan, or Chinese—can meet upon common ground.

Pantheism: "One man was true to what is in you and me; He saw that God incarnates himself in man, and evermore goes forth anew to take possession of his world. He said in this jubilee of sublime emotion, 'I am divine. Through me God acts; through me, speaks. Would you see God, see me; or see thee when thou also thinkest as I now think.' Because the indwelling Supreme Spirit cannot wholly be got rid of, the doctrine of it suffers this perversion, that the divine nature is attributed to one or two persons, and denied to all the rest, and denied with fury." Yes, truly, the divine nature is emphatically denied to all unregenerated men, and denied, too, by that divine teacher thus eulogized. Hear him: "Ye do the deeds of your father. Then said they to him, 'We be not born of fornication; we have one Father, even God.' Jesus said unto them, 'If God were your Father, ye would love me; for I proceeded forth and came from God; neither came I of myself, but he sent me. Why do ye not understand my speech? Even because ye cannot hear my word. Ye are of your father, the devil; and the works of your father ye will do. He was a murderer from the beginning, and abode not in the truth, because there is no truth in him. When he speaketh a lie, he speaketh it of his own; for he is a liar, and the father of it."

Let Pantheists, then, cease to wind their serpent coils around Christianity, and to defile the Bible with their filthy lickings. The Lord Jesus will not suffer such persons to bear even a true testimony to him, and his followers will not permit them to ascribe their falsehoods to him, without reproof. Let them stand out and avow themselves the enemies of Christ and his gospel, as they are, and cease their abominable pretences of giving to the world the ultimate development of Christianity. What concord hath Christ with Belial?

3. *Pantheism is a system of Immorality.*—It loosens all the sanctions of moral law. If there is any one point upon which all Pantheists are agreed, it is in the denial of the resurrection, the judgment, and the future punishment of the wicked. Their whole system, in all its range, from Spiritualism to Phrenology, is expressly invented to get rid of God's moral government. If man is the highest intelligence in the universe, to whom should he render an account of his conduct? Or who would have any right to call him to account? Then, if we are developments of deity, deity cannot offend against itself. Further, if our development, both o

body and mind, be the inevitable result of the laws of nature—of our organization and our position—man is but the creature of circumstances, and, therefore, as is abundantly argued, cannot be made responsible for laws and their results, over which he has no control. "I am what I am. I cannot alter my will, or be other than what I am, and cannot deserve either reward or punishment."* Before hundreds of the citizens of Cincinnati, a lecturer publicly denied the right of either God or man to invade his individuality, by taking vengeance upon him for any crime whatever. Thousands, who are not yet Pantheists, are so far infected with the poison that they utterly deny any right of vindictive punishment to God or man.

But this is not all. Again and again have we listened with astonishment to men, declaring that there was no moral law—no standard of right and wrong, but the will of the community. Of course it was quite natural, after such a declaration, to assert that a wife who should remain with a husband of inferior intellectuality, or unsuitable emotions, was committing adultery; that private property is a legalized robbery; and that when a citizen becomes mentally or physically unfit for the business of life, he confers the highest obligation on society, and performs the highest duty to himself, by committing suicide, and thus returning to the great ocean of being!

We might think that confusion of right and wrong could not be worse confounded than this; yet there is a blacker darkness still. *The distinction between good and evil is absolutely denied.* The Hindoo Pantheists declare that they cannot sin, because they are God, and God cannot offend against himself; there is no sin—it is all *maya*—delusion. So the American and English school tells us it lives only in the obsolete theology. "Evil, we are told, is good in another way, we are not skilled in."† So says the author of "Representative Men." "Evil," according to old philosophers, "is good in the making; that pure malignity can exist, is the extreme proposition of unbelief. It is not to be entertained by a rational agent. It is Atheism; it is the last profanation." "The divine effort is never relaxed; the carrion in the sun will convert itself into grass and flowers; and man, though in brothels, or jails, or on gibbets, is on his way to all that is good and true."‡ Were

---

* Atkinson's Letters, p. 190. † Festus, p. 48.
‡ Swedenborg, or the Mystic (quoted by Pierson, 41), p. 68.

these only the ravings of lunatics, or the dreamings of philosophers, we should never have hunted them from their hiding-places to scare your visions; but these doctrines are weekly propounded in your own city, and throughout our land, from platform and press, to thousands of your children and their school-teachers, of your workmen and your lawgivers, to your wives and daughters. Again and again have our ears been confounded in the squares of New York, and the streets of Philadelphia, and the market-places of Cincinnati, by the boisterous cry, *What is sin? There is no sin. It is all an old story.* Let men who fear no God, but who have lives, and wives, and property to lose, look to it, and say if they act wisely in giving their influence to a system which lands in such consequences. Let them devise some religion for the people which will preserve the rights of man, while giving license to trample upon the rights of God; or, failing in the effort, let them acknowledge that the enemy of God is, and of necessity must be, the foe of all that constitutes the happiness of man. Impiety and immorality are wedded in heaven's decree, and man cannot sunder them.

4. *Pantheism is virtually Atheism.*—It may scarce seem needful to multiply proofs on this head. How can any one imagine a being composed of the sum of all the intelligences of the universe? Such a thing, or combination of things, never was distinctly conceived of by any intelligent being. Can intelligences be compounded, or, like bricks and mortar, piled upon each other? If they could, did these finite intelligences create themselves? If the soul of man is the highest intelligence in the universe, did the soul of man create, or does the soul of man govern it? Shall we adore his soul? Some Pantheists have got just to this length. M. Comte declares, that "At this present time, for minds properly familiarized with true astronomical philosophy, the heavens display no other glory than that of Hipparchus, or Kepler, or Newton, and of all who have helped to establish these laws." *Establish* these laws! Laws by which the heavenly bodies were guided thousands of years before Kepler or Newton were born. Shall we then adore the souls of Kepler and Newton? M. Comte has invented a religion, which he is much displeased that the admirers of his Positive Philosophy will not accept, in which the children are to be taught to worship idols, the youth to believe in one God, if they can, after such a training in infancy, and the full grown men are to adore a

Grand Etre, "the continuous resultant of all the forces capable of voluntarily concurring in the universal perfectioning of the world, *not forgetting our worthy auxiliaries, the animals.*" * Our Anglo-Saxon Pantheists, however, are not quite philosophical enough yet to adore the mules and oxen, and therefore refuse worship altogether. "Work is worship," constitutes their liturgy. "As soon as the man is as one with God, he will not beg. He will then see prayer in all action."† "Labor wide as earth has its summit in heaven. Sweat of the brow, and up from that to sweat of the brain, sweat of the heart; which includes all Kepler calculations, Newton meditations, all sciences, all spoken epics, all acted heroisms, martyrdoms, up to that agony of bloody sweat, which all men have accounted divine! O brother, if this is not worship, then I say, the more pity for worship; for this is the noblest thing yet discovered under God's sky." "No man has worked, or can work, except religiously."‡ "Adieu, O church! Thy road is that way, mine is this. In God's name, adieu!" §

Such is the theory. How faithfully acted out, you can learn from the thousands who are now, publicly, upon God's holy Sabbath, working religiously upon the bridge that is to span the river, or less ostentatiously in their shops and work-rooms throughout the city. Within a circle of three miles radius of the spot you now occupy, one hundred thousand intelligent beings in this Christian city worship no God.

The abstraction, which the Pantheist calls God, is no object of worship. It is not to be loved. If it does good, it could not help it, and did not intend it. It is not to be thanked for benefits. It, the sum of all the intelligence of the universe, cannot be collected from the seven spheres to receive any such acknowledgment. It cannot deviate from its fated course of proceeding; therefore, says the Pantheist, why should I pray? It neither sees his conduct, nor cares for it; and he denies any right to call him to account. It did not create him, does not govern him, will not judge him, cannot punish him. It is no object of love, fear, worship, or obedience. It is no god. He is an Atheist. He believes not in any God.

HEAR, O ISRAEL! THE LORD OUR GOD IS ONE LORD. He is

---

* Politique Positive, vol. 2, p. 60.   † Emerson.
‡ Carlyle—Past and Present.   § Carlyle—Life of Sterling.

distinct from, and supreme over all his works. He now rules, and will hereafter judge all intelligent creatures, and will render to every one according to his works.

1. *Reason declares it.* The world did not make itself. The soul of man did not make itself. The body of man did not make itself. They must have had an intelligent Creator, who is God. God is known by his works to be distinct from them, and superior to them. The work is not the workman. The house is not the builder. The watch is not the watchmaker. The sum of all the works of any worker is not the agent who produced them. Let an architect spend his life in building a city, yet the city is not the builder. The maker is always distinct from and superior to the thing made. You and I, and the universe, are made. Our Maker, then, is distinct from, and superior to us. One plan gives order to the universe; therefore, one mind originated it. The Creator is over all his creatures.

2. *Our consciousness confirms it.* If a blind God could not make a seeing man, a god destitute of the principle of self-consciousness (if such an abuse of language may be tolerated for a moment) could not impart to man the conviction, *I am*,—the ineradicable belief that I am not the world, nor any other person; much less, every body; but that I am a person, possessed of powers of knowing, thinking, liking and disliking, judging, approving of right, and disapproving of wrong, and choosing and willing my conduct. My Maker has at least as much common sense as he has given me. He that teacheth man knowledge, shall he not know?

3. *Our Ignorance and Weakness demand a Governor of the World wiser than ourselves.* The soul of man is not the highest intelligence in the universe. It cannot know the mode of its own operation on the body it inhabits, much less the plan of the world's management. Man may know much about what does not concern him, and about things over which he has no control; but it is the will of God that his pride should feel the curb of ignorance and impotence where his dearest interests are concerned, that so he may be compelled to acknowledge that God is greater than man. He may be able to tell the place of the distant planets a thousand years hence, but he cannot tell where himself shall be next year. He can calculate for years to come the motions of the tides, which he cannot control, but cannot tell how his own pulse shall beat, or whether it shall beat at all, to-morrow. Ever as his knowledge

of the laws by which God governs the world, increases, his conviction of his impotence grows; and he sees and feels that a wiser head and stronger hand than that of any creature, planned and administers them. Ever as he reaches some ultimate truth, such as the mystery of electricity, of light, of life, of gravitation, which he can not explain, and beyond which he can not penetrate, he hears the voice of God therein, demanding him to acknowledge his impotence.

"Where is the way where light dwelleth,
"And as for darkness, what is the place thereof?
"Canst thou bind the sweet influences of the Pleiades,
"Or loose the bands of Orion?
"Canst thou bring forth Mazzaroth in his seasons?
"Or canst thou guide Arcturus, with his sons?
"Knowest thou the ordinances of heaven?
"Canst thou set the dominion thereof in the earth?
"Canst thou lift up thy voice to the clouds,
"That abundance of waters may cover thee?
"Canst thou rend lightnings, that they may go
"And say unto thee, 'Here we are?'"

4. *Our consciences convince us that God is a Moral Governor.* The distinction between brutes and men is, that man has a sense of the distinction between right and wrong. If we find a tribe of savages, or individuals, who indulge their appetites without rule, and who do wrong without any apparent remorse or shame, we designate them brutes. Even those who in words deny any difference between right and wrong, do in fact admit its existence, by their attempts to justify that opinion. Though weaker, or less regarded in some than in others, every man is conscious of a faculty in himself which sits in judgment on his own conduct, and that of others, approving or condemning it as right or wrong. In all lands, and in all ages, the common sense of mankind has acknowledged the existence and moral authority of conscience, as distinct from and superior to mere intellect. No language of man is destitute of words conveying the ideas of virtue and vice, of goodness and wickedness. When one attempts to deceive you by a wilful lie, you are sensible not only of an intellectual process of reason detecting the error, but of a distinct judgment of disapprobation of the crime. When one, who has received kindness from a benefactor, neglects to make any acknowledgment of it, cherishes

no feelings of gratitude, and insults and abuses the friend who succored him, we are conscious, not merely of the facts, as phenomena to be observed, but of the ingratitude, as a crime to be detested. And we are irresistibly constrained to believe that he who taught us this knowledge of a difference between right and wrong, does himself know such a distinction; and that he who implanted this feeling of approval of right, and condemnation of wrong, in us, does himself approve the right and condemn the wrong. And as we can form no notion of right or wrong unconnected with the idea that approbation of right conduct should be suitably expressed, and that disapprobation of wrong conduct ought also to be suitably expressed—in other words, that right ought to be rewarded, and wrong ought to be punished—so we are constrained to trace such a connection from our minds to the mind of Him who framed them. This conviction is God's law, written in our hearts. When we do wrong, we become conscious of a feeling of remorse in our consciences, as truly as the eye becomes conscious of the darkness. We may blind the eye—we may sear the conscience—that the one shall not see, nor the other feel; but light and darkness, right and wrong, will exist. The awful fact which conscience reveals to us, that we sin against God, that we know the right, and do the wrong, and are conscious of it, and of God's disapprobation of it, is conclusive proof that we are not only distinct from God, but separate from him—that we oppose our wills against his. And every pang of remorse is a premonition of God's judgment, and every sorrow and suffering which the Governor of the world has connected with sin—as the drunkard's loss of character and property, of peace and happiness, the frenzy of his soul, and the destruction of his body—is a type and teaching of the curse which he has denounced against sin.

5. *The World's History is the record of man's crimes, and God's punishments.* Once God swept the human race from earth with a flood of water, because the wickedness of man was great on the earth. Again, he testified his displeasure against the ungodly sinners of Sodom and Gomorrah, by consuming their cities with fire from heaven, and leaving the Dead Sea to roll its solemn waves of warning to all ungodly sinners, to the end of time.

By the ordinary course of his providence, he has ever secured the destruction of ungodly nations. No learning, commerce, arms, territories, or skill, has ever secured a rebellious nation against the sword of God's justice. Ask the black record of a rebel world's history for an instance. Egypt? Canaan? Nineveh? Babylon? Persia? Greece? Rome? Where are they now? Tyre had ships, colonies, and commerce; Rome an empire on which the sun never set; Greece had philosophy, arts, and liberty secured by a confederation of republics; Spain the treasures of earth's gold and silver, and the possession of half the globe. Did these secure them against the moral government of God?

No! God's law sways the universe—that law which, with the brazen fetters of eternal justice, binds together sin and misery, crime and punishment, and lays the burden on the backs of all ungodly nations, irresistibly forcing them down—down—down the road to ruin. The vain imagination that refuses to glorify God as God, leads to darkness of heart, thence to Atheism, thence to gross idolatry—onward to selfish gratification, violent rapacity, lust of conquest, and luxury, licentiousness, and effeminacy begotten of its spoils; then military tyranny, civil war, servile revolt, anarchy, famine and pestilence, and the sword of less debauched neighbors, Christ's iron scepter, hurl them down from the pinnacle of greatness, to dash them in pieces against each other, in the valley of destruction; and there they lie, wrecks of nations—ruins of empires—naught remaining, save some shivered potsherds of former greatness, to show that once they were, and were the enemies of God.

Oh, America, take warning ere it be too late! God rules the nations. "He that chastiseth the heathen, shall he not correct you?"

A day of retribution, reader, comes to you. Neither your insignificance nor your unbelief shall hide you from his eye, nor can your puny arm shield you from his righteous judgment. His hand shall find out his enemies. Oh, fly from the wrath to come!

No. 25.

HAVE WE ANY NEED OF THE BIBLE.

Religion consists of the knowledge of a number of great facts, and a course of life suitable to them. We have seen three of these: that God created the world; that He governs it; and that He is able to conquer His enemies. There are others of the same sort as needful to be known. Our knowledge of these facts, or our ignorance of them, makes not the slightest difference in the facts themselves. God is, and heaven is, and hell is, and sin leads to it, whether any body believes these things or not. It makes no sort of difference in the beetling cliff and swollen flood that sweeps below it, that the drunken man declares there is no danger, and refusing the proffered lantern, gallops on toward it in the darkness of the night. But when the mangled corpse is washed ashore, every one sees how foolish this man was to be so confident in his ignorance as to refuse the lantern, which would have shown him his danger, and guided him to the bridge where he might have crossed in safety. Some of the facts of religion lie at the evening end of life's journey—the darkness of death's night hides them from mortal eye—living men might guide their steps the better by asking counsel of one who knows the way. If they get along no better by their own counsel in the next world, than most of them do in this, they will have small cause to bless their teacher. Who can tell that ignorance, and wickedness, and wretchedness are not as tightly tied together in the world to come, as we see them here?

Solomon was a knowing man and wise: and better than that in the esteem of most people, he made money, and tells you how to make it and keep it. You will make a hundred dollars by reading his Proverbs and acting on them. They would have saved some of you many a thousand. Of course such a man knew something of the world. He was a wide awake trader. His ships coasted the shores of Asia and Africa, from Madagascar to Japan; and the overland mail caravans, from India and China, drew up in the depots he built for them in the heart of the desert. He knew the well-doing people with whom trade was profitable, and the savages who could only send apes and peacocks. He was a philosopher as well as a trader, and could not help being deeply impressed with *the great fact*, that there was a wide difference among the nations of the world. Some were enlightened, enterprising, civilized, and flourishing; others were naked savages, living in ignorance, poverty, vice, and starvation, perpetually murdering one another, and dying out off the earth.

Solomon noticed *another great fact*. In his own country, and in Chaldea, Mesopotamia, Egypt, and some others, God had revealed His will to certain persons for the benefit of their neighbors. He did so generally by opening the eyes of these prophets to see future events, and the great facts of the unseen world, and by giving them messages of warning and instruction to the nations. From this mode of revelation, by opening the prophets' eyes to see realities invisible to others, they were called seers, and the revelations they were commissioned to make were called visions; and revelation from God was called in general vision. Solomon was struck with the fact that some nations were thus favored by God, and other nations were not. The questions would naturally arise, Why this difference? What difference does it make, or does it make any difference, whether men have any revelation of God's will or not?

Solomon was led to observe a *third great fact*. The nations which were favored with these revelations were the civilized, enterprising, and comparatively prosperous nations. In proportion to the amount of divine revelation they had, and their obedience to it, they prospered. The nations that had no revelation from God were the idolatrous savages, who were sinking down to the level of brutes, and perishing off the face of the earth. He daguerreotypes these three great facts in the Proverb: "Where there is no vision the people perish; but he that keepeth the law, happy is he."

O, says the Rationalist, the world is wiser now than it was in Solomon's days. He lived in the old mythological period, when men attributed every thing extraordinary to the gods. But the world is too wise now to believe in any supernatural revelation. "The Hebrew and Christian religions like all others have their myths." "The fact is, the pure historic idea was never developed among the Hebrews during the whole of their political existence." "When, therefore, we meet with an account of certain phenomena, or events of which it is expressly stated or implied that they were produced immediately by God himself, (such as divine apparitions, voices from heaven, and the like,) or by human beings possessed of supernatural powers, (miracles, prophecies, etc.,) such an account is so far to be considered not historical." "Indeed, no just notion of the true nature of history is possible without a perception of the inviolability of the chain of finite causes, and of the impossibility of miracles."* A narrative is to be deemed mythical, 1st, "When it proceeds from an age in which there were no written records, but events were transmitted by tradition; 2d, When it presents as historical, accounts of events which were beyond the reach of experience, as occurrences connected with the spiritual world; or 3d, When it deals in the marvelous, and is couched in symbolical language."† So also De Wette, and Schelling, and Gabler, and a host of others, who pass for biblical expositors, lay it down as an axiom, that all records of supernatural events are mythical, viz.: fables, falsehoods, because miracles are impossible. Of course, from such premises the conclusion is easy. A revelation from God to man is a supernatural event, and supernatural events are impossible; therefore, a revelation from God is impossible. But it would have been much easier, and quite as logical, to have laid down the axiom in plain words at first, that a revelation from God is impossible, as to argue it from such premises; for it is just as easy to *say*, that a revelation from God is impossible, as to *say* that miracles are impossible; and as for *proof* of either one or the other, we must just take their word for it.

One cannot help being amazed at the cool impudence with which these men take for granted the very point to be proved, and set aside, as unworthy of serious examination, the most authentic records of history, simply because they do not coincide with their so-called philosophy; and at the credulity with which their followers swallow this arrogant dogmatism, as if it were self-evident truth. Let us look at it for a moment. Other religions have their myths, or fables, therefore, the Hebrew and Christian records are fables, says the Rationalist. Profundity of logic! Counterfeit bank bills are common, therefore none are genuine. "The fact is, the pure historic idea was never developed among the Hebrews," *i. e.*, Moses and the prophets were all liars. That is the fact, you may take my word for it. "Indeed, no just notion of the true nature of history is possible without a perception of the inviolability of the chain of finite causes, and of the impossibility of miracles,"—which translated into plain words is simply this: No man can understand

---

* Straus' Life of Jesus, 64, 74, 87.   † Bauer's Hebrew Mythology.

history who believes in God Almighty. "A narrative is to be deemed fabulous when it proceeds from an age in which there were no written records," such, for instance, as any account of the creation of the first man—for no event could possibly happen unless there was a scribe there to write it. Or, of the fall of man —we do not know that Adam was able to write, and no man can tell truth unless he writes a history. "A narrative is to be deemed fabulous when it presents as historical, accounts of events which were beyond the reach of experience, as events connected with the spiritual world." Is it not self-evident that you and I have had experience of every thing in the whole universe, and whoever tells us any thing which we have never seen is a liar. "When a narrative deals in the marvelous," such as Xenophon's Retreat of the Ten Thousand, Herodotus' narratives of the battles of Marathon and Thermopylæ, or Gibbon's Decline and Fall of the Roman Empire, dealing as it does in such marvelous accounts as the death of half the inhabitants of the Empire in the reign of Galerius, or any other history of any wonderful occurrence—it is of course a myth. Does not every one know that nothing marvelous ever happened, or if it did, would any historian trouble himself to record a prodigy? "Or, if it is couched in symbolical language," as is every eloquent passage in Thucydides, Robertson, Gibbon, or Guizot, the records of China, and of India, the picture-writing of the Peruvians, and especially the Egyptian hieroglyphics, which were fondly expected to do such good service against the Bible—must be at once rejected, without further examination, as mythological and unworthy of any credit whatever. Thus we are conclusively rid for ever of the Bible, for sure enough it is couched in symbolical language. Blessed deliverance to the world! But then, alas! this great deliverance is accompanied with several little inconveniences. All poetry, three-fourths of the world's history, and the largest part of its philosophy, is couched in symbolical language, and especially the whole of the science of metaphysics, from which these very learned writers have deduced such edifying conclusions, is, from the beginning to the end, nothing but a symbolical application of the terms which describe material objects, to the phenomena of mind. Alas! we must for ever relinquish "the absolute," and "the infinite," and "the conditioned," with all their "affinities and potencies," up to "the higher unity," and "the rhythm of universal existence," and all the rest of those perspicuous German hieroglyphics, whether entombed in their native pyramids for the amazement of succeeding generations, by Fichte, Schelling, or Hegel, or "worshipping in the great cathedral of the immensities," "with their heads uplifted into infinite space," or "lying on the plane of their own consciousness," in the writings of Carlyle, Emerson, and Parker. They are myths, the whole of them, for they "are couched in symbolical language,"—and Bauer, De Wette, and Strauss have pronounced every thing couched in symbolical language to be mythical. Let us henceforth deliver our minds from all anxiety about history, philosophy, or religion, and stick to the price current and the multiplication table, the only accounts that are not "couched in symbolical language."

Such is the sort of trash which passes for profound philosophy when once it is made unintelligible, and such are the canons of interpretation with which men calling themselves philosophers and Christians sit down to investigate the claims of the Bible as a revelation from God. If they would speak out their true sentiments, they would say, "There cannot be any revelation from God, because there is no God." But they could not call themselves professors of Christian colleges, and pastors of Congregational churches, and reap the emoluments of such situations, if they would honestly avow their Atheism. Besides the world would see too plainly the drift of their teaching; therefore it is cloaked under a profession of belief in God, the Creator, who however is to be carefully prevented from ever showing himself again in the world he has made.

No proof is attempted for the declaration that miracles are impossible. Yet, surely, if it implies a contradiction to say so, that contradiction could be shown. That it is not self-evident is shown by the general belief of mankind that miracles have occurred. No man who believes in a supernatural being, can deny the possibility of supernatural actings. The creation of the world is the most stupendous of all miracles, utterly beyond the power of any finite causes, and entirely beyond the reach of our experience, yet these men admit that this miracle occurred. Supernatural events then are not impossible, nor unprecedented.

The vain notion that God, having created the world at first, left it for ever after to the operation of natural laws, is conclusively demolished by the discoveries of geology. These discoveries establish the fact recorded in Scripture, that in bringing the world into its present form there were several distinct and successive interpositions of supernatural power, in the distinct and successive creations of different species of vegetable and animal life. In former periods the earth was so warm that the present races of men and animals could not have lived on it, and the plants and animals of that age could not live now. These very men are profuse in proving that the earth existed for ages before *man* made his appearance upon it. This being the case, we are compelled to acknowledge the creating power of a God above the laws of nature, for there is no law of nature which can either create a new species of plants or animals—nor yet change one kind into another—make an oak into a larch, or an ox into a sheep, or a goose into a turkey, or a megatherium into an elephant—much less into a man. Some men have dreamed of such changes as these, but no instance of such a change has ever been alleged in proof of the notion. The most distinguished anatomists and geologists are fully agreed that no such change of one animal into another ever took place; much less that any animal ever was changed into a man. Lyell says at the conclusion of four chapters devoted to an investigation of the subject: "From the above considerations it appears that species have a real existence in nature, and that each was endowed at the time of its creation, with the attributes and organization by which it is now distinguished."* Cuvier, from his comprehensive survey of the fossils of former periods, establishes the fact, "that the species now living are not mere varieties of the species which are lost." And Agassiz says, "I have the conviction that species have been created successively, at distinct intervals."† Revelations of God's special interpositions in the affairs of this world are thus written by his own finger in the fossils and coal, and engraved on the everlasting granite of the earth's foundation stones. Dumb beasts and dead reptiles start forward to give their irrefutable testimony to the repeated supernatural acts of their Creator in this world which he had made. Every distinct species of plants and animals is proof of a distinct supernatural overruling of the present laws of nature. The experience of man is not the limit of knowledge. His own existence is a proof that the chain of finite causes is not inviolable. Geology sweeps away the very foundations of scepticism, by demon-

---

* Elements of Geology, page 611, 9th edition.
† See Pearson on Infidelity, page 93, 40th edition.

strating that certain phenomena produced immediately by God himself—the phenomena of the creation of life—have occurred repeatedly in the history of our globe. Revelation is not impossible because supernatural. The world is just as full of supernatural works as of natural. Nor is it incredible because it records miracles. The miracles recorded in the coal measures are as astonishing as any recorded in the Bible.

The Spiritualist next advances to assure us, that any external revelation from God to man is *useless*, because man is wise enough without it. The vulgar exposition of this sentiment is familiar to every reader. "You need not begin to preach Bible to me. I know my duty well enough without the Bible." The more educated attempt to reason the matter after this fashion: "Miraculous phenomena will never prove the goodness and veracity of God, if we do not know these qualities in him without a miracle."* We may remark in passing, that there are some other attributes of God besides goodness and veracity—holiness and justice for instance, which are proved by miracles. "Can thunder from the thirty-two azimuths, repeated daily for centuries, make God's laws more godlike to me? Brother, no. Perhaps I am grown to be a man now, and do not need the thunder and the terror any longer. Perhaps I am above being frightened. Perhaps it is not fear but reverence that shall now lead me! Revelation! Inspirations! And thy own god-created soul, dost thou not call that a revelation?"† It is manifest however, that if Mr. Carlyle needs not the Sinai thunder to assure him that the law given on Sinai was from God, there were then, and are now many who do, and some of his own sect who doubt in spite of it. If he is above the weakness of fearing God, all the world is not so.

The claims of a divine teacher are as unceremoniously rejected as those of a divine revelation. "If it depends on Jesus it is not eternally true, and if it is not eternally true it is no truth at all," says Parker. As if eternally true and sufficiently known were just the same thing; or as if because vaccination would always have prevented the small-pox, the world is under no obligation to Jenner for informing us of the fact. In the same strain Emerson despises instruction: "It is not instruction but provocation that I can receive from another soul. What he announces, I must find

---

* Newman's Phases of Faith, 157.   † Carlyle's Past and Present, 307.

true in me, or wholly reject; and on his word, or as his second, be he who he may, I can accept nothing." Again says Parker, "Christianity is dependent on no outside authority. We verify its eternal truth in our soul."* His aim is "to separate religion from whatever is finite—church, book, person—and let it rest on its absolute truth."† "It bows to no idols, neither the church, nor the Bible, nor yet Jesus, but God only: its Redeemer is within: its salvation within: its heaven and its oracle of God."‡ The whole strain of this school of writers and their disciples is one of depreciation of external revelation, and of exaltation of the inner light which every man is supposed to carry within him. Religion is "no Morison's pill from without," but a "clearing of the inner light," a "re-awakening of our own selves from within."§ So Mr. Newman‖ abundantly argues that an authoritative book revelation of moral and spiritual truth is impossible—that God reveals himself within us and not without us—and that a revelation of all moral and religious truth necessary for us to know is to be obtained by *insight* or gazing into the depths of our own consciousness. The sum of the whole business is, that neither God or man can reveal any religious truth to our minds, or as Parker felicitously expresses it, "on his word, or as his second, be he who he may, I can accept nothing."

Now, we are tempted to ask, who are these wonderful prodigies, so incapable of receiving instruction from any body? And to our amazement we learn, that some forty odd years ago they made their appearance among mankind as little squalling babies, without insight enough to know their own names, or where they came from, and were actually dependent on an external revelation, from their nurses, for sense enough to find their mothers' breasts. And as they grew a little larger, they obtained the power of speaking articulate sounds by external revelation: hearing and imitating the sounds made by others. Further, upon a memorable day, they had a "book revelation" made to them, in the shape of a penny primer, and were initiated into the mysteries of A, B, C, by "the instructions of another, be he who he may." There was absolutely not the least "insight," or "spiritual faculty," or "self-consciousness," in one of them, by which they then could, or ever to this hour did "find true within them" any sort of necessary connection

---

* Discourse on Religion, page 209.   ‡ Ib. page 37.   ‖ Ib. page 359.
† Carlyle's Past and Present, 312.   § The Soul Passive, page 342.

between the signs, c, a, t, — d, o, g, — and the sounds *cat*, *dog*, or any other sounds represented by any other letters of the alphabet. Faith in the word of their teachers is absolutely the sole foundation and only source of their ability to read and write. On "the word of another, and as his second, be he who he may," every one of them has accepted every intelligible word he speaks or writes.

And this is not half of their indebtedness to external revelation. For they will not deny that a Feejee cannibal has just the same "insight," "spiritual faculty," "mighty and transcendent soul," "self-consciousness," or any other name by which they may dignify our common humanity, which they themselves possess. How does it happen, then, that these writers, and all the rest of our Spiritualists, are not assembled around the cannibal's oven, smearing their faces with the blood, and feasting themselves on the limbs of women and children? The inner nature of the cannibal and the spiritualist is the same: whence comes the difference of character and conduct? And the inner light, too, is the same; for they assure us that "inspiration, like God's omnipresence, is coextensive with the race." Is it not, after all, mere external revelation, in the shape of education—aye, and moral and religious teaching—that makes the whole difference between the civilized American and his inspired Feejee brother?

These gentlemen not only acknowledge, but try to repay their obligations to external revelation. As it is impossible for God to give the world a book revelation of moral and religious truth, they modestly propose to come to his assistance, it being quite possible for some men to do what it is impossible for God. Accordingly, we have a book revelation of moral and religious truth, from one, in his treatise on The Soul, an "external revelation" from another, in his Discourse concerning religion, a "Morison's pill from the outside," from a third, in his Past and Present, and "announcements" from a fourth, which assuredly the great mass of mankind never "found true within them," else his orations and publications had not been needed to convert them. It is to be understood, then, that an "external revelation," or a "book revelation" of spiritual truth is impossible, only when it comes from God, but that these gentlemen have proved it quite possible for themselves to deliver one.

In so doing they have undoubtedly attempted to meet the wishes of the greater part of mankind, who have in all lands and in all ages longed for some outward revelation from God, and testified their desire by running after all sorts of omens, auguries, and oracles, consulting witches, and treasuring Sibylline leaves, employing writing mediums, and listening to spirit rappers. The "inspiration which is limited to no sect, age, or nation—which is wide as the world, and common as God,"* has never produced a nation of Spiritualists: a fact very unaccountable, if Spiritualism be true, and one which might well lead these writers to acknowledge at least one kind of total depravity, namely, that inspired men should love the darkness of external revelations, and even of book revelations, and read Bibles, and Korans, and Vedas, and "Discourses concerning religion," and "Phases of Faith," while yet "every thing that is of use to man, lies in the plane of our own consciousness."† Surely, such a universal craving after an external revelation testifies to a felt necessity for it, and renders it probable, or at least desirable, that God would supply the deficiency. Is the religious appetite the only one for which God has provided no supply?

But we are instructed, that, "as we have bodily senses to lay hold on matter, and supply bodily wants, through which we obtain naturally all needed material things, so we have spiritual faculties to lay hold on God, and supply spiritual wants: through them we obtain all needed spiritual things." That we have both bodily senses and spiritual faculties, is doubtless true; but whether either the one or the other obtain all needed things, is somewhat doubtful. I cannot tell how it is with mankind in Boston, for I am not there; and this being a matter in which religious truth is concerned, Mr. Emerson will not allow me to receive instruction about it from any other soul; but I see from my window a poor widow, with five children, who has bodily senses to lay hold on matter, and supply bodily wants; yet in my opinion she has not obtained naturally all needed material things; and if there be a truth which lies emphatically in the plane of her own consciousness, it is, that she is in great need of a cord of wood, and a barrel of flour, for her starving children. I know, also, a man, to whom God gave bodily senses to lay hold on matter, and supply bodily wants, who, by his drunkenness, has destroyed these bodily

---

* Parker's Discourse, 171. † Ibid, 33.

senses, and brought his family to utter destitution of all needed material things. From one cause or another, I find multitudes here in poverty and destitution, notwithstanding they have bodily senses. It is reported, also, that there is a poor house in Boston, and poverty in Ireland, and starvation in Madeira, and famine in the inundated provinces of France, and misery and destitution in London; which, if true, completely overturns this beautiful theory. For, if, notwithstanding the possession of bodily senses, men do starve in this world for want of needful food and clothing, it is very possible that they may have spiritual faculties also, and yet not obtain through them all needed spiritual things. The second part of the theory is as baseless as the first. All men have spiritual faculties, and have not by them obtained all needed spiritual things. They have not in their own opinion, and surely they are competent judges of "what lies wholly in the plane of their own consciousness."

In proof of the fact that mankind have not, in their own opinion, obtained all needed spiritual things by the use of their spiritual faculties, without the aid of external revelation, we appeal to all the religions of mankind, Heathen, Mahomedan, and Christian. Every one of these appeals to revelations from God. Every lawgiver of note professed to have communication with heaven, Zoroaster, Minos, Pythagoras, Solon, Lycurgus, Numa, Mahomed, down to the chief of the present revolution in China. "Whatever becomes of the real truth of these relations," says Strabo of those before his day, "*it is certain that men did believe and think them true.*" If mankind had found the supply of all their spiritual wants within themselves, would they have clung in this way to the pretence of external revelations? Is not the abundance of quack doctors conclusive proof of the existence of disease and the need of physicians?

Not only was the need of an external revelation of some sort acknowledged by all mankind, but the insufficiency of the pretended oracles which they enjoyed was deplored by the wisest part of them. We never find men amidst the dim moonlight of tradition and the light of nature, vaunting the sufficiency of their inward light; it is only amidst the full blaze of noon-day Christianity, that philosophers can stand up and declare that they have no need of God's teaching. Had such men lived in Athens of old, they would have found men possessed of spiritual faculties, and those of

67

no mean order, engaged in erecting an altar with this inscription, "*To the Unknown God.*" One of the wisest of the heathen (Socrates) acknowledged that he could attain to no certainty respecting religious truth or moral duty, in these memorable words, "We must of necessity wait, till some one from Him who careth for us, shall come and instruct us how we ought to behave towards God and toward man." The chief of the Academy, whose philosophy concerning the eternity of matter occupies a conspicuous place in the creed of American heathens, had no such confidence in the sufficiency of his own powers of discovering religious truth. "We cannot know of ourselves what petition will be pleasing to God, or what worship we should pay to him; but it is necessary that a lawgiver should be sent from heaven to instruct us." "Oh how greatly do I long to see that man!" He further declares that "*this lawgiver must be more than man, that he may teach us the things man can not know by his own nature.*"* Whether this want of a revelation from God, was real or merely imaginary, will appear by a brief review of the opinions and practices of those who never enjoyed, and of those who reject the light of God's revelation.

They knew not God. If there is any article of religion fundamental and indispensable to its very existence, it is the knowledge of God. It is admitted by Spiritualists that the spiritual faculties are designed to lay hold on God. It has been proved in the two former tracts of this series, and will be admitted by all but Atheists, that God is an intelligent being. And further it has been proved that God is not every thing and every body, but distinct from and supreme over all his works. Besides, in this country at least, there will not be much difference of opinion as to the propriety of a rational being adoring a brute, or a log of wood, or a lump of stone. It will be allowed that such stupidity shows both ignorance and folly. Now let us enquire into the knowledge of God possessed by the people who have no vision.

The Chaldeans, the most ancient people of whom we have any account, and who had among them the immediate descendants of Noah, and whatever traditions of Noah's prophecies they preserved, were probably the best instructed of the heathen. Yet we find that they gave up the worship of God, adored the sun, and moon, and stars of heaven, and in process of time degenerated still fur-

---

* Plato. Republic. Books IV and VI., and Alcibiades II.

ther, and worshiped dumb idols. From this rock we were hewn; the common names of the days of the week, and especially of the first day of the week, will for ever keep up a testimony to the necessity of that revelation which delivered our forefathers and us from burning our children upon the devil's altars on Sun-days.

The Egyptians were reputed the most learned of mankind, and Egypt was considered the cradle of the arts and sciences. In her existing monuments, hieroglyphic inscriptions, and tomb paintings, we have presented to us the materials for forming a more correct opinion of the religion and life of the Egyptians, than of any other ancient people; and the investigation of these monuments is still adding to our information. Infidel writers and lecturers have not hesitated to allege that Moses merely taught the Israelites the religion of Egypt; and some have had the hardihood to allege that the ten commandments are found written on the pyramids, as an argument against the necessity of a revelation. If the statement were true, it would by no means prove the conclusion. Egypt was favored with divine revelations to several of her kings, and enjoyed occasional visits from, or the permanent teachings of such prophets as Abraham, Jacob, Joseph, and Moses, for four hundred years—a fact quite sufficient to account for her superiority to other heathen nations, as well as for the existence of some traces of true religion on her monuments. But the alleged fact is a falsehood. Some good moral precepts are found on the Egyptian monuments, but the ten commandments are not there. It may be charitably supposed that those who allege the contrary never learned the ten commandments, or have forgotten them, else they would have remembered that the first commandment is, "Thou shalt have no other gods before me;" and that the second is, "Thou shalt not make unto thee any graven image," etc., and would have paused before alleging that these commands were engraved upon the very temples of idols, and by the priests of the birds and beasts and creeping things which they adored. It is very doubtful if they believed in the existence of one supreme God, as most of the heathen did; but if they did, "they did not under any form, symbol, or hieroglyphic, represent the idea of the unity of God," as is fully proved by Wilkinson.* On the contrary, the monuments confirm the satirical sketch of the poet,† as to the "monsters mad Egypt

---

* Manners and Customs of Ancient Egyptians, 2d series, vol. ii., page 176, et passim.
† Juvenal, Satire XV.

worshiped: here a sea-fish, there a river-fish; whole towns adore a dog. This place fears an ibis saturated with serpents; that adores a crocodile. It is a sin to violate a leek or onion, or break them with a bite." Cruel wars were waged between different towns, as Plutarch tells us, because the people of Cynopolis would eat a fish held sacred by the citizens of Latopolis. Bulls, and dogs, and cats, and rats, and reptiles, and dung beetles, were devoutly adored by the learned Egyptians. A Roman soldier, who had accidentally killed one of their gods, a cat, was put to death for sacrilege.* Whenever a dog died, every person in the house went into mourning, and fasted till night. So low had the "great, the mighty and transcendent soul," been degraded, that there is a picture extant of one of the kings of Egypt worshiping his own coffin! Such is man's knowledge of God without a revelation from Him.

The Greeks, from their early intercourse with Egypt, borrowed from them most of their religion; but by later connections with the Hebrews about the time of Aristotle and Alexander, they gathered a few grains of truth to throw into the heap of error. After the translation of the Scriptures into Greek, in the reign of Ptolemy Philadelphus, any of their philosophers who desired, might easily have learned the knowledge of the true God. But before this period we find little or no sense or truth in their religion. And the same remarks will apply to the Romans. Their gods were as detestable as they were numerous. Hesiod tells us they had thirty thousand. Temples were erected to all the passions, fears, diseases, to which humanity is subject. Their supreme god Jupiter was an adulterer, Mars a murderer, Mercury a thief, Bacchus a drunkard, Venus a harlot, and they attributed other crimes to their gods too horrible to be mentioned. Such gods were worshiped with appropriate ceremonies, of lust, drunkenness, and bloodshed. Their most sacred mysteries, carried on under the patronage of these licentious deities, were so abominable and infamous, that it was found necessary for the preservation of any remnant of good order, to prohibit them.

It may be supposed that the human race is grown wiser now than in the days of Socrates and Cicero, and that such abominations are no longer possible. Turn your eyes, then, to India, and behold one hundred and fifty millions of rational beings, possessed

---

* Diodorus Siculus, Book 1.

of "spiritual faculties," "insight," and "the religious sentiment," worshipping three hundred and thirty millions of gods, in the forms of hills and trees, and rivers, and rocks, elephants, tigers, monkeys and rats, crocodiles, serpents, beetles and ants, and monsters like to nothing in heaven or earth, or under the earth. Take one specimen of all. There is "the lord of the world," Juggernath. "When you think of the monster block of the idol, with its frightfully grim and distorted visage, so justly styled the Moloch of the East, sitting enthroned amid thousands of massive sculptures, the representative emblems of that cruelty and vice which constitute the very essence of his worship; when you think of the countless multitudes that annually congregate there, from all parts of India, many of them measuring the whole distance of their weary pilgrimage with their own bodies; when you think of the merit-earning assiduities constantly practised by crowds of devotees and religious mendicants, around the holy city: some remaining all day with their head on the ground, and their feet in the air; others with their bodies entirely covered with earth; some cramming their eyes with mud, and their mouths with straw, while others lie extended in a puddle of water; here one man lying with his foot tied to his neck, another with a pot of fire on his breast, a third enveloped in a network of ropes;—when, besides these self-inflicted torments, you think of the frightful amount of involuntary suffering and wretchedness arising from the exhaustion of toilsome pilgrimages, the cravings of famine, and the scourgings of pestilence;—when you think of the day of the high festival— how the horrid king is dragged forth from his temple, and mounted on his lofty car, in the presence of hundreds of thousands, that cause the very earth to shake with shouts of 'Victory to Juggernath, our Lord;'—how the officiating high priest, stationed in front of the elevated idol, commences the public service by a loathsome pantomimic exhibition, accompanied with the utterance of filthy, blasphemous songs, to which the vast multitude at intervals respond, not in the strains of tuneful melody, but in loud yells of approbation, united with a kind of hissing applause;—when you think of the carnage that ensues, in the name of sacred offering— how, as the ponderous machine rolls on, grating harsh thunder, one and another of the more enthusiastic devotees throw themselves beneath the wheels, and are instantly crushed to pieces, the infatuated victims of hellish superstition;—when you think of the numerous Golgothas that bestud the neighboring plain, where the dogs, jackals and vultures seem to live on human prey; and of those bleak and barren sands that are for ever whitened with the skulls and bones of deluded pilgrims which lie bleaching in the sun,"*— you will be able to see an awful force of meaning in the words of our text, and to realize more fully the necessity of a revelation from God, for the very preservation of animal life to man. Literally, where there is no vision the people *perish*. Man doth not live by bread only, but by every word which proceedeth from the mouth of God.

Take one other illustration of ignorance of God in the minds of those who close their eyes against the light of revelation—the heathen of Europe and America, possessing that inspiration which is wide as the world, looking abroad upon all the glorious works of the great Creator, and declaring there is no God. On the other hand, we have men, possessed of this same inspiration, deifying every thing, and outrunning even the Hindoos in the multitude of their divinities, declaring that every stick, and stone, and serpent, and snail that crawls on the earth is God, and making professions of holding spiritual communings with them all. To crown the monument of folly, the chief of the Positive Philosophy comes forth with a revelation from his spiritual faculties, in which by way of improving on the proverb "both are best," and of being sure of the truth, he unites Atheism, and Pantheism, and Idolatry—teaches his child to worship idols, the youth to believe in one God, and himself and other full-grown men to adore the "resultant of all the forces capable of voluntarily contributing to the perfectioning of the universe, *not forgetting his worthy friends, the animals.*" To such darkness are men justly condemned who shut their eyes against the light of God's revelation. Where there is no vision the people perish intellectually. He who turns away his ears from the truth, must be turned unto fables. "Hear ye and give ear, be not proud, for the Lord hath spoken. Give glory to the Lord your God before he cause darkness, and before your feet stumble upon the dark mountains, and while ye look for light, he turn it into the shadow of death, and make it gross darkness."

---

* Duff's India, p. 222

Without a revelation from God, the mind of man can attain to no certainty regarding the most important of all his interests, the destiny of his immortal soul. He knows well—for every sickness, and sorrow, and calamity declares it, and quick returning troubles will not allow him to forget—that the Ruler of the world is offended with him; and conscience tells him why. The sense of guilt is common to the human race. This is, indeed, "the inspiration which knows no sect, no country, no religion, no age; which is as wide as humanity." Reason asks herself, Will God be always thus angry with me? Shall I ever feel these pangs of remorse for my sins? Will misery follow me for ever, as I see and feel that it does here? Or shall my soul exist under God's frowns, or perish under his just sentence, even as my body perishes? Does the grave hide for ever all that I loved? Have they ceased to be? Shall we ever meet again? Or must I say, "Farewell, farewell! An eternal farewell!" And in a few days myself also cease to be? The only answer reason gives, is—solemn silence.

The wisest of men could not tell. Who has not dropped a tear over the dying words of Socrates, "I am going out of the world, and you are to continue in it, but which of us has the better part is a secret to every one but God." Cicero contended for the immortality of the soul against the multitudes of philosophers who denied it in his day; yet, after recounting their various opinions, he is obliged to say, "Which of these is true, God alone knows; and which is most probable, a very great question."* And Seneca, on a review of this subject, says: "Immortality, however desirable, was rather promised than proved by these great men." †

The multitude had but two ideas on the subject. Either their ghosts should wander eternally in the land of shadows, or else they would pass into a succession of other bodies, of animals or men. From the nakedness and desolation of unclothed spirit, and the possibility which this notion held out of some close contact with a holy and just judge, the soul shrank back to the hope of the metempsychosis, and hoped rather to dwell in the body of a brute, than be utterly unclothed and mingle with spirits. This is the delusion cherished by the people of India and many other lands to this day. How unsatisfactory to the dying sinner this

---

* Tusc. Quæst, lib. 1.   † Seneca, Ep. 102.

uncertainty. "Tell me," said a wealthy Hindoo, who had given all his wealth to the Brahmins who surrounded his dying bed, that they might obtain pardon for his sins, "Tell me what will become of my soul when I die?" "Your soul will go into the body of a holy cow." "And after that?" "It will pass into the body of the divine peacock." "And after that?" "It will pass into a flower." "Tell me, oh! tell me," cried the dying man, "where will it go last of all?" Where will it go last of all? Aye, that is the question reason can not answer.

The rejectors of the Bible here, are as uncertain on this all-important subject, as the heathen of India. They have every variety of oracles, and conjectures, and suppositions about the other world; but for their guesses they offer no proof. When they give us their oracles as if they were known truths, we are compelled to ask, How do you know? The only thing in which they are agreed among themselves, is in denying the resurrection of the body—a point which they gathered from their heathen classics. A poor, empty, naked, shivering, table-rapping spirit, obliged to fly over the world at the sigh of any silly sewing girl, or the bidding of some brazen-faced strumpet, is all that ever shall exist of Washington or Newton, in the scheme of one class of Bible rejectors. To obtain rest from such a doom, others fly to the eternal tomb, and inform us that the soul is simply an acting of the brain, and when the brain ceases to act, the soul ceases also. Let us eat and drink, for to-morrow we die. But even this hog philosophy is reasonable, compared with the dogma of the large majority, that a man may blaspheme, swear, lie, steal, murder, and commit adultery, and go straight to heaven—that "many a swarthy Indian who bowed down to wood and stone—many a grim-faced Calmuck who worshiped the great god of storms—many a Grecian peasant who did homage to Phœbus Apollo when the sun rose or went down—many a savage, his hands smeared all over with human sacrifice—shall sit down with Moses and Jesus in the kingdom of God."* To such wild unreason does the mind of man descend when it rejects the Bible.

Life and immortality are brought to light by the Gospel. Where there is no vision, hope perishes. The only plausible creed for him

---

* Parker's Discourse, 93.

who rejects it, is the eternal tomb, and the heart-chilling inscription: "Death is an eternal sleep!"

Without a revelation from God, men are as ignorant how to live, as how to die. They have no rule of life having either truth or authority to direct them. Our Anglo Saxon ancestors, of the purity of whose blood we are so proud, trusted to their magical incantations for the cure of diseases, for the success of their tillage, for the discovery of lost property, for uncharming cattle and the prevention of casualties. One day was useful for all things; another, though good to tame animals, was baleful to sow seed. One day was favorable to the commencement of business, another to let blood, and others wore a forbidding aspect to these and other things. On this day they were to buy, on a second to sell, on a third to hunt, on a fourth to do nothing. If a child was born on such a day, it would live; if on another, its life would be sickly; if on another, it would perish early.* Their descendants who reject the Bible are fully as superstitious. Astrologers, and Mediums, and Clairvoyants, in multitudes, find a profitable trade among them; and one prominent anti-Bible lecturer will cure you of any disease you have, if you will only enclose, in a letter, a lock of hair from the right temple, and—a—Five Dollar Bill.

The precepts of even the wisest men, and the laws of the best regulated states, commanded or approved of vice. In Babylon prostitution was compulsory on every female. The Carthaginian law required human sacrifices. When Agathoclas besieged Carthage, two hundred children, of the most noble families, were murdered by the command of the senate, and three hundred citizens voluntarily sacrificed themselves to Saturn.† The laws of Sparta required theft, and the murder of unhealthy children. Those of ancient Rome allowed parents the power of killing their children, if they pleased. At Athens, the capital of heathen literature and philosophy, it was enacted "that infants which appeared to be maimed should be either killed or exposed."‡

Plato, dissatisfied with the constitution, made a scheme of one much better, which he has left us in his Republic. In this great advance of society, this heathen millennium, we find that there was

---

* Turner's Anglo Saxons, b. vii, chap. 13.   ‡ Aristotle, Polit. lib. vii, chap. 17.
† Diodorus Siculus, b. xx, chap. 14.

to be a community of women and of property, just as among our modern heathens. Women's rights were to be maintained by having the women trained to war. Children were still to be murdered, if convenience called for it. And the young children were to be led to battle at a safe distance, "that the young whelps might early scent carnage, and be inured to slaughter."

The teachings of all these philosophers were immoral. He may lie, says Plato, who knows how to do it. Pride and the love of popular applause were esteemed the best motives to virtue. Profane swearing was commanded by the example of all their best writers and moralists. Oaths are frequent in the writings of Plato and Seneca. The gratification of the sensual appetites was openly taught. Anstippus taught that a wise man might steal and commit adultery, when he could. Unnatural crimes were vindicated. The last dread crime—suicide—was pleaded for by Cicero and Seneca as the mark of a hero, and Demosthenes, Cato, Brutus, and Cassius, carried the means of self-destruction about them, that they might not fall alive into the hands of their enemies.

The lives of these wisest of the heathen corresponded to their teachings, so far at least as vice was concerned. The most notorious vices, and even unnatural crimes, were practiced by them. The reader of the classics does not need to be reminded that such vices are lauded in the poems of Ovid, and Horace, and Virgil; that the poets were rewarded and honored for songs which would not be tolerated for a moment in the vilest theater of New York. What, then, must the lives of the vulgar have been? In the very height of Roman civilization, Trajan caused ten thousand men to hew each other to pieces for the amusement of the Roman people; and noble ladies feasted their eyes on the spectacle. In the Augustan age, when the invincible armies of Rome gave law to half the world, fathers were in the habit of mutilating their sons rather than see them subjected to the slavery and terrible despotism of their officers. What, then, must the state of the people of the vanquished countries have been? Whole provinces were frequently given over to fire and sword by generals, not reputed inhuman; and such was the progress of war and anarchy, and their never-failing accompaniments, famine and pestilence, that in the reign of Gallienus, large cities were left utterly desolate, the public roads became unsafe from immense packs of wolves, *and it was computed that one-half of the human race perished.* This was just before the toleration of Christianity. God would allow the wisest and bravest of mankind to try the experiment of neglecting his gospel and living without his revelation, until all mankind might be convinced that such a course is suicidal to nations. "Where there is no vision, the people perish."

A brief reference to the codes of morals which the opposers of the Bible would substitute for it in Christian lands, shall conclude our proof of the necessity of such a revelation of God's law to man, as shall guide his life to peace and happiness.

The family is the basis of the commonwealth. Destroy family confidence and family government, and you destroy society, subvert civil government, and bring destruction on the human race. Mankind are so generally agreed on this subject, that adultery, even among heathens, is regarded and punished as a crime. The whole school of infidel writers and anti-Bible lecturers, male and female, apologize for, and vindicate this crime. Lord Herbert, the first of the English Deists, taught that the indulgence of lust and anger is no more to be blamed than the thirst occasioned by the dropsy, or the drowsiness produced by lethargy. Mr. Hobbes asserted that every man has a right to all things, and may lawfully get them if he can. Bolingbroke taught that man is merely a superior animal, which is just the modern development theory, and that his chief end is to gratify the appetites and inclinations of the flesh. Hume, whose argument against miracles is so frequently in the mouths of American Infidels, taught that adultery must be practiced, if men would obtain all the advantages of life, and that if practiced frequently, it would by degrees come to be thought no crime at all—a prediction as true as holy writ, the fulfilment of which hundreds of the citizens of Cincinnati can attest, who have heard a lecturer publicly denounce the Bible as an immoral book, and in the same address declare that if a woman was married to a man, in her opinion of inferior development, it was her duty to leave him and live with another. This duty is by no means neglected, as the numerous divorces, spiritual marriages, separations, and elopements among this class of persons, testify. Voltaire held that it was not agreeable to policy to regard it as a vice in a moral sense. Rousseau, a liar, a thief, and a debauched profligate, according to his own printed "Confessions," held the same high opinion of the inner light as our American Spiritualists. *"I have only to consult myself,"* said he, *"concerning what I do. All that I feel to be right, is right."* * In fact, the purport of this inner light doctrine, is exactly as Rousseau expressed it, and amounts simply to this, *Do what you like.*

On this lawless principle these men acted. Take, for example, the chief saint on the calendar of American Infidelity, whose birthday is annually celebrated by a high festival in this city, and in whose honor hundreds of men, who would like to be reputed decent citizens, parade our streets in solemn procession—Thomas Paine—the author of "The Age of Reason," as his character is depicted by one who was his helper in the work of blaspheming God and seducing men, and whose testimony, therefore, in the eyes of an infidel, is unimpeachable—William Carver.

"Mr. Thomas Paine: I received your letter, dated the 25 ult., in answer to mine, dated November 21, and after minutely examining its contents, I found that you had taken to the pitiful subterfuge of *lying* for your defence. You say that you paid me four dollars per week for your board and lodging, during the time you were with me, prior to the first of June last; which was the day that I went up, by your order, to bring you to York, from New Rochelle. It is fortunate for me that I have a living evidence that saw you give me five guineas, and no more, in my shop, at your departure at that time; but you said you would have given me more, but that you had no more with you at present. You say, also, that you found your own liquors during the time you boarded with me; but you should have said, 'I found only a small part of the liquor I drank during my stay with you; this part I purchased of John Fellows, which was a demi-john of brandy, containing four gallons, and this did not serve you three weeks.' This can be proved, and I mean not to say any thing I cannot prove, for I hold truth as a precious jewel. It is a well known fact that you drank one quart of brandy per day, at my expense, during the different times you boarded with me; the demi-john above mentioned excepted, and the last fourteen weeks you were sick. Is not this a supply of liquor for dinner and supper." * * * * "I have often wondered that a French woman and three children should leave France and all their connections, to follow Thomas Paine to America. Suppose I were to go to my native country, England, and take another man's wife and three children of his, and leave my wife and children in this country. What would be the natural conclusion in the minds of the people, but that there was some criminal connection between the woman and myself?" †

Such is the morality of those who denounce the Bible as an im-

---

* Horne's Introduction to the Scriptures, Vol. I, p. 25.

† Printed repeatedly in the New York newspapers, and given entire in the Report of the discussion between Dr. Berg and Mr. Barker. W. S. Young, Philadelphia, 1854.

moral book, and blaspheme the God of the Bible as too unholy to be reverenced or adored! "But beloved, remember ye the words which were spoken before of the apostles of our Lord Jesus Christ; how that they told you there should be mockers in the last time, who should walk after their own ungodly lusts. These be they who separate themselves, sensual, having not the spirit." In the Free Love Institute about to be established in our vicinity, we shall have the full development of these filthy principles and practices.

Let fathers and husbands look to this matter. Especially let ungodly men set to work and devise some law of man capable of binding those who renounce the law of God, and with it all human authority. For there can be no law of man, unless there is a revealed law of God. "What right," says the Pantheist, the Fourierist, the Spiritualist, the Atheist, "what right have you to command me? Right and wrong are only matters of feeling, and your feelings are no rule to me. The will of the majority is only the law of might, and if I can evade it, or overcome it, my will is as good as theirs. Oaths are only an idle superstition—there is no judge, no judgment, no punishment for the false swearer." Take away the moral sanction of law, and the sacredness of oaths, and what basis have you left for any government, save the point of the bayonet? Take away the revealed law of God, and you leave not a vestige of any authority to any human law. "We hold these truths to be self-evident," said the immortal framers of the basis of the American Confederation, "that all men are created equal; that they are *endowed by their Creator* with certain unalienable rights." It was well said. The Rights of God, are the only basis of the Rights of Man.

Once in modern times, the rejectors of the Bible had opportunity to try the experiment of ruling a people on a large scale, and giving the world a specimen of an infidel republic. You have heard one of them here express his admiration of that government, and declare his intention to present a public vindication of it. Of course, as soon as practicable, that which they admire they will imitate, and the scenes of Paris and Lyons will be re-enacted in Louisville and Cincinnati. Our Bibles will be collected and burned on a dung heap. Death will be declared an eternal sleep. God will be declared a fiction. Religious worship will be renounced; the Sabbath abolished; and a prostitute, crowned with garlands, will receive the adorations of the Mayors and Councilmen of Cincinnati and Newport. The reign of terror will commence. The guillotine shall take its place on the Fifth Street Market place. Proscription will follow proscription. Women will denounce their husbands, and children their parents, as bad citizens, and lead them to the axe; and well dressed ladies, filled with savage ferocity, will seize the mangled bodies of their murdered countrymen between their teeth. The Licking will be choked with the bodies of men, and the Ohio dyed with their blood; and those whose infancy had sheltered them from the fire of the rabble soldiery, be bayoneted as they cling to the knees of their destroyers.* The common doom of man commuted for the violence of the sword, the bayonet, the sucking boat, and the guillotine; the knell of the nation tolled, and the world summoned to its execution and funeral, will need no preacher to expound the text, *Where there is no vision the people perish.*

---

* Horne's Introduction to the Scriptures, vol. i, p. 26; where ample references to cotemporary French writers are given.

No. 26.

WHO WROTE THE NEW TESTAMENT.

"The salutation of me Paul, with mine own hand: which is the token in every epistle—so I write. The grace of our Lord Jesus Christ be with you all. Amen."—2 Thess. 3: 17.

RELIGION rests not on dogmas, but on a number of great facts. In the last Tract we found one of these to be, that people destitute of a revelation of God's will, ever have been, and now are ignorant, miserable and wicked. If it were at all needful, we might go on to show, that there are people in the world, who have decent clothing and comfortable houses—work well-tilled farms with sub-soil ploughs and McCormick reapers—yoke powerful streams to the mill wheel, and harness the iron horse to the market wagon—career their floating palaces up the opposing floods—line their coasts with flocks of white winged schooners, and show their flags on every coast of earth—invent and make every thing that man will buy, from the brass button, dear to the barbarian, to the folio of the philosopher—erect churches in all their towns, schools in every village—make their blacksmiths more learned than the priests of Egypt, their Sabbath scholars wiser than the philosophers of Greece, and even the criminals in their jails, more decent characters than the sages, heroes, and gods of the lands without the Bible; and that these people are the people who possess a Book, which they think contains a revelation from God, teaching them how to live well—which Book they call the Bible. This is the book about which we make our present inquiry, Who wrote it?

The fact being utterly undeniable, that these blessings are found among the people who possess the Bible, and only among them, we at once, and summarily, dismiss the arrogant falsehood presented to prevent any inquiry about the Book, namely, that "Christianity is just like any other superstition, and its sacred books like the impositions of Chinese, Indian, or Mohammedan impostors. They too are religious, and have their sacred books which they believe to be divine." A profound generalization indeed! Is a peach tree just like a horse-chesnut, or a scrub-oak, or a honey-locust? They are all trees, and have leaves on them. The Bible is just as like the Yi King, or the Vedas, or the Koran, as a Christian American or Briton is like a Chinaman, a Turk, or a Hindoo. But it is too absurd to begin any discussion with these learned Thebans of the relative merits of the Bible as compared with the Vedas, and the Chinese Classics, of which they have never read a single page. Let them stick to what they pretend to know.

The Bible is a great fact in the world's history, known alike to the prince and the peasant, the simple and the sage. It is perused with pleasure by the child, and pondered with patience by the philosopher. Its psalms are carolled on the school green, cheer the chamber of sickness, are chanted by the mother over her cradle, by the orphan over the tomb. Here—thousands of miles away from the land of its birth—in a world undiscovered for centuries after it was finished, in a language unknown alike at Athens and Jerusalem, it rules as lovingly and as powerfully as in its native soil. To show that its power is not derived from race or clime, it converts the Sandwich Islands into a civilized nation, and transforms the New Zealand cannibal into a British ship-owner, the Indian warrior into an American Editor, and the Negro slave into the President of a free African Republic. It does not look as if it had finished its course and ceased from its triumphs. Translated into the hundred and fifty languages spoken by nine hundred millions of men, carried by ten thousand heralds to every corner of the globe, sustained by the cheerful contributions and fervent prayers of hundreds of thousands of ardent disciples, it is still going forth conquering and to conquer. Is there any other book so generally read, so greatly loved, so zealously propagated, so widely diffused, so uniform in its results, and so powerful and blessed in its influences? Do you know any? If you can not name any book, no, nor any thousand books, which in these respects equal the Bible,—then it stands out clear and distinct, and separate from all other authorship; and with an increased emphasis comes our question: Who wrote it?

With all these palpable facts in view, to come to the examination of this question as if we knew nothing about them, or as if knowing them well, we cared nothing at all about them, and were determined to deny them their natural influence in begetting within us a very strong presumption in favor of its divine origin, were to declare that our heads and hearts were alike closed against light and love. But to enter on this inquiry into the origin of the Book which has produced such results, with a preconceived opinion that it must be a forgery and an imposition, the fruit of a depraved heart and a lying tongue, implies so much home-born deceit, that till the heart capable of such a prejudice be completely changed, no reasoning can have any solid fulcrum of truth or goodness to rest on. It is sheer folly to talk of one's being wholly unprejudiced in such an inquiry. No man ever was or could be so. As his sympathies are towards goodness and virtue, and the happiness of mankind, or towards pride and deceit, and selfishness, and savageness, so will his prejudices be for or against the Bible.

On looking at the Bible, we find it composed of a number of separate treatises, written by different writers, at various times; some parts fifteen hundred years before the others. We find, also, that it treats of the very beginning of the world before man was made, and of other matters of which we have no other authentic history to compare with it. Again, we find portions which treat of events connected in a thousand places with the affairs of the Roman Empire, of which we have several credible histories. Now, there are two modes of investigation open to us, the dogmatic and the inductive. We may take either. We may construct for ourselves, from the most flimsy suppositions, a metaphysical balloon, inflated with self-conceit into the rotundity of a cosmogony, according to which, in our opinion, the world should have been made, and we may paint it over with the figures of the various animals and noble savages which ought to have sprung up out of its fornea, and we may stripe its history to suit our notions of the progress of such a world, and soaring high into the clouds, after a little preliminary amusement in the discovery of eternal red hot fire-mists and condensing comets, and so forth, we may come down upon the summit of some of this earth's mountains, say Ararat, and take a survey of the Bible process of world making. Finding that the Creator of the world had to make his materials—a business in which no other world maker ever did engage—and further, that God's plan of making it by no means corresponds to our patent process, and that the article is not at all like what we intend to produce when we go into the business, and that it does not work according to our expectations, we can denounce the whole as a very mean affair, and the Book which describes it as not worth reading. If one wants some new subject for merriment, and does not mind making a fool of himself, and is not to be terrified by old-fashioned notions about God Almighty, and is perfectly confident that God can tell him nothing that he does not know better already, and merely wants to see whether he is not trying to pass off old fables upon wide awake people for facts—this dogmatic plan will suit him.

On the other hand, if one is tolerably convinced that he does not know every thing, and probably not much of the world he lives in, less of its history, and nothing at all about the best way of making it, and that when it needs mending it will not be sent to his workshop—that he knows nothing about what happened before he was born unless what other people tell him, and that, though men do err, yet all men are not liars—that all the blessings of education, civilization, law and liberty, from the penny primer to the Constitution of the United States, came to him solely through the channel of abundant, reliable testimony—that the only way in which he can ever know any thing beyond his eyesight with certainty, is to gather testimony about it, and compare the evidence, and enquire into the character of the witnesses—that when one has done so, he becomes so satisfied of the truth of the report that he would rather risk his life upon it than upon the certainty of any mathematical problem, or of any scientific truth, whatever—that ninety-nine out of every hundred citizens of the United States are a thousand times more certain that the Yankees whipped the British in 1776, declared the Colonies free and independent States, and made Washington President, than they ever will be that all bodies attract each other directly as their mass, and inversely as the squares of their distances, that the sum of the angles of any triangle is equal to two right angles, or that the earth is nearer the sun in winter than in summer—that certainty about the Bible History is just as attainable and just as reliable as certainty about American history, if he will seek it in the same way—and if he is really desirous to know how this Book was written, which alone in the world teaches men how to obtain peace with God, how to live well, and how to die with a firm and joyful hope of a resurrection to life eternal, and what part of it is easiest to prove either true or false—then he will take the inductive mode. He will begin at the present time, and trace the history up to the times in which the Book was written. He will ascertain what he can about that part of it which was last written—the New Testament—and begin with that part of it which lies nearest him—the Epistles. By the comparison of the documents themselves, with all kinds of history and monuments which throw light on the period, he will try to ascertain whether they are genuine or not. And from one well ascertained position he will proceed to another, until he has traversed the whole ground of the genuineness of the writings, the truth of the story, and the divine authority of the doctrine.

This is my plan of investigation. One thing at a time, and the nearest first. It is not worth while to inquire whether it be inspired by God, if it be really a forgery of impostors—nor whether the Gospel story is worthy of credit, if the only book which contains it be a religious novel of the third or fourth century? We dismiss then the questions of the Inspiration, or even the truth of the New Testament, till we have ascertained its authors. We take up the Book, and find that it purports to be a relation of the planting of the Church of Christ, of its laws and ordinances, and of the life, death and resurrection of its Founder, written by eight of his companions, at various periods and places, towards the close of the first century. There is a general opinion among all Christians that the Book was composed then, and by these persons. We want to know why they think so? In short, is it a genuine book, or merely a collection of myths with the apostles' names appended to them by some lying monks? Is it a fact, or a forgery?

In any historical inquiry, we want some fixed point of time from which to take our departure; and in this case we want to know if there is any period of antiquity in which undeniably this Book was in existence, and received as genuine by Christian societies. For I will not suppose my readers as ignorant as some of those infidels who allege that it was made by the Bible Society. It used to be the fashion with those of them who pretended to learning, to affirm that it was made by the Council of Laodicea, in A. D. 364; because, in order to guard the churches against spurious epistles and gospels, that Council published a list of those which the apostles did actually write, which thenceforth were generally bound in one volume.

. Before that time, the four gospels were always bound in one volume and called the Gospel. The Acts of the Apostles and the

Epistles universally and undoubtedly known to be written by Paul, to the Churches of Thessalonica, Galatia, Rome, Corinth, Ephesus, Philippi, Colosse, and to Philemon, a well known resident of that city—and those to Timothy and Titus, missionaries of world-wide celebrity—the First General Epistle of Peter, and the First General Epistle of John, which were at once widely circulated to check prevailing heresies—were bound in another volume and called "The Apostle." The Epistle to the Hebrews, being general, and anonymous, *i. e.*, not bearing the name of any particular church, or person, to whom any body who merely looked at it could refer for proof of its genuineness, as in the case of the other Epistles—was not so soon known by the European churches to be written by Paul. The General Epistles of James, Jude, and the Second General Epistle of Peter, lying under the same difficulty, and besides being very disagreeable to easy going Christians from their sharp rebukes of hypocrisy—the Second and Third Epistles of John, from their brevity—and the Revelation of John, being one of the last written of all the books of the New Testament, and the most mysterious—were not so generally known beyond the churches where the originals were deposited, until the other two collections had been formed. They were accordingly kept as separate books, and sometimes bound up in a third volume of Apostolical writings. Besides these, at the time of the Council of Laodicea, and for a long time before, other books written by Barnabas, Clement, Polycarp, and other companions and disciples of the apostles, and forged gospels and epistles attributed by heretics to the apostles, were circulated through the churches, and read by Christians. The Council of Laodicea did, what many learned men had done before them; it investigated the evidence upon which any of these books was attributed to an apostle—and finding evidence to satisfy them, that the gospel written by Luke had the sanction of the apostle Paul, that the gospel of Mark was revised by the apostle Peter, that the Epistle to the Hebrews was written by Paul, and the other epistles by John, Jude, James, and Peter, respectively, and not finding evidence to satisfy them about the Revelation of John, they expressed their opinion, and the grounds of it, for the information of the world.* Into these reasons we will hereafter inquire, for our faith in Holy Scripture does not rest

---

* Acta Concil, sub voce Laodicea, Canon iv. Lardner vi.; p. 368.

on their canons. We are not now asking what they *thought* but what they *did*, and we find that they did criticise certain books, reported to be written by the apostles of Jesus Christ some three hundred years before, approve some, and reject others as spurious, and publish a list of those they thought genuine. Infidels admit this, and on the strength of it long asserted that the Council of Laodicea made the New Testatament. At length they became ashamed of the stupid absurdity of alleging that men could criticise the claims, and catalogue the names of books before they were written; and they now shift back the writing—or the authentication of the New Testament—for they are not quite sure which, though the majority incline to the former—to the Emperor Constantine and the Council of Nice, which met in the year 325. Why they have fixed on the Council of Nice is more than I can tell. They might as well say the Council of Trent, or the Westminster Assembly, either of which had just as much to do with the Canon of Scripture. However, on some vague hearsay that the Council of Nice and the Emperor Constantine made the Bible, hundreds in this city are now risking the salvation of their souls.

We have in this assertion, nevertheless, as many facts admitted as will serve our present purpose. There did exist, then, undeniably, in the year 325, large numbers of Christian churches in the Roman Empire, sufficiently numerous to make it politic, in the opinion of infidels, for a candidate for the empire to profess Christianity; sufficiently powerful to secure his success, notwithstanding the desperate struggles of the heathen party; and sufficiently religious, or if you like superstitious, to make it politic for an emperor and his politicians to give up the senate, the court, the camp, the chase and the theater, and weary themselves with long prayers and longer speeches of preachers about Bible religion. Now that is certainly a remarkable fact, and all the more remarkable if we now inquire, How came it so? For these men, preachers, prince, and people, were brought up to worship Jupiter and the thirty thousand gods of Olympus, after the heathen fashion, and leave the care of religion to heathen priests, who never troubled their heads about books or doctrines after they had offered their sacrifices. In all the records of the world, there is no instance of a general council of heathen priests to settle the religion of their people. How happens it then that the human race has of a sudden waked up to such a strange sense of the folly of idolatry and the value of religion? The Council of Nice and the Emperor Constantine and his councilors making a Bible, is a proof of a wonderful revolution in the world's religion—a phenomenon far more surprising than if the Secretaries of State, and the Senate, and President Pierce, should leave the Capitol and post off to Boston, to attend the meetings of a Methodist Conference assembled to make a Hymn Book. Now what is the cause of this remarkable conversion of prince, priests, and people? How did they all get religion? How did they get it so suddenly? How did they get so much of it?

The infidel gives no answer, except to tell us * that the austerity, purity and zeal of the first Christians, their good discipline, their belief in the resurrection of the body and the general judgment, and their persuasion that Christ and his apostles wrought miracles, had made a great many converts. This is just as if I inquired how a great fire originated, and you should tell me that it burned fast because it was very hot. What I want to know is, how it happened that these licentious Greeks, and Romans, and Asiatics, became austere and pure—how these frivolous philosophers suddenly became so zealous about religion—what implanted the belief of the resurrection of the body and of the judgment to come in the sceptical minds of these heathen scoffers—and how did the pagans of Italy, Egypt, Spain, Germany, Britain, come to believe in the miracles of one who lived hundreds of years before, and thousands of miles away, or to care a straw whether the written accounts of them were true or false? According to the infidel account, the Council of Nice and the Emperor Constantine's Bible-making, is a most extraordinary business—a phenomenon without any natural cause, and they will allow no supernatural—a greater miracle than any recorded in the Bible.

If we inquire, however, of the parties attending that Council, what the state of the case is, we shall learn that they believed—whether truly or erroneously we are not now inquiring—but they believed that a teacher sent from God, had appeared in Palestine two hundred and ninety years before, and had taught this religion which they had embraced; had performed wonderful miracles, such as opening the eyes of the blind, healing lepers, raising the

---

* Gibbon's Decline and Fall, Chap. xv.

dead; that he had been put to death by the Roman Governor, Pontius Pilate, and had risen again from the dead, and had spoken to hundreds of people, and gone out and in among them for six weeks after his resurrection; that he had ascended up through the air to heaven in the sight of numbers of witnesses, and had promised that he would come again in the clouds of heaven to raise the dead, and judge every man according to his works; that before he went away he appointed twelve of his intimate companions to teach his religion to the world, giving them power to work miracles in proof of their divine commission, and requiring mankind to hear them as they would hear him; that they and their followers did so, in spite of persecutions, sufferings, and death, with so much success, that immense numbers were persuaded to give up idolatry and its filthiness, and profess Christianity and its holiness, and brave the fury of the heathen mob, and the vengeance of the Roman law—that a difference of opinion having arisen among them as to whether this teacher was an angel from heaven, or God; whether they should pray and sing the Psalms to him as Athanasius and his party believed, or only give him some lesser honor as Arius and his party believed—and this difference making all the difference between idolatry on the one hand and impiety on the other, and so involving their everlasting salvation or damnation—they had embraced the first opportunity after the cessation of persecution, and the accession of the first Christian Emperor, to assemble three hundred and eighteen of their most learned clergyman, of both sides, and from all countries between Spain and Persia, to discuss these solemn questions; and that, through the whole of the discussions, both sides appealed to the writings of the Apostles, as being then well known, and of unquestioned authority with every one who held the Christian name. These facts being utterly indisputable, are acknowledged by all persons, infidel or Christian, at all acquainted with history *.

Here then we have the books of the New Testament at the Council of Nice well known to the whole world; and the Council, so far from *giving* any authority to them, *bowing to theirs,*—both

---

* The original authorities may be found collected in the 4th vol. of Lardner's Credibility of the Gospel History. Abstracts of them, with ample references, in Mosheim and Neander's Ecclesiastical Histories.

Arian and Orthodox with one consent acknowledging that the whole Christian world received them as the writings of the Apostles of Christ. There were venerable men of fourscore and ten at that Council; if these books had been first introduced in their lifetime, they must have known it. There were men there whose parents had heard the Scriptures read in church from their childhood, and so could not be imposed upon with a new Bible. The New Testament could not be less than three generations old, else one or other of the disputants would have exposed the novelty of its introduction, from his own information. The Council of Nice then, did not make the New Testament. It was a book well known, ancient, and of undoubted authority among all Christians, ages before that Council. *The existence of New Testament Scriptures then, ages before the Council of Nice, is a Great Fact.*

We next take up the assertions, propounded with a show of learning, that the books of the New Testament, and especially the gospels, were not in use, and were not known till the third century; that they are not the productions of contemporary writers; that the alleged ocular testimony or proximity in point of time of the sacred historians to the events recorded is mere assumption, originating in the titles which Biblical books bear in our canon; that we stand here (in the gospel history), upon purely mythical and poetical ground; and that the gospels and epistles are a gradually formed collection of myths, having little or no historic reality. So Strauss, Eichorn, DeWette, and their disciples here, attempt to set aside the New Testament. In plain English, it is a collection of forgeries.

Now we might easily show that these assertions are absurd; that in the hundred years between the death of the last of the Apostles, and the beginning of the third century, there was not time to form a mythology; that the times of Trajan's persecution, and that of the philosophic Aurelius and the busy bustling age of Severus, were not the times for such a business; that bigoted Jews would not and could not have made such a character as Jesus of Nazareth—and the philosophers of that day, Celsus and Porphyry, for instance, hated it when presented to them, as heartily as either Strauss or Paine; and that there were not wanting thousands of enemies, able and willing, to expose such a forgery.

But we prefer the direct course of proving these assertions false, and we will draw the proof from enemies. It is an undeniable fact that in the close of the second century, Celsus, an Epicurean philosopher, wrote a work against Christianity, entitled, "The Word of Truth," in which he quotes passages from the New Testament, and so many of them, that from the fragments of his work which remain, we could gather all the principal facts of the birth, teaching, miracles, death, and resurrection of Jesus Christ, if the New Testament should be lost. If Paine quotes the New Testament to ridicule it, no man can deny that such a book was in existence at the time he wrote. If he takes the pains to write a book to confute it, it is self-evident that it is in circulation, and possessed of influence. So Celsus' attempt to reply to the gospels, and his quotations from them, are conclusive proofs that these books were generally circulated and believed, and held to be of authority at the time he wrote. Further, he shows every disposition to present every argument which could possibly damage the Christian cause. In fact, our modern infidels have done little more than serve up his old objections. Now nothing could have served his purpose better than to prove that the records of the history of Christ were forgeries of a late date. This would have saved him all further trouble, and settled the fate of Christianity conclusively. He had every opportunity of ascertaining the fact, living as he did so near the times and scenes of the gospel history, and surrounded by heretics and false Christians, who would gladly have given him every information. But he never once intimates the least suspicion of such a thing—never questions the gospels as books of history— nor denies the miracles recorded in them, but attributes them to magic.* Here, then, we have testimony as acceptable to an infidel as that of Strauss or Voltaire—in fact, utterly undeniable by any man of common sense—that the New Testament was well known and generally received by Christians as authoritative, when Celsus wrote his reply to it, in the end of the second century. If it was a forgery, it was undoubtedly a forgery of old standing, if he could not detect it.

But we will go back a step farther, and prove the antiquity of the New Testament by the testimony of another enemy, two generations older than Celsus. The celebrated heretic, Marcion, lived in the beginning of the second century, when he had the best opportunity of discovering a forgery in the writings of the

---

* Origen Contra Celsum, passim.

New Testament, if any such existed; he was excommunicated by the church, and being greatly enraged thereat, had every disposition to say the worst he could about it. He traveled all the way from Sinope on the Black Sea, to Rome, and through Galatia, Bithynia, Asia Minor, Greece, and Italy, the countries where the Apostles preached, and the churches to which they wrote, but never found any one to suggest the idea of a forgery to him. He affirmed that the gospel of Matthew, the epistle to the Hebrews, those of James and Peter, and the whole of the Old Testament, were books only for Jews, and published a new and altered edition of the gospel of Luke and ten epistles of Paul, for the use of his sect.* We have thus the most undoubted evidence, even the testimony of an enemy, that these books were in existence, and generally received as apostolical and authoritative by Christians, at the beginning of the second century, or within twenty years of the last of the Apostles, and by the churches to which they had preached and written.

The only remaining conceivable cavil against the genuineness of the books of the New Testament is: "That they bear internal evidence of being collections of fragments written by different persons, —and are probably merely traditions committed to writing by various unknown writers, and afterwards collected and issued to the churches under the names of the Apostles, for the sake of greater authority." This theory being received as gospel by several learned men, has furnished matter for lengthy discussions as to the sources of the four gospels. Translated into English, it amounts to this, that Brown, Smith, White, and Jones, wrote out a number of essays and anecdotes, and persuaded the churches of Ephesus, Jerusalem, Antioch, Corinth, and the rest, to receive them as the writings of their ministers, who had lived for years, or were then living among them; and on the strength of that notion of their being the writings of the Apostles, to govern their whole lives by these essays, and lay down their lives and peril their souls' salvation on the truth of these anecdotes. As though they could not tell whether such documents were forgeries or not!

It is almost incredible how ignorant dreaming book-worms are of the common business of life. Most of my readers will laugh at the idea of a serious answer to such a quibble. Nevertheless,

---

* Lardner, vol. ix, p. 358.

for the sake of those whose inexperience may be abused by the authority of learned names, I will show them that the primitive Christians, supposing them able to read, could know whether their ministers did really write the books and letters which they received from them.

If you go into the Citizens' Bank, you will find a large folio volume lying on the counter, and on looking at it you will see that it is filled with men's names in their own handwriting, and that no two of them are exactly alike. Every person who has any business to transact with the bank is requested to write his name in the book; and when his check comes afterward for payment, the clerk can tell at a glance if the signature is the same as that of which he has a single specimen. If there has been no opportunity for him to become personally acquainted with the bank, as in case of a foreigner newly arrived, he brings letters of introduction from some well known mutual friend, or is accompanied by some respectable citizen, who attests his identity. Business men have no difficulty whatever in ascertaining the genuineness of documents. It is only when people want to dispute Holy Scripture that they give up common sense.

Holy Scripture was known to be the genuine writing of the Apostles, just in the same way as any other writing was known to be genuine, only the churches who received the writings of the Apostles had ten thousand times better security against forgery than any bank in the Union. In one of the first letters Paul writes to the churches—the second letter to the Thessalonians—to whom he had been preaching only a few weeks before, sent from Athens, distant only some two days' journey, full of allusions to their affairs, commands how to conduct themselves in the business of their workshops, as well as in the devotions of the church, and explanations of some misunderstood parts of a former letter sent by the hand of a mutual friend—he formally gives them his signature, for the purpose of future reference, and comparison of any document which might purport to come from him, with that specimen of his autograph. He gives not the name merely, but his apostolic benediction also, in his own handwriting: *The salutation of me, Paul, with mine own hand, which is the token in every epistle, so I write. The grace of our Lord Jesus Christ be with you all. Amen.* It shows the heart of an Apostle of Christ; but what concerns the present question is the remark, which every business man will in a moment appreciate, how immensely the addition of these two lines adds to the security against forgery. It is a very hard thing to forge a signature, but give a business man two lines of any man's writing besides that, and he is perfectly secure against imposition.

The churches to which the epistles were written, and to which the gospels were delivered, consisted largely of business men, of merchants and traders, tent makers and coppersmiths, city chamberlains, and officers of Cæsar's household, and the like. Does any one think such men could not tell the handwriting of their minister, who had lived among them for years; or that men who were risking their lives for the instructions he wrote them, would care less about the genuineness of the documents, than you do about the genuineness of a ten dollar check? I am not as long in this city as Paul was in Ephesus, nor one-fourth of the time that John lived there, yet I defy all the advocates of the mythical theory in Germany, and all their disciples here, to write a myth half as long as this tract, and impose it on the elders and members of my church as my writing. Let it only be presented in manuscript to the congregation—there was no printing in Paul's days—and in five minutes a dozen members of the church will detect the forgery, even if I should hold my peace. And were I to leave on a mission to China or India, and write letters to the church, would any of these business men, who have seen my writing, have the least hesitation in recognizing it again? Do you think any body could forge a letter as from me, and impose it on them? What an absurdity, then, to suppose that any body could write a gospel or epistle, and just get all the members of a large church to believe that an Apostle wrote it! The first Christians, then, were absolutely certain that the documents which they received as apostolic, were really so. The Church of Rome could attest the epistle to them, and the gospels of Mark and Luke written there. The Church of Ephesus could attest the epistle to them, and the gospel, and letters, and Revelation of John written there. And so on of all the other churches; and these veritable autographs were long preserved. Says Tertullian, who was ordained A. D. 192: "Well, if you be willing to exercise your curiosity profitably in the business of your salvation, visit the apostolical churches in which the very chairs of the Apostles still preside—in which their authentic letters themselves are recited, (apud quæ *ipsæ authenticæ literæ* eorum recitantur,) sounding forth the voice and representing the countenance of each one of them. Is Achaia near you, you have Corinth. If you are not far from Macedonia, you have Philippi, you have Thessalonica. If you can go to Asia, you have Ephesus; but if you are near to Italy, you have Rome."* There can not be the least doubt about the preservation of documents for a far longer time than from Paul to Tertullian—one hundred and fifty years. I hold in my hand a Bible, the family Bible of the Gibsons —printed in 1599—two hundred and fifty-seven years old, in perfect preservation.

The only difficulty which now remains is the objection, that they might have been corrupted by alterations, and interpolations by monks in later times. We have two securities against such corruptions in the way these documents were given, and the nature of their contents. They were sacred heirlooms, and they were public documents. Could you, or could any man, have permission to alter the original copy of Washington's Farewell Address? Would not the man who should attempt such sacrilege be torn in a thousand pieces? But Washington will never be an object of such veneration as John, nor will his Farewell Address ever compare in importance with Paul's Farewell Letter to the Philippians. Besides, these gospels and letters were public documents, containing the records of laws, in obedience to which men were daily crossing their inclinations, enduring the mockery of their neighbors, losing their money, and endangering their lives. They contained the proofs and promises of that religious faith in God and hope of heaven, for the sake of which they suffered such things. Is it credible that they would allow them to be altered and corrupted? You might far more rationally talk of some southern politician altering the Declaration of Independence, or some northern man altering the Constitution of the United States. Translated into different languages—transported into Britain, Germany, France, Spain, Italy, Greece, Turkey, Carthage, Egypt, Parthia, Persia, India, and China—committed to memory by children, and quoted in the writings of Christian authors of the first three centuries, to such an extent, that we can gather the whole of the New Testament, except twenty-six verses, from their writings — appealed to as authority by heretics and orthodox in controversy—and publicly

---

* Tertullian De Præscript, cap. 36.

read in the hearing of tens of hundreds of thousands every Sabbath day in worship—we are a thousand times more certain that the New Testament has not been corrupted, than we are that the Declaration of Independence is genuine.

On this ground then we plant ourselves. The whole story of a late and gradual formation of the New Testament, or, in plain English, of its forgery, stands out as an unmitigated falsehood in the eyes of every man capable of writing his own name. The first churches could not be deceived with forgeries for apostolic writings. Nor could they, if they would, allow these writings to be corrupted. Be they true or false, fact or fiction, the books of the New Testament are the words of the Apostles of our Lord and Saviour Jesus Christ. In the next Tract we will inquire into the truth of their story.

IS THE GOSPEL FACT OR FABLE.

"For they themselves show of us what manner of entering in we had unto you, and how ye turned to God from idols, to serve the living and true God; and to wait for his Son from heaven, whom he raised from the dead, even Jesus, who delivered us from the wrath to come."—I. THESS. i: 9, 10.

IN the last Tract we ascertained that the Gospels and Epistles were not forgeries of some nameless monks of the third century—that the shopkeepers, silversmiths, tent-makers, coppersmiths, tanners, physicians, senators, town councillors, officers of customs, city treasurers, and nobles of Cæsar's household, in Rome, Antioch, Ephesus, Corinth, Athens, and Alexandria, could no more be imposed upon in the matter of documents, attested by the well known signatures of their beloved ministers, than you could by letters or sermons purporting to come from your own pastor—and that the documents which they believed to contain the directory of their lives, and the charter of that salvation which they valued more than their lives—which they read in their churches, recited at their tables, quoted in their writings, appealed to in their controversies, translated into many languages, and dispersed into every part of the known world, they neither would nor could corrupt or falsify.

The genuineness of the copies of the New Testament which we now possess, is abundantly proved by the comparison of over two thousand manuscripts, from all parts of the world; scrutinized during a period of nearly a hundred years, by the most critical scholars, so accurately that the variations of such things as would in English correspond to the crossing of a t, or the dotting of an i, have been carefully enumerated; yet the result of the whole of this searching scrutiny has been merely the suggestion of thirteen, or, as later critics say, nine unimportant alterations in the received text, of the seven thousand nine hundred and fifty-nine verses of the New Testament. This is a fact utterly unexampled in the history of manuscripts. There are but six manuscripts of the Comedies of Terence, and these have not been copied once for every thousand times the New Testament has been transcribed, yet there are thirty thousand variations found in these six manuscripts, or an average of five thousand for each, and many of them seriously affect the sense. The average number of variations in the manuscripts of the New Testament, examined, is not quite thirty for each, including all the trivialities already noticed.

We are, then, by the special providence of God, now as undoubtedly in possession of genuine copies of the Gospels and Epistles, written by the companions of Jesus, as we are of genuine copies of the Constitution of the United States, and of the Declaration of Independence. These are historic documents, of well established genuineness and antiquity, which we now proceed to examine as to their truthfulness.

There is no history so trustworthy as that prepared by contemporary writers, especially by those who have themselves been actively engaged in the events which they relate. Such history never loses its interest, nor does the lapse of ages, in the least degree, impair its credibility. While the documents can be preserved, Xenophon's Retreat of the Ten Thousand, Cæsar's Gallic War, and the Despatches of the Duke of Wellington, will be as trustworthy as on the day they were written. Yet some suspicion may arise in our minds, that these commanders and historians might keep back some important events which would have dimmed their reputation with posterity, or have colored those they have related so as to add to their fame. Of the great facts related in memoirs addressed to their companions in arms, able at a glance to detect a falsehood, we never entertain the least suspicion.

There is, however, another kind of contemporary history not so connected and regular as the formal diary or journal, which does not even propose to relate history at all, but is for that very reason entirely removed from the suspicion of giving a coloring to it; which, at the cost of a little patience and industry, gives us the most convincing confirmations of the truth, or exposures of the mistakes of historians, by the undesigned and incidental way in which the use of a name, a date, a proverb, a jest, an expletive, a quotation, an allusion, flashes conviction upon the reader's mind. I mean contemporary correspondence. If we have the private letters of celebrated men laid before us, we are enabled to look right into them, and see their true characters. Thus Macaulay exhibits to the world the proud, lying, stupid tyrant James, displayed in his own letters. Thus Voltaire records himself an adulterer, and begs his friend, D'Alembert, to lie for him; his friend replies that he has done so. Thus the correspondence of the great American herald of the Age of Reason exhibits him drinking a quart of brandy daily at his friend's expense, and refusing to pay his bill for boarding. In the unguarded freedom of confidential correspondence, the veil is taken from the heart. We see men as they are. The true man stands out in his native dignity, and the gilding is rubbed off the hypocrite. Give the world their letters, and let the grave silence the plaudits and the clamors which deafened the generation among whom they lived, and no man will hesitate whether or not to pronounce Hume a sensualist, or Washington the noblest work of God—an honest man.

If we add another test of truthfulness, by increasing the number of the witnesses, comparing a number of letters referring to the same events, written by persons of various degrees of education, and of different occupations and ranks of life, resident in different countries, acting independently of each other, and find them all agree in their allusions to, or direct mention of, some central facts concerning which they are all interested, no one can rightfully doubt that this undesigned agreement declares the truth. But if, in addition to all these undesigned coincidences, we happen upon the correspondence of persons whose interests and passions were diametrically opposed to those of our correspondents, and find that, when they have occasion to refer to them, they also confirm the great facts already ascertained, then our belief becomes conviction which cannot be overturned by any sophistry, that these things did occur. If Whig and Tory agree in relating the facts of James's flight and William's accession, if the letters of his Jacobite friends and those of the French ambassador confirm the statements of the English Historian, and if we are put in possession of the letters which James himself wrote from France and Ireland to his friends in England, does any man in his common sense doubt that the Revolution of 1688 did actually occur?

When in addition to all this concentration and convergence of documentary testimony, one finds that the matters related, being of public concern, and the changes effected for the public weal, the people of Great Britain have ever since observed, and do to this day celebrate, by religious worship and public rejoicings, the anniversaries of the principal events of that Revolution, and that he himself has been present, and has heard the thanksgivings, and witnessed the rejoicings on those anniversaries, the facts of the history come out from the domains of learned curiosity, and take their stand on the market place of the busy world's engagements. We become at once conscious that this is a practical question—a great fact which concerns us—that the whole of the law and government of a vast empire has felt its impress—that our ancestors and ourselves have been moulded under its influence, and that the Protestant religion of Europe and America, under whose guardianship we have grown to a prominent place among the people of earth, and may arrive at a better prominence among the nations of the saved, has been preserved, under God, by that Revolution. We could scarcely know whether most to pity or contemn the man who should labor to persuade us that such a Revolution had never occurred, or that the facts had been essentially misrepresented.

Now it is precisely on the same kind of evidence as that which we have for these indisputable facts of the English Revolution, that we believe the great facts of the Christian Revolution. We have contemporary histories, formal and informal; letters, public and private, from the principal agents in it, and opposers of it, dispersed from Babylon to Rome, and addressed to Greeks, Romans, Jews, and Asiatics; written by physicians, fishermen, proconsuls, emperors, and apostles. And these great facts stand out more prominently on the theater of the world's business as effecting changes on our laws and lives, and their introduction as authenticated by public commemorations, more solemn and more numerous than those resulting from the English or the American Revolution. Our main difficulty lies in selecting, from the vast mass of materials, a portion sufficiently distinct and manageable to be handled in a tract of this size.

We shall be guided by the motto already announced as the rule of inductive research. One thing at a time; and the nearest first. The Epistles being nearer our own times than the Gospels, claim our first notice, and first among these, those which stand latest on the page of sacred history, the ten letters of John; two from Peter to the Christians of Asia; and those which Paul, in chains for the gospel, dictated from imperial Rome.

From the abundant notices of the early Christians by historians and philosophers, satirists and comedians, martyrs and magistrates, Jewish, Christian, and heathen, I shall select only two for comparison with the Epistles of the Apostles; and both those heathen—the celebrated letter of Pliny to Trajan, and the well established history of Tacitus—and both utterly undeniable, and admitted by the most sceptical to be beyond suspicion. Not that I suppose that the testimony of men who did not take the trouble of making any inquiry into the reality of the facts of the Christian religion, is more accurate than that of those whose lives were devoted to its study; or that we have any just reason to attach as much weight to the assertions of persons, who, by their own showing, tortured and murdered men and women convicted of no crime but that of bearing the name of Christ, as to those of these martyrs, whose characters they acknowledged to be blameless, and who sealed their testimony with the last and highest attestation of sincerity—their blood. Considered merely as a historian, whether, as regards means of knowledge, or tests of truthfulness, by every unprejudiced mind, Peter will always be preferred to Pliny. But because the world will ever love its own, and hate the disciples of the Lord, there will always be a large class to whom the History of Tacitus will seem more veritable than that of Luke, and the Letters of Pliny more reliable than those of Peter. For their sakes we avail ourselves of that most convincing of all attestations—the testimony of an enemy. What friends and foes unite in attesting must be accepted as true.

The facts which we shall thus establish are not, in the first instance, those called miraculous. We are now ascertaining the general character, for truthfulness, of our letter writers and historians. If we find that their general historic narrative is contradicted by that of other credible historians, then we suspect their story. But if we find that, in all essential matters of public notoriety, they are supported by the concurrent testimony of their foes, and that the narrative of the miracles they relate, bears the seals of thousands who from foes became friends, from conviction of its truth, then we receive their witness as true. Even in Paul's day, heathen Greek writers bore testimony to the Apostles, what manner of entering in they had unto the converts of Thessalonica; and how they turned to God from idols, to serve the living and true God, and to wait for his Son from Heaven, whom he raised from the dead—even Jesus, who delivered us from the wrath to come. Pliny wrote forty years later.

Pliny, the younger, was born A. D. 61—was Prætor under Domitian—consul in the third year of Trajan, A. D. 100—was ex-

101

ceedingly desirous to add to his other honors that of the priesthood; was accordingly consecrated an augur, and built temples, bought images, and consecrated them on his estates; was, in A. D. 106, appointed Governor of the Roman Provinces of Pontus and Bithynia*—a vast tract of Asia Minor, lying along the shores of the Black Sea and the Propontis; and including the Province anciently called Mysia, in which were situated Pergamos and Thyatira, and in the immediate vicinity of Sardis and Philadelphia. Pliny reached his Province by the usual route, the port of Ephesus; where John had lived for many years, and indited his letters A. D., 96. The letters of Peter to the strangers scattered through Pontus, Galatia, Cappadocia, Asia, and Bithynia, bring us to the same mountainous region, eight hundred miles distant from Judea; whence, in earlier days, our savage ancestors received those Phœnician priests of Baal, whose round towers mark the coasts of Ireland nearest to the setting sun; and whence, about the period under consideration, came the heralds of the Sun of Righteousness, who brought the "*Leabhar Eoin*" † which tells their children of him in whom is the life and the light of men. Natives of these countries had been in Jerusalem during the crucifixion of Jesus, and, though only strangers, had witnessed the darkness, and the earthquake, and the rumors of what had come to pass in those days; and on the day of Pentecost had mingled with the curious crowd around the Apostles, and heard them speak, in their own mother tongues, of the wonderful works of God. The remainder of the story of their conversion we gather from the letters of Peter, John, and Pliny.

"Pliny, to the Emperor Trajan, wisheth health and happiness :‡

"It is my constant custom, Sire, to refer myself to you in all matters concerning which I have any doubt. For who can better direct me when I hesitate, or instruct me when I am ignorant?

"I have never been present at any trials of Christians, so that I know not well what is the subject matter of punishment, or of inquiry, or what strictures ought to be used in either. Nor have I been a little perplexed to determine whether any difference ought to be made upon account of age, or whether the young and tender, and the full grown and robust, ought to be treated all alike; whether repentance should entitle to pardon, or whether all who have once been

---

* Lardner, vii. p. 18, *et seq.*
† Pronounced Laar Owen—John's Book.
‡ Lib. x. Ep. 97, Lardner, vii. 22.

Christians ought to be punished, though they are now no longer so, whether the name itself, although no crimes be detected, or crimes only belonging to the name ought to be punished.

"In the mean time, I have taken this course with all who have been brought before me, and have been accused as Christians. I have put the question to them, whether they were Christians. Upon their confessing to me that they were, I repeated the question a second and a third time, threatening also to punish them with death. Such as still persisted, I ordered away to be punished; for it was no doubt with me, whatever might be the nature of their opinion, that contumacy and inflexible obstinacy ought to be punished. There were others of the same infatuation, whom, because they are Roman citizens, I have noted down to be sent to the city.

"In a short time the crime spreading itself, even whilst under persecution, as is usual in such cases, divers sorts of people came in my way. An information was presented to me, without mentioning the author, containing the names of many persons, who, upon examination, denied that they were Christians, or had even been so; who repeated after me an invocation of the gods, and with wine and frankincense made supplication to your image, which, for that purpose, I have caused to be brought and set before them, together with the statues of the deities. Moreover, they reviled the name of Christ. None of which things, as is said, they who are really Christians can by any means be compelled to do. These, therefore, I thought proper to discharge.

"Others were named by an informer, who at first confessed themselves Christians, and afterwards denied it. The rest said they had been Christians, but had left them; some three years ago, some longer, and one or more above twenty years. They all worshiped your image, and the statues of the gods; these also reviled Christ. They affirmed that the whole of their fault or error lay in this: that they were wont to meet together, on a stated day, before it was light, and sing among themselves alternately, a hymn to Christ as a God, and bind themselves by a sacrament, not to the commission of any wickedness, but not to be guilty of theft, or robbery, or adultery; never to falsify their word, nor to deny a pledge committed to them, when called upon to return it. When these things were performed, it was their custom to separate, and then to come together again to a meal, which they ate in common, without any disorder; but this they had forborne since the publication of my edict, by which, according to your command, I prohibited assemblies. After receiving this account, I judged it the more necessary to examine two maid servants which were called ministers, by torture. But I have discovered no thing besides a bad and excessive superstition.

"Suspending, therefore, all judicial proceedings, I have recourse to you for advice; for it has appeared to me a matter highly deserving consideration, especially upon account of the great number of persons who are in danger of suffering. For many of all ages, and every rank, of both sexes likewise, are accused, and will be accused. Nor has the contagion of this superstition seized cities only, but the lesser towns also, and the open country. Nevertheless, it seems to me that it may be restrained and arrested. It is certain that the temples, which were almost forsaken, begin to be frequented. And the sacred solemnities, after a long intermission, are revived. Victims, likewise, are every where bought up, whereas, for some time, there were few purchasers. Whence, it is easy to imagine, what numbers of men might be reclaimed, if pardon were granted to those who shall repent ?"

"Trajan to Pliny, wisheth health and happiness :*

"You have taken the right course, my Pliny, in your proceedings with those who have been brought before you as Christians ; for it is impossible to establish any one rule that shall hold universally. They are not to be sought after. If any are brought before you, and are convicted, they ought to be punished. However, he that denies his being a Christian, and makes it evident in fact, that is, by supplicating to our gods, though he be suspected to have been so formerly, let him be pardoned upon repentance. But in no case, of any crime whatever, may a bill of information be received without being signed by him who presents it, for that would be a dangerous precedent, and unworthy of my government."

I must request my reader now to procure a New Testament, and read, at one reading, the First General Epistle of Peter, the First General Epistle of John, and his Seven Epistles to the Churches in Ephesus, Smyrna, Pergamus, Thyatira, Sardis, Philadelphia, and Laodicea—only about as much matter as four pages of Harper's Magazine, or half a page of the Commercial—that he may be able to do the same justice to the Apostles as to the Governor. He will thus be able to see the force of the various allusions to the numbers, doctrines, morals, persecutions, and perseverance of the Christians, contained in those letters; the object which I have in view being to establish their authenticity by proving the truthfulness of their allusions to these things. If you think this too much trouble, please lay down the tract, and dismiss the consideration of religion from your thoughts. If the letters of the Apostles are not worth a careful reading, it is of no consequence whether they are true or false.

1. These letters take for granted, that the fact of the existence of large numbers of Christians, organized into churches, and meeting regularly for religious worship, at the close of the first century, is a matter of public notoriety to the world. Here, in countries eight hundred miles distant from its birth-place, in the lifetime of those who had seen its founder crucified, we find Christians scattered over Pontus, Galatia, Cappadocia, Asia, and Bithynia—

---

* Lib. x. Ep. 98, Lardner, vii. 24.

churches in seven provincial cities—the sect well known to Pliny, before he left Italy, as a proscribed and persecuted religion, the professors of which were customarily brought before courts for trial and punishment—though he had not himself been present at such trials—and now so numerous in his provinces, that a great number of persons, of both sexes, young and old, of all ranks, natives and Roman citizens, professed Christianity. Others, influenced by their example and instruction, renounced idolatry; victims were not led to sacrifice; the sacred rites of the gods were suspended, and their temples forsaken. The existence, then, of churches of Christ, consisting of vast numbers of converted heathens, at the close of the first century, is in no wise mythological or dubious. It is an established historical fact. The Epistles of the Apostles stand confirmed by the Epistles of the Governor and the Emperor.

2. The second great fact presented in the Epistles, and confirmed by the letters of the Governor and the Emperor, is, that the worship of the Christian church then, was essentially the same which it is now. We find these Christians of the first century commemorating the death and resurrection of Christ, and rendering divine honors to him, the "stated day" on which they assembled for worship, and "common meal," are as plain a description of the "disciples coming together upon the first day of the week, to break bread," as a heathen could give in few words. Their terms of communion too, to which they pledged their members by a sacrament, "not to be guilty of theft, robbery, or adultery; never to falsify their word, or deny a pledge committed to them," find their counterpart in every well regulated church at this day.

The articles of the Christian faith, then, are not the "gradual accretions of centuries," nor is the "redemptive idea, as attaching to Christ, a dogma of the post-Augustine period." The churches of the first century commemorated the death and resurrection of Jesus, as that of a divine person, "singing the hymn to him as a God," which their descendants sing at this day around his table:

"Forever and forever is, O God, thy throne of might,
  The scepter of thy Kingdom is a scepter that is right,
  Thou lovest right, and hatest ill; for God, thy God, Most High,
  Above thy fellows hath with th' oil of joy anointed thee."

And the question will force itself upon our minds, and cannot be evaded, how did these apostles persuade such multitudes of heathens to believe their repeated assertions of the death, resurrection, and glory of Jesus. In the space of three octavo pages, Peter refers to these facts eighteen times. John, in like manner, repeatedly affirms them. The Christian religion consists in the belief of these facts, and a life corresponding to them. Now, how did the apostles persuade such multitudes of heathens to believe a report so wonderful, profess a religion so novel, renounce the gods they had worshiped from their childhood, and all the ceremonies of an attractive, sensual religion; "temples of splendid architecture, statues of exquisite sculpture, priests and victims superbly adorned, attendant beauteous youth of both sexes, performing all the sacred rites with gracefulness; religious dances, illuminations, concerts of the sweetest music, perfumes of the rarest fragrance," and other more licentious enjoyments, inseparable from heathen worship. How did they persuade them to exchange all this for the assembly before daybreak, the frugal common meal, the psalm to Christ, and the commemoration of the death of a crucified malefactor? If we add, that they commemorated his resurrection, by observing the Lord's day, the question still comes up, How did they come to believe that he was risen from the dead? Could a few despised strangers, or a few citizens if you will, persuade such a community, purely by natural means, to believe such a report, to care whether the Syrian Jew died or rose, or to commemorate weekly, by a solemn religious service, either his death or resurrection? It is evident they believed what they commemorated. How did they come to do so?

But whether we can answer the question or not, the fact stands out as indisputable, that not merely the writers of the Epistles and Gospels, and a few enthusiasts, but an immense multitude of all ages, of both sexes, and of every rank—the whole membership of the primitive churches—did believe in the death, resurrection, and glory of the Lord Jesus, and did render to him divine worship. This second great fact affirmed in the Epistles, stands confirmed by the testimony of the heathen Governor, and of the Roman Emperor.

3. A mere theory of a new religion, unconnected with practice, may be easily received by those who care little about any, so long as it brings no suffering or inconvenience. But the religion of these Christians was, as you see, a practical religion. If their new worship required a great departure from the worship of their

childhood, their Christian morals required a still greater departure from their former mode of life. I need not remind you of the moral codes of Socrates, Plato, and Aristides, who taught that lying, thieving, adultery, and murder were lawful;* nor how much worse than the theory of the best of the heathen, were the lives of the worst; nor how unpopular to persons so educated would be such teaching as this—"Forasmuch, then, as Christ hath suffered for us in the flesh, arm yourselves also with the same mind; for he that hath suffered in the flesh hath ceased from sin: that he no longer should live the rest of his time in the flesh to the lusts of men, but to the will of God. For the time past of our life may suffice us to have wrought the will of the Gentiles, when we walked in lasciviousness, lusts, excess of wine, revelings, banquetings, and abominable idolatries; wherein they think it strange that ye run not with them to the same excess of riot; speaking evil of you, who shall give account to him that is ready to judge the living and the dead." "Lay aside all malice, and guile, and hypocrisies, and envies, and all evil speakings." "Whosoever abideth in Christ sinneth not. Whosoever sinneth hath not seen him, neither known him. Little children, let no man deceive you. He that doeth righteousness is righteous, even as he is righteous. He that committeth sin is of the devil." So sharp, and stern, and strictly virtuous, is apostolic religion, as displayed in these letters. Is it possible then that these converted heathens did really even approach this standard of morality? Did this gospel of Christ actually produce any such reformation of their lives?

You have the testimony of apostates, eager to save their lives by giving such information as they knew would be acceptable to the persecutor; you have the testimony of the two aged deaconesses, under torture; you have the unwilling, but yet express, testimony of their torturer and murderer, that all his cruel ingenuity could discover nothing worse than an excessive superstition and culpable obstinacy. What, then, does this philosophic inspector of entrails, and adorer of idols, call an excessive superstition and culpable obstinacy? Why, they bound themselves by the most solemn religious services, not to be guilty of theft, robbery, or adultery; not to falsify their word, nor deny a pledge committed to them; and when some senseless blocks of brass were

---

* See Tract No. 25.

carried on men's shoulders, into the court-house, to represent a mortal man, they would not adore them, nor pray to them—no, not though this philosopher compiled the liturgy, and set the example. For this refusal, and this alone, he ordered them away to death. Doubtless they heard, in their hearts, the well-known words, "Let none of you suffer as a murderer, or as a thief, or as an evil doer, or as a busy body in other men's matters. But if any man suffer as a Christian, let him not be ashamed, but let him glorify God on this behalf."

The morality of the Epistles, then, was not merely a fine theory, but an actual rule of life. The moral codes of the apostles were received as actually binding on the members of the churches of the first century. In this all-important matter of the rule of a good life—the fruits by which the tree is known—the integrity, authority, and success of the Apostles, in turning licentious heathens into moral Christians, is authenticated by the unwilling testimony of their persecutors. The Epistles of the Apostles stand confirmed as to their ethics, by the letters of Trajan and Pliny.

4. The only other fact to which I call your attention, from among the multitude alluded to in these letters, is the cost at which these converts from heathenism embraced this new religion. Every one who renounced heathenism, and professed the name of Christ, knew very well that he must suffer for it. "Beloved, think it not strange concerning the fiery trial which is to try you, as though some strange thing happened unto you, but rejoice, inasmuch as ye are partakers of Christ's sufferings, that when his glory shall be revealed, ye may be glad with exceeding joy;" this was the welcome of the Bithynian convert into the Church of Christ. Persecution by fire and sword was then the common lot of the church. "I have never been present at any trials of the Christians," says the Governor. Such trials were well known to him it seems. He was not sure whether he should murder all who ever had borne the name of Christ, or only those who proved themselves to be really his disciples, by refusing to revile him, and return to idolatry; and the merciful Emperor commands him to spare the apostates. Above twenty years before—in A. D. 86—there were apostates from the persecuted religion. In A. D. 90, John had written, "they went out from us, that it might be made manifest they were not of us; for if they had been of us,

they would no doubt have continued with us; but they went out that it might be made manifest that they were not all of us." So it seems Pliny thought: "They all worshipped your image, and other statues of the gods; these also reviled Christ. None of which things, as is said, they who are really Christians can by any means be compelled to do." What these means were he tells us: "I put the question to them, whether they were Christians. Upon their confessing to me that they were, I repeated the question a second and a third time, threatening, also, to punish them with death. Such as still persisted, I ordered away to be punished." What is very remarkable, it was, it seems, "usual in such cases, for the crime to spread itself, even whilst under persecution." In the face of such dangers, these heathens would still profess faith in Christ, and when they might have saved their lives by reviling him, refused to do so. From the published rescript of the Emperor, approving of Pliny's course, and condemning to death all who were convicted of being really Christians—from the public circulars of the Apostles, warning them of "fiery trials," "Satan casting some of them into prison," and exhorting them to "be faithful unto death;" and from such comments on these as the torture and public execution of aged women as well as men, —the terms of discipleship were well known to the whole world. Yet we see that in the face of all this, "great numbers of persons, of both sexes, and of all ages, and of every rank," in Pliny's opinion, were so steadfast in their faith, that "they were in great danger of suffering."

Here then is another well attested fact, in which the testimony of the apostles stands confirmed by the signatures of the Bithynian Governor, and the Roman Emperor—a fact which stands forth clear, prominent, most undoubted, without the smallest trace of any thing mythological or misty about it—that, in A. D. 106, great numbers of converted heathens did suffer exile, torture, and death itself, rather than renounce Christ; and that it was well known that the Christian faith enabled its possessor to overcome the world.

These four great facts of the later Epistles, being thus established beyond dispute, in pursuance of our plan, we ascend the stream of history some forty years, to the time of the earlier Epistles, when Paul lay in the Mamertine dungeons, and his faithful companion, Luke, wrote the continuation of his narrative of the things most surely believed among the Christians; when "Apostles were made as the filth of the world, and the offscouring of all things;" and Christians "were made a gazing stock, both by reproaches and afflictions;" "were brought before kings and rulers, and hated of all nations for Christ's name sake;" "endured a great fight of afflictions;" were "for his sake killed all the day long, and annointed as sheep for the slaughter;" were made a spectacle to the world, to angels, and to men." We remove the field of our investigation from a remote Province of Asia, to one equally remote from Judea, and far more unfavorable for the growth of the religion of a crucified Jew—the proud capital of the world—imperial Rome. The time shall be shortly after the burning of the city, in A. D. 64, and during the raging of the first of those systematic, imperial, and savage persecutions through which the Church of Christ waded, in the bloody footsteps of her Lord, to world-wide influence, and undying fame. Our historian shall be the well known Tacitus; and the single extract from his history, one of which the infidel Gibbon says:* "The most sceptical criticism is obliged to respect the truth of this important fact, and the integrity of this celebrated passage of Tacitus." I shall not insert quotations from Paul or Luke; that were merely to transcribe large portions of the Epistles and Gospels, which whoever will not carefully peruse, disqualifies himself for forming a judgment of their veracity. The confirmation of the four facts already established, of the existence, worship, morals, and sufferings of the Disciples of Christ; and these facts as well known within thirty years after his death, will sufficiently appear by the perusal of the following testimony of Tacitus.†

After relating the burning of the city, and Nero's attempt to transfer the odium of it to the sect "commonly known by the name of Christians, he says:"

"The author of that name was Christ, who, in the reign of Tiberius, was put to death as a criminal, under the procurator, Pontius Pilate. But this pestilent superstition, checked for awhile, broke out afresh, and spread not only over Judea, where the evil originated, but also in Rome, where all that is evil on the earth finds its way, and is practised. At first, those only were apprehended who confessed themselves of that sect; afterward, *a vast multitude* discovered by them; all of whom were condemned, not so much for the crime of burning the city, as for their enmity to mankind. Their executions

---

*Decline and Fall, vol. 2, p. 407. †Lib. xv. chap. 44.

were so contrived, as to expose them to derision and contempt. Some were covered over with the skins of wild beasts, that they might be torn to pieces by dogs; some were crucified; while others, having been daubed over with combustible materials, were set up for lights in the night time, and thus burned to death. For these spectacles Nero gave his own gardens, and, at the same time, exhibited there the diversions of the circus; sometimes standing in the crowd as a spectator, in the habit of a charioteer; and, at other times, driving a chariot himself; until at length these men, though really criminal, and deserving of exemplary punishment, began to be commiserated, as people who were destroyed, not out of regard to the public welfare, but only to gratify the cruelty of one man."

We add no comment on this remarkable passage. Take up your New Testament and read the contemporary history—Acts 22 to the end of the book—and the letters of Paul from Rome, to Philemon, Titus, the Ephesians, Philippians, Colossians, and the second to Timothy, written when the aged prisoner was ready to be offered, and the time of his departure, amidst such scenes and sufferings, was at hand. Then form your own opinion as to the origin and nature of that faith in Jesus which enabled him to say: "None of these things move me, neither count I my life dear unto me, that I may finish my course with joy, and the testimony which I have received of the Lord Jesus." "I know in whom I have believed, and am persuaded that he is able to keep that which I have committed to Him against that day."

Whatever may be your opinion of the Apostles' hope for the future, you must acknowledge that we have ascertained, beyond contradiction, these four facts of the past:

1. That without the power of force, or the help of governments, and in spite of them, they did convert vast multitudes of idolaters from a senseless worship of stocks and stones, to the worship of the one living and true God—a thing never done by the preachers of any other religion before or since.

2. That without the help of power or civil law, and solely by moral and spiritual means, they did persuade multitudes of licentious heathens to give up their vices, and obey the pure precepts of the morality contained in their Epistles—a thing never done by the preachers of any other religion before or since.

3. That these converts were so firmly persuaded of the truth of their new religion, that, with the choice of life and worldly honor, or a death of infamy and torture before them, multitudes deliberately chose to suffer torture and death rather than renounce the belief in one God, obedience to his laws, and the hope of eternal life

through Jesus Christ, which they had learned from the sermons and letters of these Apostles—a thing never done by the professors of any other religion before or since.*

4. The faith which produced such an illumination of their minds; which caused such a blessed change in their lives; which filled them with joy and hope, and enabled them even to despise torture and death, was briefly this: "That Christ died for our sins, according to the Scriptures, and that he was buried, and that he rose again on the third day, according to the Scriptures, that he ascended up into heaven, and will come again to judge the world, and reward every man according to his works, and that whosoever believes these things in his heart, and confesses them with his mouth, shall be saved; and he that believeth them not, shall be damned."

It is a fact, then, indisputably proved by history, that the New Testament does teach a religion which can enlighten men's minds, reform their lives, give peace to their consciences, and enable them to meet death with a joyful hope of life eternal. It has done these things in times past, and is doing them now. These are its undoubted fruits. Reader, this faith may be yours. It will work the same results in you as it has done in others. Like causes ever produce like effects. Jesus waits to deliver you from your sins, to fill you with joy and peace in believing, and make you abound in hope, by the power of the Holy Ghost. He has promised, if you will ask it, "I will give them a heart to know me that I am the Lord."

---

* The sufferings of the Jews, under Antiochus, are no exception. They suffered for their faith in the true God, the Messiah to come, and a resurrection to life eternal.

No. 28.

CAN WE BELIEVE CHRIST AND HIS APOSTLES!

"*That which was from the beginning, which we have seen with our eyes, which we have looked upon, and our hands have handled of the Word of Life—that which we have seen and heard, declare we unto you.*"—1 JOHN, i: 1.

WE have seen that the companions of Jesus wrote the books of the New Testament—that their statements of the existence, worship, morals, and faith of the Christian church are confirmed by their enemies, and that multitudes of heathens were turned from vice to virtue by the belief of the testimony of these men—they testified that Jesus Christ did many wonderful miracles—died for our sins, and rose again from the dead—that they saw, and heard, and felt his body, and ate, and drank, and conversed with him for forty days after his resurrection—that he ascended up to heaven in their sight—that he sent them to tell the world that he will come again in the clouds of heaven, with his mighty angels, to judge the living and the dead—that he who believes these things and is baptized shall be saved, but he that believeth not shall be damned. This is their statement. The question is, Can we believe them?

1. The first thing which strikes us in their testimony is, that it stands out utterly different from all other religions. There is nothing in the world like it, not even its counterfeits. The great central fact of Christianity—that Christ died for our sins, and rose again from the dead—stands absolutely alone in the history of religions. The priests of Baal, Brahma, or Jupiter, never dreamed of such a thing. The prophets of Mohammedanism, Mormonism, or Pantheism, have never attempted to imitate it. The great object of all counterfeit Christians is to deny it.

There is no instance in the whole world's history of any other religion ever producing the same effects. We demand any other instance of men destitute of wealth, arms, power, and learning, converting multitudes of lying, lustful, murdering idolaters, into honest, peaceable, virtuous Christians, simply by prayer and preaching. When the infidel tells us of the rapid spread of Mohammedanism and Mormonism—impostures which enlist disciples by promising free license to lust, robbery and murder, and retain them by the terror of the scimeter and the rifle ball—which reduce mankind to the most abject servitude, and womankind to the most debasing concubinage—which have turned the fairest regions of the earth to a wilderness, and under whose blighting influence commerce, arts, science, industry, comfort, and the human race itself, have withered away—he simply insults our common sense, by ignoring the difference between backgoing vice and ongoing virtue; or acknowledges that he knows as little about Mohammedanism, as he does about Christianity. The gospel stands alone in its doctrines, singular in its operation, unequaled in its success.

2. The next important point for consideration is, that the Christianity preached by Christ and his Apostles is a whole—a single system, which we must either take or leave—believe entirely, or entirely reject as an imposture. There is no middle ground for you to occupy. It is all true, or all false. For instance, you can not take one of Paul's epistles and say, "this is true," and take another of the same man's letters, containing the very same religion, and say, "this is false." If you accept the very briefest of Paul's letters, that to Philemon, containing only thirteen sentences on private business, you accept eleven distinct assertions of the authority, grace, love, and divinity of our Lord. Nor can you say you will accept Peter's letters and reject Paul's; for you will find the very same facts asserted by the one as by the other; and moreover, Peter endorses "all the epistles of our beloved brother Paul" as on the same pedestal of authority with the other Scriptures. You can not say, "I will accept the letters and reject the history," for the letters have no meaning without the history. They are founded upon it, and assume or allege its facts on every page. Were the gospels lost, we could collect a good account of the birth, teaching, death, resurrection, ascension, and almighty power of the Lord Christ from Paul's epistles; and these letters are just as confident in alleging the miraculous part of the history as the gospels themselves. Neither can you gain any advantage by saying, "I accept the gospels, but reject the letters," for there is not a doctrine of the New Testament which is not taught in the very first of them, the gospel by Matthew. Further, the gospels contain the most solemn authentication of the commissions of the Apostles, so that whosoever rejects their teach-

ing, brings upon himself guilt equal to that of rejecting Christ himself. "Lo, I am with you alway"—"He that receiveth you receiveth me, and he that receiveth me receiveth him that sent me"—"Whosoever will not receive you, nor hear your words, when ye depart out of that house or city, shake off the dust of your feet. Verily I say unto you, it shall be more tolerable for the land of Sodom and Gomorrah in the day of judgment, than for that city."

It is, if possible, more absurd to attempt to dissect the morality of the gospel from its history, and to say, "We are willing to receive the Christian code of morals as a very excellent rule of life, and to regard Jesus as a rare example of almost superhuman virtue, but we must consider the narrative of supernatural events interwoven with it as mythological," i. e., false. Which is much the same as to say, "We will be very happy to receive your friend if he will only cut his head off." Of what possible use would the Christian code of morals be without the authority of Christ, the lawgiver? If he possessed no divine authority, what right has he to control your inclination or mine? And if he will never return to inquire whether men obey or disobey his law, who will regard it? Do you suppose the world will be turned upside down, and reformed, by a little good advice? Nay, verily, the world has had trial of that vanity long enough. "We must all appear before the judgment seat of Christ, that every one may receive the things done in the body, according to that he hath done, whether it be good or bad. Knowing, therefore, *the terrors of the Lord*, we persuade men."

Take away the miraculous and supernatural from the gospel history, and there is nothing left for you to accept. There is no natural history nor worldly code of morality in it. It is wholly the history of a supernatural person, and every precept of his morality comes with a divine sanction. Further, you know nothing of either his life or his morality but from the gospel history, and if the record of the miracles which occupy three-fourths of the gospels be false, what reason have you to give any credit to the remainder? For, as the German commentator, De Wette, well says, "The only means of acquaintance with a history is the narrative we possess concerning it, and beyond that narrative the interpreter can not go. In these Bible records, the narrative reports to us only a supernatural course of events, which we must either receive or reject. If we reject the narrative, we know nothing at all about the event, and we are not justified in allowing ourselves to invent a natural course of events of which the narrative is totally silent." So, you see, you can not make a Christ to suit your taste, but must just take the Christ of the gospel, or reject him.

If you reject the testimony of Christ and his Apostles as false, and say you can not believe them in matters of fact, how can you respect their morality? Of all the absurdities of modern infidelity, the respectful language generally used by its advocates in speakng of Christ and his Apostles, is the most inconsistent. He claimed to be a Divine Person, and professed to work miracles. The infidel says he was not a Divine Person, and wrought no miracles. The consequence is unavoidable—such a pretender is a blasphemous impostor. And yet they speak of him as "a model man," an "exemplar of every virtue." What!—an impostor a model man? A blasphemer and liar an exemplar of every virtue? Is that the infidel's notion of virtue? Why, the devils were more consistent in their commendations of his character, "We know thee who thou art, THE HOLY ONE OF GOD." Let our modern enemies of Christ learn consistency from their ancient allies. We have also learned from our Master to refuse all hypocritical, half-way professions of respect for his character and teachings from those whose business is to prove him a deceiver, and whose object in speaking respectfully of such a one, can only be to gain a larger audience, and a readier entrance for their blasphemy among his professed disciples. From every man who professes respect for Christ's character and for the morality which he and his Apostles taught, we demand a straightforward answer to the questions: "When he declared himself the Son of God, the Judge of the living and the dead, did he tell the truth, or did he lie? When he promised to attest his Divine Commission by rising from the dead on the third day, had he any such power, or did he only mean to play a juggling imposture? Is Jesus the Christ the Son of the Living God, or a deceiver?" There is no middle ground. He that is not with him is against him.

The case is just the same with regard to the witnesses of his miracles, death, and resurrection. They either give a true relation of these things, or they have manufactured a series of falsehoods.

How can we believe anything from persons so habituated to lying as the narrators of the mighty works of Jesus must be, if those mighty works were never performed? How can we accept their code of morals if we refuse to believe them when they speak of matters of fact? Is it possible to respect men as moral teachers, whom we have convicted of forging stories of miracles that never occurred, and confederating together to impose a lying superstition on the world? For this is plainly the very point and center of the question about the truth of the Bible, and I am anxious you should see it clearly. A fair statement of this question is half the argument. The question then is simply this, Was Jesus really the Divine Person he claimed to be, or was he a blasphemous impostor? When the Apostles unitedly and solemnly testified that they had seen him after he was risen from the dead, that they ate and drank with him, that their hands had handled his body, that they conversed with him for forty days, and saw him go up to heaven, did they tell the truth, or were they a confederated band of liars? There is no reason for any other supposition. They could not possibly be deceived themselves in the matters they relate. They knew perfectly whether they were true or not. We are not talking about matters of dogma, about which there might be room for difference of opinion, but about matters of fact—about what men say they saw, and heard, and felt—about which no man of common sense could possibly be mistaken. "That which we have seen with our eyes, which we have heard, which we have looked upon, and our hands have handled of the Word of Life—that which we have seen and heard, declare we unto you." Such is their language. We must either take it as truth, or reject it as falsehood. It is utter nonsense to talk of the intense subjectivity of the Jewish mind, and the belief of the Apostles, that the Messiah would do wonders when he came, and the powerful impressions produced by the teaching of Jesus on their minds. We are not talking about impressions on their minds, but about impressions produced on their eyes, and ears, and hands. Did these men tell the truth when they told the world that they did eat and drink with Jesus after he rose from the dead, or did they lie? That is the question.

3. It is a hard matter to lie well. A liar has need of a good memory, else he will contradict himself before he writes far. And

he needs to be very well posted up in the matters of names, dates, places, manners and customs, else he will contradict some well known facts, and so expose his forgery to the world. Therefore writers of forgeries avoid all such things as much as possible, and as surely as they venture on specifications of that sort, they are detected. A man who is conscious of writing a book of falsehoods, does not begin on this wise: " Now in the fifteenth year of the reign of Tiberius Cæsar, Pontius Pilate being Governor of Judea, and Herod being Tetrarch of Galilee, and his brother Philip Tetrarch of Iturea and of the regions of Trachonitis, and Lysanias Tetrarch of Abilene, Annas and Caiphas being high priests, the word of God came unto John, the son of Zacharias, in the wilderness." Here in one sentence are twenty historical, geographical, political, and genealogical references, every one of which we can confirm by references to secular historians. The enemies of the Lord have utterly failed in their attempts to disprove one out of the hundreds of such statements in the New Testament. The only instance of any *public political event* recorded in the gospel, said not to be confirmed by the fragments of secular history we possess, is Luke's account of a census of the Roman Empire, ordered by Augustus Cæsar. Were it so that Luke stood alone in his mention of this, surely his credit as a historian would be as good for this fact, as the credit of Tacitus, when he states matters of which Suetonius makes no mention, or of Pliny, when he relates things not recorded by Tacitus. But we can account for the want of corroborative history in this instance, when we know that all the history of Dion Cassius, from the consulships of Antistius and Balbus to those of Messala and Cinna—that is, for five years before and five years after the birth of Christ—is lost; as also Livy's history of the same period. It is certain that some one did record the fact, for Suidas, in his lexicon upon the word *apographe,* says, "that Augustus sent twenty select men into all the provinces of the empire to take a census, both of men and property, and commanded that a just proportion of the latter should be brought into the imperial treasury. And this was the first census."

To object to the gospel history, that every thing contained in it of the doings of Christ and his Apostles in Judea, is not recorded by the historians of Greece and Italy, is much the same as to say that there are a multitude of facts recorded in D'Aubigne's History of the Reformation in Germany, of which Hume and Macaulay make no mention in their histories of England. How should they—treating of different countries, and for the most part of different periods, and writing civil and not church history? Does any body go to Macaulay to look for the history of the Westminster Assembly, or to Bancroft for an account of the Great Revival in New England? Or is the veracity of Baillie or Edwards suspected, because political history does not concern itself much about religion? It is enough, that not a single statement of the gospel history has ever been disproved.

I might give you quotations from the enemies of the Christian faith, from Josephus the Jew, and Celsus and Porphyry, heathen philosophers, and from the Emperor Julian, the apostate—who, having been raised a Christian, became a heathen, and used all his ingenuity to overturn the religion of Christ—expressly admitting the principal miracles recorded in the gospel. But I attach no such importance to the testimony of this class of persons as to suppose that it should be placed, for one moment, on a level with the testimony of the Apostles, or that their testimony to the facts of the life and death of Christ needs any confirmation from such witnesses. We have such overwhelming evidence of the sincerity and truth of the witnesses chosen by God to bear testimony to the resurrection of Christ, as we never can have of the credibility of any secular historian whatever.

You will remember that these are the writers whose accounts of the existence, the faith and worship, the numbers and morals of the Christian Church, we have seen so strikingly confirmed by their enemies; and we now inquire, can we believe the other part of their history to be as true? These are the men who taught the heathen a pure christian morality, one principal article of which was, "Lie not one to another, seeing ye have put off the old man with his deeds"—"All liars shall have their portion in the lake that burneth with fire and brimstone"—and we are to inquire if they themselves lied—lied publicly, lied repeatedly—if the very business of their lives was to propagate falsehood, and if they died with a lie in their right hands. You will remember that we proved conclusively that the belief of the death and resurrection of Jesus did turn immense multitudes of wicked men to a life of virtue, and now we are to inquire if the belief of a lie produced this blessed result, and whether, if so, there be any such thing as truth in the world, or any use in it?

4. Of no other series of events of ancient history do we possess the same number of records by contemporary historians, as of the life, death, and resurrection of the Lord Jesus. We have four direct systematic memoirs of him by four of his companions; and we have a collection of letters by four others, in which the events of the memoirs are continually referred to. At the mouth of two or three witnesses, any man's property and life will be disposed of in a court of justice, but here we have the testimony of eight eye-witnesses of the facts they relate, and they refer to five hundred other persons, the greater part of whom were then alive, who had also seen and heard Christ after his resurrection. These eight persons give us their separate and independent statements of those things they deemed worthy of record in the life and death of Christ, and of the sayings and doings of several of his friends and enemies. Now every person knows that it is impossible to make two crooked boughs tally, or two false witnesses agree. You never saw two lying reports of any considerable number of transactions agree, unless the one was copied from the other.

It is evident that the gospels were not copied from each other, for they often relate different events, and when they relate the same occurrence, each man relates those parts of it which he saw himself, and which impressed him most. Yet the utmost ingenuity of infidelity has utterly failed to make them contradict each other in any particular. Here are eight witnesses to the truth of the same story, four of whom in their letters make occasional allusions to the facts of the history as being perfectly well known, and therefore needing only to be alluded to, yet these cursory references fit into the history with every mark of truthfulness. Does the history of Matthew, written at Jerusalem, tell us that Jesus took Peter, and James, and John up into a high mountain apart, and was transfigured before them? Peter, in his letter, written from Babylon says, "We were eye-witnesses of his majesty. We were with him in the holy mount." 2 Pet. ii: 16. If the history tells how Paul was beaten and cast into prison at Philippi, and his feet made fast in the stocks, and that, nevertheless, he manfully defended his birthright as a Roman citizen, and made the tyrannical magistrates humble themselves, and apologise for their illegal conduct, we find Paul himself, in a letter to a neighboring church, appealing to their knowledge of the facts, "that after we had suffered before, and were shamefully entreated, as ye know, at Philippi, we were bold in our God to speak unto you the gospel of God with much contention. For our exhortation was not of deceit, nor of uncleanness, nor in guile. For neither at any time used we flattering words, as ye know, nor a cloak for covetousness." 1 Thess. ii: 2. Hundreds of such undesigned coincidences may be found in the New Testament, confirming the veracity of the several historians and letter writers, and giving that impression of the naturalness and truth of the story, which can neither be described nor disputed. The reader who desires to prosecute this interesting branch of the evidences of Christianity, will find an ample collection of these coincidences in Paley's Horæ Paulinæ.

This agreement of independent writers is the more remarkable, as the writers were persons of very various degrees of education, of different professions and ranks of life, born in different countries, and writing from various places in Italy, Greece, Palestine, and Assyria, without any communication with each other. Matthew was an officer of customs in Galilee—Mark a Hebrew citizen of Jerusalem—Luke a Greek physician of Antioch—James and John owned and sailed a fishing smack on Lake Tiberias—Jude left his thirty-nine acres of land, worth nine thousand denarii, to be farmed by his children when he went forth to preach the gospel—and college-bred Paul carried his sturdy independence in his breast, and his sail needles in his pocket, and dictated epistles, and cut out marquees and lug-sails in the tent factory of Aquila, Paul & Co., at Corinth. Several of his letters were written in a dungeon in Rome; the last of Peter's is dated at Babylon; Matthew's gospel was penned at Jerusalem, and John's gospel and epistles were written at Ephesus. The agreement of eight such witnesses, of such different pursuits, and so scattered over the world, in the relation of the same story, in all its leading particulars, together with their variety of style and manner, and their various relations of minor incidents, yet without a single contradiction, are most convincing proofs that they all tell truth. Nothing but truth could be thus told without contradiction.

The fact that some considerable difficulties and many minor

obscurities in these brief though pregnant narratives, prevent the combination of eight accounts so independent in their sources, and various in their style, and design, and auditors—into a flowing historical novel—a homogeneous mass, rounded and squared to our ideas of mathematical precision—is only an additional proof of their truth to nature, which abhors mathematical as much as truth does rhetorical figures. Like the variety of expression used by American, German, French, and Polish witnesses in our courts of justice, testifying the same facts in their native idioms, though in English words, the apparent discrepancy but actual harmony becomes the most decisive test of the absence of any collusion, and consequently of the verity of the facts which such various witnesses unite in testifying. Especially will any such apparent discrepancy resolve itself into our own unskilfullness or ignorance, when we remember that the mists of ages, and the drapery of a strange language, and world-wide removal of residence, and the turning of the world upside down by the progress of Christian civilization, and our consequent ignorance of the thousand little details of every day life, well known to the writer and his immediate readers, and of the force of expressive idioms, perfectly familiar to them—have rendered us not near so capable of detecting inaccuracies, as those contemporary writers and opponents, who allowed them—if they existed—to pass unchallenged. Like those antique coins, whose rust-dimmed and abbreviated inscriptions exercise the patience and historic lore of the antiquarian—though neither are needed to declare the precious material—this very rust of antiquity, through which his patience has penetrated, becomes one of the inimitable marks of historic verity. Every year throws some new light on texts difficult to us from our ignorance of those manners, customs, names, and places, which infidel malice and Christian piety have combined to explore, and from the ruins of Nineveh and the sepulchres of Egypt we receive unlooked-for testimonies to the minute accuracy of the penmen of the Bible.

5. The manner in which the Apostles published their testimony to the world, bears every mark of truthfulness. Deception and forgery skulk and try to spread themselves at first in holes and corners, but he that doeth truth cometh to the light. Had the Apostles been conscious of falsehood, would they have dared to assert that Jesus was risen from the dead in the very streets of the

city where he was crucified—in the temple, the most public place of resort of the Jews who saw him crucified—and to the teeth of the very men who put him to death? If conscious of falsehood, would they have dared, before the chief priests, and the council, and all the senate of Israel, to assert that "The God of our fathers raised up Jesus, whom ye slew and hanged on a tree. Him hath God exalted with his right hand to be a Prince and a Saviour, to give repentance to Israel, and remission of sins. And we are his witnesses of these things, and so is also the Holy Ghost which God hath given to them that obey him." Acts v: 30. Would Paul, had he been conscious that he was relating falsehood, have dared to appeal to the judge, before whom he was on trial for his life, as one who knew the notoriety of these facts, "For the king knoweth of these things, before whom also I speak freely; for I am persuaded that none of these things are hidden from him: for this thing was not done in a corner." Acts xxvi: 26. Would such appeals have been suffered to pass uncontradicted had the statements of the Apostles been false?

The boldness of their manner, however, of telling their story, is little, compared with the boldness of the design which they had in view in telling it; which was nothing less than to convert the world. Now the idea of proselyting other nations to a new religion, was absolutely unknown to the world at that time. The heathens never dreamed of any such thing. They would sometimes add a new god to their old Pantheon, but the idea of turning a nation to the worship of new deities was never before heard of. The Jews were so indignant at the project, that when Paul hinted it to them, they cried, "Away with such a fellow from the earth, for it is not fit that he should live." And this new and strange idea, of conquering the world for a crucified man, is taken up by a few private citizens, who resolve to overturn the craft by which priests have their wealth, and to bring the kingdoms of the world to become the kingdoms of our Lord and of his Christ.

Impostors would never have appealed to their power of working miracles as the Apostles did; nor could enthusiasts have done so without instant exposure. It is remarkable, that while in addressing those who believed their Divine Commission, they rarely allude to it, (fourteen of the epistles make no allusion to apostolic miracles), but dwell on a subject of far greater importance—a holy life—they never hesitate to confront a Simon Magus, or a schismatical church at Corinth, or a persecuting high priest and sanhedrim with this power of the Holy Ghost. "Tongues," says Paul, "are for a sign, not to them that believe, but to them that believe not," and this is true of all other miracles. This marks the difference between real miracles and those of pretenders, who have never attempted to establish a new religion by them, or to convert unbelievers hostile to their claims and able to examine them, without immediate exposure. But you never heard of an impostor standing up before the tribunal of his judges and alleging the miraculous cure of a well known public beggar, lame from his mother's womb, whom they had seen at the church gate every Sabbath for forty years, and bringing the man into court after such a fashion as this, "If we this day be examined of the good deed done unto the impotent man, by what means he is made whole, be it known unto you all, and to all the people of Israel, that by the name of Jesus Christ of Nazareth, whom ye crucified, whom God raised from the dead, even by him doth this man stand before you whole." Such an appeal was unanswerable. "Beholding the man that was healed standing with them, they could say nothing against it." Nay, they were compelled to acknowledge "that indeed a notable miracle hath been done by them is manifest to all them that dwell in Jerusalem—we can not deny it." Acts iv.

The denial of the miracles of the Gospel is a modern invention of the enemy. The Scribes and Priests, Emperors and Philosophers of the first centuries, who had the best opportunity of proving their falsehood, were unable to do so. The persecutors and apostates, whose malice against the church knew no bounds, never dared to utter a charge of deception against the Apostles. Why, then, you ask, did they not all become Christians? Because miracles can not convert any man against his will. Christianity is not merely a belief in miracles, but the love of Christ and a life of holiness. There are many readers of this tract who would not turn from their sins if all the dead in Spring Grove Cemetery would rise to-morrow to warn them from hell. God does not intend to force any man to become a Christian. He just gives evidence enough to try you, whether you will deal honestly and fairly with your own soul and your God, and if you are determined to hate Christ and his holy religion, you shall never want a plausible excuse for unbelief; as it is written, "Unto them which are disobedient, Christ is a stone of stumbling and a rock of offence." These ancient enemies of Christ acknowledged the reality of his miracles, but attributed them to magical power, or the help of Satan. The Jews said that he had acquired the power of miracles by learning to pronounce the incommunicable name of God. Modern infidels deny all his miracles save the greatest—the turning of men from their sins. They can not deny that—they can not ascribe it to the power of Satan or of magic, for they do not believe in either—but they follow as nearly in the footsteps of their fathers as possible, when they tell us that multitudes of men, in every age, and in every land, have been turned from falsehood to truth by the belief of a lie, and from vice to virtue by the example of an impostor!

6. But the strongest proof of the truth of the facts of the gospel, is the existence, the labors and sufferings of the Apostles themselves. Nobody denies that such men lived, and preached, and were persecuted on account of their preaching that Jesus died and rose again. Now, if this was a falsehood, what motive had they to tell it? It was very displeasing to their rulers who had crucified him, and who had every inclination to give them the same treatment. To preach another king, one Jesus, to the Romans, was to bring down the power of the empire upon them. Nothing could be more absurd in the eyes of the Grecian philosophers than to speak of the resurrection of the body. Nor could any plan be devised more certain to arouse the fury of the pagan priesthood, than to denounce the craft by which they had their wealth, and to preach that they are no gods which are made by hands. The most degraded wretch who perishes by the hand of the hangman, is not so contemptible in our eyes, as the crucified malefactor was in the eyes of the Roman people; nor could any thing more disagreeable to the Jewish nation be invented, than the declaration that the Gentiles should become partakers of the kingdom of God. What then should induce any man in his senses to provoke such an opposition to a new religion, and to make it so contemptible and disagreeable to those whom he sought to convert, if he were manufacturing a lie to gain power and popularity?

The religion they preached was not adapted to please sensual men, nor to allow its preachers in sensual gratifications. "Our exhortation," says Paul—and every reader of the New Testament knows that he says truth—"Our exhortation was not of deceit, nor of uncleanness, nor of guile." Infidels admit that they preached a pure morality. But it is a long time since men learned the proverb, "Physician heal thyself." "Thou that preachest a man should not steal, dost thou steal? Thou that sayest a man should not commit adultery, dost thou commit adultery? Thou that abhorrest idols, dost thou commit sacrilege?" It could not, then, be to obtain license for lust that these men preached holiness.

There is only one other conceivable motive which should induce men to confederate together for the propagation of falsehood—the design of making money by it. But their new religion made no provision for any such thing. One of their first acts was to desire the church to elect deacons who might manage its money matters, and allow them to give themselves wholly to prayer and to the ministry of the word. Twenty-five years after that they could appeal to the world that "Even to this present hour, we, (the Apostles,) both hunger and thirst, and are naked, and are buffeted, and have no certain dwelling place, and labor working with our hands; being reviled, we bless; being persecuted, we suffer it: we are counted as the filth of the world, and the offscouring of all things to this day." Their book opens with the story of their Master's birth in a stable, with the manger for his cradle, and one of its last pictures is that of his venerable Apostle chained in a dungeon, and begging his friend to bring his old cloak from Troas, and to do his diligence to come before winter.

Unpopular, pure, and penniless, if the gospel story were not true, how could it have had preachers? They at least believed it.

The last and most convincing testimony which any man can give to the truth of a statement of fact, is to suffer rather than deny it. Many have wondered why God allowed his dear servants to suffer so much persecution in the first ages of the church. One principal reason was to give future ages an irresistible proof of the sincerity and faithfulness of the witnesses for Christ. The Apostles lived lives of persecution and suffering for the name of Jesus—sufferings which they might have avoided if they had only abstained from preaching any more in this name. But, said they,

"We can not but speak the things we have seen and heard. One who had no personal acquaintance with Jesus, and whose first interview with him was while he was breathing out threatening and slaughter against the disciples of the Lord, is converted and called to be an Apostle; and behold the prospect Jesus presents to him, "I will show him *how great things he must suffer for my name.*" "The Holy Ghost testifieth, says Paul, that in every city bonds and afflictions abide me. Yet none of these things move me." That at least was a true prophecy. "Seven times," says Clement, "he was in bonds, he was whipt, he was stoned; he preached both in the east and west, leaving behind him the glorious report of his faith, and so having taught the whole world righteousness, and for that end traveled even to the utmost bounds of the west, he at last suffered martyrdom by the command of the governors, and went to his holy place, having become a most eminent pattern of patience to all ages.* Hear his own appeal to those who envied his authority in the church, "Are they ministers of Christ, I am more: in labors more abundant, in stripes above measure, in prisons more frequent, in deaths often. Of the Jews five times received I forty stripes save one. Thrice was I beaten with rods, once was I stoned, thrice I suffered shipwreck, a night and a day I have been in the deep: in journeyings often, in perils of waters, in perils of robbers, in perils by my own countrymen, in perils by the heathen, in perils in the city, in perils in the wilderness, in perils in the sea, in perils among false brethren; in weariness and painfulness, in watchings often, in hunger and thirst, in cold and nakedness." 1 Cor. ii: 23.

Man can give no higher proof of his veracity, than a life such as this, unless it be to seal it with his blood; and this crowning testimony to the truth the Apostles gave. Save the aged disciple, who, after torments worse than death, survived to address the persecuted church as—"Your companion in tribulation, and in the kingdom and patience of Jesus Christ," they all suffered martyrdom for the truth of the gospel history.

Let me again remind you that the gospel is not a collection of dogmas, but a relation of facts—that these twelve men did not preach the death and resurrection of Jesus, because they had read them in a creed, but because they had seen them with their own eyes—that they lived holy lives of toil, and hardship, and poverty,

---

* Wake's Trans. of Clement, Ep. ad Cor. v.

and suffering, in preaching these facts to the world: and, that they died painful and shameful deaths, as martyrs for their truth. You admit these things. Then I demand of you, "What more could either God or man do to convince you of their truthfulness?"

The faithful and true witness himself has given you this last, undeniable, test of veracity. With the certainty of an ignominious death before him, he solemnly swears to the truth of this fact, and dies for it. "And the high priest answered and said unto him, I adjure thee by the living God, that thou tell us whether thou be the Christ, the Son of God? Jesus saith unto him, thou hast said. Hereafter ye shall see the Son of man sitting on the right hand of power, and coming in the clouds of heaven."

Unbeliever, are you prepared to meet him there, and prove him a perjured impostor?

No. 29.

PROPHECY.

"IN fifty years all Europe will be either Cossack or Republican." So prophesied the most sagacious of modern politicians, without any pretence to Divine inspiration, other than the inspiration of genius, when calculating the prospects of the future by the light of his past experience. "All genius is prophetic, inasmuch as it grasps general laws, universal in their range, and invariable in their operation, the application of which to particular events constitutes prediction. The Hebrew prophets were sagacious observers of human nature, and made very shrewd calculations of the future progress of events, by a careful induction of the invariable laws of nature from the history of the past. But there was nothing supernatural in that. Every poet, philosopher, and politician is more or less of a prophet. Men of profound genius are rare in any department of science, and ignorance ascribes to supernatural inspiration the sagacity derived from extensive observation; but philosophy traces to the same source the inspiration of Moses and Solon, of Apollo and Ezekiel, of Newton and Napoleon." So says the modern sceptic.

This prediction of Napoleon's is a fair specimen of the oracles of human sagacity, as well as a test of the wisdom of those philosophers who risk their eternal destiny on the sagacity of a man ignorant of his own fate one week ahead, and peril their souls on the chance that, ten years hence—when the affairs of Europe may be of as little consequence to them as they are now to Napoleon—Europe will bring forth from the throes of revolution either a despotism or a republic. No chance, it seems, of a birth of twins falsifying this sage prediction.

Suppose, however, that during the six thousand years during which statesmen have gambled with the liberties of mankind, as many as half-a-dozen should have guessed the shape of some coming event from the shadow which it cast before it—as Cayotte is reported to have predicted the fate of Charles for Louis the XVI., and the atrocities of the Parisian rabble during the Reign of Terror—what then? Is such a guess of any use to the world? Does it, or should it, command any respect when uttered? Does it profess to come from the Disposer of all events, as his seal authenticating any revelation of moral duty to man?

O yes! We are told by men who could not read one of Apollo's oracles to save their lives, nor recite one of Isaiah's prophecies to save their souls—Apollo's oracles no less than Isaiah's were inspired. Could such persons be prevailed upon to read carefully any single prophetic book of Scripture, with the historic facts to which it refers, or even the briefest abridgment of these facts, such as that contained in Scott's, or the Comprehensive Commentary, they would not thus expose their ignorance alike of heathen and Christian oracles.

The differences between them are too numerous to be easily enumerated. The oracles of the heathen are always sources of gain to their prophets. The ancient Pythoness must have a hecatomb, the writing medium a dollar, and the modern Pythoness of the platform a dime. But under the inspiration of God even a Balaam becomes honest, and the leprosy of Naaman marks the sordid Gehazi and his seed for ever.

The oracles of the heathen are always immoral in their tendency. From the first spiritual communication through the serpent medium in the tree of knowledge, down to the last spiritual marriage rapped out by the oracle, they are all in favor of pride, ambition, lying, lust, and murder. The oracles of God begin with a prohibition of curiosity, pride, covetousness, and theft: "In the day thou eatest thereof thou shalt surely die." And they are uniformly of the same tenor, forbidding, reproving, threatening vice, and encouraging virtue, down to the last: "Blessed are they that do his commandments, that they may have right to the tree of life, and may enter in through the gates into the city; for without are dogs, and sorcerers, and whoremongers, and murderers, and idolaters, and whosoever loveth and maketh a lie."

This last mark of falsehood belongs to all heathen oracles, from the first utterance by the serpent down to the last response rapped out by the medium. Take any one heathen oracle of which we have any definite account—and the number is very small—and you will find that, if it is not "as equivocal as Apollo," *it is false.* For instance, infidels very confidently refer to the augury of Vettius Valens, that, "if it be true, as historians say, that Romulus saw twelve vultures at the founding of Rome, that signified that it should exist twelve centuries." It very properly begins with an if, for the story of Romulus and the vultures is exceedingly apocryphal. But whether the story be false or no, the augury certainly is. If it refers to the material city then building, it was false. Brennus, the Gaul, burned it to the ground before it was four centuries old. If it prophesied the permanence of the political constitution, every school-boy knows that within twelve centuries half a dozen revolutions falsified the augury. If it referred to the ultimate duration of the city of that name, or of the Roman people, it is self-evidently false; for now, after the lapse of twenty-six centuries, Rome is larger, its territory wider, and its people more numerous, than for centuries after Romulus saw the twelve vultures. Yet men who have read Roman history present Vettius Valens as a prophet. It is written, "He frustrateth the tokens of the liars."

But it is objected that "the prophecies of Scripture are as obscure as the oracles; are all wrapped up in symbolical language; that many of them have a double meaning; that no two interpreters are agreed as to the meaning of the unfulfilled predictions; and that no man can certainly foretell any future event by means of them." The objection proceeds on a total mistake of the nature and design of prophecy, which is not to unvail the future for the gratification of your curiosity, but to give you direction in your present duty—precisely the reverse of the oracles referred to, which proposed to tell their votaries what would happen—but rarely condescended to direct them how to behave themselves so that things might happen well. The larger part of the prophecies of Scripture is taken up with directions to men how to regulate their conduct, rather than with information how God means to regulate his. There is just as much of the latter as is sufficient to show us that the God who gave the Bible governs the world, and even that always urges the same moral lesson: "Say ye to the righteous that it shall be well with him, for he shall eat the fruit of his doings." "Woe to the wicked; it shall be ill with him, for the reward of his hands shall be given him." Whenever a vision relates to what God will do in the distant future, it is dark and mysterious; but whenever any directions are given necessary for our immediate duty, then the "vision is written and made plain on tables, *that he may run that readeth it.*" The possessors of a clearly engrossed title-deed have surely no reason to complain that the president has chosen that his seal appended to it shall consist of a device, which, by reason of its being hard to read and harder to imitate, secures both himself and them against forgery. The double meaning of some prophecies is a double check. So far from resembling the equivocations of heathen oracles, by taking either of two opposite events for a fulfilment, they require both of two corresponding ones; and some prophecies, like a master key, open several successive events, and thus show that the same mind planned both locks and key. When the prediction is fulfilled all mystery vanishes, and men see plainly that thus it was written—that is to say, men who look—for the man who will not open his eyes will never see any thing that it concerns him to know. But the man who thinks that it concerns him so much to know what God will do with the world a hundred years after he is dead, that unless the prophecies of the Bible are all made plain to him, he will neither read God's word nor obey his law, may go on his own way. We expound no mysteries to such persons; for it is written, "None of the wicked shall understand."

As to the objection taken from the symbolical language of prophecy, and which seems to a number of our modern critics so weighty that they remove to the purely mythologic ground every thing "couched in symbolical language," and account nothing to be prediction unless "literal history written in advance"—I would merely ask, How is it possible to reveal heavenly things to earth-born men but by earthly figures? Do you know a single word in your own, or any other language to express a spiritual state or mental operation, that is not the name of some material state or physical operation, used symbolically? Heart, soul, spirit, idea, memory, imagination, inclination, &c., every one of them a figure of speech—a symbol. Nay, is there a letter in your own or in any other alphabet, that was not originally a picture of something? I demand to know in what way God or man could teach you to know anything you have never seen, but by either showing you a picture of it, or telling you what it is like? That is simply by type or symbol; and these are the only possible media of conveying heavenly truth, or future history to our minds. When, therefore, the sceptic insists that prophecy be given literally in the style of history written in advance, he simply requires that God would make it utterly unintelligible. We can gather clear and definite ideas from the significant hieroglyphics of symbolic language, but the literalities of history written in advance would be worse to decipher than the arrow-headed inscriptions of Nineveh. Just imagine to yourself Alexander the Great reading Guizot, instead of Daniel; or Hildreth, as being less mysterious than Ezekiel; and meeting, for instance, such a record as this: "In the year of Christ 1847, the United States conquered Mexico, and annexed California." "In the year of Christ—what new Olympiad may that be?" he would say. "The United States of course means the States of the Achæan League, but on what shore of the Euxine may Mexico and California be found?" What information could Aristotle gather from the record that, "In 1857, the Transatlantic Telegraph was in operation?" Could all the augurs in the seven-hilled city have expounded to Julius Cæsar the famous despatch, if intercepted in prophetic vision, "Sebastopol was evacuated last night, after enduring for three days an infernal fire of shot and shell?" Nay, to diminish the vista to even two or three centuries, what could Oliver Cromwell, aided by the whole Westminster Assembly, have made of a prophetic vision of a single newspaper paragraph of history written in advance, to inform them that, "Three companies of dragoons came down last night from Berwick to Southampton, by a special train, traveling 54½ miles an hour, including stoppages, and embarked immediately on arrival. The fleet put to sea at noon, in the face of a full gale from the S. W.?" Why, the intelligible part of this single paragraph would seem to them more impossible, and the unintelligible part more absurd, than all the mysterious symbols of the Apocalypse.

The world has accepted God's symbols thousands of years ago, and it is too late in the day for our reformers to propose new laws of thought and forms of speech, to the human race. David's prophetic lyrics, and Christ's lovely parables, Isaiah's celestial anthems and Ezekiel's glorious symbols, Solomon's terse Proverbs, will be recited and admired, ages after the foggy abstractions of mystified metaphysicians have vanished from the earth. The Thirst of Passion, The Cup of Pleasure, The Fountain of the Water of Life, The Blood of Murder, the Rod of Chastisement, The Iron Scepter, The Fire of Wrath, The Balance of Righteousness, The Sword of Justice, The Wheels of Providence, The Conservative Mountains, and The Raging Seas of Anarchy, The Golden, Brazen, and Iron Ages, will reflect their images in Truth's Mirror, and photograph their lessons on Memory's Tablet, while the mists of the "positive philosophy," "the absolute," and "the conditioned," float past unheeded, to the land of forgetfulness. God's prophetic symbols are the glorious embodiments of living truths, while man's philosophic abstractions are the melancholy ghosts of expiring nonsense.

The prophetic symbols are sufficiently plain to be distinctly intelligible *after* the fulfillment, as we shall presently see; sufficiently obscure to baffle presumptious curiosity before it. Had they been so written as to be fully intelligible beforehand, they must have interfered with man's free agency, by causing their own fulfillment. They hide the future sufficiently to make man feel his ignorance; they reveal enough to encourage faith in the God who rules it.

The revelation of future events, however, is not the principal design of the prophecies of the Bible; they bear witness to God's powerful present influence over the world now. For God's prophecy is not merely his foretelling something which will certainly happen at some future time, but over which he has no control—as an astronomer foretells an eclipse of the sun, but can neither hasten nor hinder it—but it is his revealing of a part of his plan of this world's affairs, to show that God, and not man, is the sovereign of this world. For this purpose he tells beforehand the actions which wicked men, of their own free will, will commit contrary to his law, and the measures he will take to thwart their designs, and fulfill his own. Nay, he declares he will so manage matters that without their knowledge, and even contrary to their intentions, heathen armies and infidel scoffers shall serve his purposes and show his power; while yet they are as perfectly voluntary in all their movements as if they, and not God, governed the world. Every fulfilled prophecy thus becomes an instance and evidence of a supernatural government; and is to a thinking mind a greater miracle than casting mountains into the sea. The style of prophecy corresponds to this design. It is not by any means apologetic or supplicating; but, on the contrary, majestic, convincing, and terrifying to the ungodly.

"*Remember this and show yourselves men.*

"*Bring it again to mind, O ye transgressors.*

"*For I am God, and there is none else.*

"*I am God, and there is none like me.*

"*Declaring the end from the beginning,*

"*And from ancient times the things that are not yet done,*

"*Saying,* 'MY COUNSEL SHALL STAND, AND I WILL DO ALL MY PLEASURE.'" *

---

* Isaiah, chap. 46: 8-11.

Infidels feel the power of this manifestation of God in his word; and are driven to every possible denial of the fact, and evasion of the argument drawn from it. They feel instinctively that Bible prophecies are far more than mere predictions. They would rather endow every human being on earth with the power of predicting the future than allow the God of heaven that power of ruling the present which these prophecies assert. Hence the attempt to admit their predictive truth, and yet deny their Divine authority, by ascribing them to human sagacity.

Transatlantic steam navigation has produced a remarkable change in the tone of infidel writers and speakers in regard to the prophecies of the Bible. You could not converse long with an infidel on this subject, a few years ago, until he would assure you, with all confidence, that the prophecies were all written after their fulfillment, and so were not prophecies at all. But now that travelers of all classes, scoffers, sailors, and doctors of divinity, scientific expeditions, and correspondents of daily newspapers, have flooded the world with undeniable attestations that many of them are receiving their fulfillment at this day, none but the most grossly ignorant and stupid attempt to deny that the prophecies of the Bible were written thousands of years since, and that many of them have since been accomplished; and that so many have been fulfilled that their accomplishment cannot be ascribed to chance. But the force of the argument for the Divine inspiration of the prophets is met by the assertion that there is nothing supernatural in prophecy, and that it is only one form of the inspiration of genius.

Calculating securely on that profound ignorance of the Bible which characterizes their followers, modern writers inform them that "none of the prophets ever uttered any distinct, definite, unambiguous prediction of any future event which has since taken place, which a man without a miracle could not equally well predict." It is alleged that the prophecies, in predicting the overthrow of the nations of antiquity, predicted nothing beyond the ken of human sagacity, enlightened by a careful study of the experience of the past and the invariable laws of nature—that it requires no inspiration to foretell the decay of perishing things—that the invariable progress of all things, empires as well as individuals, is first upward, through a period of youthful vigor and energy, then onward through a period of ripe maturity, and then downward, through a gradual decay and final dissolution, to the inevitable grave. The world's history is but a history of the decline and fall of nations.

I. Now, if this be true, it is an awful truth for the infidel, for *it sweeps away the last vestige of a foundation of his hope for eternity.* The only reason any unbeliever in Revelation could ever give, or that modern spiritualists do give, for their hope of a happy eternity, is the analogy of Nature—the alleged constant progress of all things toward perfection in this world. It is an awkward truth that individually we must die and the worms crawl over us; but then the wretched fate of the individual was to be compensated by the glorious progress of the race onward and ever onwards and upward—from the fungus to the frog, and from the frog to the monkey, from the monkey to the man, from the noble savage wild in woods, to the pastoral tribe; thence to the empire and the federal republic; and finally to the reign of individual and passional attraction, and union with the sum of all the intelligences of the universe, through a constant progress towards infinite perfection.

But, alas! it seems it was a false analogy, an ill-observed fact, a delusion; the course of nature is all the other way. The tendency of all perishing things is not to perfection, but to perdition; and it needs no inspiration to tell that man's loftiest towers and strongest cities and proudest empires will come to ruin; or that the most polished, powerful, and populous nations of antiquity will dwindle down into Turks, Moors, and Egyptians. Here is a fact of awful omen. Death reigns in this world of ours—death moral, social, political, and physical, has ever trampled upon man, proud man, learned man, civilized man, over all the plans of man, over every man and over every association of men, even the largest, the wisest, the mightiest. And now the infidel, having taken away our hope of help from heaven, comes with the serpent's hiss and fiendish sneer to taunt the perishing world with this miserable truism—that the tendency of every thing on earth is to perdition, and that it needs no inspiration to tell it. Truly it does not. Were that all the prophets of God had to tell us—as it is all the prophets of infidelity can prophecy—we had as little need for the one as for the other. Earthquake and hurricane, volcano and valley flood, autumn frosts and winter blasts, fever, consumption, war, and pestilence, the grave-yard and the charnel-house, the

Parthenon and the Pyramids, and the mounds of Mexico and Assyria, unite to attest this awful doom.

But what reason has the skeptic to believe that this invariable law of nature shall ever be repealed, and this inevitable progress of all things to perdition be arrested? Why may not men be as selfish and filthy, and grasping and murderous in the other world as they are in this? Why may not the course of nature be as fatal to the sinner's prosperity there, as it is here? Why may not the progress of the proud empires and spheres of futurity, be such as the skeptic declares the progress of the past to have been, so invariably towards dissolution and death, that it shall need no inspiration to predict its course downward, downward, ever downward, to endless perdition? Stand forward skeptic, and point the world to an instance in which an ungodly nation has stemmed this all-destroying torrent of ruin; or acknowledge that all you can promise the nations of the world to come, from your experience of the invariable laws of nature, is *perdition, endless perdition.*

II. It is manifest, however, that this destruction of nations and desolation of empires must have had a beginning some time or other. Nations could not perish before they had grown, nor empires be destroyed till they had accumulated; and during all this period of their growth and vigor, the experience of mankind would never lead them to predict their ruin. The sagacious observer, beholding Babylon, Nineveh, Damascus, and Tyre, growing and flourishing during a period of a thousand years past, would have no reason from such an experience to expect any thing else than a thousand years of prosperity to come. Especially impossible is it for human sagacity, enlightened by experience, to predict *unexampled* desolations—destructions such as the world had never witnessed.

Now the predictions of the Bible are predictions of unexampled desolations, and unparalleled ruin of empires. The desolation of any extensive region of the earth, or the overthrow of any great nation, was an event absolutely unknown to the world when the prophets of the Bible began to utter their predictions; unless the skeptic will allow the truth of the Bible record of the prediction and execution of the deluge, and the destruction of Sodom. War and conquest had indeed caused some provinces to change masters; one nation had made marauding invasions on others, and carried off cattle and slaves; but the result of the greatest military operation of which we have any record, at the commencement of the prophetic era—the conquest of Palestine by the Israelites—so far from desolating the region, or exterminating the people, had been merely to increase its productiveness, and drive its former occupants to new settlements, where at that era they were fully able to cope with their former conquerors. Whatever the experience of thirty centuries may have since taught the nations concerning the certainty of the connection between national crime and national ruin, a long suffering God had not then given any such signal examples of it, as those of which he gave warning by the prophets.

The course of the nations and cities founded after the deluge had been regularly onward and prosperous, and they were just rising to the maturity of their power and splendor when Jonah, Micah, Hosea, and Isaiah, began to pronounce their sentences. They denounced desolation and solitude against nations more populous than this continent, one of whose cities enumerated more citizens than some of our proud commonwealths, and displayed buildings, a sight of whose crumbling ruins is deemed sufficient recompense for the perils of a journey of six thousand miles. The hundred churches of Cincinnati could all have been conveniently arranged in the basement of the temple of Belus; on the first floor our hundred thousand non-church going citizens might have assembled to listen to a lecture on spiritualism from some eloquent Chaldean soothsayer; and the remaining seven stories would have still been open for the accommodation of the natives of the original Queen City. Every product of earth was trafficked in the markets of Tyre—a single Jewish house imported annually more gold than all the banks of this continent possess—and the whole coinage of the United States since 1793 would want a hundred millions of dollars of the value of the golden furniture of a single temple in Babylon. In fact, in the suburbs of Babylon or Nineveh, Washington or Cincinnati would have been insignificant villages; and the stone-fronted brick palaces of Broadway and the Fifth Avenue, would make passable stables and haylofts for the mansions of Thebes or Petra.

So far, therefore, from being the teaching of experience, the calculation of sagacity, there was nothing more utterly unexampled and unparalleled than the complete desolation of any nation at the time the prophets of Israel predicted such things. If the world has grown wiser since regarding the decline and fall of empires, it has gathered the best part of its sagacity from the prophecies.

III. The prophecies of the Bible are not vague general denunciations of natural decline and extinction to all the nations of the world, which, if they were merely the exposition of a universal *natural* law of national death, they would be—nor yet the application of any such natural and inevitable law to some particular nation, denouncing its destruction, without any specification of time, manner, instrument, or cause of its infliction. They are all the applications of *moral law*—sentences pronounced on account of national wickedness. In every case the prophecy charges the crimes, and specifies the punishment selected by the Judge of all the earth. The nations selected as examples of Divine justice are as various as their sentences are different—covering a space as long as from Eastport to San Francisco, and climes as various as those between Canada and Cuba; peopled by men of every shade of color and degree of capacity, from the negro servant of servants, to the builders of the Colosseum and the pyramids. They minutely describe, in their own expressive symbols, the nations yet unfounded and kings unborn, who should ignorantly execute the judgments of the Lord. They predict the futures of over thirty states—*no two of which are alike*, each prediction embracing a large number of minute particulars, any one of which was utterly beyond the range of human sagacity. To predict that a man will die may require no great sagacity, but to tell the year of his death, that he will die as a criminal, allege the crime for which he will be sentenced, the time, place, and manner of his execution, and the name of the sheriff who will execute the sentence, is plainly beyond the skill of man. Such is the character of Bible predictions. Zedekiah's sentence was thus pronounced; and thus, too, the sentences of nations doomed to ruin for their crimes are recorded in the Bible, that men may know that the mouth of the Lord hath spoken them. If, for instance, a prophet should declare that New York should be overturned, and become a little fishing village, and that her stones and timber, and her very dust, should be scraped off and thrown into the East River—that Philadelphia should become a swamp, and never be inhabited, from generation to generation—that Columbus should be deserted, and become a hog-pen—that Louisville should become a dry, barren desert, and New Orleans be utterly consumed with fire, and never be built again—that learning should depart from Boston, and no travelers ever pass through it any more—that New England should become the basest of the nations, and no native American ever be President of the Union, but that it should be a spoil and a prey to the most savage tribes, and that the Russians should tread Washington under foot for a thousand years, but that God would preserve Pittsburg in the midst of destruction—and if all these things should come to pass, would any man dare to deny that the prophet spake not the dictates of human sagacity, or the calculations of genius, but the words of God?

To attempt to illustrate the Divine wisdom displayed in a system of connected predictions, covering the destiny of the nations of the world, and extending from the dawn of history to the end of time, by presenting two or three instances of the fulfillment of specific predictions, would be something like exhibiting a fragment of a column as a monument of the skill of the architect of a temple; yet, as such a fragment may excite the curiosity of the traveler to visit the structure whence it was taken, I shall present two or three prophecies in which specific predictions are given, concerning the *geographical, political, social, and religious condition* of three of the great nations of antiquity—*Egypt, Judea, and Babylon*—the fulfilment of which is spread over the surface of empires and the ruins of cities, patent to all travelers at the present hour, and abundantly attested in hundreds of volumes. An interesting collection of such testimonies will be found in *Keith on the Prophecies;* while the curious in history will find an invaluable collection of extracts from authentic historians, illustrating the specific fulfillment of prophecy in the past, in *Newton on the Prophecies.* I do earnestly hope hundreds of my young readers will purchase and peruse both these volumes.

Could human sagacity have calculated that Egypt—the most defensible country in the world, bounded on the south by inaccessible mountains, on the east by the Red Sea, on the west by the trackless, burning desert; able to defend the mouths of her river with a powerful navy, and to drown an invading army every year by the inundation of the Nile; which had not only maintained her independence, but extended her conquests for a thousand years past—Egypt, which had given learning, arts, sciences, and idolatry to half the world, and which had not risen to the hight of its fame or the extent of its influence for twenty-five years after the prediction—should be invaded, conquered, spoiled, become a prey to strangers and evermore to strangers, never have a native prince, sink into barbarism, renounce idolatry, and become famous for her desolations? Yet the Bible predictions are specific on all these matters: "*I will make the rivers dry, and sell the land into the hand of the wicked; and I will make the land waste, and all that is therein by the hand of strangers. I the Lord have spoken it. Thus saith the Lord God, I will also destroy the idols, and I will cause the images to cease out of Noph, and there shall be no more a prince of the land of Egypt.*"*

Let infidels read the fulfillment of these predictions: "Such is the state of Egypt. Deprived twenty-three centuries ago of her natural proprietors, she has seen her fertile fields successively a prey to the Persians, the Macedonians, the Romans, the Greeks, the Arabs, the Georgians, and at length the race of Tartars distinguished by the name of the Ottoman Turks. The Mamelukes, purchased as slaves and introduced as soldiers, soon usurped the power and selected a leader. If their first establishment was a singular event, their continuance is not less extraordinary; they are replaced by slaves brought from their original country.† Says Gibbon: "A more unjust and absurd constitution can not be devised than that which condemns the natives of the country to perpetual servitude under the arbitrary dominion of strangers and slaves. Yet such has been the state of Egypt above five hundred years. The most illustrious sultans of the Baharite and Beyite dynasties were themselves promoted from the Tartar and Circassian bands; and the four and twenty beys, or military chiefs, have ever been succeeded, not by their sons, but by their servants." ‡ Mehemet Ali cut off the Mamelukes, but still Egypt is ruled by the Turks, and the present ruler (Ibrahim Pasha) is a foreigner. It is needless to remind the reader that the idols are cut off. Neither the nominal Christians of Egypt, nor the iconoclastic Moslem, allow images to appear among them. The rivers, too, are drying up. In one day's travel forty dry water-courses will be crossed in the Delta; and water-skins are needed now around the ruined cities whose walls were blockaded by Greek and Roman navies.

---

* Ezekiel, chap. xxx.   ‡ Decline and Fall, chap. lix.
† Volney's Travels, 1, 74, 103.

"*It shall be the basest of the kingdoms, neither shall it exalt itself any more above the nations, for I will diminish them that they shall no more bear rule over the nations.*" * Every traveler will attest the truth of this prediction. The wretched peasantry are rejoiced to labor for any who will pay them five cents a day, and eager to hide the treasure in the ground from the rapacious tax-gatherer. I have seen British horses refuse to eat the meal ground from the mixture of wheat, barley, oats, lentiles, millet, and a hundred unknown seeds of weeds and collections of filth, which forms the produce of their fields. For poverty, vermin, and disease, Egypt is proverbial. Let us hear a scoffer's testimony, however: "In Egypt there is no middle class, neither nobility, clergy, merchants, nor landholders. A universal air of misery in all the traveler meets points out to him the rapacity of oppression, and the distrust attendant upon slavery. The profound ignorance of the inhabitants equally prevents them from perceiving the causes of their evils, or applying the necessary remedies. Ignorance, diffused through every class, extends its effects to every species of moral and physical knowledge. Nothing is talked of but intestine troubles, the public misery, pecuniary extortions, and bastinadoes." †

Here, then, we have conclusive proof of the fulfillment at this day of four distinct, specific, and improbable Bible predictions: concerning the country—the rulers—the religion—and the people of Egypt.

Let us note now a distinct and totally different judgment pronounced against the transgressors of another land. Pre-eminent in inflicting destruction on others, her retribution was to be extreme. Degradation and slavery were to be the portion of the learned Egyptians, but utter extinction is the doom of mighty Babylon. It is written in the Bible concerning the land where the farmer was accustomed to reap two hundred fold: "*Cut off the sower from Babylon, and him that handleth the sickle in the time of harvest. Every purpose of the Lord shall be performed against Babylon, to make the land of Babylon a desolation without an inhabitant. Behold the hindermost of the nations shall be a dry land and a desert. Because of the wrath of the Lord it shall not be inhabited, but it shall be wholly desolate.*‡

---

* Ezekiel, chap. xxix.
† Volney, I. 190.
‡ Jeremiah, chap. 50 and 51.

PROPHECY. 15

Proofs in abundance of the fulfillment of these predictions present themselves in every volume of travels in Assyria and Chaldea. "Those splendid accounts of the Babylonian lands yielding crops of grain of two and three hundred fold, compared with the modern face of the country, afford a remarkable proof of the *singular desolation* to which it has been subjected. The canals at present can only be traced by their decayed banks. The soil of this desert consists of a hard clay, mixed with mud, which at noon becomes so heated with the sun's rays, that I found it too hot to walk over it with any degree of comfort."* "That it was at some former period in a far different state is evident from the number of canals by which it is traversed, now dry and neglected; and the quantity of heaps of earth, covered with fragments of brick and broken tiles, which are seen in every direction—the indisputable traces of former cultivation.† "The abundance of the country has vanished as clean away as if the besom of desolation had swept it from north to south; the whole land, from the outskirts of Babylon to the farthest stretch of sight, lying a melancholy waste. *Not a habitable spot appears for countless miles.* ‡

As the desolation of the country was to be extraordinary, so the desolation of the city of Babylon was to be remarkable. When the prophet wrote, its walls had been raised to the hight of three hundred and fifty feet, and made broad enough for six chariots to drive upon them abreast. From its hundred brazen gates issued the armies which trampled under foot the liberties of mankind, and presented their lives to the nod of a despot, who slew whom he would, and whom he would allowed to live. Twenty years' provisions were collected within its walls, and the world would not believe that an enemy could enter its gates. Nevertheless the prophets of God pronounced against it a doom of destruction as extraordinary as the pride and wickedness which procured it. Tyre, the London of Asia, was to *become a place for the spreading of nets*, § and the infidel Volney tells us its commerce has declined to *a trifling fishery*; but even that implies some few resident inhabitants. Rabbah, of Ammon, was to become *a stable for camels and a couching place for flocks.* ‖ Lord Lindsay reports that "he could not sleep amidst its ruins for the bleating of sheep,

---

* Mignon's Travels, 31.
† Trans. Bombay Lit. Soc., I. 123.
‡ Porter's Babylonia, ii. 285.
§ Ezekiel, chap. 26.
‖ Ezekiel, chap. 25.

143

that the dung of camels covers the ruins of its palaces, and that the only building left entire in its Acropolis is used as a sheepfold." * Yet sheepfolds imply that the tents of their Arab owners are near, and that some human beings would occasionally reside near its ruins. But desolation, solitude, and utter abandonment to the wild beasts of the desert is the specific and clearly predicted doom of the world's proud capital. The most expressive symbols are selected from the desert to portray its desertion.

"*Babylon, the glory of the kingdoms, the beauty of the Chaldees' excellency, shall be as when God overthrew Sodom and Gomorrah. It shall never be inhabited, nor dwelt in, from generation to generation. Neither shall the Arabian pitch tent there; neither shall shepherds make their folds there; but wild beasts of the desert shall be there, and their houses shall be full of doleful creatures; and owls shall dwell there, and satyrs shall dance there; and the wild beasts of the islands shall cry in their desolate houses, and dragons in their pleasant places.*" †

Every traveler attests the fulfillment of this strange prediction. "It is a tenantless and desolate metropolis," says Mignon, who, though fully armed, and attended by six Arabs, could not induce them by any reward to pass the night among its ruins, from their apprehension of evil spirits. So completely fulfilled is the prophecy, "*The Arabian shall not pitch his tent there.*" The same voice which called camels and flocks to the palaces of Rabbah, summoned a very different class of tenants for the palaces of Babylon. Rabbah was to be a sheepfold, Babylon a menagerie of wild beasts—a very specific difference, and very improbable. One of the later Persian kings, however, after it was destroyed and deserted, repaired its walls, converted it into a vast hunting-ground, and stocked it with all manner of wild beasts; and to this day the apes of the Spice Islands, and the lions of the African deserts meet in its palaces, and howl their testimony to the truth of God's word. Sir R. K. Porter saw two majestic lions in the Mujelibe, (the ruins of the palace,) and Fraser thus describes the chambers of fallen Babylon: "There were dens of wild beasts in various places, and Mr. Rich perceived in some a strong smell, like that of a lion. Bones of sheep and other animals were seen in the cavities, with numbers of bats and owls."

---

* Lindsay's Travels, ii. 78, 117. † Isaiah, chap. 13.

Various destructions were predicted for Babylon. "*I will make it a habitation for the bittern, and pools of water,*"* says one prophecy. "*Her cities are a desolation, a dry land, and a wilderness,*"† says another. How can such contradictions be true? says the scoffer.

But the scoffer's contradiction is a fact. God can cause the most discordant agencies to agree in effecting his purpose. Babylon is alternately an overflowed swamp from the inundations of the obstructed Euphrates, and an arid desert under the scorching rays of an eastern sun. Says Mignon: "Morasses and ponds tracked the ground in various places. For a long time after the subsiding of the Euphrates great part of this place is little better than a swamp." At another season it was "a dry waste and burning plain." Even at the same period, "one part on the western side is low and marshy, and another an arid desert." ̸

Another, and widely different agent, to be employed in the destruction of the great center of tyranny and idolatry, is thus specifically and definitely indicated in the prediction: "*Behold I am against thee, O destroying mountain, that destroyest all the earth; and I will stretch out my hand against thee, and roll thee down from the rocks, and make of thee a burnt mountain; and they shall not take of thee a stone for a corner, or a stone for foundations, but thou shalt be desolate for ever, saith the Lord.*" ‖

"There is one fact," says Fraser, "in connection with the most remarkable of these relics, (the Birs Nimrod,) which we can not dismiss without a few more observations. All travelers who have ascended the Birs have taken notice of the singular heaps of brickwork scattered on the summit of this mound, at the foot of the remnant of the wall still standing. To the writer they appeared the most striking of all the ruins. That they have undergone the most violent action of fire is evident from the complete vitrification which has taken place in many of the masses. Yet how a heat sufficient to produce such an effect could have been applied at such a hight from the ground is unaccountable. They now lie on a spot elevated two hundred feet above the plain, and must have fallen from some much more lofty position, for the structure which still remains, and of which they may be supposed originally to have formed a part, bears no marks of fire. The building originally

---

* Isaiah, chap. 14.   ‡ Jeremiah, chaps. 50 and 51.   ‖ Jeremiah, chap. 51.
† Jeremiah, chap. 51.   ̸ Mignon, 139.

can not have contained any great proportion of combustible materials, and to produce so intense a heat by substances carried to such an elevation, would have been almost impossible, for want of space to pile them on. Nothing, we should be inclined to say, short of the most powerful action of electric fire, could have produced the complete, yet circumscribed fusion which is here observed. Although fused into a solid mass, the courses of bricks are still visible, identifying them with the standing pile above, but so hardened by the power of heat, that it is almost impossible to break off the smallest piece; and, though porous in texture, and full of air-holes and cavities, like other bricks, they require, on being submitted to the stone-cutter's lathe, the same machinery as is used to dress the hardest pebbles." *

Egypt was to be reduced to slavery and degradation, Babylonia to utter barrenness and desolation; but a different and still more incredible doom is pronounced in the Bible upon Judea and its people. The land was to be emptied of its people, and remain uncultivated, retaining all its former fertility, while the people were to be scattered over all the earth, yet never to lose their distinct nationality, nor be amalgamated with their neighbors: *"I will make your cities waste, and bring your sanctuaries into desolation; and I will bring the land unto desolation, and your enemies which dwell therein shall be astonished at it. And I will scatter you among the heathen, and will draw out a sword after you, and your land shall be desolate and your cities waste. Then shall the land enjoy her Sabbaths as long as it lieth desolate, and ye be in your enemies' land, even then shall the land rest, and enjoy her Sabbaths.* † *Until the cities be wasted without inhabitant, and the houses without man, and the land be utterly desolate, and the Lord have removed men far away, and there be a great forsaking in the midst of the land. But yet in it shall be a tenth, and it shall return and shall be eaten, as a teil tree and as an oak, whose substance is in them when they cast their leaves.* ‡ *The generation to come of your children,* AND THE STRANGER FROM A FAR LAND, *shall say, 'Wherefore hath the Lord done thus to this land? What meaneth the heat of this great anger?'* " §

It is superfluous to adduce proof of the undeniable and acknowledged fulfillment of these predictions, but as an example of the

---

* Fraser's Mesopotamia and Assyria, 145. ‡ Isaiah, chap. 6.
† Leviticus, chap. 26. § Deuteronomy, chap. 29.

way in which God causes scoffers to fulfil the prophecies, let us again hear Volney: "I journeyed in the empire of the Ottomans, and traversed the provinces which were formerly the kingdoms of Egypt and Syria. I enumerated the kingdoms of Damascus and Idumea, of Jerusalem and Samaria. This Syria, said I to myself, now almost depopulated, then contained a hundred flourishing cities, and abounded with towns, villages, and hamlets. What has become of so many productions of the hand of man? What has become of those ages of abundance and of life? *Great God! from whence proceed such melancholy revolutions? For what cause is the fortune of these countries so strikingly changed? Why are so many cities destroyed?* Why is not that ancient population reproduced and perpetuated? A mysterious God exercises his incomprehensible judgments. He has doubtless pronounced a secret malediction against the earth. He has struck with a curse the present race of men in revenge of past generations."* The malediction is no secret to any who will read the twenty-ninth chapter of Deuteronomy; nor is the avenging of the quarrel of God's covenant confined to the sins of past generations. The philosopher who would understand the fates of cities and empires, should read the prophecies.

The word of God specifies no less distinctly and definitely the destiny of the Jewish than of the Babylonian capital, but fixes on a widely different kind of destruction. Babylon was never to be built again, but devoted to solitude—busy Tyre to become a place for spreading nets—the caravans, which once brought the wealth of India through Petra were to cease, and the doom was to "cut off him that passeth by and him that returneth." But Jerusalem, it was predicted, should long feel the miseries of a multitude of oppressors, should never enjoy the luxury of solitary woe, but "*be trodden down of the Gentiles.*† Saracens, Tartars, Turks, and Crusaders, Gentiles from every nation of the earth, fulfilled the prediction of old, even as hosts of pilgrims from all parts of the earth do at this day.

So minute and specific are the predictions of Scripture, that the fate of particular buildings is accurately defined. One temple to the living God, and only one, raised its walls in this world, which he had made for his worship. Its frequenters perverted it from its

---

* Volney's Ruins of Empires, Book I.   † Luke, chap. 21.

proper use of leading them to confess their sinfulness, seek pardon through the promised Savior to whom its ceremonies pointed, and learn to be holy, as the God of that temple was holy. They hoped that the holiness of the place would screen them in the indulgence of pride, formality, and wickedness. The temple of the Lord, instead of the Lord of the temple, was the object of their veneration. But the doom went forth, "*Therefore for your sakes shall Zion be plowed as a field, and Jerusalem shall become as heaps, and the mountain of the house like the high places of the forest.*" * History has preserved, and the Jews to this day curse, the name of the soldier, Terentius Rufus, who plowed up the foundations of the temple. It long continued in this state. But the emperor Julian the Apostate conceived the idea of falsifying the prediction of Jesus, "*Behold your house is left unto you desolate,*" † and sent his friend Alypius with a Roman army and abundant treasure, to rebuild it. The Jews flocked from all parts to assist in the work. Spades or pickaxes of silver were provided by the vanity of the rich, and the rubbish was transported in mantles of silk and purple. But they were obliged to desist from the attempt, for "horrible balls of fire breaking out from the foundations with repeated attacks, rendered the place inaccessible to the scorched workmen, and the element driving them to a distance from time to time, the enterprise was dropped." ‡ Such is the testimony of a heathen, confirmed by Jews and Christians. The enclosures of the mosque of Omar forbidding them all access to the spot on which it stood, leave it desolate to the Jews to this day.

IV. No sane man can believe that such minute and accurate predictions of various and improbable events, could be the result of human calculations; yet there is another feature of the Bible prophecies still farther removed beyond the reach of human sagacity, and that is remarkable and unaccountable *preservation amidst the general ruin*. If, as skeptics allege, destruction is the natural and inevitable doom, then preservation is supernatural and miraculous—a miracle of Divine power controlling nature; and its prediction is a miracle of Divine wisdom. Now the prophecies of the Bible contain several very definite, and widely different predictions of the preservation of people and cities from the general destruction. We shall refer in this case also to those of whose ful-

---

* Micah, chap. 3.   ‡ Ammian Marcell. lib. 23, chap. 1
† Matthew, chap. 23.

fillment there can be no manner of doubt, for the facts are palpable and undeniable at the present day.

Of the Israelitish nation God predicted, that it should be a peculiar, distinct people, separate from the other nations of the world: *"Lo the people shall dwell alone, and shall not be reckoned among the nations."* * In apparent contradiction to this separation, he further threatened to punish them for their sins, by dispersing them over the world: *"I will scatter you among the heathen, and will draw out a sword after you.* † *For lo, I will command, and I will sift the house of Israel among all nations, like as corn is sifted in a sieve; yet shall not the least grain fall upon the earth."* ‡ It was further threatened, as if to make sure of their national destruction, *"And among these nations thou shalt find no ease, neither shall the sole of thy foot have rest, but the Lord shall give thee a trembling heart and failing of eyes, and sorrow of mind; and thy life shall hang in doubt before thee, and thou shalt fear day and night, and have none assurance of thy life.* ‖ Contrary to all appearances, and in spite of all this dispersion and persecution, it is predicted that Israel shall still exist as a nation, and be restored to the favor of God, and that prosperity which ever accompanies it: *"And yet, for all that, when they be in the land of their enemies, I will not cast them away, neither will I abhor them to destroy them utterly, and to break my covenant with them; for I am the Lord their God."* §

Here are four distinct predictions—of national peculiarity—universal dispersion—grievous oppression—and remarkable preservation. The fulfillment is obvious and undeniable. You need no commentary to explain it. Go into any clothing-store on Western Row, or into the synagogue in Broadway, and you will see it. The infidel is sorely perplexed to give any account of this great phenomenon. How does it happen that this singular people is dispersed over all the earth, and yet distinct and unamalgamated with any other? How does it happen that for eighteen hundred years they have resisted all the influences of nature, and all the customs of society, and all the powers of persecution, driving them towards amalgamation, and irresistible in all other instances? In the face of the power of the Chinese Empire, in spite of the

---

* Numbers, chap. 23.   ‡ Amos, chap. 9.   ‖ Leviticus, chap. 26.
† Leviticus, chap. 26.   § Deuteronomy, chap. 32.

tortures of the Spanish Inquisition, amidst the chaos of African nationalities and the fusion of American democracy, in the plains of Australia, and in the streets of San Francisco, the religion, customs, and physiognomy of the children of Israel are as distinct this day as they were three thousand years ago, when Moses wrote them in the Pentateuch, and Shishak painted them on the tombs of Medinet Abou. How does the infidel account for it? It will not do to allege the favorite story about purity of blood and Caucasian race; for the question is, How does it happen that this people, and this people alone, have kept the blood pure; while all other races are so mingled that no other race can be found pure on earth? Besides, lest any should suppose such a cause sufficient for their preservation, another nation descended from the same father and the same mother—the children of Jacob's twin brother, have utterly perished, and there is not any remaining of the house of Esau.

Human sagacity, with all the facts before its face, can not give any rational account of the causes of this anomaly. It can not tell to-day, why this people exists separate from, and scattered through all nations, from Kamschatka to New Zealand; how, then, could it foretell, three thousand years ago, this singular exception to all the laws of national existence? While the sun and moon endure, the nation of Israel shall exist as God's witness to God's word—an undeniable proof that the mouth of the Lord hath spoken it.

Take another instance of preservation, so remarkable amidst the surrounding destruction, that it arrested the attention and admiration of the author of the Decline and Fall of the Roman Empire, skeptic and scoffer though he was.

The seven churches of seven of the most considerable cities of Asia, were then, as the churches of Christ still are, the salt of the earth. Ten righteous men would have averted God's judgments from Sodom. Jesus pronounced the sentences of these churches seventeen hundred and sixty years ago, and the present condition of the cities attests the Divine authority of the record containing them. They are various and specific. Three were to be utterly destroyed. Against two no special threatening is denounced. To the remaining two promises of life and blessing are given.

Ephesus, famous for its magnificence, the busy avenue of travel, the seat of the temple of Diana, long the residence of an apostle, and afterward of Christian bishops—"one of the eyes of Asia,"—as it stood first on the roll of cities, first receives the doom of abused privileges: *"I will remove thy candlestick out of its place, unless thou repent."*

Says Gibbon:* "The captivity and ruin of the seven churches of Asia was consummated (by the Ottomans) A. D. 1312; and the barbarous lords of Ionia and Lydia still trample on the monuments of classic and Christian antiquity. In the loss of Ephesus, the Christians deplored the fall of the first angel, and the extinction of the first candlestick of the Revelation. *The desolation is complete*, and the temple of Diana or the Church of Mary will equally elude the search of the curious traveler."

"A few unintelligible heaps of stones," says Arundell, "with some mud cottages untenanted, are all the remains of the great city of the Ephesians. Even the sea has retired from the scene of desolation, and a pestilential morass, covered with mud and rushes, has succeeded to the waters which brought up the ships laden with merchandise from every country." Some parts of the site of the city are cultivated; and Fisk, who entered into conversation with the Greek peasants, men and women whom he found pulling up the tares and weeds from the corn, ascertained that they all belonged to *distant villages*, and came there to labor.

Had the twenty thousand patrons of the drama in the thirty-one theatres of New York, honored the theatre of Laodicea with their presence, its polite citizens would have accommodated them all on the reserved seats, retiring themselves to ten thousand less commodious sittings, and to two less gigantic theatres. While yet busy in the erection of their splendid places of public amusement, Jesus said, *"I will spew thee out of my mouth."* "The circus and three stately theatres of Laodicea are peopled with wolves and foxes," says Gibbon.

A Lydian capitalist once deposited in the vaults of Sardis more specie than is now in circulation in this whole continent. But Jesus said, *"Thou hast a name that thou livest and art dead. If, therefore, thou shalt not watch, I will come upon thee as a thief, and thou shalt not know what hour I will come upon thee."*

"Sardis," says Gibbon, "is a miserable village." A later writer

---

* Chapter 64.

(Durbin) tells us that the Turks say, "Every one who builds a house in Sardis dies soon, and avoid the spot." Arundell, in his account of his visit to the seven churches, says: "If I were asked what impresses the mind most strongly on beholding Sardis, I should say "its indescribable *solitude*, like the darkness of Egypt, that could be felt. So deep the solitude of the spot, once the lady of kingdoms, produces a feeling of desolate abandonment in the mind which can never be forgotten." Connect this feeling with the message of the Apocalypse to the church of Sardis, "Thou hast a name that thou livest and *art dead*, and then look around and ask, Where are the churches? Where are the Christians of Sardis? The tumuli beyond the Hermus reply, *"All dead!"*—suffering the infliction of the threatened judgment of God for the abuse of their privileges. Let the unbeliever, then, be asked, Is there no truth in prophecy?—no reality in religion?"

Only twenty-seven miles north of this desolate metropolis, the manufactories of Thyatira despatch weekly to Smyrna, cloths, as famous over Asia for the brilliancy and durability of their hues as those which Lydia displayed to the admiration of the ladies of Phillippi. Two thousand two hundred Greek Christians, two hundred Armenian, and a Protestant Church under the care of the missionaries of the American Board of Commissioners of Foreign Missions, assemble every Sabbath to commemorate the resurrection of Him who said to the Church of Thyatira: *"I will put upon you no other burden; but that which ye have already hold fast till I come."*

The fragrant citron still flourishes around the birth-place of Galen; but the ruins of the famous library of 200,000 manuscripts are far less durable memorials of the city of booksellers than those beautifully dressed skins, which, taking their name (*Pergamena*) from the place of their manufacture, will preserve the name and fame of Pergamos as long as parchment can preserve man's memorials or God's predictions. Though famous for fragrance, physic, and philosophy, Pergamos was infamous for idolatry, licentiousness, and persecution; yet still endeared to Jesus as the scene of the martyrdom of faithful Antipas, and the dwelling-place of a hidden church; and widely different sentences are recorded against those opposite classes. The public memorials are to perish, but the hidden word to endure. "The fanes of Jupiter and Diana, and Venus and Esculapius, (worshipped under the symbol of a live snake,) were prostrate in the dust, and where they had not been carried away by the Turks to cut up into tombstones or pound into mortar, the Corinthian columns and the Ionic, the splendid capitals, the cornices and the pediments, all in the highest ornament, were thrown in unsightly heaps;"* is the comment on the threatening of Jesus, "*I will fight against them—the idolaters—with the sword of my mouth.*" The 3,000 Greek and 300 Armenian Christians, and even the 10,000 Turkish inhabitants of the modern Pergamos, have received hundreds of copies of the promise, "*To him that overcometh I will give to eat of the hidden manna, and will give him a white stone, and in the stone a new name written, which no man knoweth, saving he that receiveth it.*" But whether the hidden church of Pergamos shine forth or not, Gibbon was inaccurate in stating, in the face of facts, that "the god of Mohammed without a rival is invoked in the mosques of Pergamos and Thyatira." God's providence is as discriminating as his prophecy, though unbelief may overlook both.

We have noted here instances of the prediction of remarkable destruction to Sardis, Ephesus, and Laodicea—of continued existence to Pergamos and Thyatira—let us now note a prediction of remarkable escape and preservation from the universal doom. If it requires no inspiration to prophecy destruction—the universal fate of humanity, according to the infidel—surely it requires more than human skill to say that any city shall escape this universal fate, and more than human power to avert this destruction. Of Philadelphia—but twenty-five miles distant from the ruins of Sardis—Jesus said, and the Bible records the prophecy: "*I know thy works; behold I have set before thee an open door, and no man can shut it, for thou hast a little strength, and hast kept my word, and hast not denied my name. Behold I will make them of the synagogue of Satan, which say they are Jews and are not, but do lie; behold I will make them to come and worship before thy feet, and to know that I have loved thee. Because thou hast kept the word of my patience, I also will keep thee from the hour of temptation which shall come upon all the world, to try them that dwell upon the earth. Behold I come quickly, hold that fast thou hast, that no man take thy crown. Him that overcometh will I make a pillar in the temple of my God, and he shall go no more out; and I will write*

---

* Macfarlane's Seven Apocalyptic Churches.

upon him the name of my God, and the name of the city of my God, which is, New Jerusalem, which cometh down out of heaven from my God; and I will write upon him my new name."

"Philadelphia alone," says Gibbon, "has been saved by prophecy, or courage. At a distance from the sea, forgotten by the emperors, encompassed on all sides by the Turks, her valiant sons defended their religion and their freedom alone for fourscore years, and at length capitulated with the proudest of the Ottomans. Among the Greek colonies and churches of Asia, Philadelphia is still erect—*a column in a scene of ruins*—a pleasing example that the paths of honor and safety may be the same."

In the pages of this eloquent writer it would be hard to discover another instance of unqualified hearty commendation of soldiers or sufferers for Christianity and liberty, such as Gibbon here bestows on Philadelphia's valiant sons. But it was written, "*I will make them come and worship before thy feet,*" and the skeptic and scoffer must fulfill the word of Jesus; even as the unbelieving Mohammedan also does, when he writes upon it the modern name, Allah Sehr—*The City of God. A majestic solitary pillar,* of high antiquity, arrests the eye of the traveler, and reminds the worshippers of the six modern churches of Philadelphia, of the beauty and faithfulness of the prophetic symbol. Heaven and earth shall pass away, but Jesus' word shall not pass away.

Improbable to human sagacity as this preservation must have seemed, the resurrection of a fallen city is more utterly beyond man's vision. In the Bible, however, tribulation and recovery was foretold to Smyrna: "*Fear none of those things which thou shalt suffer. Behold the devil shall cast some of you into prison, and ye shall have tribulation ten days. Be thou faithful unto death, and I will give thee a crown of life.*" "The populousness of Smyrna is owing to the foreign trade of the Franks and Armenians," says the scoffer. No matter to what it is owing; he who dictated the Bible foresaw it, and made no mistake in foretelling it. Says Arundell: "This, the other eye of Asia, is still a very flourishing commercial city, one of the very first in the present Turkish empire in wealth and population, containing 130,000 inhabitants. The continued importance of Smyrna may be estimated from the fact that it is the seat of a consul from every nation in Europe. The prosperity of Smyrna is now rather on the increase than the decline, and the houses of painted wood, which were most unworthy of its ancient fame and present importance, are rapidly giving way to palaces of stone rising in all directions; and probably, ere many years have passed, the modern town may not unworthily represent the ancient city, which the ancients delighted to call the crown of Ionia. Commercial activity and architectural beauty, however, are but a small part of the glorious destiny of the community to which Jesus says, "I will give thee a crown of life." Deliverance from the curse of sin, and communion with the Lord of Life, alone can secure either a nation's or an individual's immortality. Smyrna possesses the gospel of salvation. Several devoted English and American missionaries proclaim salvation to its citizens. From its printing presses thousands of copies of the word of life issue to all the various populations of the Turkish empire. A living church of Christ in Smyrna holds forth for the acceptance of the dying nations around her, that crown of life promised and granted by the word of God, not to her only, but to all who love his appearing and his kingdom.

V. This is the grand distinction of God's word of prophecy, *that it is the word of life*. It is the only word which promises life, the only word which bestows it on fallen humanity. Recognizing no inevitable law of destruction but the sentence of God, no invariable law of nature superior to the counsel of Jehovah, nor any progress of events which his Almighty arm can not arrest and reverse, it points a despairing world to sin as the cause of all destruction, to Satan as the author of sin, to ungodly men in league with him as the foes of God and man, and to Christ pledged to perpetual warfare with such until the last enemy be destroyed. This word of prophecy tells us, that the battle-fields Messiah has won are earnests of that great victory; points to the columns which he has preserved erect amidst scenes of ruin, as assurances that he is able to save to the uttermost all that come unto God by him; goes to the grave-yards, where fallen Smyrnas, idolatrous Saxons, debased Sandwich Islanders, and cannibal New Zealanders have buried the image of the living God, and in Jesus' name proclaims, "*I am the resurrection and the life: he that believeth in me, though he were dead, yet shall he live;*" and, amidst the very ruins of destroyed cities, and the crumbling heaps of their perished memorials, beholds the assurances that Satan's rule of ruin shall not be perpetual, anticipates the day when the course of sin and misery shall be reversed, and teaches Adam's sons to face the foe, and chant forth that heaven-born note of victorious faith, "*O thou enemy! destructions are come to a perpetual end.*"

Come forth, trembling skeptic, from the cave of thy dark invariable experience of death and destruction, and from the vain sparks of thy misgiving hopes of an ungodly eternity to come less miserable than the past, and lift thine eyes to this heavenly sunrising on the dark mountain tops of futurity, the like of which thou didst never dream of in all thy Pantheistic reveries. Search over all the religions of the world—the hieroglyphics of Egypt, the arrow-headed inscriptions of Assyria, the classic mythologies of graceful Greece and iron Rome, the monstrous shasters of thine Indian Pundits, or the more chaotic clouds of thy German philosophies—in none of them wilt thou ever find this divine thought, *an end of destructions—a perpetual end.* Cycles of ruin and renovation, and of renovation and ruin, vast cycles, if you will, but evermore ending in dire catastrophes to gods and men—an everlasting succession of death and destructions, is the fearful vista which all the religions of man, and thine own irreligion, present to thy terrified vision. But thou wast created in the image of the living God, and durst not rest satisfied with any such prospect. Now I come in the name of the Lord to tell thee that, "God so loved the world that he gave his only begotten Son, that whosoever believeth on Him *should not perish, but have everlasting life*"— and I demand of thee that thou acknowledge this promise of life everlasting to be the word of that living God, and to show cause, if any thou hast, why thou dost relinquish thy birthright, and spurn the gift of everlasting life which is in Christ Jesus our Lord?

But, if thou hast no sufficient cause why thou shouldest choose death rather than life, then hear, and your soul shall live, while I relate the promises which God hath made of old to our fathers, and hath fulfilled to us their children, by raising up his Son Jesus Christ from the dead, and sending him to bless you, by turning away every one of you from your iniquities. For there can be no deliverance from misery and destruction but by means of delivery from sin and Satan.

It is quite in agreement with the manner of our deliverance from any of the evils of our fallen condition, that our deliverance from the power of sin and Satan be effected by the agency of a deliverer. Our ignorance is removed by the knowledge of a teacher—our sickness by the skill of a physician—the oppressed nation hails the advent of a patriotic leader, and oppressed humanity acknowledges the fitness and need of a Divine deliverer, even by the ready welcome it has given to pretenders to this character, and by the longing desire of the wisest and best of men for a divinely-commissioned Savior—a desire implanted by the great prophecy, which stands at the portal of hope for mankind, in the very earliest period of our history, that "*the seed of the woman should bruise the serpent's head,*" and so leave man triumphant over the great destroyer.

The prophecies regarding the Messiah are so numerous, pointed, various, and improbable, as to set human sagacity utterly at defiance; while they are also connected so as to form a scheme of prophecy, which gradually unrolls before us the advent, the ministry, the death, resurrection, and ascension of the Lord, the progress of his gospel over all the world, and the blessed effects it should produce on individuals, families, and nations. It closes with a view of the second coming of Jesus to conquer the last of his enemies, and take possession of the earth as his inheritance. I can only lop off a twig or two from this blessed tree of life, in the hope that the fragrance of the leaves may allure you to take up the Bible, and eat abundantly of its life-giving promises. As I have in the three previous Tracts abundantly proved the veracity of the New Testament history, I shall now with all confidence refer to its account of the birth, life, and death of Jesus, as illustrating the prophecies.

The time, the place, the manner of his birth, his parentage and reception, were plainly declared, hundreds of years before he appeared.

When Herod had gathered all the chief priests and scribes of the people together, he demanded of them where Christ should be born, and they said unto him, "in Bethlehem of Judea, for thus it is written by the prophet: '*And thou Bethlehem, in the land of Judah, art not the least among the princes of Judah, for out of thee shall come a Governor, that shall rule my people Israel.*" The first verse of this chapter records the fact, "Now when Jesus was born in Bethlehem of Judea."*

The throne of Judah was to be occupied by strangers, and the line of native princes was to cease upon the coming of this Gover-

---

* Matthew, chap. 2.

nor, and not till his coming: "*The scepter shall not depart from Judah, nor a lawgiver from between his feet, till Shiloh come, and to him shall the gathering of the people be.*" On the day of his crucifixion the rulers of the Jews made this formal and public announcement of the fact, "We have no king but Cæsar." *

He was to address a class of people whom no other religious teacher had condescended to notice before, and very few save those sent by him ever since: "*The Spirit of the Lord God is upon me, because the Lord hath anointed me to preach good tidings to the meek, to bind up the broken hearted, to proclaim liberty to the captives, and the opening of the prison to them that are bound.*" Hear Jesus' words: "Come unto me, all ye that labor and are heavy laden, and I will give you rest. Go and tell John those things ye do hear and see. The blind receive their sight, the lame walk, the lepers are cleansed, the deaf hear, the dead are raised up, *and the poor have the gospel preached unto them.* And blessed is he whosoever shall not be offended in me." †

Yet, notwithstanding his feeding of thousands, and healing of multitudes, and teaching of the lowest of the people, it was foretold he should be unpopular: "*He is despised and rejected of men, a man of sorrows, and acquainted with griefs, and we hid, as it were, our faces from him. He is despised, and we esteemed him not.*" The brief records are: "Then all his disciples forsook him and fled." "Then began Peter to curse and to swear, saying, 'I know not the man.' Pilate saith unto them, 'Ye have a custom that I release unto you one at the passover: will ye, therefore, that I release unto you the King of the Jews?' Then they all cried again, saying, 'Not this man, but Barabbas.' Now Barabbas was a robber." ‡

All the prophets agree in predicting that for the sins of his people, and to atone for their guilt, he should be put to death by a shameful public execution: "*In the midst of the week Messiah shall be cut off, but not for himself. He was wounded for our transgressions, he was bruised for our iniquities, the chastisement of our peace was upon him, and by his stripes we are healed. He was numbered with the transgressors, and he bore the sin of many, and he made intercession for the transgressors. They pierced my hands and my*

---

* Gen., 49: 10. John, 19: 15.   † Isaiah, 61. Matthew, 11: 2.
‡ Isaiah, 53: 3. Matthew, 26: 56, 74; 27: 15. John, 18: 40.

feet." * The record says: "The Son of Man came not to be ministered unto, but to minister, and to give his life a ransom for many." "And when they were come to the place which is called Calvary, there they crucified him and the malefactors, one on the right hand and the other on the left. Then said Jesus, *'Father, forgive them, for they know not what they do.'*"

The one grand unparalleled fact, one which demands the hope of dying men for a victory over the great destroyer, and a resurrection from the tomb—the fact that one man born of a woman died, and did not see corruption, but rose again from the dead and went up into heaven, and dieth no more—forms the theme of many a prophetic psalm of triumph: *"Thou wilt not leave my soul in hell, nor wilt thou give thine Holy One to see corruption. Thou wilt show me the path of life. Thou wilt make me full of joy with thy countenance. Thou hast ascended on high. Thou hast led captivity captive."* Often did Jesus predict this prodigy before friend and foe: "Sir, we remember that that deceiver said, when he was yet alive, 'After three days I will rise again." The last chapters of the gospels relate the proofs by which he convinced his incredulous disciples that the prophecy was fulfilled: "Behold my hands and my feet, that it is I myself. Handle me and see, for a spirit hath not flesh and bones, as ye see me have. And when he had thus spoken, he showed them his hands and his feet. And while they yet believed not for joy, and wondered, he saith unto them, 'Have ye here any meat?' And they gave him a piece of a broiled fish, and of an honey comb. And he took it and did eat before them; and said unto them, 'Thus it is written, and thus it behooved Christ to suffer, and to rise from the dead the third day; and that repentance and remission of sins should be preached in his name among all nations, beginning at Jerusalem. And ye are witnesses of these things. And behold I send the promise of my Father upon you, but tarry ye in the city of Jerusalem until ye be endued with power from on high. And he led them out as far as to Bethany, and he lifted up his hands and blessed them. And while he was blessing them he was parted from them, and carried up into heaven. And while they looked steadfastly toward heaven, as he went up, behold two men stood by them in white apparel, which said, 'Ye men of Galilee, why stand ye gazing up into heaven?

---

* Daniel, 9: 26.   Isaiah, 53: 5, 12.   Psalm 22: 16.   Matthew, 20: 28.   Luke, 23: 33.

This same Jesus, which is taken up from you into heaven, shall so come in like manner as ye have seen him go into heaven.' " *

With your own eyes you shall see the fulfillment of this prophecy. Every eye shall see him. The clouds of heaven shall then reveal the vision now sketched on the page of revelation: "And I saw a great white throne, and Him that sat on it, from whose face the earth and the heaven fled away, and there was found no place for them. And I saw the dead, small and great, stand before God; and the books were opened; and another book was opened, which is the book of life; and the dead were judged out of those things which were written in the books, according to their works. And the sea gave up the dead which were in it; and death and hell delivered up the dead which were in them; and they were judged every man according to their works. And death and hell were cast into the lake of fire. This is the second death. And whosoever was not found written in the book of life was cast into the lake of fire. And I saw a new heaven and a new earth: for the first heaven and the first earth were passed away; and there was no more sea. And I John saw the holy city, New Jerusalem, coming down from God, out of heaven, prepared as a bride adorned for her husband. And I heard a great voice out of heaven saying, 'Behold the tabernacle of God is with men, and he will dwell with them, and they shall be his people, and God himself shall be with them, and be their God. And God shall wipe away all tears from their eyes; and there shall be no more death, neither sorrow nor crying: neither shall there be any more pain; for the former things are passed away.' And he that sat upon the throne said, '*Behold, I make all things new.*' And he said unto mé, 'WRITE, FOR THESE WORDS ARE TRUE AND FAITHFUL.'

---

* Psalm 16: 10; 68: 18. Matthew, 28: 63. John, 20: 24. Luke, 20: 36. Acts, 1: 9.

No. 30.
MOSES AND THE PROPHETS.

In the foregoing tracts of this series we have found that we have great need of God's teaching; that he has sent his son, Jesus Christ, to show us the way of life: that the gospel preached by Him and His Apostles has proved itself the power of God by saving men from their sins; and that this gospel is truly recorded in the New Testament. From these facts, already settled, we proceed, according to our plan of investigation, to examine those which may be more obscure—to examine the Old Testament by the light of the New.

The great majority of Jews and Christians have always believed, that the world was in as great need of God's teaching before the coming of Christ as it has been since—that God did put his words into the mouths of certain persons, called prophets; and that he caused them to tell them truly to their neighbors—that he enabled these prophets to make predictions of future events beyond the skill of man to calculate, and to do miracles which the power of man could not perform, as proofs that they spake the word of God—that he caused them truly to record in writing a great many of these revelations, and so much of the history of the times in which, and of the people to whom, they were given, as was needful for a right understanding of them—that he has so managed matters since, as that these revelations and narratives have been faithfully preserved in the books of the Old Testament—that we are bound to believe these revelations to be true, not because we can otherwise demonstrate their truth, but because God, who can not lie, has declared it; and that we are bound to do the things they command, not merely because we see them to be right, but because God commands us.

It is needful to consider the Divine Authority of the Old Testament distinctly from that of the New, not only because it is a distinct subject in itself,—and because our plan of investigation leads us backward from the known and established fact of the Divine Authority of the New Testament to the discovery or disproof of the like character in the Old,—but because a great many persons admit, in words at least, that Christ was a teacher sent from God, who, either in so many words or in effect, deny the Divine Authority of the Old Testament. Some of the modern Spiritualists have revived the creed of the Gnostics of the first century—that the Hebrew Jehovah was a being of very different character from the Deity revealed by Jesus Christ. They will extol to the skies the world-wide benevolence, compassion and kindness, of the gospel of Christ, in contrast with the alleged national pride, bigotry, and exclusiveness of the Hebrew prophets. Others are desirous of appearing remarkably candid in bestowing on the Old Testament a liberal commendation as a collection of religious tracts of merely human origin, and of various degrees of merit—some of them of extraordinary literary excellence, well suited to the infancy of the human intellect, and highly useful in their time in raising men from fetichism and idolatry to the worship of one God; but which, containing many errors along with this grand truth, have been set aside by the more perfect teachings of Christ and his Apostles, much in the same way as the old Ptolemaic Astronomy was displaced by the discoveries of Newton. Others still are willing to acknowledge the Old Testament as inspired, provided we will allow Shakspeare and the Koran to be inspired also. Besides all these there are several scores of scholars anxious to conceal its nakedness under theories of inspiration made and trimmed in a great many styles, but all cut from the same doctrine, to wit: that God revealed his truth aright to Moses and the Prophets, but they went wrong in the telling of it. Now, all these notions will be refuted by the fact, that God is the Author of the Bible.

When we say that God is the Author of the Bible, and that it carries with it a Divine Authority because it is the Word of God, we do not mean that God is the Author of every saying in it, and that every sentiment recorded in it is God's mind, any more than we mean to make D'Aubigne responsible for every sentiment of priests, popes, and monks he has faithfully recorded in his History of the Reformation. On the contrary, we find, in the very beginning of the Bible, a very full expression of the Devil's sentiments recorded in the Devil's own words—*Ye shall not surely die*: and they are not one whit less devilish and lying, though recorded in the Bible, than when expounded by any modern Universalist preacher. But we mean that it is very true that the Devil was the preacher of that first Universalist sermon; and that God thought it needful to let mankind know the shape of the doctrine, the character of the preacher, and the consequences of listening to error; and therefore directed Moses to record it truly for the information of all whom it may concern. So there are many other sayings of wicked men, and even of good men, recorded in the Bible, which are very false; but the Bible gives a true record of them, by God's direction, that we may not be ignorant of Satan's devices.

Nor, when we say that God directed the Prophets what to write and how to write it, so that they did not go wrong in the writing of his word, do we mean that he also so guided every piece of their behavior, as that they never went wrong in doing their own actions. Nor that the sins of the saints, recorded in the Bible, are any thing the less sinful for being recorded there, or for being performed by men who ought to have known better. There is not a perfect man upon the earth, that doeth good, and sinneth not. If the Bible had left the faults of its writers undiscovered, it would not have been a true history. But these very writers of the Bible tell us their own transgressions, under the direction of the spirit of God: a thing writers in general are very shy about. Moses tells us how he spake unadvisedly with his lips, and was punished for it. David's penitential psalms record the bitter tears he wept over his transgression; tears which could not wash out the sentence against the man after God's own heart.—" *The Sword shall never depart from thy house.*" An overburdened people, a rotten court, a falling empire, continual strife, a family of scolding women, only one son, and he a fool—might have been considered sufficient marks of God's displeasure, without causing the wisest of men to pen and publish to the world, such a minute record of his madness, folly, and misery, as we find in Ecclesiastes. But these shipwrecked mariners were divinely directed to pile up the sad memorials of their errors, on the reefs where they were wrecked, as beacons of warning to all inexperienced voyagers on life's treacherous sea. The light-house is built by the same authority as the custom-house.

Now let us take note of the objects of our investigation. We are not in search of the literary beauty or poetic inspiration of the Bible; but we inquire by what right does it command our obedience? Nor are we about to inquire whether, when we have tried the Bible at the tribunal of our reason, we shall give it a diploma to commend it to the patronage of other critics; but whether it comes to us attested by such evidence of being the word of God, that our reason shall reverently bow down before it as a higher authority, and seek light from it by which to judge of all spiritual and moral matters.

Attempts are continually made to confuse these great questions, by concessions of the literary excellence of the Bible, on the part of those who deny its Divine authority. For instance, one of the modern oracles of infidelity says, and his admirers incessantly repeat the grand discovery: "The writings of the Prophets contain nothing above the reach of the human faculties. Here are noble and spirit-stirring appeals to men's conscience, patriotism, honor, and religion; beautiful poetic descriptions, odes, hymns, expressions of faith almost beyond praise. But the mark of human infirmity is on them all, and proofs or signs of miraculous inspiration are not found in them."*

But what do the toiling millions of earth care about beautiful poetic descriptions of a heaven and a hell that have no reality? Or what does it signify to you or me, reader, that the Bible raises its head far above the other cedars of earthly literature—if its top reaches not to heaven, can it make a ladder long enough to carry us there? The Bible contains predictions beyond the reach of the human faculties, as we have fully proved.† These predictions at least are from God, and have no mark of human infirmity on them.

It does not at all meet this question to grant, as many Pantheists do, that the Bible is inspired—just as every work of genius is inspired; nor to profess that they believe the Bible to be from God—just as every pure and holy thought, and every good work, proceed from him. When the asserters of the Divine authority of the Bible speak of it as inspired, they mean that it is so as no other book is; and when they speak of it as coming from God, they mean that it does not come simply as a gift of God's bounty, as the soldier's land-warrant comes from the government; but that it comes like the laws of Congress, carrying authority with it to command our obedience.

We feel no interest whatever in the discussion of an inspiration, "like God's omnipotence, not limited to the few writers claimed by the Jews, Christians and Mahommedans, but as extensive as the race;" ‡ or perhaps as extensive as all creation, and leading us to regard even "the solemn notes of the screech owl" as inspired.∥

---

* Parker's Absolute Religion, p. 205. † See Tract 29.
‡ Parker's Discourses on Religion, p. 161.
∥ Macknight's Doctrine of Inspiration, p. 161, and seq.

What manner of use could the Bible be to an ignorant soul groping its way to truth and holiness, or to a dying sinner hastening to the judgment seat of God, if it were true, that, "the Bible's own teaching on the subject is that every thing good in any book, person, or thing, is inspired? Milton and Shakspeare, and Bacon and the Canticles, the Apocalypse, and the Sermon on the Mount, and the Eighth Chapter of the Romans are all inspired. How much inspiration they respectively contain must be gathered from their results."*

This liberal grant of inspiration, alike to Moses and Mahommed, to Christ and to Shakspeare, is evidently a denial of Divine Authority to any of them. If Hamlet, and the Sermon on the Mount, and the Koran, are all of a like Divine Authority, or all alike without any, it is merely a matter of taste whether I worship at Niblo's or the Tabernacle, or keep a harem in my house, or a prayer meeting. Most men, however, find it hard to believe that Christ and Mahommed taught exactly the same religion, or that the church and the theater are precisely equal and alike in their influences on the heart and life; and so they reject several of these inspired men and cleave to the one they like best. Whereas, if this Pantheist theory be true, they ought not to act in such a disrespectful way toward any inspired man; but ought to attend the church, the theater, and the harem with equal regularity, and serve God, mammon, and Belial with equal diligence.

"Oh," it is replied, "they are not all inspired in the same degree. It does not follow that because Byron, and Shakspeare, and Paul are all inspired, that their writings will produce exactly the same results, or that they are alike suitable for every constitution and temper. How much inspiration they severally possess must be determined by their results. The tree is known by its fruits; and experience is the price of truth."

But truth may be bought too dear. I am sick and need some medicine, but know not exactly what kind, or how much to take. "Here," says my Pantheist friend, "is a whole drug store for you. Every drawer, and pot, and bottle is full of medicine. Help yourself." But, my good sir, how am I to know what kind will suit me? There are poisons here as well as medicines; and I can not tell the difference between arsenic and calomel. One of my neighbors died

---

* Macknight's Doctrine of Inspiration, ps. 192, etc.

the other day from swallowing oxalic acid instead of Glauber's Salts. Be kind enough to put the poisons on one shelf and the medicines on the other, or, at least, to label them, so that I may know which to choose and which to refuse. "Oh," says my Pantheist friend, this distinction between medicines and poisons is all an antiquated, vulgar prejudice. What you call poisons are really medicines. Medical virtue is not confined to the few specifics recognized by the Homœpathics, the Regular Faculty, or the Hydropathics, but is as extensive as the world. Every thing on earth has a medical virtue; but how much, and of what sort, must be determined by experience. In fact, you must just try for yourself whether any particular drug will kill you or cure you. So here is the whole drug store to begin your cure with." A valuable gift, truly! "In the day we eat thereof, our eyes will be opened, and we shall be as gods, knowing good and evil." I think, reader, you and I will let somebody else try that experiment.

"Quite right! Why should men throw away their common sense and swallow every thing as inspired?" says our friend of the rationalistic school. "God has given us reason to discern between good and evil, and commanded us to use it. *Prove the Spirits whether they be of God. I speak as to wise men. Judge ye what I say*—is the language of Scripture. The right of private judgment is the inalienable inheritance of Protestants. I am for examining the Bible according to the principles of reason and truth. 'That only is to be regarded as true and valid which is matter of personal conviction.' The Old Testament is in many places contrary to my convictions of truth and reason. I find that it consists of a great variety of treatises of various degrees of merit. Even in the same book it presents often strange contrasts—sublime moral precepts on one page; on the next, solemn requirements of frivolous ceremonies, utterly unworthy of God; or solemn narrations of miraculous interferences with the established course of nature, which, taken literally, are absolutely incredible. The judicious reader must therefore discriminate between those divine precepts of morality which were infused into the minds of the Hebrew sages, and those Jewish prejudices which their education and character inclined them to regard as equally important; and he must divest the narrative of facts as they actually occurred, from the national legends and traditions which the compilers of the Pentateuc' lded to adorn the history."

166

This, it will be seen, at once raises another and very important question, namely: By what standard are the writings of the Old Testament to be judged? Or rather it settles the question by taking it for granted that every inquirer is to judge them according to his own notions of reason and truth. But this does not help me out of my difficulty; for it supposes me already to possess the knowledge and the virtue which a revelation from God is needed to communicate. If I am able, by my own reason, to construct a perfect standard of morals to judge the Bible by, what need have I for the Bible revelation? And if I have the right to refuse obedience to any commands I may judge frivolous or unreasonable, before I know whether they came from God or not, and am bound to obey only those which agree with my notions of right, what authority has the law of God? A revelation from God which should submit its truths to be judged by the ignorance, and its commands by the inclinations, of sinful men, would by that very submission declare its worthlessness. The use of a Divine Revelation is either to tell us some truth of which we are ignorant, or to enjoin some duty to which we are disinclined.

Besides, it is not possible to make any such dissection of the moral precepts of the Bible, from the miraculous history which forms their skeleton, as will leave them either truth or authority. It is the miraculous history that gives sanction to the Divine morality, and without it, the ten commandments would have no more hold on any man's conscience, than the wise saws which Poor Richard says. Take for instance, one of the first and most important of the Bible moralities—the sacredness of marriage—which is wholly based upon a narrative of events utterly unparalleled; and if judged by the usual course of nature, perfectly incredible. The original difference in the formation of man and woman, and God's making at first one man and one woman, and joining them together with his blessing, constitute the reasons, and consecrate the pledge of marriage. "*For this cause shall a man leave his father and mother*—although the claims of the parental relation are very strong—*and cleave to his wife*—with whom it may be he has but a few weeks' acquaintance—*and they two shall be one flesh. What therefore God hath joined together let not man put asunder.*" But if the cause had no existence, save in the brain of some antediluvian novel-writer, and God did not so unite them, the consequence is only a notion also, and any man may leave his wife whenever he likes.

By far the most incredible narrative in the Bible is contained in the first verse: "*In the beginning God created the heavens and the earth.*" All the other miracles recorded in it, sink into familiarity compared with this stupendous display of the supernatural. To the believer of this first great miracle, none of its subsequent narratives can seem incredible. But it is precisely upon this unexampled and incredible narrative, that the whole structure of Bible morality is built. If this extraordinary narrative be rejected as false, all the moral precepts of the Bible are not worth a feather. The morality of the Bible, then, stands or falls with its history.

If we proceed now to examine the facts of the history, it is evident neither your reason or mine, nor our personal convictions, can be any rule of what is true and valid. The most that reason can say about history is, that the story seems probable; but so does any well-written novel: or that it is improbable; but truth is often stranger than fiction; and every genuine history relates wonderful events. Neither does our personal knowledge enable us to tell what was the original historical fact, how much was added by the Hebrew prejudices of Moses, and which are the legends with which it was afterward adorned; for neither you nor I were there to see. Nor can any two of those critics, who have undertaken to divide the facts from the fables according to their personal convictions of what is true and valid, agree upon any common principle of gleaning, or in gathering in their results. And if they could, the crop would not be worth barn-room; for the only conclusion in which they seem at all likely to agree is, that the story of creation in the beginning of the book is a myth, like one of Ovid's Metamorphoses; and that the prophecy of the resurrection at the end, is another; and that there are a great many legends in the middle. Now, if so, why winnow such chaff?

But while the Jewish people exist as a distinct race, it is impossible rationally to deny some extraordinary origin of their extraordinary character and customs; and the Bible is the only history which pretends to tell it. The utter failure of Rationalistic criticism to give any rational account of the facts which must be admitted to account for the existence of the Jews as a distinct people, is ludicrously apparent in the attempts generally made to explain the plagues of Egypt, the passage of the Red Sea, and the miracles of the desert, as merely natural phenomena, dextrously used by Moses and Aaron to suit their purpose.

It is alleged that these enthusiastic patriots, full of the superstitions of an early age, which attributed all prodigies to God, and placed all heroes under his guidance, succeeded by their fiery eloquence in inspiring their captive countrymen with the love of liberty; and had political dexterity enough to create a faction in their favor in the Egyptian cabinet. Then taking advantage of a fortunate succession of calamities arising from natural causes,—such as an extraordinary rising of the Nile, in consequence of which it was more deeply colored than usual with the red mud of Nubia, and overflowed the country to a greater extent than usual, leaving on its retreat numerous ponds which of course bred swarms of frogs and gnats, and raised malaria, spreading various sicknesses over the land both to man and beast; a devastating visit of locusts, the well-known scourge of Africa; a remarkable thunderstorm, accompanied with hail, causing great havoc of growing crops, as such hail storms always do; followed by the chamsin, or dust-storm from the desert, darkening the air with clouds of dust and sand; and by an extraordinary mortality, the natural result of these various causes,—they persuaded the superstitious Egyptians that these calamities were tokens of the displeasure of the God of the Hebrews, and improved the opportunity to escape while the resources of the Egyptians were exhausted, and their minds confounded by these various misfortunes. Leading them to that part of the Red Sea south of Suez, where a succession of shoals, or rather a bar, stretches across from the Egyptian to the Arabian side, they crossed safely at low water, while the Egyptian army perished by the rising of the tide; and the Israelites betaking themselves to a wandering, pastoral life in the wilderness of Arabia, lived, as the Bedouins do at this day, on the milk of their flocks and the manna which was spontaneously produced by the tamarisk trees of Sinai,—where they remained until they had framed a civil and religious code, and whence they prosecuted their conquests in various directions for fifty years, until their invasion of Palestine. This is the sum of what, with various modifications, Rationalist writers and preachers present us, as the genuine historic basis of the Mosaic narrative.

It really does seem to have been very fortunate for the Israelites, that so many misfortunes should happen to fall upon their oppressors, all in one season, and just at the time that men of such cleverness as Moses and Aaron were among them; and that the Egyptians should luckily have imbibed the superstition, that all nature was under the direction of a Supreme Moral Governor, who was able and willing to wield all the elements for the punishment of oppressors. Would it not be for the interests of liberty if American slaveholders were also infected with this superstition?

It was also very lucky for these poor, overworked, and oppressed slaves,—the class which in all other ages and countries suffers most from hard times,—that they should have escaped unhurt by these calamities; for if they had suffered by them as well as the Egyptians, they could not have persuaded them that God favored Israel.

Here one can not but wonder that these learned Egyptians, whose colleges of priests were planted on the banks of the Nile, and who had made the climate, soil, and productions of their native land their constant study, should have been so ignorant of these natural causes of the plagues—so easily discovered now-a-days by any body who makes a summer trip to Egypt—as to be terrified into emancipating their slaves by a stormy season. Just imagine to yourself a couple of Abolitionist lecturers proceeding to Lexington and commanding the slaveholders of Kentucky to liberate their slaves immediately, on pain of the Ohio being muddy during high water, and the swamps of the river-bottom being full of frogs and mosquitoes! But this interpretation does not reach the climax of absurdity till our Rationalist Punch, by way of signalizing his deliverance from Egyptian bondage, makes Pharaoh and his army forget that the tide ebbs and flows in the Red Sea, raises the tide over a shoal faster than cavalry could gallop away from it, gathers an annual crop of twenty millions of bushels of manna from the thornbushes of Sinai, and feeds three millions of men, women, and children for forty years upon purgative medicine!!!

"We must then give up the problem as insoluble; for if reason be insufficient to give authority to the Bible, and criticism fails to discover its truth, how are we to know that it possesses either?"

Just as you would discover the truth of any other history, or the authority of any other law. You do not say, "The tale of the successive swellings of the Catawba, the Yadkin, and the Dan,—three times in a fortnight, in Feb., 1781, immediately after the American army had retreated across these rivers, preventing Cornwallis and the

British forces from crossing till the little handful of weary and famished patriots had escaped—savors of the marvelous and leans so much toward the superstition of a special providence, that it must be rejected as not historical." You inquire if there be sufficient testimony to the fact. You do not say, "The Revised Statutes present internal evidence of being a collection of political tracts by various authors, written at different times, differing also in style, and of various degrees of merit, many of them contrary to my inmost personal convictions; therefore I can not acknowledge them as true and valid." You simply ask if this be a true copy of the laws passed by the Legislature and signed by the Governor? Our inquiry about the truth of the history, and the authority of the laws of the Bible, must be of the same kind—an inquiry after testimony. Is this book genuine or a forgery? Is it a true history or a lying romance? Have we any testimony on the subject?

It is important at the outset to know how long these documents have undoubtedly existed. No one denies that they were in existence 1800 years ago. Indeed, the first literary attack on them which has been recorded was made about that time; and Josephus' defence of the Scriptures against Apion still exists. The very same writings which the Protestant churches now acknowledge as canonical, and none other, were then acknowledged to be of Divine authority by the Jews. It is true they bound their Bibles differently from ours, but the contents were the very same. They made up their parchments of the 39 books in 22 rolls or volumes, one for every letter of their alphabet—putting Judges and Ruth, the two books of Samuel, the two books of Kings, the two books of Chronicles, Ezra and Nehemiah, Jeremiah's Prophecy and Lamentations, and the twelve minor prophets, in one volume respectively. They also distinguished the Five Books of Moses as *The Law;* the Psalms, Proverbs, Ecclesiastes, and Song of Solomon, as *The Psalms;* and all the remainder as, *The Prophets.** Moreover, it is well known that 282 years before the Christian Era, these writings were translated into Greek and widely circulated in all parts of the world. They were, in fact, not only popular, but received as of Divine authority by the Jews at that time, read in their Synagogues in public worship, and regarded with sacred reverence. How did they come to receive them in this manner?

---

* Josephus against Apion, book 1, sec. 8. Horne's Introduction, chap. 2, sec. 1.

These books are not such as any person would forge to gain popularity or make money by. There is nothing in them to bribe the good opinion of influential people, or catch the favor of the multitude. On the contrary, their stern severity and unsparing denunciation of popular vice and profitable sin must have secured their rejection by the Jewish people, had they not been constrained by undeniable evidence to acknowledge their Divine Authority. They set out with the assertion of the Divine Authority of the Law of Moses, and every where sharply reprove princes, priests, and people for breaking it. The Prophets, so far from seeking popularity, are fool-hardy enough to denounce the bonnets, hoops, and flounces of the ladies, and to cry, Woe! against the regular business of the most respectable note-shavers*—to croak against the march of intellect, and shake public confidence in the prosperity of their great country†—to ally themselves with fanatic abolitionists, and introduce agitating political questions into the pulpit; crying, *Woe to him that useth his neighbor's service without wages, and giveth him not for his work.*‡ To crown all, they organized Abolition clubs to procure immediate emancipation, and published incendiary proclamations in the cities of the slaveholders: § and, strange to say, they were allowed to escape with their lives; and their writings were held sacred by the children of those very men and women they so unsparingly denounced—a conclusive proof that the calamities they predicted had compelled them to acknowledge these prophets as the heralds of God. The proof must have been conclusive indeed, which compelled the Jews to acknowledge the writings of the Prophets as sacred.

Another very striking feature of these writings is their mutual connection with each other. They were written at various intervals, during a period of a thousand years' duration, by shepherds and kings, by prophets and priests, by governors of states and gatherers of sycamore fruit; in deserts and in palaces, in camps and in cities, in Egypt and Syria, in Arabia and Babylon; under the iron heel of despotic oppression and amid the liberty of the most democratic republic the world ever saw: yet, amid all this variety of authorship, and change of circumstances, and lapse of time, they ever hold to one great theme, always assert the same

---

* Isaiah, iii: 16.   Ezek., xviii: 12.   † Jere., 21 ch., and xxii: 16.
‡ Jere., xxii: 13.   § Jere., chap. 34.

great principles, and perpetually claim connection with the writers who have preceded them. There is nothing like this in the histories of other nations. Two centuries will work such changes of opinion, that you can not find now-a-days any historian who approves the sentiments of Pepys or Clarendon, whatever use he may make of their facts. But the historians of the Bible not only refer to their predecessors' writings, but refer to them as of acknowledged Divine authority. Thus the very latest of these books gives the weight of its testimony to the first—"*And they set the priests in their divisions, and the Levites in their courses for the service of God, which is at Jerusalem, as it is written in the book of Moses.*"* And Daniel speaks of the books of Moses as well known when he says, "*Therefore the curse is poured upon us, and the oath that is written in the Law of Moses, the servant of God.*" † The shortest book in the Old Testament—the prophecy of Obadiah, consisting only of twenty sentences—contains twenty-five allusions to the preceding histories and laws. The last of the Prophets shuts up the volume with a command to "*Remember the law of Moses.*" In fact, just as the Epistles prove the existence and acknowledged authority of the Gospels; so do the Prophets prove the existence and acknowledged authority of the Law of Moses. They were acknowledged not merely by one generation of the Jewish people, but by the nation during the whole period of its national existence: and they are of such a character, and so closely connected by references from one to the other, that they must then, and now, be taken as one whole—all accepted, or all rejected together.

The reader of the Old Testament will speedily find that these writings are not merely a connected history of the nation, of great general interest, like Bancroft's or Macauley's, but of no such special interest to any individual as to force him, by a sense of-self-interest, or the danger of loss of liberty or property, to correct their errors. On the contrary, every farmer in Palestine was deeply concerned in the truth and accuracy of the Bible; for it contained not only the general boundaries of the country, and of the particular tribes; like the survey of the Maine boundary, or of Mason and Dixon's line; but it delineated particular estates also, and was in fact, the Report of the Surveyor-General, deposited in the county

---

* Ezra, 6; 18.   † Daniel, 9: 11.

court for reference, in case of any litigation about sale or inheritance of property.* The genealogies of the tribes and families were also preserved in these writings; and on the authenticity and correctness of these records, the inheritance of every farm in the land depended; for as no lease ran more than fifty years, every farm returned to the heirs of the original settler, at the year of jubilee.† Thus every Jewish farmer had a direct interest in these sacred records; and it would be just as hard to forge records for the county courts of Ohio, and pass them off upon the citizens as genuine, and plead them in the courts as valid, as to impose at first, or falsify afterward, the records of the Commonwealth of Israel.

This will appear more clearly, when we consider that they contained also the laws of the land—the Constitution of the United States of Israel, with the statutes at large—according to which, every house and farm and garden in the whole country was possessed—every court of justice was guided ‡—every election was held, from the election of a petty constable, to that of governor of the state §—and the militia enrolled, mustered, officered, and called out to the field of battle. ‖ These laws prescribed the way in which every house must be built, regulated the weaver in weaving his cloth, and the tailor in making it, and the cooking of every breakfast, dinner and supper eaten by any Israelite over the world, from that day to this.¶ Now, let any one who thinks it would be an easy matter to forge such a series of documents, and get people to receive and obey them, try his hand in making a volume of Acts of Assembly, and passing it off upon the people of Ohio for genuine. Let him bring an action into one of the courts, and persuade the judges to give a decision in his favor, upon the strength of his forged or falsified statutes, and then he may hope to convince us that the Laws of Moses are simply a collection of religious tracts, which came to be held sacred through lapse of time, nobody knows how or why.

To a Jew living before the coming of Christ, who received the unanimous testimony of his nation, handed down from generation to generation, confirmed by all the commemorative ceremonies of the Passover and the Sacrifices, the observance of the Sabbath, and the reading of the Law and the Prophets in the Synagogue, the

---

* Joshua, chs. 13, 14, 15, 16, 17, 18, 19.   † 1 Chron., chs. 1, 2, 3, 4, 5, 6, 7, 8, 9; Lev. 25.
‡ Exo., xxi: 6.   Deut., i: 16, ch. 19.   § Exo., xviii: 21.   ‖ Deut. 20 ch.   Numb. x: 9.
¶ Deut., xxii: 8, 11, 12.   Lev., ch. 11.

singing of the historical Psalms in the Temple, and the execution of the Laws of Moses in the courts of justice, and by the very existence of the Jewish nation as a distinct people, no doubt could remain that truths so unpopular, and laws so burdensome, could never have been received by any nation, unless constrained by some superior power; nor that the miracles by which these laws were authenticated, and the national existence of the people of Israel was secured, were genuine and divine. The chain of historical and internal evidence is too strong to be broken, while the Jewish nation exists.

But yet this historical and internal evidence of the authority of the Old Testament is but the smallest part of that which we possess, who have the testimony of Christ on this subject. For this testimony removes the question from the mists of antiquity, and even from the debatable ground of historic certainty, and resolves the whole process of searching for, and comparing and examining a host of second-hand witnesses, into the easy and certain one of hearing the author himself say whether he acknowledges this book to be his or not. Christians receive the Old Testament as the Word of God, because Jesus says so.

Now, reader, it is of the utmost importance that you should stop just here, and give a plain, confident answer to these questions:— Dost thou believe upon the Son of God? Is Jesus the Messiah of whom Moses in the Law, and the Prophets, did write? Are you perfectly satisfied of the truth of the New Testament, and willing to venture your eternal salvation upon the words of Christ contained in it? For if not, of what use is it for you to trouble yourself about the Old Testament? You might as well waste your time in examining the genuineness of the bills of a broken bank: they may be genuine or they may be forgeries; but who cares? They will never be paid. If the first promises of the Bank of Heaven, to send the Messiah 1800 years ago, have been fulfilled, its other paper may be also valuable: if not, it must be equally worthless. If the New Testament be not of Divine Authority, you may place the Prophets on the same shelf with the Poems of Ossian: and then follows the serious consequence, that there is not a grain of hope left for you or for any man on earth. If Jesus be indeed an Almighty Savior, and if he has indeed risen from the dead, then, through the power of his mighty love, your filthy soul may be washed from its sins, and your mortal body may be raised from the rottenness of the grave. But if Christ be not risen, you are yet in your sins. You have no notion that any of the gods of the heathen, or the precepts of the Koran, can purify your heart. You know well that Infidelity never sanctified any of your comrades. Conscience tells you that you are not any better now than you were a year ago, but worse. You are yet in your sins; and in them you must live and die! Aye, while your immortal soul lives, while the laws of human nature continue, you must carry those brands of infamy on your character, and daily progress from bad to worse—sinking deeper and deeper in the contempt of all intelligent beings; and, were there no other avenger, in the remorse and despair of your own mind, you must experience the horrors of perdition. Jesus, able to save to the uttermost all that come unto God by him, is your only hope. There is none other name given under heaven among men whereby we must be saved. If his gospel be true, you may be saved: if it is false, you must be damned.

If you have the shadow of a doubt of the truth of the New Testament, go over the subject again; re-read the former Tracts of this series; pray to God for light and truth: above all, read the Book itself again and again: and if, in your case, as in that of one of the most famous teachers of German Neology—De Wette—the careful study of the New Testament impels you to rush through all the mists of doubt to the higher standpoint of a lofty faith, and the sunshine of real religion; and if with him you can now say, "Only this one thing I know, that in no other name is there salvation than in the name of Jesus Christ the crucified, and that for humanity there is nothing higher than the incarnation of Deity set before us in him, and the Kingdom of God established by him,"* you may then go on with your inquiry into the Divine authority of the Old Testament. With the Master himself before you, the Author, the Inspirer, by whom, and for whom, the Prophets spake, and to whom all the Scriptures point, you will not think of wasting time in examining second-hand evidence; but go direct to Jesus himself. His testimony will not be merely so much additional testimony—another candle added to the chandelier by whose light you have perused the evidences of the Scriptures: it will shine out on your soul as the light of the Sun of Righteousness with healing on his wings. Every word from his lips will awaken in your heart

---

* Preface to Exposition of the Apocalypse.

the voice from heaven, "*This is my beloved Son. Hear him.*" What saith Christ, then, respecting the Old Testament?

The moment you open the New Testament to make this inquiry, you are met by a reference to the Old. "*The book of the generation of Jesus Christ, the Son of David, the Son of Abraham,*" is its formal title: and the most cursory perusal tells you that you have taken up, not a separate and independent work, which you can profitably peruse and understand without much reference to some foregoing volumes—as one might read Abbott's Life of Napoleon without needing at the same time to study The History of the Crusades—but that you have taken up a continuation of some former work,—the last volume in fact of the Old Testament,—and that you can not understand even the first chapter without a careful reading of the foregoing volumes. Before you have finished the first chapter you meet with the most unequivocal assertion of the harmony of the gospels and the prophecies, and of the Divine authority of both—"*Now all this was done that it might be fulfilled which was spoken of the Lord by the prophet, etc.*" The whole tenor of the New Testament corresponds to this beginning, teaching that the birth, doctrine, miracles, life, death, resurrection, ascension, and second coming of the Lord, are the fulfillments of the Old Testament promises and prophecies; of which no less than a hundred and thirty-nine are expressly quoted, beginning with Moses and ending with Malachi.

We can not explain this by saying, with the mythical school of interpreters, that this was merely the opinion of the writers of the gospels and of the Jews of their age; whose longings for the Messiah led them to imagine some curious coincidences between the events of Christ's life and the utterances of these ancient oracles to be really fulfillments; and that Christ did not deem it needful in all cases to undeceive them. For to suppose that Christ—the Truth—would sanction or connive at any such sacrilegious deception, is at once to deprive him, not only of his Divine character, but of all claim to common honesty. So far from the Jews longing for any such events as those which fulfilled the prophecies, they despised the Messiah in whom they were fulfilled, and refused to believe in him; and his disciples were as far from the gospel ideal of the Messiah, when Jesus needed to reproach them with, "*O, fools, and slow of heart to believe all that the prophets have spoken.*"*

---

* Luke, xxiv; 25.

It was not the Jews, nor yet the disciples, but the Lord himself who perpetually insisted on the Divine authority of the Old Testament, as *The Word* of his Father, and the sufficient attestation of his own Divine character, after this manner: *Ye have not his word abiding in you, for whom he hath sent, him ye believe not. Search the Scriptures, for in them ye think ye have eternal life; and they are they which testify of me. Had ye believed Moses, ye would have believed me, for he wrote of me; but if ye believe not his writings, how shall ye believe my words?**

His first recorded sermon contains a remarkable and solemn attestation to the Divine authority of the Old Testament, and of his own relation to it as its substance and supporter. *Think not that I came to destroy the Law or the Prophets; I came not to destroy, but to fulfill. For, verily I say unto you, till heaven and earth pass, one jot, or one tittle shall in no wise pass from the Law till all be fulfilled.*† The whole of this discourse is an exposition of the true principles of the Old Testament, stripping off the rubbish by which tradition had made void the Law of God, and enforcing its precepts by the sanction of his own authority. And in one of his last discourses after his resurrection: *Beginning at Moses, and all the Prophets, he expounded to them in all the Scripture, the things concerning himself. And he said unto them, These are the words which I spake unto you, while I was yet with you—that all things which were written in the Law of Moses, and in the Prophets, and in the Psalms, concerning me, should be fulfilled. Then, opened he their understandings, that they might understand the Scriptures.*‡

In this distinct enumeration of the whole of the Scriptures of the Old Testament; the assertion, that they all treated of him, and that their principal predictions were fulfilled in him; and in his bestowal of divine illumination to enable them to understand these divine oracles, we have such an endorsement of their character by the Truth himself, as must command the faith and obedience of every believer in him. Had no objections been raised against particular doctrines or features of the Old Testament, we would stop here; perfectly satisfied with the attestations to the truth of its history, given by the continual references, and to the authority of its precepts, by the solemn formal declarations

---

* John, v; 38-47.   † Mat., v; 17, etc.   ‡ Luke, ch. 24 throughout.

of the Son of God. But some popular objections to its completeness and perfection, demand a brief notice.

1. The general character of the Old Testament being then ascertained beyond doubt, our first inquiry must be as to the integrity and completeness of the collection. For it is manifest that their Divine authority being admitted, any attempt to add to them any human writings, or to take away those which were from God, would be a crime so serious in its consequences, that it could not escape the notice of him who severely rebuked even the verbal traditions by which the Jews made void the law of God. Now we are told by some that a great many inspired books have been lost; and they enumerate the Prophecy of Enoch; the Book of the Wars of the Lord; the Book of Joshua; the Book of Iddo, the Seer; the Book of Nathan, the Prophet; the Acts of Rehoboam; the Book of Jehu the son of Hanani; the Five Books of Solomon, on trees, beasts, fowls, serpents, and fishes—which are alluded to in the Bible.

If the case were so, it is difficult to see what objection could be raised against the Divine authority of the books we have, because of the Divine authority of those we have not; for it is not supposed that one divinely inspired book would contradict another. Nor yet can we see how the loss of these books should disprove their inspiration, much less the inspiration of those which remain, any more than the want of a record of the multitude of words and works of Jesus himself which were never committed to writing,* should be an argument against the Divine authority of the Sermon on the Mount. It will hardly be asserted that God is bound to reveal to us every thing that the human race ever did, and to preserve such records through all time, or lose his right to demand our obedience to a plain revelation of his will; or that we do well to neglect the salvation of our own souls until we obtain an infallible knowledge of the Acts of Rehoboam.

But there is not the shadow of a proof that any of these were inspired books, or that some of them were books at all. The Bible no where says that Enoch wrote his prophecy, or that Solomon read his lectures on natural history; nor of what religious interest they would have been to us any more than the hard questions of the Queen of Sheba, and his answers to them. Though the loss of these ancient chronicles may be regretted by the antiquarian,

---

* John, xx; 30.

the christian feels not at all concerned about it; knowing as he does on the testimony of Christ, that the Holy Scriptures, as he and his Apostles delivered them to us, contain all that we need to know in order to repent of our sins, lead holy lives, and go to heaven; and that we have the very same Bible of which Jesus said *They have Moses and the Prophets; let them hear them. If they believe not Moses and the Prophets, neither would they believe though one rose from the dead.**

2. Another objection is, that the religion of the Old Testament was essentially different from that of the New. It is at once acknowledged, that the light which Christ shed on our relations to God and to our brethren of mankind is so much clearer than that of the Old Testament that we see our duties more plainly, and are more inexcusable for neglecting them, than those who had not the benefit of Christ's teaching. And no objection can be raised against God for not sending his Son sooner, or for not giving more light to the world before his coming, unless it can be shown that he is debtor to mankind, and that they were making a good use of the light he gave them. So that the question is not, Did God give as full and expanded instructions to the church in her infancy as he has given in her maturity? but, Did he give instructions of a different character? It is not, Did Christ reveal more than Moses? but, Did Christ contradict Moses? And here at the very outset we are met by Christ's own solemn formal disclaimer of any such intention; "*Think not that I come to destroy the Law and the Prophets. I come not to destroy, but to fulfill.*" And as to the actual working of the Christian religion, when Paul is asked, "*Is the Law then against the promises of God?*"† he indignantly replies " *God forbid!*"

But it is urged, "Judaism is not Christianity. You have changed the sabbath, abolished the sacrifices, trampled upon the rules of living, eating and visiting only with the peculiar people, you neglect the passover, and drop circumcision, the seal of the covenant, all on the authority of Christ. Do you mean to say that these are not essential elements of the Old Testament religion?"

Undoubtedly. Outward ceremonies of any kind never were essential parts of religion: "*I will have mercy and not sacrifice,*" is an Old Testament proverb, which clearly tells us that outward ceremonies are merely means toward the great end of all religion

---

* Luke, xvi: 29.   † Gal., iii: 21.

"*The law,*" says the Holy Ghost, by the pen of Paul, "*was our schoolmaster to bring us to Christ.*" The bread of heavenly truth is served out to God's children now on ten thousand wooden tables instead of one brazen altar; but it is made of the same corn of heaven, it is dispensed by the same hand of love, to a larger family, it is true, but received and eaten in the exercise of the very same religious feelings, by any hearer of the gospel in New York, as by Abraham on Moriah. By faith in Christ the sinner now is justified, "*Even as Abraham believed God and it was imputed to him for righteousness.*"* So says one who knew both law and gospel well. "*Do we then make void the law through faith? God forbid! Yea we establish the law!*"* The Epistles to the Romans and to the Hebrews, are just demonstrations of this truth, that the law was the blossom—the gospel the fruit.

But it is alleged that the religion of the Old Testament could not but be defective, as it wanted the doctrines of immortality and the resurrection; of which it is alleged, the Old Testament saints were ignorant. It were easy to prove, from their own words and conduct, that Job, Abraham, David and Daniel, were not ignorant of these great doctrines.† But the manner in which our Lord proves the truth of the resurrection, by a reference to it as undeniably taught in the Old Testament, must ever silence this objection. "*But as touching the resurrection of the dead, have ye not read that which was spoken unto you by God, saying, 'I am the God of Abraham, and the God of Isaac, and the God of Jacob.' God is not the God of the dead, but of the living.*"‡

3. Again, however, it is contended, "that the morality of the Old Testament was narrow and bigoted; requiring indeed, the observance of charity to the covenant people, but allowing Israel to hate all others as enemies, and as well expressed in the text, *Thou shalt love thy neighbor and hate thine enemy.*" §

But let it be noticed, that this is no text of Scripture, nor does our Lord so quote it. He does not say it is so written, but, *ye have heard it said by them of old time.* The first part is God's truth: the second is the devil's addition to it, which Christ clears away and denounces. It were easy to quote multitudes of passages from the Old Testament, commanding Israel to show kindness to the

---

* Romans, chs. iv, v, and vi. † Job, xix; 25. Psalm, xvi: 10. Hebrews, xi: 13-16. Daniel, xii: 2-3.   ‡ Matthew, xxii: 32.   § Matthew, v: 43.

stranger, and a whole host of promises, that in them all the families of the earth should be blessed; any one of which would sufficiently refute the foolish notion, that the morality of the Old Testament was geographical, and its charity merely national. But the simple fact, that the most sublime sanction of world-wide benevolence which ever fell even from the lips of Christ himself, was uttered by him as the sum and substance of the teachings of the Old Testament, conclusively confutes this dogma. The Golden Rule was no new discovery, unless its author was mistaken, for he says: *Therefore all things that ye would that men should do to you, do ye even so to them,* FOR THIS IS THE LAW AND THE PROPHETS.* He declares the very basis and foundation of the whole Old Testament religion to be those eternal principles of godliness and charity, which he quotes in the very words of the Law: *Then one of them which was a lawyer asked him a question, tempting him, and saying, Master, which is the great commandment in the law? Jesus said unto him, thou shalt love the Lord thy God with all thy heart, and with all thy soul, and with all thy mind. This is the first and great commandment. And the second is like unto it; thou shalt love thy neighbor as thyself. On these two commandments hang all the Law and the Prophets.*† The Law and the Prophets then taught genuine world-wide benevolence, Christ being witness; and the moral law of the Old Testament is the moral law of the New Testament, if we may believe the Lawgiver.

4. "Still, it is alleged, it can not be denied that the writers of the Old Testament breathed a spirit of vindictiveness, and imprecated curses on their enemies, utterly at variance with the precepts of the gospel, which commands us to bless and curse not; and even in their solemn devotions uttered sentiments unfit for the mouth of any Christian; nor that their views of the character of God were stern and gloomy, and that they represented the Hebrew Jehovah as an unforgiving and vengeful being, utterly different from the kind and loving Father whom Christ delighted to reveal."

This, if the truth were told, is the grand objection to the Old Testament. The holy and righteous sin-hating God presented in its history, is the object of dislike. The God who drowned the old world—destroyed Sodom and Gomorrha by fire from heaven—

---

* Matthew, vii: 12. † Matthew, xxiii: 35.

commanded the extermination of the lewd and bloody Canaanites—thundered his curses against sinners of every land and every age, saying "*Cursed be he that confirmeth not all the words of this law to do them*"—requiring all the people to say *Amen**—is not the God whom Universalists can find in their hearts to adore. A mild, easy, good-natured being, who would allow men to live and die in sin without any punishment, would suit them better. They try to think that he is altogether such an one as themselves, and an approver of their sin.

But it is worth while to inquire whether the Father of our Lord Jesus Christ be in this respect any thing different from the Hebrew Jehovah, or whether the gospel has in the least degree lessened his displeasure against iniquity. Paul thought not that he was a different person, when he said, "*We know him who hath said, Vengeance belongeth unto me, I will repay saith the Lord.*"† Jesus thought not that he was more lenient to sinners when he cried, "*Woe unto thee, Chorazin! Woe unto thee, Bethsaida! Thou Capernaum, which art exalted to heaven shalt be brought down to hell. It shall be more tolerable for the land of Sodom in the day of judgment than for thee.*"‡ It is not in the Old Testament, but in the New, that we are told that Jesus himself shall come "*In flaming fire, taking vengeance on them that know not God, and obey not the gospel of our Lord Jesus Christ; who shall be punished with everlasting destruction from the presence of the Lord and from the glory of his power.*"§ It is not an old, bigoted Hebrew Prophet giving a vision of the Hebrew Jehovah, but the beloved disciple who leaned on Jesus' breast, picturing the Savior himself, who says, "*He was clothed in a vesture dipped in blood; and his name is called the Word of God. And the armies which were in heaven followed him upon white horses, clothed in fine linen, white and clean; and out of his mouth goeth a sharp sword, that with it he should smite the nations; and he shall rule them with a rod of iron; and he treadeth the wine-press of the fierceness and wrath of Almighty God.*"‖

Let no man imagine that the New Testament offers impunity to the wicked, or that the Old Testament denies mercy to the repenting sinner, or that Christ exhibited any other God than the God of Abraham, Isaac and Jacob—the same Hebrew Jehovah

---

* Deut. xxvii: 26. † Heb. x: 30. ‡ Matthew xi: 21.
§ 2 Thes. 1 ch. ‖ Revelation 19 ch.

who *commands the wicked to forsake his way, and the unrighteous man his thoughts; and to return unto the Lord, and he will have mercy upon him; and to our God and he will abundantly pardon.** It is exceedingly strange that those who dwell upon the paternal character of God, as a distinctive feature of Christ's personal teaching, should have forgotten that the hymns of the Old Testament church, a thousand years before his coming, were full of this endearing relation; that it was by the first Hebrew Prophet that the Hebrew Jehovah declared, "*Israel is my Son, my first born; therefore I say unto thee let my Son go that he may serve me;*"† and that by the last of them he urges Israel to obedience by this tender appeal. "*If I be a Father where is mine honor?*"‡ It was not Christ, but David—one of those gloomy, stern, Hebrew Prophets—who penned that noble hymn to our Father in heaven, which Christ illustrated in his Sermon on the Mount:

> "The Lord is merciful and gracious,
> Slow to anger and plenteous in mercy.
> He will not always chide,
> Neither will he keep his anger for ever.
> He hath not dealt with us after our sins,
> Nor rewarded us according to our iniquities;
> For as the heaven is high above the earth,
> So great is his mercy to them that fear him;
> As far as east is from the west,
> So far hath he removed our transgressions from us.
> Like as a father pitieth his children,
> So the Lord pitieth them that fear him."
>
> Psalm 103.

It is utter ignorance of the Old Testament which prompts any one to imagine that it presents any other character of God than "*The Lord, the Lord God, merciful and gracious, and long suffering, and abundant in goodness and truth, keeping mercy for thousands, forgiving iniquity and transgression and sin, and that will by no means clear the guilty.*"§ This is the name which God proclaimed to Moses, and this is the character which he proclaimed in Christ, when he cried on the cross, "*My God! My God! Why hast thou forsaken me? But thou art holy, thou that inhabitest the praises of Israel.*"‖ Justice and mercy are united in Christ dying for the ungodly.

---

* Isaiah, ch. 55. † Exodus iv: 22. ‡ Mal. i. § Exodus, ch. xxxiv. ‖ Psalm, xxii.

It is untrue to say that the Prophets of the Old Testament were actuated by a spirit of malice, or of revenge for personal injuries as such, in praying for, or prophesying destruction on the inveterate enemies of God and his cause.* Of all scripture characters, David has been most defamed for vindictiveness; but surely never was man more free from any such spirit, than the persecuted fugitive, who, with his enemy in his hand in the cave, and his confidential advisers urging him to take his life, cut off his skirt instead of his head; and on another occasion prevented the stroke which would have smitten the sleeping Saul to the earth, and sent back even the spear and the cruse of water, the trophies of his generosity. When cursed himself, and defamed as a vengeful shedder of blood by the Benjamite, he could restrain the fury of his followers, protect the life of the ruffianly traitor, and thus appeal to God as the witness of his innocence:

"O Lord, my God! if I have done this,
If there be iniquity in my hands.
If I have rewarded evil to him that was at peace with me,
Yea I have delivered him that without cause was mine enemy."†

It is true that he does bitterly curse several living persons; of whom it is observable that some had done him no sort of personal injury; as Doeg the Edomite—the Nena Sahib of his day—who anticipated the scenes of Cawnpore in the streets of Nob; by mercilessly butchering unoffending men, helpless women, and innocent babes. But surely no friend of humanity can imagine that it is improper that the chief magistrate of Israel, anointed for the very purpose of being a terror to evil doers, should express his righteous indignation against such atrocities; nor confound such public execration with the petty gnawings of private revenge. Still less can the fearer of God doubt the propriety of his expressing by the mouth of his Prophet, that displeasure which he signally displayed by his providence, scathing and blasting the accursed wretch into a terror to all bloody and deceitful men who shall read their own warning in his doom.

"God shall likewise destroy thee for ever,
He shall take thee away and pluck thee from thy dwelling,
And root thee out of the land of the living."‡

---

* 2 Tim. iv: 14.   † Psalm vii.
‡ Psalms, 7 and 52, and 2 Samuel, xvi ch., and xxi and xxii chs.

We have the most solemn assurance that every one of the historical incidents of scripture is recorded for our instruction, and that every prophecy gives a lesson to all ages. *Now all these things happened unto them for ensamples, and they are written for our admonition, upon whom the ends of the world are come.** The imprecations of the Bible against individual sinners are the gibbets on which these malefactors are hung up for warning to all men to flee the crimes that brought them to that fate.

It is put beyond the possibility of doubt, by the combined testimony of the Lord and his Apostles, that by far the greater number of the curses which David úttered, he spoke in the person of Christ himself, of whom he was a type; and with direct reference to the crimes and punishment of his enemies. Thus the 69th Psalm, and the 109th, pre-eminently the cursing Psalms, are most explicitly and repeatedly asserted by Christ, by Peter and by John, to belong to Christ, and to express his very words; *This scripture must needs have been fulfilled, which the Holy Ghost, by the mouth of David, spake before concerning Judas, which was guide to them that took Jesus. For it is written in the book of Psalms,* "*Let his habitation be desolate, and let no man dwell therein.*" *And,* "*His bishopric let another take.*"† If any one feels reluctant to imagine that such cursings should fall from the lips of the merciful Savior, let him remember that the most awful curse which shall ever fall on the ears of terrified men, shall be pronounced by Jesus himself, "*Depart ye cursed into everlasting fire, prepared for the Devil and his angels.*"‡ The solemn facts of the Bible will not accomodate themselves to our likes and dislikes. Christ loves righteousness and hates iniquity; in the Bible he takes leave to say so, and he expects his people to share his feelings, and be willing to express them on fit occasions.

Personal revenge and curses for mere personal injuries are forbidden in the New Testament as well as in the Old. But it was an Apostle of Jesus Christ who cried, "*If any man love not our Lord Jesus Christ, let him be accursed. Though we or an angel from heaven bring any other gospel unto you, let him be accursed.*" Nor until we can in some measure feel this holy indignation against sin, and this burning desire to see all tyranny, superstition, oppres-

---

* 1 Cor., x ch.;
† John, ii: 17, xv: 25. xix: 28; Acts, i: 20; Matthew, xxv: 41.
‡ Gal. i: 9. 1 Cor., xvi: 22. Rev., chs. xxix, xx and xxi.

sion, licentiousness and profanity, crushed and banished from the earth, can we pray in truth "*Thy kingdom come.*" Still less can we be prepared for the rejoicings of heaven over the conquest of the enemies of God and man; *Rejoice over her thou heaven, and ye holy Apostles and Prophets, for God hath avenged you on her.*

Reader you hope to go to heaven; but it may be a very different place from what you dream of. Did you ever study the employment of the saints there? Are you washed from your sins? Is your mind purified from your carnal notions? Unless a man be born again he can not see the kingdom of God. Are your likes and dislikes, your sentiments and sympathies, your understanding and your will, all brought into subjection to Christ? Can you heartily love and adore a sin-hating, sin-avenging God? Or do you shrink back in terror or dislike from God's denunciations of wrath against the wicked? Would your benevolence lead you to deal alike with the righteous and the wicked; and to abhor the thought of destroying them that destroy the earth? Then how will you join in the hallelujahs of heaven; for God's judgments are the themes of thanksgiving and praise from saints and angels there, and this is their song:

"*Hallelujah, salvation, and glory, and honor, and power, unto the Lord, our God, for true and righteous are his judgments; for he hath judged the great whore, which did corrupt the earth with her fornication, and hath avenged the blood of his servants at her hands. And again they said, Hallelujah! And her smoke rose up for ever and ever. And the four and twenty elders, and the four living creatures fell down and worshiped God, that sat on the throne, saying, Amen! Hallelujah! And a voice came out of the throne saying, Praise our God all ye his servants; and ye that fear him, both small and great. And I heard, as it were, a great multitude, and as the voice of many waters, and as the voice of mighty thunders, saying, Hallelujah!* For the Lord God Omnipotent reigneth."*

And now, if this be the character of God—if he be indeed one who hates iniquity, and punishes impenitent sinners, we need not wonder that those who spake his word should utter imprecations, either in the Old Testament or in the New; but rather bless the mercy which warns before justice strikes, and seeks by the terrors

---

* Revelation, chs. xix, xx, xxi.

of the Lord to persuade men from perdition. The curses of the Bible are all denounced against the enemies of God, with the design of showing sinners their danger, and leading them to repentance.

The conclusion then of our investigation is, that the Old Testament is the word of God no less than the New—that it is in no respect contrary to it—that all its parts—the Law and the Prophets, and the Psalms—are of Divine authority—that all its contents were written by Divine direction, whether prophecy or history, ceremony or morality, promise or threatening, curses or blessings. It is of the Old Testament principally that the Holy Ghost declares "*All Scripture is given by inspiration of God; and is profitable for doctrine, for reproof, for instruction, and correction in righteousness; that the man of God may be perfect, thoroughly furnished unto all good works.*"*

---

* 2 Timothy, iii: 16.

No. 31.

INFIDELITY AMONG THE STARS.

A little or superficial knowledge of philosophy may incline a man's mind to Atheism; but depth in philosophy bringeth men's minds about to religion. BACON.

WHEN skeptics, who are determined not to believe in the Bible, find the historical evidences of its genuineness, authority, and inspiration, impregnable against the assaults of criticism, they turn their attention to some other mode of attack, and of late years have selected their weapons from the physical sciences. The argument thus raised is, that the Bible cannot be the word of God, because it asserts facts contrary to the teachings of science. Of this warfare Voltaire may be considered the leader, in his celebrated attack on the chemical processes recorded in scripture; in which he exposed himself to the ridicule of all the chemists and metallurgists in Europe, by denying the possibility of dissolving the golden calf: the solution of gold being actually found in every gilder's shop in Paris, and known even to coiners and forgers for hundreds of years before he made this notable discovery. The result was ominous.

The whole circle of the sciences has been ransacked for such arguments, and especially has every new discovery been hailed by skeptics as an ally to their cause, until further acquaintance has demonstrated that the stranger, too, was in alliance with religion. Thus, when Geology began to upheave his Titanic form, he was eagerly greeted as a being undoubtedly not of celestial, but rather of subterranean, or even infernal origin, and so willing to employ his gigantic powers in the assault upon heaven, and able to overwhelm the Bible and the Church under the ruins of former worlds. But now that skeptics have discovered the proofs he gives of the presence of the Almighty on this world of ours, they are getting shy of his acquaintance, and are cultivating the society of some new and juvenile visitors from the chambers of Animal Magnetism and Biology. The same scene will doubtless be acted over again; and these infantile strangers, when able to give distinct utterance to the facts of their developed consciousness, will bear testimony to the truth of God.

Such objections to the Bible are very rarely brought forward by truly scientific men. It is a phenomenon, like the advent of a great comet, to find a man profoundly versed in any science, attack the Bible. Your third or fourth rate men of learning attain distinction in this field. An anti-Bible writer or lecturer always has been promoted to that high eminence from the school-room, or the editorial sanctum of an unsuccessful newspaper; or his patients have not sufficiently appreciated his physic, or he has failed in getting a patent-right for his wonderful perpetual motion, or possibly he has enlarged his practical knowledge of science in the laboratory of some Western College, and had his head turned by being asked to hear the mathematical recitations during the sickness of some professor. But to hear of men like Galileo, Kepler, Boyle, Newton, and Leibnitz, or of Lyell, Mantell, Herschell, Agassiz, Hitchcock, Balbo, Nichol, or Rosse, heading an attack upon Christianity, would be an unprecedented phenomenon. Such men are profoundly impressed with the thorough agreement between the facts of nature rightly observed, and the declarations of the Bible rightly interpreted.

Nevertheless, the other class being both the most numerous and the most noisy, make up by perseverance for their deficiency of information, and counterbalance their ignorance by their assurance. Such writers, assuming that they have outstripped all the philosophers of former days, will tell you how foolishly David and Kepler, and Bacon and Newton, and Herschell dreamed of the heavens declaring the glory of the Lord, and the firmament showing his handy work; "while at the present time, and for minds properly familiarized with true astronomical philosophy, the heavens display no other powers than those of natural laws, and no other glory than that of Hipparchus, of Kepler, of Newton, and of all who have helped to discover them." Theology belongs only to the infancy of the human intellect; metaphysical philosophy is the amusement of youth; but the full grown man has learned to relinquish both religion and reason, and comes to the "positive state of science in which the human mind, acknowledging the impossibility of obtaining absolute knowledge, abandons the search after the origin and destination of the universe, and the knowledge of the secret causes of phenomena." The crown of modern science is ultimately to be placed upon the brow of Atheism; but long before that eagerly-desired achievement, the old Bible theology is to be buried beyond the possibility of a resurrection, under mountains of natural laws, and monuments of scientific discovery. These assertions, confidently made, and perseveringly reiterated in the ears of ungodly men ignorant of the facts, of impetuous youths eager to throw off the restraints of religion, of christians weak in the faith, and even poured into the unsuspecting mind of childhood, produce the most painful, and often fatal results; and it becomes the imperative duty of the bishops of the Church of Christ not to allow them to pass unchallenged, but to convince the gainsayers, and stop the mouths of these unruly and vain talkers; or, if that be not possible, to make their folly manifest to all men. The weapons for such a service are well tried and abundant, and the difficulty lies only in making a proper selection.

At first view, the extinction of religion by science seems very unlikely. It is as unlikely that any thing that an infidel says about religion should be true, as that a blind man should describe the sun correctly. Did you ever know one who could quote three verses of scripture correctly, or even read a chapter accurately and attentively, with the book before him? I shall show you presently that learned infidels make the grossest blunders respecting the plainest scripture records of scientific facts. It is very unlikely that infidels, who lay no claim to prophetic inspiration, should make any predictions about religion more reliable than those they have been telling so abundantly for two hundred years past, respecting the immediate overthrow of Christianity and the Bible; which, nevertheless, has been going on conquering new kingdoms every year, its missionaries outstripping scientific ardor in exploring the mysteries of African Geography, honorably receiving the prizes which the infidel Volney instituted for philological proficiency, and printing Bibles from Voltaire's printing-press. And it is very unlikely that these physical sciences, so long worshipers in the temple of God, should now become impious: as unlikely as that John Angel James, or D'Aubigne, or Buchanan, or Hodge, or Barnes should now, in their old days, renounce the Bible, and blaspheme God. What! Astronomy, and Geology, and Zoology, and Botany, and Ethnography, that were suckled at the breast of the Bible, raise their hands against the mother that bore them! Incredible! These young sciences made an early profession of religion; taught sabbath-school in the days of Job, Zophar, and Elihu; wrote sacred poetry, and were licensed to preach, in the days of Solomon; poured forth prophetic raptures in the days of Uzziah, Jotham, Ahaz, and Hezekiah; wrote volumes on the politics of Christianity in Babylon, and painted glorious visions of the victories of the Lamb of God, and dazzling views of the landscapes of paradise restored in Patmos; employed the gigantic intellect of Newton, the elegant pen of Paley, the eloquence of Chalmers, Herschell's heaven-piercing eye, and Miller's muscular arm, to guard the outer courts of the sanctuary, while they sung sublime anthems to the music of David's harp within; and have they now, after such a life of devotion, relinquished all these sublimities and beatitudes, taken lodgings in the stye, and renounced their faith in God, and hope of heaven, for the infidel maxim, "Let us eat and drink, for to-morrow we die"? God forbid!

No rational man will be easily convinced of the truth of such an unlikely accusation. Least of all will he believe it, on the say-so of men of whom he knows little, save that they are not much acquainted with either religion or the sciences. I, for one, mean to enquire for the truth from reliable informants. The object of this and the following Tracts is to interrogate these physical sciences themselves whether they are really becoming skeptical of the being of the Living God, and hostile to Holy Scripture; or whether they have lately given any utterances which would give occasion to such a suspicion. I do not propose, of course, to attempt giving an outline of Astronomy, Geology, Zoology, Ethnography, &c., in the limits of this or subsequent Tracts; but confining our attention to Astronomy, I shall assume that my readers are possessed of such a knowledge of the principles of that science as our common schools afford every intelligent youth—or, should their early education be defective in this respect, I entreat them to do themselves the justice, and enjoy the high gratification, of perusing some of the lucid and interesting popular works on the subject to be found in every bookstore, or in our public libraries*—and proceed to select from the

---

* *Kendall's Uranography and Atlas of the Heavens* is a cheap and useful manual. Sir John Herschell's *Outlines of Astronomy* is a larger and more scientific work. Somerville's *Connection of the Physical Sciences* displays the wide range of modern discovery in Astronomy, and its connected sciences. The attractive works of the Christian Philosopher, Thos. Dick, L.L. D., *The Siderial Heavens, The Solar System*, and *Celestial Scenery*, will ever be as popular as they are perspicuous and original. The condensed, lucid, frigid *Cosmos* of the encyclopediac Humboldt, will interest those who understand the technology of the science. The discoveries of Lord Rosse's magnificent telescopes are described with a simple, majestic eloquence not unworthy of the grandeur of the theme, by J. P. Nicholl, L.L. D., in *Contemplations on the Solar System*, and the

vast mass of modern discoveries those which have a bearing upon the question, *Is the progress of astronomical discovery hostile, or favorable, to natural and revealed religion?*

The progress of astronomical science has swept away the alleged facts on which all systems of Atheism have been based.

1. *It has refuted the fundamental dogma of Atheism, that the universe is infinite, and therefore self-existent.* The assertion is confidently made by Atheists and Pantheists, that the universe has no boundaries; not merely none which we can see, but that it actually fills all immensity: suns succeeding suns, and firmament clustering beyond firmament, throughout infinite space.

It is indispensable for the Atheist not only to assert, but to prove this to be the fact, if he would convince himself, or any other person, that the universe had no Creator, but exists by the necessity of its own nature; for that which exists by the necessity of its own nature, must exist in all time, and in every place. No reason can be given why self-existent suns, planets, and moons, should exist in any one portion of space, and not exist in any other similar portion of space. For if such a reason could be given, that reason must show a cause for their existence in the one place, and their non-existence in another; and that cause must have existed before the universe, and must have been a cause sufficient to produce the effect. This sufficient cause includes ability to produce, wisdom to arrange, and force to put in motion all the powers of the universe: qualities which reside only in an intelligent being. This is the cause which the Bible asserts when it says, "In the beginning GOD created the heavens and the earth," and which Atheists deny when they assert that "the universe is eternal and infinite."

Now, this fundamental article of the creed of infidels is utterly incapable of proof. If the fact were really so, they never could prove it. They acknowledge no revelation from an infinite understanding, but found their belief on the knowledge of a number of finite and ignorant beings. Before they are competent to pronounce upon the extent of the universe, they must explore it thoroughly; which, when they shall have done, they will have demonstrated that it has boundaries, seeing they have discovered them;

Architecture of the Heavens. The Annual of Scientific Discovery, as its name imports, records the latest discoveries.

but, if they have not thoroughly explored the universe, they can not say that it is infinite, because they do not know. The very utmost, then, which could possibly be asserted on the matter would be, not that the universe has no boundaries, but that man has never reached them. As in the case of ocean soundings, if we cannot find bottom, we are not therefore to conclude that there is none, but that our line is not long enough, or our lead not heavy enough to reach it.

For, it were a logical absurdity to say, that the whole is greater than the sum of its parts—that any number of finite parts could compose an infinite universe. Each sun or planet is a finite object, and any possible number of them can be counted in a sufficient time. It is impossible that any number can be infinite; for we are not using the word infinite here in the loose sense in which it is used by mathematicians, when they speak of an infinite series; that is, a series which, though it has no end, has a beginning; but in the strict sense of something having neither beginning nor end. A beginning of the universe, either in space or time, is the very thing the Atheist denies.

While reason thus enables us to show this dogma of the infinity of the universe to be theoretically improbable, and logically irrational, science has lately taken a more decisive step, and demonstrated it to be actually false. The universe has boundaries, and we have seen them. The proof is simple, and easily demonstrable, since the discovery that nebulæ are clusters of stars. That broad band of luminous cloud which stretches across the heaven, called the Milky Way, consists of millions of stars, so small and distant that we cannot see the individual stars, and so numerous that we cannot help seeing the light of the mass: just as you see the outline of the forest at a distance, but are unable to distinguish the individual trees. Besides this mass of stars to which our solar system belongs, there are thousands of smaller similar clouds in various parts of the heavens, which have successively been shown to consist of multitudes of stars. But all around these star-clouds the clear blue sky is discovered by the naked eye.

Now, it is easy to perceive, that if all the regions of infinite space were filled either with self-luminous suns, or planets capable of reflecting light, or comets of gaseous consistency, at such distances as the Milky Way, or any other star-cloud demonstrates to be safe and practicable, we should see no blue sky at all; but the whole vault of heaven would present that whitish light resulting from the mingling of the rays of multitudes of stars, planets, and comets, which the Milky Way does actually exhibit. No matter how small or how distant these stars, *if they were only infinitely numerous*, it is impossible that there could be any point in the heavens unilluminated by their rays, even although the stars themselves were invisible to our eyes, or even to our telescopes. The whole heaven would be one vast Milky Way.

Though the telescope discovers multitudes of stars where the naked eye sees none, yet they are, in far the greater number of instances, "*seen projected on a perfectly dark heaven, without any appearance of intermixed nebulosity.*"* And even through the Milky Way, and the other nebulæ, the telescope penetrates, through "*intervals absolutely dark, and completely void of any star, of the smallest telescopic magnitude.*"† It may assist us to understand the full import of this declaration, to remember that Lord Rosse's large telescope clearly defines any object on the moon's surface as large as the Custom House. Its power of penetrating space surpasses our power of imagination, but is represented by saying, that light, which flashes from San Francisco to London quicker than you can close your eye and open it again, requires *millions of years* to travel to our earth from the most distant star-cloud discoverable by this telescope.‡ If a galaxy like this of ours existed any where within this amazing distance, that telescope would discover its existence. It has, in fact, augmented the universe visible to us, 125,000,000 times, and thus made us feel that not merely this world, which constitutes our earthly all, and yon glorious sun, which shines upon it, but all the host of heaven's suns, and planets, and moons, and firmaments, which our unaided eyes behold, are but as a handful of the sand of the ocean shore, compared with the immensity of the universe. But ever, and along with this, it has shown us the ocean as well as the shore, and revealed boundless regions of darkness and solitude stretching around and far away beyond these islands of existence. The telescope, then, enlarges and confirms our views of the extent of the unoccupied portions of space.

If there were only one dark point of the heavens no larger than

---

* Herschell's Outlines, ch. xvii., ₴ 887.   † Cosmos, iii. 197.
‡ Architecture of the Heavens, 9th ed., p. 180.

the apparent magnitude of the smallest star, this one unoccupied space would sufficiently disprove the infinity of the universe, inasmuch as there would be a portion of space of boundless length, and of a diameter not less than the diameter of the earth's orbit, say 190,000,000 miles, in which stars might exist, as they do in its borders, but yet do not. But the argument becomes utterly overwhelming, when the attempt is made to calculate the proportion of space occupied by the stars to that left unoccupied. Whether we take Herschell's computation, that the nebulæ cover one 270th part of the superficies of the visible heaven,* or Struve's supposition of the existence of a star subtending no measurable angle, in every part of the visible sky as large as the surface of the moon, the vast disproportion of the universe to the space in which it is placed, forces itself upon our notice. For, upon the largest of these computations, the proportion of existence to empty space is mathematically proved to be not greater than as the cube of 1 to the cube of 269; that is to say, there is room for 19,395,109 such universes as this of ours in that small part of infinite space open to the view of Herschell's telescopes. But when we come to consider the vastness of these regions of darkness, over which no light has traveled for twenty millions of years, and remember also that astronomers have looked clear through the nebulæ, and find that they bear no more cubical proportion to the infinite darkness behind them than the sparks of a chimney do to the extent of the sky against which they seem projected, so far from imagining the universe to be infinite, we stand confounded at its relative insignificance, and are convinced that it bears no more proportion to infinite space than a fishing-boat does to the Atlantic Ocean.

There is no possible evasion of this great fact, by any contradictory hypothesis. It cannot be objected "that stars may exist at infinite distances, whose light has not yet reached the limits of our universe." If they do, they did not exist from eternity, for there is no possible distance over which light could not have traveled, during eternal duration. But their eternal existence is the very thing which the Atheist is concerned to prove. Grant that infinite space is filled with worlds *which had a beginning*, and their necessary existence instantly falls, and we are compelled to seek for a cause of their beginning of existence: that is to say, a Creator.

---

* Cosmos, iv. 292.

Nor will it answer the purpose to say, "that for any thing we know to the contrary, these dark regions may be filled with dark stars."

If the fact were so, it is equally fatal to the dogma of self-existence. Some stars shine: others are dark. Why so? Wherefore this difference? Variety is an effect, and demands a prior cause. Were there only two stars in the sky, or two substances on the earth, and those unlike in any particular, that plurality and that variety would prove that they could not be infinite or self-existent, but dependent upon some cause for their existence, and their various forms.

But we do know many things contrary to the notion that the dark regions of infinite space may be full of dark stars. Light is not the only indication of the presence of a star. The attraction of gravity, which is wholly independent of light, is a proof quite as certain and satisfactory to the astronomer. The presence of stars and planets too faint to be discovered by the naked eye, and of one, the planet Neptune,* as far distant from the planet disturbed by its attraction as the earth is from the sun, was ascertained, and its place pointed out to a degree, by Adams and Leverrier, *before it was seen*. If the dark interplanetary spaces, then, were full of dark attracting bodies, the perturbations of the other planets would discover their existence. So the presence of some invisible stars at much greater distances from their visible associates has been discovered by Bessel,† and it is quite possible that a dark firmament may yet be discovered, containing as great a number of dark stars as we now behold of luminaries: another group of islets in the ocean of infinite space. But the very facts which will prove their existence will disprove their infinity; for we can know their presence only by their perturbation of the proper motions of the visible stars; but if infinite space were full of dark bodies, the visible stars would have no room to move at all. It is easily demonstrable, that if infinite space were filled with dark stars, the equilibrium and coherence of our galaxy, and of all other clusters of stars, would be destroyed. The existence of nebulæ and clusters, and the revolutions of the binary stars, are conclusive proof that the dark parts of infinite space are not full of dark attracting bodies.

---

* Nicholl's Contemplations on the Solar System, xxx.
† Cosmos, iii. 253.

Nor can the Atheist here raise his usual argument from unknown facts, and say that, "far beyond the range of our most powerful telescopes, a boundless expanse of firmaments may exist." It concerns not our present argument whether such exist or not. Whatsoever discoveries may be made to eternity, of firmaments, ten thousand times ten thousand times larger than we now behold, *they can never bear the smallest proportion to the infinite space in which they exist.* Beyond these islets will extend gulfs and oceans immeasurable. Our argument, however, has no concern with the unknown possible, but with the actual fact—visible to the naked eye, and confirmed by the telescope—that there is a portion of space in which millions of universes such as this might exist with safety, yet they do not. Worlds, therefore, do not exist by the necessity of their own nature, wherever there is room for them, but must have had some pre-existent, external, and supernatural cause of their existence in this place and not in other places. This implies choice—will—God.

The physical refutation of the self-existence of the universe is completed by the discovery, that all the orbs of heaven, as well as the earth, are in motion, and that an orderly and regulated motion.* The fact need not be illustrated, for it is not denied. The consequence is inevitable. That which is self-existent must be unchangeable: for change is an effect, and demands a cause; and the cause must exist before the effect, and produce it. Whatsoever is changeable, then, is a product of a prior cause, and so not self-existent. But the universe is changeable, for it is in motion, which is a change of place; therefore, the universe is not self-existent, but the product of a prior cause.

No mechanical law is a sufficient cause for this motion. To allege that a power of orderly, regulated motion—and there is no other sort of motion in heaven or earth—is an inherent property of matter, is simply to insult our common sense, and overturn the foundation of all reason. For we have no knowledge of matter, and can have none, more certain than we have of the constitution of our own minds, which requires us to trace up every change among material objects to *the energy and will of a person* capable of planning and effecting the change. To refer us to the law of gravity is not to give us a *cause* for the motions of the heavenly bodies, but

---

* Herschell's Outlines, ch. xvi.

only a *name*; for law is only *a rule of action*. We demand a lawgiver—an agent—a *force*, capable of producing effects. When the law of projectiles makes a cannon ball, and projects it, we will believe that the law of gravity made the worlds, and moves them.

"Descending within the mind's interior chambers, I find no conviction so sure of the existence of an external world, as is my belief in the reality of *power*—of something that sustains succession, and causes order. Again, then, whence this idea, and what is it? What this attribute with which I endow material laws, and raise them into *forces?* Now, in my apprehension, the strictest scrutiny cannot obtain for these inquiries any reply save one: we *primarily* connect the idea of *power* with no change or movement, except an act or determination of the FREE WILL; but from such acts, that idea is inseparable. If, therefore, in order to explain the progress of material things, we require the agency of *efficient causes*, is not this a direct and solemn recognition—through all form and transiency—of the necessity of an *ever present creative power:* a power requisite and necessary to uphold—to renew the universe every moment—or, rather, to prolong creation by the persistence of the creative act? And, in very truth, startling though it be, such is the only and ultimate scientific idea of the Divine Omnipresence. Law is not even the Almighty's minister; the order of the material world, however close and firm, is not merely the Almighty's ordinance. The *forces*, if so we name them, which express that order, are not powers which he has evolved from the silences, and to whose guardianship he has committed all things, so that He himself might repose. No! above, below, around, *there* is God: there his universal presence, speaking to finite creatures, in finite forms, a language which only the living heart can understand. In the rain and the sunshine; in the soft zephyrs; in the cloud, the torrent, and the thunder; in the bursting blossom, and the fading branch; in the revolving season, and the rolling star: there is the Infinite Essence, and the mystic development of HIS WILL." *

2. *Scientific Astronomy inexorably demolishes the Atheistic scheme for the arrangement of the Solar System by accident, commonly known as Buffon's cosmogony.*

"Buffon supposes that the force of a comet falling obliquely on the sun has projected to a distance a torrent of the matter of which

---

* Nicholl's Architecture of the Heavens, 9th ed., 272.

it is composed, as a stone thrown into a basin causes the water which it contains to splash out. This torrent of matter, in a state of fusion, has broken into several parts, which have been arrested at different distances from the sun, according to their density, or the impetus they received. They then united in spheres, by the effect of motion of rotation, and condensing by cold, have become opaque and solid planets and satellites.*"

This formation of worlds by accident, it is true, gave no reason for the form of their orbits, for their rotation on their axes, in one direction, and that, too, the direction of their motion, nor for several other matters, of which infidels make little account, but about which plain men like to ask, namely: Where did the sun come from? What melted it down into a fluid state, fit to be splashed about? Where did the comet come from? And who threw it with so correct an aim through infinite space as exactly to hit the sun *in an oblique direction.* Creation, it seems, was nearly missed, after all. This chaotic theory never gained much respect from men of science, though its simplicity speedily opened its way among the vulgar, and it has ever been a favorite with the most ignorant class of infidels, numbering thousands of warm advocates, even at the present day.

It was thought to be very much corroborated by the discovery of the asteroids, and their supposed formation by the explosion of a larger body. There is a certain proportion observed in the distances of the orbits of the planets from each other—a breadth of guage, as it were, on the celestial railroad. But there was the breadth of a track between the orbits of Mars and Jupiter on which no train ran, and this vacancy excited the curiosity of astronomers. In the first seven years of this century, three very small planets were discovered, running near this track; and Dr. Olbers, the discoverer of Pallas, finding that they were nearly in the same track, and sometimes crossed each other, and that they were diminutively small—bearing about the same proportion to a regular planet which a hand-car does to a freight train—imagined that they were formed by the explosion of a large planet: that the boiler of the large locomotive had burst, the fragments had all lighted upon the track again, in the shape of hand-cars, and the hand-cars had magnanimously resolved to keep running, and do the business of the

---

* Pontecoulant in System of the World, p. 70.

line; and that, as there must have been material enough in the original planet to make some thousands of them, more would be discovered by watching two depots, at the crossings of the tracks, in the constellations Virgo and the Whale, where they must all pass. In fact, he did himself find another, very near one of these nodes; and quite lately, thirty-eight others have been found; and astronomers now expect to hear of one or two more every year. At first sight, his theory seemed strengthened by every new discovery. It is true, reflecting men could not help wondering at such a marvellously regular explosion as would produce beautiful little orderly planets, going so regularly and curiously too, and all by accident. They never heard of the blowing up of a palace producing cottages, or the explosion of a steamboat throwing off the hurricane deck in the shape of whaleboats, or the bursting of a locomotive producing model engines, or even hand-cars. However, as the theory removed God out of sight it was generally accepted, and freely used by infidels, to show that the world had no need of a creator.

But astronomers saw, that as each new asteroid had a track of its own, and ran to a different terminus, and the roads in which they ran were of different guages and grades—one little asteroid, Pallas, running up and down a track inclined 35 degrees, just as speedily as the others—every new discovery increased the difficulty of accounting for their origin by explosion. But the discovery of the planet Hygeia, at a vast distance from the others, utterly overturned the explosion theory. Loomis says:

"The difficulties in the way of our regarding these small planets as fragments of a single body, were well nigh insuperable before the discovery of Hygeia. This last discovery has probably given the death blow to the theory of Olbers. The orbit of Hygeia completely encloses the orbits of several of the asteroids, its perihilion distance—that is, its least distance from the sun—exceeding the aphelion—or greatest distance—of Flora by *twenty-five millions of miles. No change of position of the orbits could, therefore, bring these orbits to a coincidence.*"

The matter has been finally settled by the greatest of modern mathematicians, Leverrier, who has subjected the eccentricities, distances, and inclinations of the orbits of the asteroids to a mathematical investigation, the result of which is as follows:

---

* Progress of Astronomy, 70.

"In the present state of things, these eccentricities and these inclinations are totally incompatible with Olber's hypothesis, which supposed that the small planets—some of which were discovered even in his day—were produced from the wreck of a larger star, which had exploded. The forces necessary to launch the fragments of a given body in such different routes (whose existence we should be obliged to suppose), would be of such an improbable intensity, that the most limited mathematical knowledge could not but see its absurdity." He concludes the memoir by advancing four propositions, "which forever annihilate Olber's hypothesis." *

The Buffonian theory, thus deprived of the only apparently analogous fact by which it was supported, was restored to its birthplace, in the regions of foggy hypothesis. But science, indignant that such nonsense should ever have dared to assume her livery, will not allow it to linger even among the shades. Those irregular world-breaking comets, which, while their density was unknown, formed such convenient sledge-hammers for the Atheist's world-factory, have been literally dissipated into smoke by powerful telescopes. In fact, a respectable wreath of smoke is quite a substantial being compared with the densest of the comets.

"The smallest comets, such as are visible only in telescopes, or with difficulty by the naked eye, and which are by far the most numerous, offer very frequently no appearance of a tail, and appear only as round or somewhat oval vaporous masses, more dense towards the center, where, however, they appear to have no distinct nucleus, or any thing which seems entitled to be considered a solid body. Stars of the smallest magnitude remain distinctly visible, though covered by what appears to be the densest portion of their surface; although the same stars would be completely obliterated by a moderate fog extending only a few yards from the surface of the earth. And since it is an observed fact, that even those larger comets, which have presented the appearance of a nucleus, have yet exhibited no phases, though we cannot doubt that they shine by the reflected solar light, it follows that even these can only be regarded *as great masses of thin vapor*, susceptible of being penetrated through their whole substance by the sunbeams, and reflecting them alike from their interior parts and from their surfaces.

---

* Memoir to the French Academy, by M. Leverrier; from The Annual of Scientific Discovery, for 1855, p. 376.

Nor will any one regard this explanation as forced, or feel disposed to resort to a phosphorescent quality in the comet itself, to account for the phenomena in question, when we consider (what will hereafter be shown) the enormous magnitude of the space thus illuminated, and the extremely small mass which there is ground to attribute to these bodies. It will then be evident that the most unsubstantial clouds which float in the highest regions of our atmosphere, and seem at sunset to be drenched in light, and to glow throughout their whole depth, as if in actual ignition, without any shadow or dark side, *must be looked upon as dense and massy bodies, compared with the filmy and all but spiritual texture of a comet.*" *

3. *The progress of Astronomical discovery has utterly refuted the notion of creation by natural law, known as the Development Theory, or the Nebular Hypothesis.*

Scientific infidels knew that there was too much order and regularity in the motions of the planets to allow any rational mind to ascribe these motions to accident, according to Buffon's notion. They saw that these movements must be regulated by law. La Place, an eminent mathematician, saw that there are at least five great regularities pervading the system, for which Buffon's theory gave no reason:

1. The planets all move in elliptical orbits, nearly circular. They might, on the contrary, have been as elongated as those of comets.

2. They revolve in orbits nearly in the plane of the sun's equator. They might have revolved in orbits inclined to it at any angle, or even in the plane of his poles.

3. They revolve around the sun all in the same direction, which is the direction of his rotation on his axis.

4. They rotate on their axes, also, so far as known, in the same direction.

5. The satellites (with the exception of those of Uranus) revolve around their primary planets, and also rotate on their axes, in the same normal direction.

It was evident, even to the believers in chance, that so many regularities were not produced by accident. La Place found, by computing the chances by the formula of probabilities, that the chances were two millions to one against these regularities happen-

---

* Herschell's Outlines of Astronomy, p. 553, ed. of 1853.

ing by chance, *and four millions to one in favor of these motions having a common origin.* The grand phenomenon being a motion of rotation in the whole system, of which the rotation of the sun is the central part, he thought if he could account for this, he could explain all the rest.

He set out by supposing that the sun and planets originally existed as a vast cloud of gaseous matter, intensely heated—a vast fire mist—placed in a region of space much cooler, and that this cloud, by gradual cooling, and the pressure of its parts, settled down into solid forms. It was supposed that some portions of this cloud would begin to cool sooner than others, and so become solid sooner, and that the hot gas, rushing to the solid part, would form a vortex, which would set the cloud in motion around its center. As the speed of its rotation would increase, and the outside condense and grow solid before the inside, the cloud would whirl off the rings of solid matter, which would keep revolving in the same orbits in which they were cast off, and would revolve faster and faster as they grew cooler and more solid, till they broke up, by the force of their velocity, into smaller pieces; which fragments, in their turn, repeated the process, until the present number of planets and their satellites was produced.

This theory differs from Buffon's much as a low pressure engine, deriving most of its power from the condenser, differs from one of high pressure. La Place does not explode the boiler to make his planets, but merely runs his train so fast as to break an axle every now and then, when the wheel runs off with the velocity it had got, and keeps its track as well as if it had an engineer to guide it, grows into a little locomotive by dint of running, and after a while breaks an axle too,—breaking is a hereditary failing of these suns and planets that had no God to make them—and the wheels thus thrown off supply it with moons and rings, like Saturn's. The illustration is not nearly so absurd as the theory, inasmuch as a locomotive is an incomparably less complicated contrivance than a planet. However, the nonsense was cradled in the halls of philosophy in the manner following.

Herschell had discovered numbers of nebulæ, or luminous clouds, in the distant heavens, shining with a distinct light, but which, with the highest magnifying power he could apply, presented no trace of stars. Some nebulæ, it is true, his largest telescope resolved, like our own Milky Way, into beds of distinct stars; but there were others—for instance, one in the belt of Orion—visible to the naked eye as a cloud, but which his forty feet telescope only displayed as a larger cloud, without any shape of stars. Now, reasoning upon the matter, he found that if these nebulæ were composed of stars as large as those distinctly visible, they must be immensely distant to be indistinguishable by his telescope, and exceedingly numerous and close together to give a cloud of light visible to the naked eye. In fact, the suns of those firmaments must be so close to each other as to present a blaze of glory, and complexities of revolution inconceivable to the dwellers on earth. But as this daring idea seemed incredible, even to his giant mind, he thought the appearance of these nebulæ might be more rationally accounted for by supposing that they were not stars at all, but simply clouds of gaseous matter, like the matter of comets, from which he supposed that stars were formed by a long process of condensation and solidification. He thought this theory was favored by the fact, that nebulæ are generally seen in those portions of the heavens that are not thickly strewn with stars; and also by the various forms of these clouds. Some were merely loose clouds, without any definite form; others seemed gathering towards the center. In some, of a roundish, or oval form, the central mass seemed well defined. In a few, the process seemed nearly complete, a bright star shining in the midst of a faint nebulous halo. Here, then, it was said, we see the whole progress of the growth of stars: their development from the gaseous nebulous fluid into solid, brilliant suns. La Place accepted Herschell's discoveries as conclusive proof of the truth of his theory, and it was generally accepted by the scientific world. Oddly enough, nobody seems to have noticed that those appearances of *condensation toward the centre*, which seemed to Herschell so strongly in favor of his theory of the nebulous fluid, were diametrically opposed to La Place's requirements of *condensation at the circumference;* and these two contradictory notions were supposed to support each other, and to furnish a solid basis for the Development Hypothesis.

This theory, as stated by Herschell, and expounded by Nicholl, Dick, and other Christian writers, is not necessarily Atheistical. On the contrary, they allege that it furnishes us with greater evidences of the power of God, and gives us higher ideas of his wisdom, to suppose a system of creation by development, under natural law, than by a direct exercise of his will. Undoubtedly, had God so pleased, he could somehow have made suns from Fire Mists, but not according to La Place's plan, as we shall presently see. Or he could have caused firmaments to grow from seeds, as forests do, according to some sublime and uniform law of such celestial vegetation. In such a case, we should have had the same kind of evidence of his being, power, wisdom, and goodness, in creation by natural law, which we now have from his providence by natural law, when he sends us rain from heaven, and fruitful seasons; and so much greater an amount of it, as the heavens are greater than the earth. The first creation of primeval elements demands a creator, and the contrivance of the law of development a contriver; and the force, either of gravity, chemical attraction, or any other, by which it operates, must proceed from an agent. The Development Theory, then, cannot exist without God.

However, as it seems to remove him a few steps from his works, and as all ungodly men desire his absence, Atheists and Pantheists of all kinds have earnestly laid hold of it as the foundation of their system of the development of the universe from eternal, self-existent matter, without an intelligent creator. It is at this moment, with thousands, the substitute for the Living God.

Like most errors, this is the product of ignorance. Herschell, with his large telescope, did not see well enough the objects which he pronounced to be clouds of nebulous fluid. Lord Rosse has seen them better, with his larger telescope, and these clouds are hosts of very small and distant stars, clearly projected against the dark sky.* That nebula in Orion, which was considered the test specimen, has been resolved, and the whole nebular hypothesis is dissipated. Says Sir David Brewster, "It was certainly a rash generalization to maintain, that nebulæ differed from clusters of stars, because existing telescopes could not resolve them. The very first application of Lord Rosse's telescope to the heavens overturned the hypothesis; and with such unequivocal facts as that instrument has brought to light, we regard it as a most unwarrantable assumption to suppose, that there are in the heavenly spaces any masses of matter different from solid bodies composing planetary systems."* Nichol, formerly an eloquent supporter of the nebular hypothesis, thus expresses the opinion of the scientific world:

"It has been asked, Are not many such masses in the heavens

---

* North British Review, No. III, p. 477.

still irresolvable, even by the great mirrors of Parsonstown? It cannot, indeed, be doubted, that nebulæ defying the most energetic of these instruments, exist in numbers in the sky; but, nevertheless, *every shred of that evidence which induced us to accept as a reality accumulations in the heavens of matter not stellar, is for ever and hopelessly destroyed.* The logical state of the question is simply this: On the ground of a certain characteristic, Herschell felt disposed to divide unresolved nebulæ into two classes. He declined to believe one class to be stellar, because that conclusion would have constrained his acceptance of what seemed opposed by all analogy, viz., the existence of aggregations of stars in a state of compression to which he had found nothing even approximately similar, in the course of his previous examination of the universe. Now, the nebula of Orion, being an eminent instance of the latter class, its decisive resolution broke down the force of the characteristic; it showed that to be *a fact*, on the presumed improbability of which the entire theory depended." † "The effects of the removal of the nebular theory on our views of the general structure of the heavens, I have explained in another work; and I refer to it here only in its bearings on La Place's celebrated theory of the origin of our solar system. *The basis of that theory, considering it as a matter of observation, is obviously destroyed. No such fact as the condensing of nebulous matter into organized stars, can now be seen in the heavens;* so that La Place's fundamental tenet, that the sun originated in the gradual condensing of a gaseous or vaporous mass, must henceforth be regarded as a pure hypothesis.‡"

It never was any thing more than pure hypothesis—a mere notion. Granting to this theory all the benefit of Herschell's supposed discovery, it never could become any thing more than a theory, utterly incapable of proof as a fact; for it is evident that no man could possibly ascertain the nature of clouds thousands of millions of miles distant, or know whether they were hot or cold, or whether they were growing hotter or colder. It was not pretended that anybody ever did see them scaling off into rings, and the rings

---

* Cosmos, IV, p. 304. Herschell's Outlines, xvii, ₴ 870. Annual of Scientific Discovery, for 1853, p. 363.
† Nicholl's Architecture of the Heavens, 9th ed. p. 145.
‡ Nicholl's Solar System, 3d ed., p. 9.

breaking up into planets and moons, nor was it likely anybody ever would see such a phenomenon. Its author merely put it forth as a probable theory, and no scientific man ever pretended to demonstrate it as a discovered fact. Among scientific astronomers it was *merely a notion.*

It was always an unsatisfactory notion. It made us no wiser about the origin of things. It gave no answer to the all-important questions, Where did the gaseous matter come from? How did it get to be so hot, while the space around it was so cold? Whence came the fire that heated it? Did it contain within itself all the principles of things now found in the resulting planets, such as attraction, repulsion, chemical affinity, animal and vegetable life, and intellect? If so, how came they there? If not, where did they come from?

Besides, it was an impracticable notion, contrary to the known principles of mechanics. The great requirement of the whole system—the power to work the engine—the motion of rotation upon which the whole world-turning business depends—never could, by any possibility, be raised, either by La Place's, or any other mechanical plan. If he had the moving power, no doubt he could scatter off pieces of matter from his rotating sun, as drops of water are scattered from a rotating grindstone; but his theory is a plan to make the grindstone turn itself, and is precisely of the same value as any of the hundreds of ingenious schemes for a perpetual motion, whose inventors have dreamed of creating power by machinery, in defiance of the fundamental law of mechanics, that "Action and reaction are equal." The power is to be raised by making his gas cool at one part of the surface faster than at another, and so make a vortex around that spot, which would set the whole revolving. No conceivable reason can be assigned why it should begin to cool at one place of the surface faster than another; or, indeed, why, if eternally hot, it ever should begin to cool at all. But, to make the required vortex for the rotation of the mass, it should not begin to cool at any part of the surface, but near the middle, where, as every engine driver who ever saw a condenser, and every woman who has cooled a dish of mush, knows, it could not begin to cool at all; and so no motion could be produced. This is so well known in the machine shops and dockyards, that it is very rare to find an intelligent millwright or machinist acknowledge the theory.

Even were the rotation and the cooling process to take place, as is supposed, no such results would proceed from these combined operations as the case requires; for, according to the theory, as the cooling and contracting rings revolve in the verge of a vortex of fluid less dense than themselves, one of these two results must take place: either, as is most probable, from their exceeding tenuity, the rings will break at once into fragments, when, instead of flying outwards, they will sink towards the center, and, as long as they are heavier than the surrounding fluid, *they will stay there;* and, as the cooling goes on on the outside, so will the concentration of the heavier matter, till we have *one* great spheroid, with a solid center, liquid covering, and gaseous atmosphere. A vortex will never make, nor allow to exist beyond its center, planets heavier than the fluid of which it is composed. The other alternative, and the one which La Place selected, was the supposition that the cooling and contracting rings did not at first break up into pieces, but retained their continuity; but, contrary to all experience and reason, he supposed that these cooling rings kept contracting, and widening out from the heated mass, at the same time. The only fluid planetary rings which we can examine—those of Saturn— have been closing in on the planet since the days of Huygens, and, in a dozen years or so, will be united with the body of the planet;* and every boy who has seen a blacksmith hoop a cart-wheel, has learned the principle that a heated ring contracts as it cools, and in doing so presses in upon the mass around which it clings. But, according to this Nebular Notion, the Fire Mist keeps cooling and shrinking up, while the rings, of the very same heat and material, keep cooling faster, and widening out from it: a piece of schismatical behavior without a parallel among solids or fluids, either in heaven or earth, or under the earth.

Plateau's experiment of making a globule of oil rotate and disperse into drops, by centrifugal force communicated by clockwork, while floating in a mixture of alcohol and water, *all of the same density*, is no illustration of the Nebular Theory, the essential condition of which is, that the cooling contracting rings be of a *different density* from the rest of the mass. Their divergence from the more fluid portion is supposed to arise from their growing heavier

---

* Bond, of Cambridge, U. S., quoted by Sir David Brewster, in More Worlds than One, 35.

as they cool, and therefore capable of a greater centrifugal force; in consequence of which, they rotate so much faster than the fluid from which they derived their motion, that finally they fly out of it. The only other instance of such a performance, which I can remember, is that of the Yankee's mill-wheel, which traveled three times as fast as the stream which drove it, while the latter was swift enough to make the saw-logs fly up out of the water, merely by the force of the current.

This Nebular Notion was always as contrary to Astronomical facts, as to mechanical principles. The orbits of the comets being inclined at all angles to the sun's equator, are often out of the plane of his rotation, and so in the way of the theory. The moons of Uranus revolve in a direction contrary to all the other bodies, and fly right into the face of the theory. According to the nebular theory, the outer planets first cast off from the sun, ought to be lighter than those nearer him, as these had longer pressing near the middle of the mass; and the sun himself, having been pressed by the weight of all the rest of the system, should be the densest body of the whole. And the author of the Vestiges of Creation, in expounding the theory, manufactures a set of facts to suit it, and tells his readers that the planets exhibit a progressive diminution in density from the one nearest the sun to that which is most distant. Our solar system could not have lasted thirty years had that been the case. The Earth, Venus, and Mars, are nearly of the same density. Uranus is more dense than Saturn, which is nearer the Sun. Neptune is more dense than either. The Sun, which ought to be the heaviest of all, according to the theory, is only one fourth the density of the earth. La Place himself has demonstrated that these densities and arrangements are indispensable to the stability of the system. But they are plainly contradictory to his theory of its formation.*

The palpable difference of luminosity between the Sun and the planets, which, as they are all made of the very same materials, and by the same process, according to this theory, ought to be equally self-luminous, is in itself a self-evident refutation of the Nebular Hypothesis, or of any other process of creation by mere

---

* Taking water as the unit of density, Mercury is 6.71; Venus, 5.11; Earth, 5.44; Mars, 5.21; Saturn, 0.76; Uranus, 0.97; Neptune, 1.25; the Sun, 1. 37.—COSMOS, iv., p. 447.

mechanical law. "The same power, whether natural or supernatural, which placed the Sun in the center of the six primary planets, placed Saturn in the center of the orb of his five secondary planets; and Jupiter in the center of his four secondary planets; and the Earth in the center of the Moon's orbit; and, therefore, had this cause been a blind one, *without contrivance or design*, the Sun would have been a body of the same kind with Saturn, Jupiter, and the Earth; that is, *without light or heat.* Why there is one body in our system qualified to give light and heat to all the rest, I know no reason, but because the Author of the system thought it convenient." So says the immortal Newton.*

The great expounder of modern science—Humboldt—is equally explicit in enumerating the decisive marks of choice and will in the construction of the solar system, and in contemptuously dismissing the notion of development and creation by natural law from the halls of science.

"Up to the present time, *we are ignorant, as I have already remarked, of any internal necessity—any mechanical law of nature—* which (like the beautiful law which connects the square of the periods of revolution with the cube of the major axis) represents the above named elements—the absolute magnitude of the planets, their density, flattening at the poles, velocity of rotation, and presence or absence of moons—of the order of succession of the individual planetary bodies of each group, in their dependence upon the distances. Although the planet which is nearest the sun is densest—even six or eight times denser than some of the exterior planets: Jupiter, Saturn, Uranus, and Neptune—the order of succession in the case of Venus, the Earth, and Mars, is very irregular. The absolute magnitudes do, generally, as Kepler has already observed, increase with the distances; but this does not hold good when the planets are considered individually. Mars is smaller than the Earth; Uranus smaller than Saturn; Saturn smaller than Jupiter, and succeeds immediately to a host of planets, which, on account of their smallness, are almost immeasurable. It is true, the period of rotation generally increases with the distance from the Sun; but it is in the case of Mars slower than in that of the Earth, and slower in Saturn than in Jupiter."†

"*Our knowledge of the primeval ages of the world's physical*

---

* Newton's Optics, iv. p. 438.   † Cosmos, iv. 425.

history does not extend sufficiently far to allow of our depicting the present condition of things as one of development.*"

4. *Astronomy not only exposes the folly of past cosmogonies, but demonstrates the impossibility of framing any true theory of creation, and thus refutes all future cosmogonies.*

The grand error of all cosmogonies lies in the arrogant assumption, on which every one of them must be founded, that the theorist is acquainted with all substances and all forces in the universe, and with all the modes of their operation: not only at the present period, and on this earth, but in all past ages, and in worlds in widely different and utterly unknown situations; for, if he be ignorant of any substance, or of any active force in the universe, his generalization is avowedly imperfect, and necessarily false. That unknown force must have had its influence in framing the world. Its omission, then, is fatal to the theory which neglects it. A theory of creation, for instance, which would neglect the attraction of gravitation, would be manifestly false. But there are other laws, as far reaching, whose omission must be equally fatal; for instance, the power of repulsion.

A conviction of this truth has given rise to a constant effort to simplify matters down to the level of our ignorance, by reducing all substances to one, or at most two, simple elements, and all forces to the form of one universal and irrational law; but the progress of science utterly blasts the attempt. Instead of simplifying matters, the very chemical processes undertaken with that view revealed new substances, and every year increases our knowledge of nature's variety. No scientific man now dreams of one primeval element. In the same way, astronomy, which, it was boasted, would enable us to account for all the operations of the universe, by reducing all motion to one mechanical law, has revealed to us the existence of other forces as far reaching as the attraction of gravitation, and more powerful; and substances whose nature and combinations are utterly unknown. But every cosmogony is just an attempt to simplify matters, by ignoring the existence of these unknown substances and mysterious forces; a process which science condemns, as utterly unphilosophical and absurd.

The Sun's heat, at its surface, is 300,000 times greater than at the surface of the earth; but a tenth of this amount, collected in the

---

* Cosmos, iii. 28.

focus of a lens, dissipates gold and platina in vapor. When the most vivid flames which we can produce are held up in the blaze of his rays, they disappear. If a cataract of icebergs, a mile high, and wider than the Atlantic Ocean, were launched into the Sun with the velocity of a cannon ball, the small portion of the Sun's heat expended on our earth would convert that vast mass into steam as fast as it entered his atmosphere, without cooling its surface in the least degree. "The great mystery, however, is to conceive how so enormous a conflagration (if such it be) can be kept up. Every discovery in chemical science here leaves us completely at a loss, or rather seems to remove farther the prospect of probable explanation." * Yet, the Sun is the nearest of the fixed stars, and by far the best known, and most nearly related to us. In fact, we are dependent on his influences for life and health. But if the theorist cannot tell his substance, or the nature and cause of the light and heat he sends us, how can he presume so far on the world's credulity as to present a theory of his formation?

"Astronomical problems accumulate unsolved upon our hands, because we cannot, as mechanicians, chemists, or physiologists, experiment on the stars. Are they built of the same material as our planet? Are Saturn's rings solid, or liquid? Has the moon an atmosphere? Are the atmospheres of the planets like ours? Are the light and heat of the sun begotten of combustion? And what is the fuel which feeds these unquenchable fires? These are questions which we ask, and variously answer, *but leave unanswered after all.*" † But, till he can answer these, and a thousand questions like these, let no man presume to describe the formation of these unknown orbs.

Comets constitute by far the greatest number of the bodies of our solar system. Arago says seven millions frequent it, within the orbit of Uranus.‡ They are the largest bodies known to us, stretching across hundreds of millions of miles. They approach nearer to this earth than any other bodies, sometimes even involving it in their tails, and generally exciting great alarm among its inhabitants. But the nature of the transparent luminous matter of which they are composed is utterly unknown. As they approach the Sun, they come under an influence directly the opposite of

---

* Herschell's Outlines, vi., ₴400.
† Dr. George Wilson, F. R. S. E., in Edinburg. Phil. Journal, v., 53.
‡ Somerville's Connection of the Physical Sciences, 360.

attraction. The tail streams away from the sun, over a distance of millions of miles, *and yet, the rate of the comet's motion towards the sun is quickened,* as though it were an immense rocket, driven forward by its own explosion.

Further, while the body of the comet travels towards the Sun, sometimes with a velocity nearly one-third of that of light, the tail sends forth coruscations in the opposite direction, with a much greater velocity. The greatest velocity with which we are acquainted on earth is the velocity of light, which travels a million of times faster than a cannon ball, or at the rate of 195,000 miles per second; but here is a substance capable of traveling twenty-three times faster, and here is a force propelling it, twenty-three times greater than any which exists on earth. Its existence was first discovered by the coruscations of the comet of 1807. "In less than one second, streamers shot forth, to two and a half degrees in length; they as rapidly disappeared, and issued out again, sometimes in proportions, and interrupted, like our northern lights. Afterwards, the tail varied, both in length and breadth; and in some of the observations, the streamers shot forth from the whole expanded end of the tail, sometimes here, sometimes there, in an instant, two and a half degrees long; *so that within a single second they must have shot out a distance of* 4,600,000 *miles.** Similar exhibitions of this unknown force were made by the comet of 1811, by Halley's comet, and several others.

In these amazing disclosures of the unknown forces of the heavens, do we not hear a voice rebuking the presumption of ignorant theorists, with the questions, Knowest *thou* the ordinances of heaven? Canst *thou* set the dominion thereof in the earth? Hear one of the most distinguished of modern astronomers expound the moral bearings of such a discovery: "The intimation of a new cosmical power—I mean of one so unsuspected before, but which yet can follow a planet through all its wanderings—throws us back once more into the indefinite obscure, and checks all dogmatism. How many influences, hitherto undiscovered by our ruder senses, may be ever streaming toward us, and modifying every terrestrial action. And yet, because we had traced one of these, we have deemed our astronomy complete! Deeper far, and nearer to the root of things, is that world with which man's destiny is entwined."†

---

* Dick's Siderial Heavens, ch. xx.   † Nicholl's Solar System, 70.

We can have no reason, save our own self-sufficient arrogance, to believe that the discovery of these two forces exhausts the treasures of infinite wisdom. Humboldt thus well refutes the folly of such an imagination: "The imperfectibility of all empirical science, and the boundlessness of the sphere of observation, render the task of explaining the forces of matter by that which is variable in matter, an impracticable one. What has been already perceived, by no means exhausts that which is perceptible. If, simply referring to the progress of science in our own times, we compare the imperfect physical knowledge of Robert Boyle, Gilbert, and Hales, with that of the present day, and remember that every few years are characterized by an increasing rapidity of advance, we shall be better able to imagine *the periodical and endless changes which all physical sciences are destined to undergo. New substances and new forces will be discovered.*"*

Thus, all true science, conscious of its ignorance, ever leads the mind to the region of faith. Its first lesson, and its last lesson, is humility. It tells us that every cosmogony which the children of theory so laboriously scratch in the sand, must be swept away by the rising tide of science. When we seek information on the great questions of our origin and destiny, and cry, Where shall wisdom be found, and what is the place of understanding? the high priests of science answer, in her name, "It is not in me; the measure thereof is longer than the earth, and broader than the sea."

We receive this honest acknowledgment as an inestimable boon. We are saved thereby the wearying labor of a vain and useless search after knowledge which lies not in her domain. We come down to the Bible with the profound conviction that science can give us no definite information of our origin, no certainty of our destiny, and but an imperfect acquaintance with the laws which govern this present world. If the Bible cannot inform us on these all-important questions, we must remain ignorant. Science declares she cannot teach us. The Word of God remains, not merely the best, but absolutely the only—the last resource of the anxious soul.

The Bible gives us no theory of creation. It simply asserts the fact, that "In the beginning God created the heavens and the earth," but does not tell us *how* he did so. The knowledge could

---

* Cosmos, iii. 27.

be of no use to us, for he never means to employ us as his assistants in the work of creation. Nor could we understand the matter. The force by which he called the worlds into being, and upholds them in it, exists in no creature. "He stretcheth forth the heavens alone. He spreadeth abroad the earth by himself." "He upholdeth all things by the word of his power."

But it presents anxious, careworn, humbled souls with something infinitely more precious than cosmogonies: even an explicit declaration of the love towards them of Him who made these worlds.

"Thus saith the Lord, THY REDEEMER,

"And he who formed thee from the womb:

"I am the LORD, who maketh all things;

"Who stretcheth forth the heavens alone,

"And spreadeth abroad the earth, by myself."

Yes, the Creator of Heaven and Earth, who upholds all things by the word of his power, became a man like you, and dwelt on earth, and suffered the sorrow, the shame, the pain, the death, that sinful man deserved; and when he had by himself purged our sins, sat down on the right hand of the Majesty on high. From that heavenly throne his voice now sounds, Reader, in your ear, "Come unto me, all ye that labor and are heavy laden, and *I will give you rest.*"

No. 32.

DAYLIGHT BEFORE SUNRISE.

In the last Tract we saw Astronomy demonstrating our need of a revelation from God. In this we shall see how it illustrates and confirms that revelation. Seen through the telescope, the Bible glows with celestial splendor. Even its cloudy mysteries are displayed as clouds of light, and its long-misunderstood phrases are resolved, by a scientific investigation, into galaxies of brilliant truths, proclaiming to the philosopher that the Book which describes them is as truly the Word of God, as the heavens which it describes are his handiwork.

If, once in a century, a profound practical astronomer is found denying the inspiration of the Bible, he will either acknowledge, or discover himself, not familiar with its contents. For the most part, the charges brought against the Bible, of contradicting the facts of Astronomy, are based upon misstatements and mistakes of its teachings, and so do not fall within the range of the telescope, or the department of the observatory. The Sabbath-school teacher, and not the astronomer, is the proper person to correct such errors. A few months' instruction, in the Bible class of any well conducted Sabbath-school, would save some of our popular anti-Bible lecturers from the sin of misrepresenting the Word of God, and the shame of hearing children laugh at their blunders.

A favorite field for the display of their knowledge of science, and ignorance of the art of reading, by our modern infidels, is the Bible account of creation, in the first chapter of Genesis, which is alleged to be utterly irreconcilable with the known facts of Astronomy and Geology. Leaving the latter out of view, for the present, the astronomical objections may all be arranged under four heads. First, that the Bible account of the creation of man, only some six or seven thousand years ago, must be false—because the records of astronomical observations, taken more than seventeen thousand years ago, by the Hindoos and Egyptians, are still in existence, and have been verified. Second, that the light of some of the stars, now shining upon us, and especially of some of the distant nebulæ, must have left them millions of years ago, to have traveled over the vast space which separates them from us, and be visible on our globe now; whereas, the Bible teaches that the universe was created only some six or seven thousand years ago. Third, that the Bible represents God as creating the sky a solid crystal, or metallic sphere, or hemisphere (they are not agreed which), to which the stars are fastened, and with which they revolve round the earth; which, every schoolboy knows to be absurd. Fourth, that the Bible represents God as creating the Sun and Moon only two days before Adam, and as creating light before the Sun; which is also held to be absurd.

1. The first of these objections—that the Hindoos and Egyptians made astronomical observations thousands of years before Adam, and that the accuracy of these observations has been verified by modern calculations—*is simply untrue.* No such observations were ever made. The pretended records of such have been proved, in the case of the Hindoo astronomy, to be forgeries, and in the case of the Egyptian records, blunders of the discoverers. There is not an authentic uninspired astronomical observation extant for three thousand years after Adam.

The objection, however, is worth noticing, and its history worth remembering, as a specimen of the way in which ignorant men swallow impudent falsehoods, if they only seem to contradict the Word of Truth. When the labors of Oriental Scholars had made the Vedas and Shasters—the sacred books of the Hindoos—accessible to European philosophers, a wonderful shout was raised among infidels. "Here," it was said, "is the true chronology. We always knew that man was not a degenerate creature, fallen from a higher estate, some few thousand years ago, but that he has existed from eternity, in a constant progress toward his present lofty position; and now we have the authentic records of the most ancient and civilized people in the world—the people of India—reaching back for millions of years before the Mosaic cosmogony, and allowing ample time for the development of the noble savage into the cultivated philosopher. These records have every mark of truth, giving minute details of events, and histories of successive lines of princes; and, moreover, record the principal astronomical facts of the successive periods—eclipses, comets, positions of stars, &c.—which attest their veracity. Henceforth, the Hebrew records must hide their heads. Neither as poetry nor history can they pretend to compare with the Vedas."

The Hindoo Shasters were accordingly, for a time, in high repute, among people who knew very little about them. Even Dr.

Adam Clarke was so far led away with the spirit of the age, as to pollute his valuable commentary by the insertion of the *Gitagovinda*, after the Chaldee Targum on the Song of Solomon; where the curious reader can satisfy himself as to the scientific value of such Pantheistic dotings. By the infidels of Britain and America they were appealed to as standard works, of undoubted authority; and hundreds, who declared that it was irrational credulity to believe in the Bible, risked their souls on the faith of the Vedas, *of which they never had read a single sentence!*

Now, when we remember that these veracious chronicles reach back through *maha yugs* of 4,320,000 years of mortals, a thousand of which, or 4,320,000,000, make a *kalpa*, or one day of the life of Brahma, while his night is of the same duration, and his life consists of a hundred years of such days and nights, about the middle of which period the little span of our existence is placed;—that among the facts of the history, are the records of the seven great continents of the world, separated by seven rivers, and seven chains of mountains, four hundred thousand miles high (reaching only to the moon); of the families of their kings, one of whom had a hundred sons, another only ten thousand, another sixty thousand, who were born in a pumpkin, nourished in pans of milk, reduced to ashes by the curse of a sage, and restored to life by the waters of the Ganges;—and that among the astronomical observations by which the accuracy of these extraordinary facts is confirmed, are accounts of deluges, in which the waters not only rose above the tops of earth's mountains, but above the seven inferior and three superior worlds, *reaching even to the Pole Star**—we may well wonder at the faith which could receive all this as so true, that on the strength of it they rejected the miracles of the Bible as false. Even Voltaire ridiculed these stories.

But a visionary man, named Baillie, calculated the alleged observations backwards, and found them sufficiently correct to satisfy him that all the rest of the story was equally true. It never seems to have occurred to him, that if he could calculate eclipses *backwards*, so could the Hindoos. It is just as easy to calculate an eclipse, or the position of a planet, backwards, as forwards. If I watch the motion of the hands of a clock accurately, and find that the little hand moves over the twelfth of a circle every hour, and

---

* Duff's India, 127.

the large hand around the circle in the same time, and that the large hand, now at noon, covers the little one, I can calculate that at sixteen minutes and a quarter past three it will nearly cover it again; but then, it is just as easy to count that the two hands were covered at sixteen minutes and a quarter before nine that morning, or that they were exactly in line at 6 A. M. If my clock would keep going at the same rate for a thousand years, I could predict the position of the hands at any hour of the 29th of March, of the year 2857; but it is evident that the very same calculation applied the other way would show the position that the hands would have had a thousand years ago, or five thousand years ago, just as well. And if I were to allege that my clock was made by Tubal Cain, before the flood, and for proof of the fact declare, that on the first of January, 3857, B. C., at 6 o'clock, P. M., I had seen the two hands directly in line, and some wiseacre were to calculate the time, and find that at that hour the hands ought to have been just in that position, and conclude thence that I was undoubtedly one of the antediluvians, and the clock no less certainly a specimen of the craft of the first artificer in brass and iron, the argument would be precisely parallel to the infidel's argument from the Tirvalore Tables, and the astronomy of the Vedas.

But suppose my clock ran a little slow: say half a minute in the month, or so; or that it was made to keep siderial time, which differs by a little from solar time, and that I did not know exactly what the difference was; it is evident that on a long stretch of some hundreds or thousands of years, I would get out of my reckoning, and the hands would not have been in the positions I had calculated. Now, this was just what happened with the Brahmins and their calculations. The clock of the heavens keeps a uniform rate of going, but they made a slight mistake in the counting of it; and so did their infidel friends. But our modern astronomers have got the true time, set their clocks, and made their tables by it; and on applying these tables to the pretended Hindoo observations, find that they are all wrong, and that no such eclipses as they allege ever did, or possibly could have happened in our solar system.* So the Hindoo astronomy is now consigned to the same tomb with the Hindoo chronology and cosmogony, except when a missionary, on the banks of the Ganges exhibits it to the pupils of his English

---

* Connection of the Physical Sciences, p. 83.

school, as a specimen of the falsehoods which have ever formed the swaddling bands of Pantheism; or when some Louisiana planter astonishes a Yankee schoolmaster in search of employment, with an exhibition of the profound philosophy sheltered among the canebrakes.

Failing in the attempt to substitute Brahminism for Christianity, infidels beat a retreat from India, and went down into Egypt for help. Here they made prodigious discoveries of the scientific and religious truths believed by the worshipers of dogs and dungbeetles, recorded upon the coffins of holy bulls, and the temples sacred to crows and crocodiles. The age was favorable for French discoveries.

Napoleon and his savans cut out of the ceiling of a temple, at Dendera, in Egypt, a stone covered with uncouth astronomical, astrological, and hieroglyphic figures, which they insisted was a representation of the sky at the time the temple was built; and finding a division made between the signs of the Crab and the Lion, and marks for the Sun and Moon there, they took it into their heads that the Sun must have entered the Zodiac at that spot, on the year this Zodiac was made; and calculating back, found that must be at least seventeen thousand years ago. Hundreds of thousands visited the wonderful antediluvian monument, in the National Library, in Paris, where it had been brought; and where infidel commentators were never wanting to inform them that this remarkable stone proved the whole Bible to be a series of lies. A professor of the University of Breslau published a pamphlet, entitled *Invincible Proof that the Earth is at least ten times older than is taught by the Bible.* Scores of such publications followed, and for forty years infidel newspapers, magazines, and reviews, kept trumpeting this great refutation of the Bible. From these it descended to the vulgar, with additions and improvements; and it is now frequently alleged as proving that "ten thousand years before Adam was born, the priests of Egypt were carving astronomy on the pyramids." There is scarcely one of my French or German readers who has not heard of it.

It did not shake the skeptic's credulity in the least that no two of the savans were agreed, by some thousands of years, how old it was—that they could not tell what the Egyptian system of astronomy was—*and that none of them could read the hieroglyphics which explained it.* Whatever might be doubtful, of one thing they were all perfectly sure: that it was far older than the creation. But in 1832 the curious Egyptian astronomy was studied, and it appeared that the Sun and Moon were so placed on the Zodiac to mark the beginning of the year there; and the dividing line fenced off one-half of the sky under the care of the Sun, while the other was placed under the Moon's patronage. Then it was discovered that the positions of the stars were represented by the pictures of the gods whose names they bore—Jupiter, Saturn, &c.—and by calculating the places of these pictures back, it was found that this Zodiac represented their places in the year of our Lord 37: the year of the birth of Nero, a great temple-builder and repairer. Finally, Champollion learned to read the hieroglyphics, and the names, surnames, and titles of the emperors Tiberius, Claudius, Nero, and Domitian, were found on the temple of Denderah; and on the portico of the temple of Esneh, which had been declared to be a few thousand years older than that of Denderah, the names of Claudius and Antoninus Pius; while the whole workmanship and style of building have satisfied all antiquarians that these buildings were erected during the declining days of art in the Roman Empire. The Roman title, *autocrat*, engraved on the Zodiac itself, attests its antiquity to be not quite two thousand, instead of seventeen or twenty-seven thousand years.

But, not satisfied with merely demolishing the batteries of infidelity, astronomy has been employed to ascertain the dates of numbers of events recorded on Egyptian monuments to have happened to one or other of the Pharaohs, "beloved of Ammon, and brother of the Sun," when such a star was in such a position. Mr. Poole has spent years in gathering such inscriptions, and in calculating the dates thus furnished. The astronomer royal, at Greenwich, Mr. Airy, has reviewed the calculations, and finds them correct. Wilkinson, the great Egyptologist, agrees with their conclusions. And the result is, that *the astronomical chronology of the Egyptian monuments sustains the Bible Chronology.** Geology comes forward to confirm the testimony of her elder sister, and assures us that the alleged vast antiquity of the Egyptian monuments is impossible, as it is not more than 5,000 years since the soil of Egypt first appeared above water, as a muddy morass.† The learned Adrian Balbo thus sums up the whole question: "No

---

* Poole's Horæ Egyptiacæ.   † Henri L'Egypte Pharonique.

monument, either astronomical or historical, has yet been able to prove the books of Moses false; *but with them, on the contrary, agree, in the most remarkable manner, the results obtained by the most learned philologists, and the profoundest geometricians.*

2. To the second objection—That astronomers have discovered stars whose light must have been millions of years traveling to this earth, and that consequently these stars must have existed millions of years ago, and therefore the Bible makes a false declaration when it says that the universe was created only some six or seven thousand years ago—I reply by asking, *Where does the Bible say so?*

"What," says our objector, "is not that the good old orthodox doctrine of Christians and commentators? Do they not unanimously denounce geologists and astronomers as heretics, for asserting the vast antiquity of the earth?"

We shall see presently that no such unanimity of denunciation has ever existed, and that some of the most ancient and learned Christian commentators taught the antiquity of the earth, from the Bible, before geology was born. But that is not the question before us just now. We are not asking what the good old orthodox doctrine of Christians, or the unanimous opinion of commentators may have been, but what is the reading of the Bible—*What does this book say?*—not, "What does somebody think?"

"Well," replies our objector, "does not the Bible say, in the first of Genesis, that God created the heavens and the earth in six days, and Adam on the sixth; and are not chronologists agreed that that was not more than seven thousand years ago, at the very utmost?"

If the Bible had said that God created the heavens and the earth in six days, and that the end of that period was only seven thousand years ago, it would by no means follow that the beginning of it was only a few hours before that; for every Bible reader knows, that the most common use of the word *day*, in scripture, is to denote, not a period of twenty-four hours, but a period of time which may be of various lengths.† In this very narrative, (Gen. 2: 5) it is used to denote the whole period of the six days' work: "In the day the Lord God made the earth and the heavens." Does it mean just twenty-four hours there? In the first of Genesis, its duration is defined to consist of "the evening and the morning." Before our infidel chronologist finds out the Bible date of creation, he must be

---

* Atlas Ethnographique, Eth. I. † See Cruden's Concordance, Art. *Day.*

able to tell us *of what length was the evening which preceded the first morning*, and with it constituted the first day? God has of set purpose placed stumbling blocks for scoffers at the entrance and the exit of the Bible, as a rebuke to pride and vain curiosity.*
He nowhere says that the first of the six days of Genesis was the *first* day, absolutely, of the earth's existence. And lest any one should think so, from the use of the ordinal adjective *first*, he does not use that word; but while each of the other days is called "day second," "day third," &c., the first of the series is distinguished by the cardinal numeral, as "day one;" literally, "*And evening was and morning was day one.*" The first day and the last day are hidden from man.

But if our objector had read the Bible attentively, he would have seen that it *does not say that God created the heavens and the earth in six days.* Before it begins to give any account of the six days' work, it tells us of a previous state of disorder; and going back beyond that again, it says, "*In the beginning*, God created the heavens and the earth." It is as self-evident that this *beginning* was before the six days' work, as that the world must have existed before it could be adjusted to its present form. How long before, the Bible does not say, nor does the objector pretend to know. It may have been as many millions of years as he assigns to the stars, or twice as many, for any thing he knows to the contrary. He must have overlooked the first two verses of the Bible, else he had never made this objection; which is simply a blunder, arising from incapacity to read a few verses of Scripture correctly.

But it is replied, "Does not the Bible say, in the fourth commandment, 'In six days the Lord made heaven, and earth, and the sea, and all that in them is," &c. ? True. But we are speaking just now of a very different work: the work of *creation*. If any one does not know the difference between *create* and *make*, let him turn to his dictionary, and Webster will inform him that the primary literal meaning of *create* is, "To produce; to bring into being, from nothing; to cause to exist." The example he gives to illustrate his definition is this verse, "In the beginning God *created* the heavens and the earth." But the primary meaning of *make* is, "To compel: to constrain;" thence, "to form of materials;" and he illustrates the generic difference between these two words by a

---

* Dan. 12: 10. Job, 38: 4. Col. 2: 18.

quotation from Dwight: "God not only *made*, but *created:* he not only made the work, but the materials." Both words are as good translations of the Hebrew originals, *bra*, and *oshe*, as can be given.

If any of my readers has not a dictionary, he can satisfy himself thoroughly as to the different meanings of these two words, and of their equivalents in the original Hebrew, by looking at their use in his Bible. Thus, he will find *create* applied to the creation of the heavens and the earth, in the beginning, when there could have been no pre-existent materials to make them from; unless we adopt the Atheistic absurdity, of the eternity of matter—that is to say, *that the paving-stones made themselves.** Then it is applied to the production of animal life—v. 21—which is not a product or combination of any lifeless matter, but a direct and constant resistance to the chemical and mechanical laws which govern lifeless matter: "God created great whales, and every living creature that moveth."† Next it is applied to the production of the human race, as a species distinct from all other living creatures, and not derived from any of them. "God *created* man in his own image." ‡ It is in like manner applied to all God's subsequent bestowals of animal life and rational souls, which are directly bestowed by God, and are not in the power of any creature to give. "Thou sendest forth thy spirit: they are *created*." "Remember now thy *Creator*, in the days of thy youth." § In all these instances, the use of the word determines its literal meaning to be what Webster defines it: "To bring into being from nothing."

The metaphorical use of the word is equally expressive of its literal meaning, for it is applied to the production of new dispositions of mind and soul utterly opposite to those previously existing. "Create in me a clean heart;" which God thus explains: "A new heart will I give you, and a new spirit will I put within you; and I will take away the stony heart out of your flesh, and I will give you an heart of flesh." ‖ The Hebrew word *bra* has as many derivative meanings as our English word *create;* as we speak of "creating a peer," "long abstinence creating uneasiness," &c.; but these no more change the primitive idea in the one case than in the other.

---

* Tract 23, *Did the World make itself?* § Psalm 104: 30. Eccl. 12: 1.
† Gen. 1: 21. ‖ Psalm 51: 10. Ezekiel, 36: 26.
‡ Gen. 1: 27.

From this word *create*, the Bible very plainly distinguishes the words *make* and *form*, using them as the complement of the former, in many passages which speak of both creation and making. Thus, man was both created and made. His life and soul are spoken of as a creation; his body as a formation from the dust; his deputed authority over the earth also implies a primal creation, and subsequent investiture; and so both terms are applied to it. So the words *make* and *form* are applied to the production of the bodies of animals from pre-existing materials, while animal life is ever spoken of as a product of creative power. But, that we may see that these processes are distinct, and that the words which express them have distinctive meanings, *the Author of the Bible takes care to use them both* in reference to this very work, in such a way that we cannot fail to perceive he intends some distinction, unless we suppose that he fills the Bible with useless tautologies. For instance, "On the seventh day, God rested from all his work, which God *created* and *made*." "These are the generations of the heavens and the earth, when they were *created;* in the day the Lord God *made* the earth and the heavens." "But now thus saith the Lord that *created* thee, Jacob, and he that *formed* thee, O Israel." "For thus saith the Lord, that *created* the heavens, God himself, that *formed* the earth, and *made* it; He hath established it; He *created* it not in confusion; he *formed* it to be inhabited."* In all these passages *creation* is clearly distinguished from *formation* and *making*, if the Bible is not a mass of senseless repetitions. If *create*, and *make*, and *form*, have all the same meaning, why use them all in the same verse. These, and many similar passages, show that the Bible teaches the work of *creation*—calling things into being—to be previous to and distinct from the work of *making* —forming of materials already created.

Between these two widely different processes—of the original creation of the universe, and the subsequent preparation of the habitable earth, by the six days' work—two intervening periods are indicated by scripture, both of indefinite length. The first of these is that which intervened between the original creation and the period of disorder indicated in the second verse. The second is that disordered period during which the earth continued without form and void.

---

* Gen. 2: 1-5. Isa. 43: 1-7; 45: 1, 2.

That original chaos which some would find in the second verse, never had any existence, save in the brains of atheistic philosophers. It is purely absurd. God never created a chaos. Man never saw it. The crystals of the smallest grain of sand, the sporules of the humblest fungus on the rotten tree, the animalculæ in the filthiest pool of mud, are as orderly in their arrangements, as perfect after their kind, and as wisely adapted to their station, as the angels before the throne of God. And as man never saw, so he has no language to describe a state of original disorder; for every word he can use implies a previous state of regularity; as, disorder tells of order dissolved; con-fusion of previous forms melted together. So the poets who have tried to describe a chaos have been obliged to represent it as the wreck of a former state.

Both the Bible language and the Bible narrative correspond to the philosophy and philology of the case; for, by the use of the substantive verb, in the past tense, implying progressive being, according to the usual force of the word in Hebrew, we are told literally, "the earth *became* without form and void." God did not create it so, but after it was created, and by a series of revolutions not recorded, it became disordered and empty. The Holy Spirit takes care to explain this verse, by quoting it in Jer. 4: 23, as the appropriate symbolical description of the state of a previously existing and regularly constituted body politic, reduced to confusion by the calamities of war. Again, he explains both the terms used in it in Isa. 34: 11, by using them to describe, not the rude and undigested mass of the heathen poet, but the wilderness condition of a ravaged country, and the desolate ruins of once beautiful and populous cities: "He will stretch out upon it the line of *confusion*, and the stones of *emptiness*." In both these cases the previous existence of an orderly and populous state is implied. And finally, we are expressly assured, that the state of disorder mentioned in the 2d verse of Gen. 1, was not the original condition of the earth— Isaiah, 45: 18—where the very same word is used as in Gen. 1: 2, "He created it not, *teu, disordered*, in *confusion*." The period of the earth's previous existence in an orderly state, or that occupied by the revolutions and catastrophes which disordered its surface, is not recorded in scripture.

The second period is that of disorder, which must have been of some duration, more or less, and is plainly implied to have been of considerable length, in the declaration that "the Spirit of the

Lord moved"—literally *was brooding* (a figure taken from the incubation of fowls)—"upon the face of the waters." But no portion of Scripture gives any intimation of the length of this period.

If, then, astronomers and geologists assert that the earth was millions, or hundreds of millions of years in process of preparation for its present state, by a long series of successive destructions and renovations, and gradual formations, there is not one word in the Bible to contradict that opinion; but, on the contrary, very many texts which fully and unequivocally imply its truth. But, as the knowledge of the exact age of the earth is by no means necessary to any man's present happiness, or the salvation of his soul, it is no-where taught in the Bible. God has given us the Stars to teach us Astronomy, the Earth to teach us Geology, and the Bible to teach us Religion, and neither contradicts the other.

This is no new interpretation, evoked to meet the necessities of modern science. The Jewish Rabbins, and those of the early Christian fathers who gave any attention to criticism, are perfectly explicit in recognizing these distinctions. The doctrine of the creation of the world only six or seven thousand years ago, is a product of monkish ignorance of the original language of the Bible. But Clemens of Alexandria, Chrysostom, and Gregory Nazianzen, after Justin Martyr, teach the existence of an indefinite period between the creation and the formation of all things. Basil and Origen account for the existence of light before the Sun, by alleging that the Sun existed, but that the chaotic atmosphere prevented his rays from being visible till the first day, and his light till the third.* Augustine, in his first homily, represents the first state of the earth, in Gen. 1: 1, as bearing the same relation to its finished state, that the seed of a tree does to the trunk, branches, leaves, and fruit. Horsley, Edward King, Jennings, Baxter, and many others, who wrote during the last two centuries, but before the period of geological discovery, explained the 2d verse substantially as did Bishop Patrick, a hundred and fifty years ago. "How long all things continued in confusion, we are not told. *It might have been, for any thing that is here revealed, a very great while.*" †

Some persons, however, have supposed that the chaos of the second verse succeeded immediately to the creation of the first, and

---

* Wiseman's Lectures on the Connection of Science and Revealed Religion, 1—297.
† Commentary on Gen. 1: 2.

that the six days' work in like manner followed that instantaneously, or at least after a very brief interval, because the records of these cycles are connected by the word *and*, which they think, precludes the idea of any lengthened periods or intervals. But the slightest reflection upon the meaning of the word will show that *and* cannot of itself be any *measure* of time, its use being to indicate merely *sequence* and *connection*. When used historically, it always implies an interval of time; for there can be no succession without an interval; but the length of that interval must be determined from the context, or some other source. A very cursory perusal of the Bible, either in English or Hebrew, will show that very often in its brief narratives, the interval indicated by *and*, and its Hebrew originals, is a very long time. The descent of Jacob and his children into Egypt is connected with the record of their deaths, in the very next verse, by this word *and*, which thus includes nearly the lifetime of a generation. That event, again, is connected with a change of dynasty in Egypt, and the oppression and multiplication of the Israelites there, recorded in the next verse, by the same word, *vai, and;* while the period over which it reaches was over two hundred years.* So in the brief record of the family of Adam, after reciting the birth of Seth, the historian adds, in the next verse, "And to Seth also was born a son, and he called his name Enos;" while the interval thus indicated by the word *and* was a hundred and five years. The command to build the ark, recorded in the last verse of the sixth chapter of Genesis, is connected with the command to enter into it, in the first verse of the seventh chapter, by this same word *and*, although we know, from the nature of the case, that the interval required for the construction of such a huge vessel must have been considerable; and from the third verse of the sixth chapter, we learn that it was a hundred and twenty years. So the births and deaths of the antediluvians are connected by this same word, *and*, throughout the fifth chapter of Genesis; while the interval, as we see from the narrative, was often eight or nine hundred years. The descent of the Holy Spirit upon Christ, to qualify him for judging the world, is connected with the actual discharge of that office, in the destruction of Antichrist by the breath of his mouth, by this word *and*,† although the interval has been over eighteen hundred years. If

---

* Exo. 1: 5, 8. † Isa. 11: 3, 4.

in the records of the generations of mortal men, the word *and* is customarily employed as a connecting link in the narrations of events separated by an interval of hundreds of years, it is quite consistent with the strictest propriety of language to employ it, with an enlargement proportioned to the duration of the subject of discourse, to connect intervals of millions, in the narrative of the generations of the heavens and the earth.

The Bible uniformly attributes the most remote antiquity to the work of creation. So far from supposing man to be even approximately coeval with it, the emphatic reproof of human presumption is couched in the remarkable words, "Where wast thou, when I laid the foundations of the earth?" In majestic contrast with the frail human race, Moses glances at the primeval monuments of God's antiquity, as though by them he could form some faint conceptions even of eternity, and sings, "Before the mountains were brought forth, or ever thou hadst formed the earth and the universe, even from everlasting to everlasting thou art God." *

The very word here used, *the beginning*, is in itself an emphatic refutation of the notion that the work of creation is only some six or seven thousand years old. Geologists have been unable to invent a better, and have borrowed from the Bible this very form of speech, to designate those strata beyond which human knowledge cannot penetrate—*the primary formations*. But, with far greater propriety, the Holy Spirit uses this word with regard to ages, compared with which the utmost range of the astronomer's or geologist's reasonings is but as the tale of yesterday. For this word, in Bible usage, marks the last promontory on the boundless ocean of eternity: the only positive word by which we can express the most remote period of past duration. It is not a date—a point of duration. It is a period—a vast cycle. It has but one boundary: that where creation rises from its abyss. Created eye has never seen the other shore. It is that vast period which the Bible assigns to the manifestations of the Word of God, "whose goings forth have been of old, from everlasting." Carrying our astonished gaze far back beyond the era of his creature, man, and ages before the "all things" that were made by him, the Bible places this *beginning* on the very shore of the eternity of God, when it declares, "*In the beginning* was the Word, and the Word was with God, and

---

* Psalm 90.

the Word was God."* Thus, both by the use of the imperfect tense, *was*, denoting continued existence, and by the connection of this *beginning* with the eternity of the Word, does the Bible teach us to dismiss from our thoughts all narrow views of the period of duration employed in manifesting the glory of the self-existent Eternal One, and to raise our conceptions to the highest possible pitch, and then feel that far beyond the grasp of human calculation lies that *beginning*, which includes the years of the right hand of the Most High, and is even used as one of the names of the eternal: "I AM THE BEGINNING and *the Ending, saith the Lord, Who is, and Who was, and Who is to come*—THE ALMIGHTY."†

In another Bible exhibition of the eternity of the Son of God, we are conducted from that *beginning*, downward, stage by stage, from those periods of remote antiquity prior to the formation of water, the upheaval of the mountains, the alluvial deposits, the subsidence of the existing sea basins, and the adornment of the habitable parts of the earth, to that comparatively recent event, the existence of the sons of men. Our ideas of the eternity of the love of Christ are thus enhanced, by the vastness of the ages which stretch out between the human race and that beginning when he was, as it were, "The Lamb slain from before the foundations of the world."

"The Lord possessed me *in the beginning of his way*,
"*Before his works of old.*
"I was set up from everlasting,
"*From the beginning, or ever the earth was.*
"When there were no depths, I was brought forth;
"When there were no fountains, abounding with water;
"Before the mountains were settled,
"Before the hills, was I brought forth;
"While as yet he had not made the earth, nor the fields,
"Nor the highest part of the dust of the world.
"When he prepared the heavens, I was there;
"When he described a circle upon the face of the deep;
"When he established the clouds above;
"When he strengthened the fountains of the deep;
"When he gave to the sea his decree,
"That the waters should not pass his commandment;
"When he appointed the foundations of the earth:

---

* John, 1: 1.   † Rev. 1: 4.

"Then was I by him, as one brought up with him;
"And I was daily his delight, rejoicing always before him:
"Rejoicing in the habitable parts of his earth;
"And my delights were with the sons of men.*"

Let the geologist, then, penetrate as deeply as he can into the profundities of the foundations of the earth, and bring forth the monuments of their hoary antiquity: we will follow with the most unfaltering faith, and receive with joy these proofs of his eternal power and Godhead. Let the astronomer raise his telescope, and reflect on our astonished eyes the light which flashed from morning stars, on the day of this earth's first existence, or even the rays which began to travel from distant suns, millions of years ere the first morning dawned on our planet: we will place them as jewels in the crown of Him who is the bright and morning star. They shall shed a sacred luster over the pages of the Bible, and give new beauties of illustration to its majestic symbols. But never will geologist penetrate, much less exhaust, the profundity of its mysteries, nor astronomer attain, much less explore, the sublimity of that beginning revealed in its pages; for eye hath not seen, nor ear heard, nor hath it entered into the heart of man to conceive, either the antiquity, or the nature, or the duration of the things which God hath prepared for them that love him. Human science will never be able to reach the Bible era of creation. It is placed in an antiquity beyond the power of human calculation, in that sublime sentence with which it introduces mortals to the Eternal: "*In the beginning, God created the heavens and the earth.*"

3. The third objection we have named is equally unfounded. *The Bible no-where teaches that the sky is a solid sphere, to which the stars are fixed, and which revolves with them around the earth.* I know that infidels allege that the word *firmament*, in the first chapter of Genesis, conveys this meaning. It does not. Neither the English word, nor the Hebrew original, has any such meaning. As to the meaning of the English word, I adhere to the dictionary. Infidels must not be allowed to coin uncouth meanings for words, different from the known usage of the English tongue, for which Webster is undeniable authority. His definition of *firmament* is, "The region of the air; the sky, or heavens. In scripture, the word denotes an expanse—a wide extent; for such is the significa-

---

* Proverbs, 8: 22.

tion of the Hebrew word, coinciding with *regio, region,* and *reach.* The original, therefore, does not convey the sense of solidity, but of stretching—extension. The great arch or expanse over our heads, in which are placed the atmosphere and the clouds, and in which the stars *appear* to be placed, and are *really* seen." The word *firmament,* then, conveys no such meaning as the infidel alleges, to any man who understands the English tongue.

No Hebrew speaking man or woman ever did, or ever could understand the original Hebrew word *reqio* in any other sense than that of *expanse;* for the verb from which it is formed means to extend, or spread out, as even the English reader may see, by a few examples of its use, in the following passages of scripture; where the English words by which the verb *reqo* is expressed, are marked in italics. "Then did I beat them small as the dust of the earth, and did stamp them as the mire of the street, and *did spread them abroad."* "The goldsmith *spreadeth it over* with gold." "Thus saith the Lord: He that created the heavens, and stretched them out; He that *spread forth* the earth." "I am the Lord, that maketh all things; that stretcheth forth the heavens alone, and *spreadeth abroad* the earth by myself." "To him that *stretcheth out* the earth above the waters." "The censers of these sinners against their own souls, let them *make them broad* plates, for a covering for the altar. *And they were made broad."* "Hast thou with him *spread out* the sky;"* or, in Humboldt's elegant rendering, "the pure ether, *spread* (during the scorching heat of the south wind) as a melted mirror over the parched desert." † We might refer to the opinions of lexicographers, all unanimous in ascribing the same idea to the word; but the authorities given above are conclusive. The meaning, then, of the Hebrew word rendered firmament, is so utterly removed from the notion of compactness, or solidity, or metallic or crystalline spheres, that it is derived from the very opposite: the fineness or tenuity produced by processes of expansion. Science has not been able to this day to invent a better word for the regions of space than the literal rendering of the original Hebrew word used by Moses—*the expanse.*

The inspired writers of the New Testament, though they found the world full of all the absurdities of the Greek philosophy, and

---

* 2 Sam. 22: 43.   Isa. 40: 19; 44: 24; 42: 5; Ps. 136: 6.   Numbers, 17: 38.   Job, 37: 18.

† Cosmos, v. 2, p. 60.

their Greek translations of the Bible continually using the word *stereoma*, which expressed these notions, *never used it* but once, and then not for the sky, but for the *steadfastness of faith* in Christ. Their thus using it once, shows that they were acquainted with the word, and its proper meaning, and that their disuse of it was intentional; while their disuse of it, and choice of another word to denote the heavens, proves decisively that they disapproved of the absurdity which it was understood to express. Now, whether you account for this fact by admitting their inspiration, or by alleging that they drew their language from the Hebrew original, and not from the Greek translation, it is in either case perfectly conclusive as to the scriptural meaning of the word. Indeed, it is marvellous how any man who is familiar with his Bible, and knows that the scriptures usually describe the sky by metaphors conveying the very opposite ideas to those of solidity or permanence — as, "stretched out like a curtain," "spread abroad like a tent to dwell in," "folded up like a vesture," and the like—should allow himself to be imposed on by the impudent falsehood of Voltaire, that the Bible teaches us that the sky is a solid metallic or crystal hemisphere, supported by pillars.

Those beautiful figures of sacred poetry in which the universe is represented as the palace of the Great King, adorned with majestic "pillars," and "windows of heaven," whence he scatters his gifts among his expectant subjects in the courts below, have been grossly abused for the support of this miserable falsehood. We are assured, that so ignorant was Moses of the true nature of the atmosphere, and of the origin of rain, that he believed and taught that there was an ocean of fresh water on *the outside* of this metal hemisphere, which covered the earth like a great sugar-kettle, bottom upwards, and was supported on pillars; and at the bottom of the ocean were trap-doors, to let the rain through; which trap-doors in the metal firmament are to be understood, when the Bible speaks of the windows of heaven. Now, the bottom of an ocean is an odd place for windows, and a trap-door is rather a strange kind of watering-pot; and if Moses put the ocean of fresh water on the *outside* of his metal hemisphere, he must have changed his notions of gravity materially from the time he planned the brazen hemisphere for the tabernacle, which he turned mouth upwards, and put the water in the *inside*.

While such writers are quite clear about the metal trap-doors and the ocean, they have not yet fully fathomed the construction and arrangement of the pillars. Whether the Bible teaches that they are "pillars of salt," like Lot's wife, or of flesh and blood, like "James, Cephas, and John," or such "iron pillars and brazen walls" as Jeremiah was against the house of Israel—whether they consisted of "cloud and fire," like the pillar Moses describes in the next book as floating in the sky over the camp of Israel, or are "pillars of smoke," such as ascend out of the wilderness—whether they are those "pillars of the earth which tremble" when God shakes it, or "the pillars of heaven which are astonished at his reproof"—whether they are the pillars of the earth and its anarchical inhabitants, which Asaph bore up, or are composed of the same materials as Paul's "pillar and basis of the truth," or the pillars of victory which Christ erects "in the temple of God"*— they have not yet decided. Whether the Hebrews understood these pillars to be arranged on the outside of the metal hemisphere, and if so, to imagine any use for them there; or in the inside, and in that case whether they kept the sky from falling upon the earth, or only supported the earth from falling into the sky, these learned men are by no means agreed. Having trampled the pearl into fragments, their attempts to combine them into another shape are more amusing than successful; and it is hard to say which of the seven opinions ascribed to the Bible by infidel commentators is least probable. That opinion, however, will, doubtless, after more vigorous and protracted rooting, be discovered and greedily swallowed amid grunts of satisfaction: an appropriate reward of such laborious stupidity.

The absurdities of the Greek philosophers were not drawn from the Bible. Had the Greeks read the Bible more, they would have preserved the common sense God gave them a great deal longer, and would not, while professing themselves to be wise, have become such fools as to adore blocks and stones, and dream of metal firmaments. But they turned away their ears from the truth, and were turned unto such fables as infidels falsely ascribe to the Bible. A thousand years before the cycles and epicycles of the Ptolemaic astronomy were invented, and before learned Greeks had learned to talk nonsense about crystal spheres, and trap-doors in the bottom

---

* Gen. 10: 26.   Exo. 13: 20; 33: 10.   Jere. 1: 18.   Gal. 2: 7.   Song, 3: 6.   Job, 9: 6; 26: 11.   Ps. 75: 3.   1 Tim. 3: 15.   Rev. 3: 12.

of celestial oceans, the writers of the Bible were recording those conversations of pious philosophers concerning stars, and clouds, and rain, from which Galileo derived the first hints of the causes of barometrical phenomena. The origin of rain, its proportion to the amount of evaporation, and the mode of its distribution by condensation, could not be propounded by Humboldt himself with more brevity and perspicuity than they are expressed by the Idumean philosoper: "He maketh small the drops of water; they pour down rain according to the vapor thereof, which the clouds do drop and distil upon man abundantly. Also, can any understand the spreadings of the clouds, or the noise of his tabernacles."* The cause of this rarefaction of *cold water*—the clouds are not steam—is as much a mystery to the British Association as it was to Elihu; and even were all the mysteries of the electrical tension of vapors disclosed, "the balancings of the clouds" would only be more clearly discovered to be, as the Bible declares, "the wonderful works of Him who is perfect in wisdom." But the gravity of the atmosphere, the comparitive density of floating water, and its increased density by discharges of electricity, were as well known to Job and his friends as they are to the wisest of our modern philosophers. "He looketh to the ends of the earth, and seeth under the whole heaven, *to make weight to air, and regulate waters by measure, in his making a law for the rain, and a path for the lightning of thunder.*" † Three thousand years before the theory of the trade winds was demonstrated, or before Maury had discovered the rotation and revolutions of the wind-currents, it was written in the Bible, "The wind goeth towards the south, and turneth about to the north. *And the wind returneth again, according to his circuits.*" ‡

Thousands of years before Newton, Galileo, and Copernicus were born, Isaiah was writing about the "orbit of the earth," and its insignificance in the eyes of the Creator of the host of heaven. ₴ Job was conversing with his friends, on the inclination of its axis, and its equilibrium in space: "He spreadeth out the north over the empty space, and hangeth the earth upon nothing." ||

The "waters above the heavens," which the Holy Ghost harmonizes with other Cosmical bodies—Sun, Moon, Fixed Stars, and

---

* Job, 36: 27.
† Job, 28: 24—literal reading.
‡ Eccl. 1: 6.

₴ Isa. 40th ch.
|| Job, 26: 7.

distant Galaxies, Heavens of Heavens—in his arrangement of choristers for the grand anthem of the universe, have no reference to, or connection with our earth. They refer to such phenomena as are indicated by the atmosphere loaded with vapors of Mercury and Venus, the "polar snows" and "greenish seas" of Mars, the trade winds of Jupiter, and the rings of Saturn, "composed of a fluid a little denser than water," in our own system, and to analogous collections of water in more distant firmaments.*

So far from entertaining the least idea of the waters of the atmosphere being contained either on the outside or the inside of a metal or solid hemisphere, the writers of the Bible never once use, even figuratively, any expression conveying it. On the contrary, the well known scriptural figures for the fountains of the rain, are the soft, elastic, leathern waterskins of the east, "the bottles of the clouds," or the wide, flowing shawl or upper garment wherein the people of the east are accustomed to tie up loose, scattering substances.† "He bindeth up the waters in his thick cloud, and the cloud is not rent under them." "Who hath bound the waters in a garment;" "As a vesture thou shalt change them;" or the loose, flowing curtains of a royal pavilion; or the extended covering of a tent: "his pavilion around him were dark waters, and thick clouds of the skies;" "the spreadings of the clouds, and the noise of his tabernacles;" "he spread a cloud for a covering." ‡ Instead of the notion of a single ocean, the "number of the clouds" is proverbial in the scriptures ‖ for a multitude; and in direct opposition to the permanence of a vast metallic arch, the chosen emblems of instability and transitoriness, and of the utmost rapidity of motion, suitable even for the chariot of Jehovah, are selected from the heavens.§

In short, there is not the slightest vestige of any foundation in scripture for the notions long afterwards introduced by the Greek philosophers. Yet Christians, who have read these passages of scripture over and over again, allow themselves to give heed to infidels, who have not, asserting, without the shadow of proof, that

---

* Psalm 148. Herschell's Outlines, § 509, 510, 512. Annual of Scientific Discovery, 1842, p. 376.
† Ruth, 3 : 15.
‡ Job, 38 : 37; 26 : 8; 38 : 9; 36 : 29. Ps. 105 : 39; 77 : 17.
‖ Isa., 44 : 22. Jere., 4 : 13. Job, 38 : 37. Prov., 30 : 4.
§ Eccl., 11 : 4. Ps. 104 : 3. Mat. 24 : 30.

Moses taught absurdities which were not invented for a thousand years after his death. The Bible gives hints of many profound scientific truths; it teaches no absurdities; *and, instead of countenancing the notion that the sky is a solid metal hemisphere, it teaches, both literally and figuratively, directly the contrary.*

4. We come now to the fourth objection, that the Bible represents God as creating light before the Sun, which is supposed to be an absurdity, and as creating the Sun, Moon, and Stars only two days before Adam. This is the only Astronomical objection to the Bible account of creation which has any foundation of scripture statement to rest upon; but we shall soon see that here, also, infidels have not done themselves the justice of reading the Bible with attention.

I have already corrected that confusion of ideas and carelessness of perusal which confounds the two distinct and different words, *create* and *make,* so as to make both mean the same thing. God *created* the heavens, as well as the earth, *in the beginning:* a period of such remote antiquity that, in Bible language, it stands next to eternity. The Sun and Moon then came into being. Through what changes they passed, or when they were endowed with the power of giving light to the universe, the Bible no-where declares; but on the fourth day, it tells us, they *were made lights,* or, literally, *light-bearers,* to this earth. The comparatively insignificant place allotted to the stars, in the narrative of this earth's formation, corresponds, with the strictest propriety, to the nature of the discourse; which is not an account of the system of the universe, but of the process of preparation of this earth for the abode of man. Compared with the influences of "the two great light-bearers," those of the stars are very insignificant; since the Sun sheds more light and heat on the earth in one day, than all the fixed stars have done since the creation of Adam. It is evident, from the words, that Moses is not speaking either of their original creation, or of their actual magnitude, but of their appointment and use in relation to us, when he says, "And God made two great light-bearers (the greater light-bearer to rule the day, and the lesser light-bearer to rule the night), and the stars. And God set them in the firmament of the heavens, to give light upon the earth, and to rule over the day and the night, and to divide the light from the darkness."

Neither here nor elsewhere does he say they were *created* at this time, but in all the subsequent references uses other words, such as "prepared," "divided," "made," "appropriated," "made for ruling," "gave:" a studious omission, which shows that the author of the Bible had not forgotten how long it was since he had called them into being. *The Bible, then, does not say that God created the Sun and Stars only two days before Adam.*

Another correction of careless Bible reading is necessary, that we may be satisfied about what the Bible *does not say*, ere we begin to defend what it does say. The Bible does not say, nor lead us to believe, that the darkness spoken of in the second verse of the first of Genesis had existed from eternity. Darkness is not eternal: it requires the exercise of creative power for its production; but light is the eternal dwelling of the Word of God.* The darkness which brooded over our earth, at the period of its formation, is very plainly described in the Bible as a temporary phenomenon, incident to and necessary for the birth of ocean. It is confined by the adverb of time, *when*, to the period of condensation, upheaval, and subsidence, occupied by the birth of that gigantic infant, "*when* it burst forth as though it had issued from the womb; *when* I made the cloud a garment for it, and thick darkness a swaddling band for it, and broke up for it my decreed place, and set bars and doors." † The Sun may have shone for millions of years before upon the earth, or might have been shining with all his brilliance at that very time, while not a single ray penetrated the thick darkness of the vapors in which earth was clothed. But whether or not, darkness must, from its very nature, be limited, both in space and time. To speak of infinite and eternal darkness is as unscriptural as it is absurd. The source of light is Uncreated and Eternal.‡

Further—if my readers are not tired with these perpetual corrections of careless reading and mistaken meaning—the light called into existence in the third verse of the first chapter of Genesis is as evidently a different word from *the two lights* spoken of in the fourteenth verse, as the singular is different from the plural; and the thing signified by it is as distinct from the things spoken of in the fourteenth verse, as the abstract is from the concrete: as, when I say of the first, "light travels 195,000 miles per second," but

---

* Isa. 45:7. 1 John, 1:5, Dan. 2:22. 1 Tim. 6:16.
† Job, 38:9, 10. Literally, *In my making*, &c.
‡ Rev. 21:23; 22:5. Isa. 60:19.

239

mean a totally distinct subject when I say, "Extinguish the lights." The Hebrew words are even more palpably different, the word for *light*, in the third verse, being *aur*, while the words for *the lights*, in the fourth days' work, are *maurt* and *at emaur:* words as distinct in shape and sense as our English words, *light* and *the lighthouses*.

The locality of the light of the third verse is, moreover, wholly different from that of the light-bearers of the fourteenth verse. That was placed on earth—these in heaven. It was of the earth alone the writer was speaking, in the second verse; the earth alone is the subject of the following verses. It was the darkness of earth that needed to be illuminated; but there is not the remotest hint, in any portion of scripture, that any other planet or star was shrouded in gloom at this time. But, on the contrary, we are most distinctly informed that the wonders which God was performing in this world at that very time were distinctly visible amidst the cheerful illumination of other orbs, "when the morning stars sang together, and all the sons of God shouted for joy," * as this earth emerged from its temporary darkness. It was not from the light of heaven, but out of this darkness of earth, that God, who still draws the lightning's flash from the black thunder-cloud, commanded the light to shine.† And it was upon this earth, and not throughout the universe, that it produced alternate day and night. To extend this command for the illumination of the darkened earth, so as to mean the production of light in general, and the lighting of the most distant telescopic, and even invisible stars—which are neither specified in the command itself, nor by any necessity of language or scripture implied in it, but, on the contrary, excluded, by the express scripture declarations of the pre-existence of light, and of morning stars—is an outrage alike against all canons of criticism, laws of grammar, and dictates of common sense. The command, "Let there be light," had respect to this earth only.

The Bible does represent this earth as illuminated at a time when the Sun was not visible from its surface—perhaps not visible at all. Now, if any one will undertake to scoff at the Bible for speaking of light without sunshine, or of the sun shining upon a dark earth—as infidels abundantly do—we demand that he tell us,

---

* Job, 38: 7.   † 2 Cor. 4: 6.

What is light, and how is it connected with the Sun? If he can not, let him cease to scoff at matters too high for him.

If he can tell, he knows that the retardation of Encke's comet, which every year falls nearer and nearer the Sun, has discovered the existence of an attenuated ether in the expanse or firmament; and that the experiments of Arago on the polarization of light have finally demonstrated, that our sensation of light is exerted by a series of vibrations or undulations of this fluid.* He will then be able to perceive the propriety with which the Author of light and of the Bible speaks, not of *creating* light, as if it were a material substance, but of *forming* or commanding its display. And he will be better able to comprehend the beauty and scientific propriety with which he selected the active participle of the verb *to flow*, as the name for the undulations of this fluid; for the primary meaning of the Hebrew verb *ar* is *to flow*, or, when used as a noun, *a flood*. "It shall be cast out and drowned, as by the *flood* of Egypt." † And of the like import are the nouns, *iar* and *aur*, formed from it. "Who is this that covereth up like *a flood*—whose waters are moved as the rivers." ‡ The philosopher, even though he be a skeptic, will cease to mock the Bible when he reads there, that 6000 years ago its author termed light *the flowing—the undulation*. "In the words of the 'Son of God,' and 'the Son of Man,' no less than in his works, with all their adaptation to the circumstances of the times and persons to whom they were originally delivered, are things inexplicable—concealed germs of an infinite development, reserved for future ages to unfold.∥" To the man of learning and reflection, this progressive fullness and unfathomable depth of the Scripture, is a most conclusive proof that it was dictated by him in whom are hid all the treasures of wisdom and knowledge.

But the ignorant scoffers—the great majority—will mock on, and speak evil of the things they know not. Their mockery is founded on two assumptions, which they believe to be irrefutable: that the Sun is the only possible source of light to the earth; and that it is impossible for the Sun to exist without illuminating the earth. Unless they can *prove* both these assumptions to be true, they can

---

* Somerville's Connection of the Physical Sciences, Sec. 19—23.
† Amos, 8:8.
‡ Jere. 46:7. Gen. 41:1—18. See Parkhurst's Hebrew Lexicon, sub voce.
∥ Neander.

not prove the Bible account of creation to be false, nor even show it to be impossible. Neither of these assumptions can possibly be proved true; for none of them can explore the universe, to discover the sources of light, nor put the Sun through every possible experiment, to discover that his light is an inseparable quality. The only thing infidels can truly allege against the Bible account of the origin of light is, *their ignorance of the process.* The argument is simply this: "God could not cause light without sunshine, *because I don't know how he did it.* Nor *can I understand* how the Sun shone on a dark earth; therefore, it is impossible."

These arguments from ignorance need no other answer than the questions, Do you know how the Sun shines at all? Is your ignorance the measure of God's wisdom?

But I shall demonstrate the utter falsehood of both these assumptions, by showing the actual existence of many sources of light besides the Sun, and the perfect possibility of the existence of the Sun without sunshine, and of sunshine without any light reaching the earth. Thus, both the alleged *impossibilities* upon which the argument against the truth of the Bible is based will be removed, and the gross ignorance of natural science displayed by professedly scientific scoffers at the Bible, exposed.

Light, so far from being solely derived from the Sun, exists in, and can be educed from, almost any known substance. Even children are familiar with the light produced by the friction of two pieces of quartz; and no one needs to be informed how light may be produced by the combustion of inflammable substances. But the number of these substances is far greater than is generally supposed, and light can be produced by processes to which we do not generally apply the idea of burning. Resins, wool, silks, wood, and all kinds of earths and alkalies, are capable of emitting light in suitable electrical conditions; so that the surface of our earth may have been a source of light in past ages, as it even now is [*] near the poles and the equator, flashing its Aurora Borealis and Aurora Australis, and sending out its belts of Zodiacal light (which is now ascertained to be a telluric phenomenon, like Saturn's ring[†]), far into the surrounding darkness. Further, the metallic bases of all the earths are highly inflammable, and a brilliant flame can be produced by the combustion even of water. All the metals can

---

[*] Cosmos, vol. 1, p. 196. [†] Annual of Scientific Discovery, 1856.

be made to flash forth lightnings, under suitable electric and magnetic excitements, and the crystals of several rocks give out light during the process of crystallization. Thousands of miles of the earth's surface must once have presented the lurid glow of a vast furnace of melted granite. Even at a far later era of its history, it may have shone with a luster little inferior to that of the Sun; for lime—of which unknown thousands of miles of its strata consist—when subjected to a heat much less than that produced by contact with melted granite or lava, emits a brilliant white light, of such intensity that the eye cannot support its luster.* Even now, the copper color of the moon during an eclipse shows us that the earth is a source of light.† The mountains on the surface of Venus and the Moon, and the continents and oceans of Mars, attest the existence of upheaval and subsidence, and of volcanic fires, capable of producing such phenomena, and of course of sources of light in those planets, such as exist on the earth. We know, then, most certainly, that there are many other bodies capable of producing light besides the Sun. That God could command the light to shine out of darkness, and convert the very ocean into a magnificent illumination, the following facts clearly prove. "Capt. Bonnycastle, coming up the Gulf of St. Lawrence, on the 7th of September, 1826, was roused by the mate of the vessel, in great alarm, from an unusual appearance. It was a starlight night, when suddenly the sky became overcast, in the direction of the high land of Cornwallis County, *and an instantaneous and intensely vivid light, resembling the Aurora, shot out of the hitherto gloomy and dark sea*, on the lee bow, which was so brilliant that it lighted every thing distinctly, even to the mast-head. The light spread over the whole sea, between the two shores, and the waves, which before had been tranquil, now began to be agitated. Captain Bonnycastle describes the scene as that of *a blazing sheet of awful and most brilliant light*. A long and vivid line of light, superior in brightness to the parts of the sea not immediately near the vessel, showed the base of the high, frowning, and dark land abreast; the sky became lowering, and more intensely obscure. Long tortuous lines of light showed immense numbers of large fish, darting about as if in consternation. The topsail yard and mizen boom were lighted by the

---

* Johnson's Turner's Chemistry, § 160.
† Cosmos, vol. 1, p. 196. Nicholl's Solar System, 184.

glare, as if gas-lights had been burning directly below them; and until just before day-break, at four o'clock, the most minute objects were distinctly visible." *

The other assumption, that the Sun could not possibly have existed without giving light to the earth, is contradicted by the most familiar facts. The earth and each of the planets might have been, and most probably were, surrounded by a dense atmosphere, through which the Sun's rays could not penetrate. It is not at all necessary to prove that such was the fact. I am only concerned to prove the *possibility*; for the infidel's objection is founded on the presumed *impossibility* of the co-existence of a dark earth and a shining sun. Any person who has ever been in Pittsburg, Glasgow, or the manufacturing districts of England, and has seen how the smoke of even a hundred factory chimneys will shroud the heavens, can easily comprehend how a similar discharge, on a larger scale, from the thousands of primal volcanoes,† would cover the earth with the pall of darkness. By the eruption of a single volcano, in the island of Sumbawa, in 1815, the air was filled with ashes, from Java to Celebes, darkening an area of more than 200,000 square miles; and the darkness was so profound in Java, three hundred miles distant from the volcano, that nothing equal to it was ever witnessed in the darkest night.‡ Those who have witnessed the fogs raised on the Banks of Newfoundland, in the Gulf of St. Lawrence, and in the Bay of Fundy, by the mingling of currents of water of slightly different temperatures, can be at no loss to conceive the density of the vapors produced by the boiling of the sea around and over the multitude of volcanoes ‖ which have produced the countless *atolls* of the Pacific, and by the vast upheavals of thousands of miles of heated rocks of the primary formations into the beds of primeval oceans. While such processes were in progress, it was impossible but that darkness should be upon the face of the deep.§ Even now, a slight change of atmospheric density and temperature would vail the earth with darkness. We see this substantially done every time that God "covereth the light with clouds, and commandeth it not to shine by the cloud that cometh betwixt," although the Sun continues to shine with all his

---

* Connection of Physical Sciences, 288.   ‖ Cosmos, vol. 1, p. 250.
† Cosmos, vol. 1, p. 250.   § Cosmos, vol. 1, pp. 198, 216.
‡ Lyell's Principles of Geology, 465.

usual splendor. To understand how there may be day without sunshine, we need only conceive the whole earth temporarily enveloped in the vapors of the unastronomical atmosphere of Peru, thus described by Humboldt:

"A thick mist obscures the firmament in this region for many months, during the period called *tiempo de la garua*. Not a planet —not the most brilliant stars of the southern hemisphere—are visible. It is frequently almost impossible to distinguish the position of the moon. If, by chance, the outline of the Sun's disc be visible during the day, it appears devoid of rays, as if seen through colored glasses. According to what modern geology has taught us to conjecture concerning the ancient history of our atmosphere, its primitive condition in respect to its mixture and density *must have been unfavorable to the transmission of light*. When we consider the numerous processes which, in the primary world, may have led to the separation of the solids, fluids, and gases around the earth's surface, the thought involuntarily arises, *how narrowly the human race escaped being surrounded with an untransparent atmosphere*, which, though not greatly prejudicial to some classes of vegetation, would yet have completely vailed the whole of the starry canopy. All knowledge of the structure of the universe could then have been withheld from the enquiring spirit of man."* The Sun, then, may have shone with all his brilliancy, for thousands of years, and a single ray never have penetrated the darkness upon the face of the deep.

But there is another well ascertained fact, which equally refutes the infidel's assumption. There is no necessary connection between the Sun and sunshine. The Sun may have existed for thousands of years as the center of the solar system, and the planets may have revolved around him, as they do now, while so far from shedding a single ray of light on any of them, he may have derived a feeble illumination from their beams. Modern science has discovered the astonishing fact, that at this moment the globe of the Sun is not a source of light to itself, much less to us; that, in fact, light is no more connected with the Sun than with a candlestick; and that the Bible description of the Sun as a *light-bearer*, expresses the results of the latest researches of Herschell, Encke, and Arago.

---

* Cosmos, vol. 3, p. 139.

The Sun consists mainly of a dark nucleus, like the body of the earth, and other planetary globes, surrounded by two atmospheres, of enormous depths, the one nearest to him being cloudy and dense, like our atmosphere, while the loftier stratum consists of those dazzling phosphorescent zephyrs that bestow light and heat on so many surrounding spheres. This phosphorescent atmosphere, or *photosphere*, as it is called, is by no means inseparably attached to the surface of the nucleus, or in any degree stable, but is subject to extensive fluctuations, and the most violent commotions; being frequently swayed and whirled aside, laying bare the surface of the dark globe beneath, for thousands of miles, to the observation of astronomers, and even to the naked eye. So far from being necessarily a source of light to the universe, the Sun's light is but very faintly visible on his own globe. "We approach the question" (of the inhabitability of the Sun,) says Sir David Brewster, "with the certain knowledge that the Sun is not a red hot globe, but that its nucleus is a solid, opaque mass, receiving very little light and heat (only seven rays out of a thousand) from its luminous atmosphere." Outside of this photosphere another gaseous, transparent atmosphere has been discovered.*

Any one of these facts is fatal to the assumption, that the Sun could not exist without shining, and that his light must have necessarily been visible through the universe ever since the creation of the heavens and the earth. His dark, solid nucleus may have existed for millions of years, as the center of gravity, around which the solar system revolved, and have given out no more light or heat than it does this day, or than the dark suns do around which Procyon and Sirius now revolve.† His luminous photosphere may either not have existed at all, or its gases not have been inflamed or electrically excited into luminosity. No man can adduce the shadow of a proof that the Sun shone nine minutes before the first recorded observation—namely, that recorded by the Author of the Bible, in the first of Genesis. The Sun's outer atmosphere may have been as dense as his inner one: in which case this radiance of his photosphere would have been as effectually veiled as a gas lamp by a London fog. And the simple possibility of any of these

---

* Nicholl's Solar System, 174. Herschell's Outlines, ₴389. More Worlds than One, 98. Cosmos, vol. 4, p. 372.

† Cosmos, vol. 3, p. 253.

events, or indeed of any contingency by which the Sun could exist as a dark body, is quite sufficient to vindicate the Bible from the charge of contradicting the facts of science, and teaching impossibilities. But we will go further, and show that so far from light being an essential property of suns, it is a very variable attribute, and that in several cases suns have ceased, and others begun to shine, before our eyes.

The fixed stars are self luminous bodies, similar to our Sun, only immensely distant from us. Their numbers, magnitudes, and places, are known and recorded. But new stars have frequently flashed into view, where none were previously seen to exist; and others have gradually grown dim and disappeared, without changing their place; and a few, which had disappeared, have re-appeared in the same spot they formerly occupied; while others have changed their color since the era of astronomical observation. In short, there is no permanence in the heavens, any more than on the earth; but a perpetual progress and change is the destiny of suns and stars, of which the most conspicuous indication is the variability of their powers of giving light, of which I shall transcribe a few instances.

"On the 11th of November, 1572, as the illustrious Danish astronomer, Tycho, was walking through the fields, he was astonished to observe a new star in the constellation Cassiopea, beaming with a radiance quite unwonted in that part of the heavens. Suspecting some delusion about his eyes, he went to a group of peasants, to ascertain if they saw it, and found them gazing at it with as much astonishment as himself. He went to his instrument, and fixed its place, from which it never after appeared to deviate. For some time it increased in brightness—greatly surpassed Sirius in luster, and even Jupiter. It was seen by good eyes in the day time: a thing which happens only to Venus, under very favorable circumstances; and at night it pierced through clouds which obscured the rest of the stars. After reaching its fullest brightness, it again diminished, passed through all degrees of visible magnitude, assuming in succession the hues of a dying conflagration, and then finally disappeared." "It is impossible to imagine any thing more tremendous than a conflagration that could be visible at such a distance." *

Astronomers now recognize a class of such *Temporary Stars*,

---

* Nicholl's Solar System, 188. Connection of Physical Sciences, 363.

which have appeared from time to time in different parts of the heavens, blazing forth with extraordinary luster, and after remaining awhile, apparently immovable, have died away, and left no trace.* Twenty-one of such appearances of new suns are on record.†

Still further, many familiar suns have ceased to shine. "On a careful re-examination of the heavens, *many stars are found to be missing.*" ‡ "There are many well authenticated cases of the disappearance of old stars, whose places had been fixed with a degree of certainty not to be doubted. In October, 1781, Sir William Herschell observed a star, No. 55 in Flamstead's Catalogue, in the constellation Hercules. In 1790 the same star was observed by the same astronomer, but since that time no search has been able to detect it. The stars 80 and 81 of the same catalogue, both of the fourth magnitude, have likewise disappeared. In May, 1828, Sir John Herschell missed the star numbered 42, in the constellation Virgo, which has never since been seen. Examples might be multiplied, but it is unnecessary." §

The demonstration of the variableness of the light-giving power of suns is completed by the phenomena of the class emphatically called *variable stars;* though the best astronomers are now agreed that *variability, and not uniformity,* in the emission of light, is the general character of the stars. ‖ But the variations which occur before our eyes impress us more deeply than those which require centuries for their completion. Sir John Herschell has observed and graphically described one such instance of variation of light.

"The star Eta Argus has always hitherto been regarded as a star of the second magnitude; and I never had reason to regard it as variable. In November, 1837, *I saw it, as usual.* Judge of my surprise to find, on the 16th of December, that *it had suddenly become a star of the first magnitude,* and almost equal to Rigel. It continued to increase. Rigel is now not to be compared with it. It exceeds Arcturus, and is very near equal to Alpha Centauri, being, at the moment I write, the fourth star in the heavens, in the order of brightness.¶ It has since passed through several variations of luster. Humboldt gives a catalogue of twenty-four of such stars, whose variations have been recorded."

---

* Herschell's Outlines, § 827.
† Cosmos, vol. 8, p. 210.
‡ Herschell's Outlines, § 832.
§ Mitchell's Planetary and Stellar Worlds, 294.
‖ Cosmos, vol. 3, p. 253.
¶ Astronomical Observations, 351.

"A strange field of speculation is opened by this phenomenon. Here we have a star fitfully variable to an astonishing extent, and whose fluctuations are spread over centuries, apparently in no settled period, and with no regularity of progression. What origin can we ascribe to these sudden flashes and relapses? What conclusions are we to draw as to the comfort or habitability of a system depending for its supply of light and heat on such an uncertain source? Speculations of this kind can hardly be termed visionary, when we consider that, from what has been before said, we are compelled to admit a community of nature between the fixed stars and our own Sun; and when we reflect, that geology testifies to the fact of extensive changes having taken place, at epochs of the most remote antiquity, in the climate and temperature of our globe: changes difficult to reconcile with the operation of secondary causes, such as a different distribution of sea and land, but which would find an easy and natural explanation in a slow variation of the supply of light and heat afforded by the Sun himself."* "I cannot otherwise understand alterations of heat and cold so extensive as at one period to have clothed high northern latitudes with a more than tropical luxuriance of vegetation, and at another to have buried vast tracts of Europe, now enjoying a genial climate, and smiling with fertility, under a glacier crust of enormous thickness. Such changes seem to point to causes more powerful than the mere local distribution of land and water can well be supposed to have been. In the slow secular variations of our supply of light and heat from the Sun, *which, in the immensity of time, may have gone to any extent, and succeeded each other in any order, without violating the analogy of siderial phenomena which we know to have taken place*, we have a cause, not indeed established as a fact, but readily admissible as something beyond a bare possibility, fully adequate to the utmost requirements of geology. A change of half a magnitude on the luster of our Sun, regarded as a fixed star, spread over successive geological epochs—now progressive, now receding, now stationary—*is what no astronomer would now hesitate to admit as a perfectly reasonable and not improbable supposition.*†

The most eminent astronomers are perfectly unanimous in their deductions from these facts. They regard *variability as the gen-*

---

* Outlines, § 830.   † Astronomical Observations, 351.

eral characteristic of *suns and stars, our own Sun not excepted.* "We are led, says Humboldt, by analogy to infer, that as the fixed stars *universally* have not merely an apparent, but a real motion of their own, so their surfaces or luminous atmospheres are generally subject to those changes (in their "light process") which recur, in the great majority, in extremely long, and therefore unmeasured, and probably undeterminable periods, or which, in a few, recur without being periodical, as it were, by a sudden revolution, either for a longer or a shorter time." And he asks, *Why should our Sun differ from other suns?*

In reference to the extinction of suns, he says: "What we no longer see is not necessarily annihilated. It is merely the transition of matter into new forms—into combinations which are subject to new processes. Dark cosmical bodies may, by a renewed process of light, again become luminous."* In confirmation of the fact adduced in support of this view, by La Place, "that those stars which have become invisible, after having surpassed Jupiter in brilliancy, have not changed their place during the time they continued visible," he adds, "The luminous process has simply ceased. Bessel asserts † that, *"No reason exists for considering luminosity an essential property of these bodies."* And Nicholl sums up the matter in the following emphatic words: "No more is light *inherent* in the Sun than in Tycho's vanished star; and with it and other orbs, a time may come when, through the consent of all the powers of nature, he shall cease to be required to shine. *The womb which contains the Future is that which bore the Past."* ‡

Here, then, we behold astronomy presenting to our observation facts and processes so similar to those which revelation presents to our faith, that all those men who are most profoundly versed in her lore, reasoning solely from the facts of science, and without any reference to the Bible, unanimously conclude that there was such a state of darkness and confusion before our era as the Bible declares —that its causes were most probably such as the Bible implies— and that the sudden illuminating of dark bodies, and their extinction, and even re-illumination, are facts so perfectly well authenticated as matters of observation in regard to other suns, that no reasonable man can hesitate to believe any credible assurance that our Sun has passed through such a process. With what feelings,

---

* Cosmos, vol. 3, p. 222-232.   † Cosmos, vol. 3, p. 246.   ‡ Solar System, 190.

then, are we to regard the ignorance and brazen-faced impudence of men who, in defiance of the most common facts, and in contradiction to the demonstrations of science, blaspheme the God of truth as a teacher of falsehood, because he speaks of light distinct from that of the Sun? Surely, such men are those whom he describes as "having the understanding darkened, being alienated from the life of God, through the ignorance that is in them, because of the blindness of their hearts. In whom the God of this world hath blinded the minds of them that believe not." *

These facts of the sudden kindling of stars, their gradual passage through all the hues of a dying conflagration, and their final extinction and present blackness of darkness, are facts of fearful omen to the enemies of God. They are the original threatenings of Heaven, whence the fearful language of Bible warning is derived. They attest its truth, and illustrate its import.

The favorite theory of the unbeliever is the uniformity of nature. "Where," says he, "is the promise of Christ's coming to judgment; for since the fathers fell asleep, all things continue as they were since the beginning of the world?" But the telescope dispels the illusion, exhibits the course of nature as a succession of catastrophes, displays the conflagration of other worlds, and the extinction of their suns, before our eyes, and asks, *Why should our Sun differ from other suns?* It is not the preacher, but the philosopher, who has turned prophet, when—looking back on the period when the Siberian elephant and rhinoceros were frozen amidst their native jungle, and icebergs visited the plains of India—he proclaims, "*The womb that bore the Past contains the Future.*"

The threatenings of God's word are invested with a mantle of terrible literality by the facts we have been contemplating. Raised at the day of resurrection, in these bodies, and with these senses, and this capability of rejoicing in the light, and shuddering and pining amidst outward gloom, physical darkness will be the terrible prison of those who chose darkness rather than light, because their deeds were evil. The Father of Lights shall withdraw his blessed influences from the hearts, the dwellings, the eyes, of those who say to him, "Depart from us, for we desire not the knowledge of thy ways." The Sun shall cease to vivify God's corn, and wine, and oil, which ungodly men consume upon their lusts. The Moon shall cease to shine upon the robber's toil, and the Stars to illumine

---

* Eph. 4: 18. 2 Cor. 4: 4.

the adulterer's path. The light of Heaven shall cease to gild the field of carnage, where men perform the work of Hell. In the very midst of your worldliness and business, Unbeliever, when you are in all the engrossment of buying and selling, and planting and building, and marrying and giving in marriage, without warning or expectation, "the Sun shall go down at noon, and the stars shall be darkened in the clear day." As in the warning and example given to the enemies of the Lord in Egypt, thick darkness, that may be felt, shall wind its inevitable chains around you, preventing your escape from the judgment of the great day, and giving you a fearful foretaste of that "blackness of darkness for ever" of which you are now forewarned in the Word of Truth.

"The Sun shall be darkened, and the Moon shall not give her light,
"And the stars shall fall from the heavens,
"And the powers of the heavens shall be shaken;
"And then shall appear the sign of the Son of Man in the heavens,
"And then shall all the tribes of the earth mourn;
"And they shall see the Son of Man coming in the clouds of heaven,
"With power and great glory."
"Cast ye the unprofitable servant into outer darkness;
"There shall be weeping and gnashing of teeth."
"Hear ye, and give ear; be not proud,
"For the Lord hath spoken.
"Give glory to the Lord, your God,
"Before he cause darkness,
"And before your feet stumble upon the dark mountains;
"And while ye look for light,
"He turn it into the shadow of death,
"And make it gross darkness."
"I am the light of the world;
"He that followeth me shall not walk in darkness,
"But shall have the light of life." *

---

* Matthew, 24: 29. John, 8: 12. Jere. 13: 15. Matt. 22: 13, and 25: 30.

No. 33.

TELESCOPIC VIEWS OF SCRIPTURE.

No kind of knowledge is more useful to man than the knowledge of his own ignorance; and no instrument has done more to give him such knowledge than the telescope. Faith is the believing of facts we do not know, upon the word of one who does. If any one knows every thing, or thinks he does, he can have no faith. A deep conviction of our own ignorance is, therefore, indispensable to faith. The telescope gives us this conviction, in two ways. It shows us that we see a great many things we do not perceive, tells us the size and the distances of those little sparks that adorn the sky, and leads us to reason out their true relations to our earth. Then it tells us that what we see is little of what is to be seen; that our knowledge is but a drop from the great ocean—a rushlight, sparkling in the vast darkness of the unknown. It tells us that we do not see right, and that we do not see far; and that there may be things, both in heaven and earth, not dreamed of in our philosophy. Further, it confirms the Bible testimony concerning the facts of its own province, by removing all improbability from some of its most wonderful narratives, attesting the accuracy of its language, and confirming, by some of its most recent discoveries, the truth of its statements. Our space will only allow us to select five illustrations of the tendency of faith in the telescope, to produce faith in the Bible.

1. One of the latest astronomical discoveries throws light upon one of the most ancient scientific allusions of the Bible, and one which has perplexed both commentators and geologists: *that which hints at the second causes of the deluge.* Not that it is at all needful for us to be able to tell where God Almighty procured the water to drown the ungodly sinners of the old world, before we believe his word that he did so; unless, indeed, somebody has explored the universe, and knows that there is not water enough in it for that purpose, or that it is so far away that he could not fetch it; for, as to the fact itself, geology assures us that all the dry land on earth has been drowned, not only once, but many times. It is not the province of the commentator, but of the geologist, to account for the phenomenon.

Several solutions of the difficulty of finding water enough for the purpose have been proposed. One of these supposes that, as the earth is known by its density not to be solid, some of its internal caverns are filled with water, which, when heated by neighboring volcanic fires, would expand one twenty-third of its bulk, and flow out, and raise the ocean. When the volcanic fire was burnt out, and the water cooled, it would of course contract to its former dimensions, and the ocean recede. These caverns they suppose to be meant by "the fountains of the great deep," in Genesis vii : 11.

But the Bible describes another, and plainly a very important source of the waters of the deluge, in the rain which fell for forty days and forty nights. At present, all the water in our atmosphere comes from the sea, by evaporation; and the quantity is too insignificant to cover the globe to any considerable depth. Divines and philosophers were perplexed to give any adequate explanation of this language, and considered it simply as Noah's description of the appearance of things as viewed from the ark, rather than an accurate explanation of the actual causes of the deluge. Now, it is certainly true, that the Bible does describe things as they appear to men. It is, however, beginning to be discovered, that these popular appearances are far more closely connected with philosophical reality than a self-sufficient pedantry will allow. Our purblind astronomy and prattling geology may be as inadequate to expound the mysteries of the Bible philosophy, as was the incoherent science of Strabo and Ptolemy. The experience of another planet, now transacting before our eyes, admonishes us not to limit the resources of Omnipotence by our narrow experience, or to suppose that our young science has catalogued all the weapons in the arsenal of the Almighty.

The planet Saturn is surrounded by a revolving belt, consisting of several distinct rings, containing an area a hundred and forty-six times greater than the surface of our globe, with a thickness of a hundred miles. From mechanical considerations it had been proved that these rings could not be of a uniform thickness all around, else when a majority of his seven moons were on the same side, the attraction would draw them in upon him, on the opposite side; and once attracted to his surface, they could never get loose again, if they were solid.* It was next ascertained that the mo-

---

* Kendall's Uranography, 268.

tions of the moons and of the rings were such, that if the inequality was always in the same place, the same result must follow; so that the ring must be capable of changing its thickness, according to circumstances. It must be either composed of an immense number of small solid bodies, capable of shifting freely about among themselves, or else be fluid. Finally, it has been demonstrated that this last is the fact; that the density of this celestial ocean is nearly that of water; and that the inner portion, at least, is so transparent, that the planet has been seen through it.* "The ring of Saturn is, then, a stream or streams of fluid, rather denser than water, flowing about the primary." † The extraordinary fact, which shows us how God can deluge a planet when he pleases, I give not in the words of a divine, but of a philosopher, whose thoughtless illustration of scripture is all the more valuable, that it is evidently unintentional.

"M. Otto Struve, Mr. Bond, and Sir David Brewster, are agreed that Saturn's third ring is fluid, that it is not of very recent formation, and that it is not subject to rapid change. And they have come to the extraordinary conclusion, that the inner border of the ring has, since the day of Huygens, been gradually approaching to the body of Saturn, and that we may expect, sooner or later—perhaps in some dozen years—to see the rings united with the body of the planet. *With this deluge impending, Saturn would scarcely be a very eligible residence for men, whatever it might be for dolphins."* ‡

Knowing, as we most certainly do, that the fluid envelopes of our own planet were once exceedingly different from the present, § here is a possibility quite sufficient to stop the mouth of the scoffer. Let him show that God did not, or prove that he could not, suspend a similar series of oceans over the earth, or cease to pronounce a universal deluge impossible.

2. That sublime ode, in which Deborah describes *the stars in their courses as fighting against Sisera,*‖ has been rescued from the grasp of modern scoffers and impostors, by the progress of astronomy. By both these classes has it been alleged as lending its support to the delusions of judicial astrology; the one class desiring to damage the Bible as a teacher of superstition, and the

---

* Annual of Scientific Discovery, 1856, p. 380.   † Ib., 1852, p. 376.
‡ Ib., 1856, p. 377.   § Cosmos, vol. 1, pp. 198-215.   ‖ Judges, 5.

other to help their trade by pleading its authority. The Bible reader will doubtless be greatly surprised to hear it asserted, that the Bible lends its sanction to this antiquated, and, as he thinks, exploded superstition. He knows how expressly the Bible forbids God's people to have any thing to do with it, or with its heathenish professors. "Thus saith the Lord, Learn not the way of the heathen, and be not dismayed at the signs of heaven, for the heathen are dismayed at them."* And they will be still more surprised to learn, that those who object against the Bible, that it ascribes a controlling influence to the stars, are firm believers in Reichenbach's discovery of *odyle:* an influence from the heavenly bodies so spiritual and powerful, that they imagine it able to govern the world, instead of God Almighty.†

The passage thus variously abused is a description, in highly poetic strains, of the battle between the troops of Israel and those of Sisera: of the defeat of the latter, and of an earthquake and tempest, which completed the destruction of his exhausted troops. The glory of the victory is wholly ascribed to the Lord God of Israel; while the rain, the thunder, lightning, swollen river, and "the stars in their courses," are all described, in their subordinate places, as only his instruments—the weapons of his arsenal.

"Lord, when thou wentest out of Seir,

---

* Jeremiah, 10.

† Some of my readers may deem any notice of such a subject, in the nineteenth century, entirely unnecessary; but having lived for some years within sight of the dwelling of a woman who publicly advertised herself in the newspapers as a professor of astrology, and seen the continual flow of troubled minds to the promised light—the humble serving-girl stealing up the side entrance, and the princely chariot discharging its willing dupes at the door, and rolling hastily away, to await them at the corner—I know of a certainty that folly is not yet dead. There are women—aye, and men too—who are above the folly of reading the Bible, but just wise enough to pay five dollars for, and spend hours in the study of, an uncouth astrological picture, representing a collocation of the stars, which was never witnessed by any astronomer—men who would not give way to the superstition of supposing that their destiny was regulated by the will of Almighty God, yet believe that every living creature's fate is regulated by the aspect of the stars at the hour of his nativity; the same stars always causing the same period of life and mode of death; though every day's experience testifies the contrary. The same stars presided over the birth of the poor soldier, who perished in an instant at Austerlitz; of his Imperial Master, who pined for years in St. Helena; of the old gentleman who died in his own bed, of gout; and of the batch of puppies, whereof old Towser was the only surviving representative, the other nine having found their fate in the horse-pond, in defiance of the controlling stars. They were all born at the same hour, and under the same auspices, and destined to the same fate, by the laws of astrology.

"When thou marchedst out of the field of Edom,
"The earth trembled, and the heavens dropped,
"The clouds also dropped down water;
"The mountains also melted from before the Lord,
"Even that Sinai, from before the Lord God of Israel."

Then, after describing the battle, she alludes to the celestial artillery, and to the effects of the storm in swelling the river, and sweeping away the fugitives who had sought the fords:

"They fought from heaven;
"The stars in their courses fought against Sisera;
"The river Kishon swept them away:
"That ancient river, the river Kishon." *

After describing some further particulars, the hymn concludes with an allusion to the clearing away of the tempest, and the appearance of the unclouded Sun over the field of victory:

"So let all thine enemies perish, O, Lord;
"But let them that love thee be as the Sun, when he goeth forth
  in his might."

Where is there the least allusion here to any controlling influence of the stars? You might just as well say, "The Bible ascribes a controlling influence over the destinies of men, to the river Kishon;" for they are both spoken of, in the same language, as instruments in God's hand for the destruction of his enemies.

But it is objected, "Even by this explanation you have the Bible representing the stars as causing the rain." Not so fast. If a man were very ignorant, and had never heard of any thing falling from the sky but rain, he might think so. And if the Bible did attribute to the stars some such influence over the vapors of the atmosphere, as experience shows the moon to possess over the ocean, are you able to demonstrate its absurdity?

Deborah, however, when she sang of the stars *in their courses* fighting against Sisera, was describing a phenomenon very different from a fall of rain—was, in fact, describing a fall of ærolites upon the army of Sisera. Multitudes of stones have fallen from the sky, and not less than five hundred such falls are recorded.

"On Sept. 1st, 1814, a few minutes before midday, while the sky was perfectly serene, a violent detonation was heard in the department of the Lot and Garonne. This was followed by three or four

---

* Judges, 5th ch.

others, and finally by a rolling noise, at first resembling a discharge of musketry, afterwards the rumbling of carriages, and lastly that of a large building falling down. Stones were immediately after precipitated to the ground, some of which weighed eighteen pounds, and sunk into a compact soil, to the depth of eight or nine inches; and one of them rebounded three or four feet from the ground."

"A great shower of stones fell at Barbatan, near Roquefort, in the vicinity of Bordeaux, on July 24th, 1790. A mass fifteen inches in diameter penetrated a hut and killed a herdsman and bullock. Some of the stones weighed twenty-five pounds, and others thirty pounds."

"In July, 1810, a large ball of fire fell from the clouds, at Shahabad, which burned five villages, destroyed the crops, and killed several men and women." *

Astronomers are perfectly agreed as to the character of these masses, and the source whence they come. "It appears from recent astronomical observations that the Sun numbers among his attendants not only planets, asteroids, and comets, but also immense multitudes of meteoric stones and shooting stars." † Aerolites are, then, really stars. They are composed of materials similar to those of our earth: the only other star whose materials we can compare with them. They have a proper motion around the Sun, in orbits distinct from that of the earth. They are capable of emitting the most brilliant light, in favorable circumstances. Some of them are as large as the asteroids. One, of 600,000 tons weight, passed within 25 miles of the earth, at the rate of 20 miles a second. A fragment of it reached the earth.‡ "That aerolites were called *stars* by the ancients, is indisputable. Indeed, Anaxagoras considered the stars to be only stony masses, torn from the earth by the violence of rotation. Democritus tells us that invisible dark masses of stone move with the visible stars, and remain on that account unknown, but sometimes fall upon the earth, and are extinguished, as happened with the stony star which fell near Aegos Potamos.§

---

* Dick's Celestial Scenery, p. 57, Applegate's edition, where many such instances are related.

† Vaughn's Report to the American Association for the advancement of Science, in Annual of Scientific Discovery for 1855, p. 364.

‡ Somerville's Connection of the Physical Sciences, 382.

§ Cosmos, vol. 1, p. 122; vol. 4, p. 569.

When Deborah, therefore, describes the *stars in their courses* as fighting against Sisera, it is an utterly unfounded assumption to suppose that she has any allusion to the baseless fancies of an astrology every-where condemned by the religion she professed, when a simple and natural explanation is afforded by the fact, that stars do fall from the heavens to the earth, and *that they do so in their courses*, and just by reason of their orbital motion; and that the ancients both knew the fact, and gave the right name to those bodies. Let no reasonable man delude himself with the notion that God has no weapons more formidable than the dotings of astrology, till he has taken a view of the arsenals of God's artillery, which he has treasured up against the day of battle and of war.

Here it may be well to notice the illustration which the remarkable showers of November meteors, particularly those of November, 1833, shed upon several much ridiculed texts of scripture. Scientific observation has fully confirmed and illustrated the scientific accuracy of the Bible in such expressions as, "the stars shall fall from heaven;" "there fell a great star from heaven, burning as it were a lamp;" "and the stars of heaven fell unto the earth, even as a fig-tree casteth her untimely figs, when she is shaken of a mighty wind." Whatever political or ecclesiastical events these symbols may signify, there can be no question, now, that the astronomical phenomenon used to prefigure them is correctly described in the Bible. Most of my readers have seen some of these remarkable exhibitions; but for the sake of those who have not, I give a brief account of one. "By much the most splendid meteoric shower on record, began at nine o'clock, on the evening of the 12th of November, 1833, and lasted till sunrise next morning. It extended from Niagara, and the northern lakes of America, to the south of Jamaica, and from 61° of longitude, in the Atlantic, to 100° of longitude in Central Mexico. Shooting stars and meteors of the apparent size of Jupiter, Venus, and even the full moon, darted in myriads towards the horizon, *as if every star in the heavens had darted from their spheres.*" They are described as having been as frequent as the flakes of snow in a snow-storm, and to have been seen with equal brilliancy over the greater part of the continent of North America.*

The source whence these meteors proceed is distinctly ascer-

---

* Connection of the Physical Sciences, 383.

tained to be, as was already remarked with regard to the aerolites, a belt of small planetoids, revolving around the Sun in a little less than a year, and in an orbit intersecting that of the earth, at such an angle, that every thirty-three years, or thereabouts, the earth meets the full tide on the 12th of November. These meteors are true and proper stars. "All the observations made during the year 1853 agree with those of previous years, and confirm what may be regarded as sufficiently well established: the cosmical origin of shooting stars." *

3. The language of the Bible with respect to *the circuit of the Sun* is found to have anticipated one of the most sublime discoveries of modern astronomy. True to the reality, as well as to the appearance of things, it is scientifically correct, without becoming popularly unintelligible.

There is a class of aspirants to gentility who refuse to recognize any person not dressed in the style which they suppose fashionable among the higher classes. A Glasgow butcher's wife, in the Highlands, attired in all the magnificence of her satins, laces, and jewelry, returned the courteous salute of the little woman in the gingham dress and gray shawl with a contemptuous toss of the head, and flounced past, to learn, to her great mortification, that she had missed an opportunity of forming an acquaintance with the Queen. So a large class of pretenders to science refuse to become acquainted with Bible truth, because it is not shrouded in the technicalities of science, but displays itself in the plain speech of the common people to whom it was given. They will have it, that because its author used common language, it was because he could not afford any other; and as he did not contradict every vulgar error believed by the people to whom he spoke, it was because he knew no better; and because the Hebrews knew nothing of modern discoveries in astronomy, geology, and the other sciences, and the Bible does not contain lectures on these subjects, the God of the Hebrews must have been equally ignorant, and the Bible consequently beneath the notice of a philosopher.

You will hear such persons most pertinaciously assert, that Moses believed all the absurdities of the Ptolemaic astronomy: that the earth is the immovable center, around which revolve the crystal sphere of the firmament, and the Sun, and Moon, and stars,

---

* Annual of Scientific Discovery, 1854, p. 361.

which are attached to it, after the manner of lamps to a ceiling; and that he, and the world generally in his day, had not emerged from the grossest barbarism and ignorance of all matters of natural science. Yet these very people will probably tell you, in the same conversation, of the wonderful astronomical observations made by the Egyptians, ten thousand years before the days of Adam! So beautiful is the consistency of infidel science. But when you enquire into the source of their knowledge of the philosophy of the ancients, you discover that they did not draw it from the writings of Moses, of which they betray the grossest ignorance, nor of any one who lived within a thousand years of Moses' time. Voltaire is their authority for all such matters. He transferred to the early Asiatics all the absurdities of the later Greek philosophers, and would have us believe that Moses, who wrote before these Greeks had learned to read, was indebted to them for his philosophy. Of the learning of the ancient patriarchs Voltaire does not tell them much, for a satisfactory reason.

Yet it might not have required much learning to infer, that the eyes, and ears, and nerves of men who lived ten times as long as we can, must have been more perfect than ours; that a man who could observe nature with such eyes, under a sky where Stoddart now sees the ring of Saturn, the crescent of Venus, and the moons of Jupiter, with the naked eye,* and continue his observations for eight hundred years, would certainly acquire a better knowledge of the appearance of things than any number of generations of short-lived men, called away by death before they have well learned how to observe, and able only to leave the shell of their discoveries to their successors; that unless we have some good reason for believing that the mind of man was greatly inferior, before the flood, to what it now is, the antediluvians must have made a progress in the knowledge of the physical sciences, during the three thousand one hundred and fifty-five years which elapsed from the creation to the deluge, much greater than the nations of Europe have effected since they began to learn their A, B, C, about the same number of years ago; and that though Noah and his sons might not have preserved all the learning of their drowned contemporaries, they would still have enough to preserve them from the reproach of ignorance and barbarism; at least until their sons have succeeded in building

---

* Letter to Herschell, from Oroomiah, in Persia—Annual of Scientific Discovery, 1854, p. 367.

a larger ship than the ark, or a city which would not look contemptible in the suburbs of Babylon.

When we know that the Chaldeans taught the Egyptians the expansive power of steam, and the induction of electricity by pointed conductors;—that from the most remote antiquity the Chinese were acquainted with decimal fractions, electro-magnetism, the mariner's compass, and the art of making glass;—that lenses have been found in the ruins of Nineveh, and that an artificial currency was in circulation in the first cities built after the flood;*—that astronomical observations were made in China, with so much accuracy, from the deluge till the days of Yau, B. C., 2357, that the necessary intercalations were made for harmonizing the solar with the lunar year, and fixing the true period of $365\frac{1}{4}$ days;—and that similar observations were conducted to a like result within a few years of the same remote period, in Babylon;—if he does not conclude that the world may have forgotten as much ancient lore during eighteen hundred years of idolatrous barbarism before the coming of Christ, as it has learned in the same number since—will, at least, satisfy himself that the ancient patriarchs were not ignorant savages.† "Whole nations," says La Place, "have been swept from the earth, with their languages, arts, and sciences, leaving but confused masses of ruins to mark the place where mighty cities stood. Their history, with a few doubtful traditions, has perished; *but the perfection of their astronomical observations marks their high antiquity, fixes the periods of their existence, and proves that even at that early time they must have made considerable progress in science."* ‡ The infidel theory, that the first men were savages, is a pure fiction, refuted by every known fact of their history.

That, however, is not the matter under discussion. We are not enquiring, now, what Moses and the prophets *thought*, but what the author of the Bible *told them to say*. The scribe writes as his

---

* "These tablets (of unbaked clay, with inscriptions, found in the tombs of Erech, the city of Nimrod—Gen. 10:10—and deciphered by Rawlinson,) were, in point of fact, the equivalent of our bank notes, and prove that a system of artificial currency prevailed in Babylon and Persia at an unprecedentedly early age: centuries before the introduction of paper and writing.

Rawlinson, in News of the Churches, February, 1857. *p.* 50.

† Wilkinson's Manners and Customs of the Egyptians, vol. 3, p. 106; Cosmos, vol. 1, pp. 173, 182; Chinese Repository, v. 9, p. 573; Williams' Middle Kingdom, vol. 2, p. 147.

‡ Connection of Physical Sciences, 82.

employer dictates. "I will put my words in thy mouth," said God to Jeremiah. "My tongue is as the pen of a ready writer," said David. The prophets began, not with "Thus saith Isaiah," but "Thus saith the Lord." Unless the Word of God was utterly different from all his other works, it must transcend the comprehension of man in some respects. The profoundest philosopher is as ignorant of the cause of the vegetation of wheat, as the mower who cuts it down; but their ignorance of the mysteries of organic force is no reason why the one may not harvest, and the other eat and live. Just so God's prophets conveyed precious mysteries to the Church, of the full import of which they themselves were ignorant; even as Daniel heard but understood not; and the prophets to whom it was revealed that they did not minister to themselves, but to us, enquired and searched diligently into the meaning of their own prophecies; which meaning, nevertheless, continued hid for ages and generations.* If the prophets of the old economy might be ignorant of the privileges of the gospel day, of which they prophesied, at God's dictation, they might very well be ignorant, also, of the philosophy of creation, and yet write a true account of the facts, from his mouth.

Let us suppose, then, that the ancient Hebrews and their prophets were, if not quite as ignorant of natural science as modern infidels are pleased to represent them, yet unacquainted with the discoveries of Herschell and Newton; and, as a necessary consequence, that their language was the adequate medium of conveying their imperfect ideas, containing none of the technicalities invented by philosophers to mark modern scientific discoveries; and that God desired to convey to them some religious instruction, through the medium of language. Must we suppose it indispensable for this purpose that he should use strange words, and scientific phrases, the meaning of which would not be discovered for thirty-three hundred years? Could not Dr. Alexander write a sabbath-school book, without filling it full of such phrases as "right ascension," "declination," "precession of the equinoxes," "radius vector," and the like? Or, if some wiseacre did prepare such a book, would it be very useful to children? Perhaps even we, learned philosophers of the nineteenth century, are not out of school yet. How many discoveries are yet to be made in all the

---

* Dan. 12: 8; 1 Pet. 1: 10; Eph. 1; 3.

sciences: discoveries which will doubtless render our fancied perfection as utterly childish to the philosophers of a thousand years hence, as the astronomy of the Greeks seems to us; and demand the use of technical language, which would be as unintelligible to us as our scientific nomenclature would have been to Aristotle. If God may not use popular speech in speaking to the people of any given period, but must needs speak the technical language of perfect science,—and if science is now, and always will be, of necessity, imperfect,—we are led to the sage conclusion, that every revelation from God to man must always be unintelligible!

Does it necessarily follow, that because the author of the Bible uses the common phrases, "sun rising," and "sun setting," in a popular treatise upon religion, that therefore he was ignorant of the rotation of the earth, and intended to teach that the Sun revolved around it? He is certainly under no more obligation to depart from the common language of mankind, and introduce the technicalities of science into such a discourse, than mankind in general, and our objectors in particular, are to do the like in their common conversation. Now, I demand to know whether they are aware that the earth's rotation on its axis is the cause of day and night? But do you ever hear any of them use such phrases as "earth rising," and earth setting?" But if an infidel's daily use of the phrases, "*sun rising,*" "*sun setting,*" and the like, does not prove, either that he is ignorant of the earth's rotation as the cause of that appearance, or that he intends to deceive the world by those phrases, why may not Almighty God be as well informed and as honest as the infidel, though he also condescends to use the common language of mankind.

Do you ever hear astronomers, in common discourse, use any other language? I suppose Lieut. Maury, and Herschell, and Leverrier and Mitchell, know a little of the earth's rotation; but they, too, use the English tongue very much like other people, and speak of sunrise and sunset; yet nobody accuses them of believing in the Ptolemaic astronomy. Hear the immortal Kepler, the discoverer of the laws of planetary revolution: "We astronomers do not pursue this science with the view of altering common language; but we wish to open the gates of truth, without affecting the vulgar modes of speech. We say with the common people, "The planets stand still, or go down;" "the sun rises, or sets;" meaning only that so the thing appears to us, although it is not truly so, as all astronomers are agreed. How much less should we require that the Scriptures of Divine Inspiration, setting aside the common modes of speech, should shape their words according to the model of the natural sciences, and by employing a dark and inappropriate phraseology about things which surpass the comprehension of those whom it designs to instruct, perplex the simple people of God, and thus obstruct its own way towards the attainment of the far more exalted end to which it aims."

It is evident, then, that God not only may, *but must* use popular language in addressing the people, in a work not professedly scientific; and that if this popular language be scientifically incorrect, such use of it neither implies his ignorance or approval of the error.

But it may be worthy of enquiry whether this popular language of mankind, used in the Bible, be scientifically erroneous. If the language be intended to express an absolute reality, no doubt it is erroneous to say the sun rises and sets; but if it be only intended to describe an appearance, and the words themselves declare that intention, it cannot be shown to be false to the fact. Now, when the matter is critically investigated, these phrases are found to be far more accurate than those of "earth rising," and "earth setting," which infidels say the author of the Bible should have used. For, as up and down have no existence in nature, save with reference to a spectator, and as the earth is always down with respect to a spectator on its surface, neither rising towards him, nor sinking from him, in reality, nor appearing to do so, unless in an earthquake, the improved phrases are false, both to the appearance of things, and to the cause of it. Whereas, our common speech, making no pretensions to describe the causes of appearances, cannot contradict any scientific discovery of these causes, and therefore cannot be false to the fact, while it truly describes all that it pretends to describe—the appearance of things—to our senses. And so, after all the outcry raised against it by sciolists, the vulgar speech of mankind, used by the Author of the Bible, must be allowed to be philosophical enough for his purpose, and theirs: at least till somebody favors both with a better.

Though we are in no way concerned, then, to prove that every poetical figure in Scripture, and every popular illustration taken from nature, corresponds to the accuracy of scientific investigation, before we believe the Bible to be a revelation of our duty to God

265.

and man, yet it may be worth while to enquire, further, whether we really find upon its sacred pages such crude and egregious scientific errors as infidels allege. We have seen in the last Tract, that they are not able to read even its first chapter without blundering. Indeed, they generally boast of their ignorance of its contents. It is a very good rule to take them at their word, and when they quote Scripture, to take it for granted *that they quote it wrong*, unless you know the contrary. The first thing for you to do when an infidel tells you the Bible says so and so, is to get the book, and see whether it does or not. You will generally find that he has either misquoted the words, or mistaken their meaning, from a neglect of the context; or perhaps has both misquoted and mistaken. Then, when you are satisfied of the correct meaning of the text, and he tells you that it is contrary to the discoveries of science, the next point is to ask him, *How do you know?* You will find his knowledge of science and scripture about equal. Both these tests should be applied to scientific objections to the Bible, as they are all composed of equal parts of Biblical blunders and philosophical fallacies.

In the objection under consideration, for instance, both statements are wrong. The Bible does not represent the earth as the immovable center of the universe, or as immovable in space at all. It does not represent the Sun and stars as revolving around it. Nor are the facts of astronomy more correctly stated. It is not the Bible, but our objector, that is a little behind the age in his knowledge of science.

If we enquire for those texts of Scripture which represent the earth as the immovable center of the universe, we shall be referred to the figurative language of the Psalms, the book of Job, and other poetical parts of Scripture, which speak of the "foundations of the earth," "the earth being established," "abiding for ever," and the like, when the slightest attention to the language would show *that it is intended to be figurative.* The accumulation of metaphors and poetical images in some of these passages, is beautiful and grand in the highest degree; but none, save the most stupid reader, would ever dream of interpreting them literally. Take, for instance, Psalm 104: 1–6, where, in one line, the world is described as God's house, with beams, and chambers, and foundations; but in the very next line the figure is changed, and it is viewed as an infant, covered with the deep, as with a garment.

"Bless the Lord, O my soul.
"O Lord my God thou art very great;
"Thou art clothed with honor and majesty:
"Who coverest thyself with light, as with a garment:
"Who stretchest out the heavens like a curtain:
"*Who layeth the beams of his chambers upon the waters:*
"Who walketh upon the wings of the wind:
"Who maketh his angels spirits:
"His ministers a flaming fire:
" *Who laid the foundations of the earth,*
" *That it should not be removed for ever.*
"Thou coveredst it with the deep, as with a garment:
"The waters stood above the mountains."

But if any one is so gross as to insist on the literality of such a passage, and to allege that it teaches the absolute immobility of the earth, let him tell us what sort of immobility the 3d verse teaches, and how a building could be stable, the beams of whose chambers are *laid upon the waters*—the chosen emblems of instability. "He hath founded it upon the seas: he hath established it upon the floods," says the same poet, in another Psalm: 24: 1. This, and all other expressions quoted as declaring the immobility of the earth *in space*, are clearly proved, both by the words used, and the sense of the context, to refer to an entirely different idea: namely, *its duration in time*. Thus, Eccl. 1: 4, "One generation passeth away, and another cometh; but the earth abideth for ever," is manifestly contrasting the duration of earth with the generations of short-lived men, and has no reference to motion in space at all.

Again, in Psalm 119: 89–91, our objectors find another Bible declaration of the immobility of the earth in space:

"For ever, O Lord, thy word is settled in heaven;
" Thy faithfulness is unto all generations;
"Thou hast established the earth, and it abideth.
" *They continue to this day*, according to thine ordinances."

The same permanence is here ascribed to the heavens (to which, as our objectors argue, the Bible ascribes a perpetual revolution) as to the earth. The next verse explains this permanence to be *continuance to this day*: durability, not immobility. That the word establish does not necessarily imply fixture, is evident from its application, in Prov. 8: 28: "He *established* the clouds," the most fleeting of all things. Nor is the Hebrew word, *kun* (whence our

English word, cunning), inconsistent with motion; else, the Psalmist had not said that "a good man's footsteps are *established* by the Lord." * "He *established* my goings." Wise arrangement is the idea, not permanent fixture.

The same remarks apply to Psalm 93: 1,—96: 10,—1 Chron. 16: 30, and many other similar passages.

"The world is established, that it cannot be moved;
"Thy throne is established of old:
"Thou art from everlasting."

Where the establishment, which is contrasted with the impossible removal, and which explains its import, is evidently not a local fixing of some material seat, in one place, but the everlasting duration of God's authority. The idea is not that of position in space, at all, but continued duration.

Space does not allow us to quote all the passages which refer to this subject; but after an examination of every passage in the Bible usually referred to in this connection, and of a multitude of others bearing upon it, I have no hesitation in saying, that it does not contain a single text which asserts or implies the immobility of the earth in space. The notion was drawn from the absurdities of the Greek philosophy, and the superstitions of Popery, but was never gathered from the word of God.

But it is alleged that other passages of scripture do plainly and unequivocally express the motion of the Sun, and his course in a circuit; as, for instance, the nineteenth Psalm:

"In them he hath set a tabernacle for the Sun,
"Which is as a bridegroom coming out of his chamber,
"And rejoiceth as a strong man to run a race.
"His going forth is from the end of heaven,
"And his circuit unto the ends of it."

And again, in the account of Joshua's miracle, in the tenth chapter of his book, it is quite evident that the writer supposed the Sun to be in motion, in the same way as the Moon, for he commanded them both to stand still: "Sun, stand thou still upon Gibeon, and thou Moon in the valley of Ajalon. And the Sun stood still, and the Moon stayed, until the people had avenged themselves upon their enemies." Now, it is said, if the writer had known what he was about, he would have known that the Sun

---

* Ps. 40: 1, and 37: 23, margin.

was already standing still, and would have told the earth to stop its rotation. And if the earth had obeyed the command, we should never have heard of the miracle; for, as the earth rotates at the rate of a thousand miles an hour, the concussion produced by such a stoppage would have projected Joshua, and Israelites, and Amorites, beyond the Moon, to pursue their quarrel among the fixed stars.

When we hear men of some respectability bring forward such stuff, we are constrained to wonder, not merely were they ever at school, but if they ever traveled in a railroad car, or whether they suppose their hearers to be so ignorant of the most common facts, as to believe that there is no way of bringing a carriage to a stand but by a sudden jerk, or that God is more stupid than the brakesman of an express train. We will do them the justice, however, to say, that they did not invent it, but merely shut their eyes, and opened their mouths, and swallowed it for philosophy, because they found it in the writings of an infidel scoffer, and of a Neological professor of theology*—an edifying example of infidel credulity!

Let it be noticed, that in neither of these texts, nor in any other portion of scripture, does the Bible say a single word about the revolution of the Sun *round the earth*, as the common center of the universe; on which, however, the whole stress of the objection is laid. The passages do not prove what they are adduced to prove. They speak of the Sun's motion, and of the Sun's orbit, *but they do not say that the earth is the center of that orbit.* These texts, then, do not prove the author of the Bible ignorant of the system of the universe.

The objection is based upon utter ignorance of one of the most important and best attested discoveries of modern astronomy: the grand motion of the Sun and Solar System through the regions of space, and the dependence of the rotation of all the orbs composing it, upon that motion. It is not the author of the Bible who is ignorant of the discoveries of modern astronomy—when he speaks of the orbit of the Sun, and his race from one end of the heavens to the other, and of the need of a miraculous interposition to stop his course for a single day—but his correctors, who have ventured to decry the statements of a book which commands the respect of such astronomers as Herschell and Rosse, while ignorant of those

---

* M. Voltaire; M. Cheneviere; Theol. Essays, vol. 1, p. 456.

elements of astronomy which they might have learned from a perusal of the books used by their children, in our common schools. For the benefit of such, however, I will present a brief explanation of the grounds upon which astronomers are as universally agreed upon the belief of the Sun's motion around a center of the firmament, as they are upon the belief of the revolution of the earth round the Sun.

When you are passing in a carriage, at night, through the street of a city lighted up by gas-lamps in the streets, and lights irregularly dispersed in the windows, or passing in a ferry-boat, from one such city to another, at a short distance from it, you observe that the lights which you are leaving appear to draw closer and closer together, while those towards which you are approaching widen out, and seem to separate from each other. If the night were perfectly dark, so that you could see nothing but the lights, you could certainly know not only that you were in motion, but also to what point you were moving, by carefully watching their appearances. So, if all the fixed stars were absolutely fixed, and the Sun and planets, including our earth, were moving in any direction—say to the north—then the stars towards which we were moving would seem to widen out from each other, and those which we were leaving would seem to close up; so that the space which appeared between any two stars in the south, in a correct map of the heavens, a hundred years ago, would be smaller, and that between any two stars in the north would be larger, than the space between the same stars upon a correct map now. Now, such changes in the apparent positions of stars are actually observed. The stars do not appear in the same places now as they did a hundred years ago.

The fixed stars, then, are either drifting past our Solar System, which alone remains fixed; or, the fixed stars are all actually at rest, and our Sun is drifting through them; or, our Solar System and the so called fixed stars are both in motion. One or other of these suppositions must be the fact. The first is simply the old Ptolemaic absurdity, only transferring the center of the universe to the Sun. The second is contrary to the observed fact, that multitudes of the stars which were supposed to be fixed, are actually revolving around each other, in systems of double, triple, and multiple suns. And both are contrary to the first principles of gravitation; for, as every particle of matter attracts every other, directly as the mass, and inversely as the square of the distance, if any one particle of matter in the universe is in motion, the square of its distance from every other particle varies, and its attraction is increased in one direction, and diminished in another; and so every particle of matter in free space, as far as the force of gravitation extends, will be put in motion too. But our earth, and the planets, and the double and triple stars, are in motion, and the law of gravitation extends to every known part of the universe; therefore, every known particle of matter in the universe is in motion too, our Sun included.

The third supposition, then, is most indisputably true: our Solar System, and all the heavenly bodies, are in motion. To this conclusion all the observed facts conform. The Bible does say that the Sun moves, and moves in a curve. All mathematicians prove that it must of necessity do so. All astronomers assert that it does so. The unanimous verdict of the scientific world is thus rendered by Nicholl: "*As to the subject itself, the grand motion of the Sun, as well as its present direction, must be received now as an established doctrine of Astronomy.*" * But the discovery was anticipated, three thousand years ago, by the Author of the Bible.

But, as will readily be perceived, the difficulty of determining either the direction or the rate of this motion is immensely increased in this case; for we are now not like persons riding in a carriage, watching the fixed lights in the street to determine our direction and rate of progress; but we are watching the lamps of a multitude of carriages, moving at various distances, and with various velocities, and, for any thing we can tell at first sight, in various directions. We are on board a steamer, and are watching the lights of a multitude of other steamers, also in motion; and it is not easy to find out, in the darkness, how either they or we are going. If each were pursuing its own independent course, without any common object or destination, the confusion would be so great that we could learn nothing of the rate or direction either of our own motion or theirs.

But astronomers are not content to believe that the universe is governed by accident. The whole science is based upon the as-

---

* Humboldt's Cosmos, vol. 1, p. 139; Herschell's Outlines, 380; Kendall's Uranography, 205.
† Architecture of the Heavens, 9th ed., p. 252.

sumption, that a presiding mind has impressed the stamp of order and regularity upon the whole cosmos. They are deeply convinced that God's law extends to all God's creation: that all his works display his intelligence, as well as his power, and proceed according to a wise plan. Having seen that all the stellar motions previously known are orderly motions, in circular or elliptical orbits, and that the most of the solid bodies belonging to our own system revolve in one direction, they reasoned from analogy that this might be the case with the Sun and fixed stars, and went to work with great diligence, to see whether it was or not; and, by comparing a great multitude of observations, ancient and modern, made both in the northern and southern hemisphere, and on all sorts of stars, they have come to the unanimous conclusion, that our own Sun, and all the bodies of the Solar System, are flying northward, at the rate of a hundred and fifty millions of miles a year—a thousand times faster than a railway train—towards the constellation Hercules, in R. A. 259° Dec. 35°.

Further, as the direction of this motion is slowly and regularly changing, just as the direction of the head of a steamer in wearing, or of a railway train running a curve, it is certain that the Sun is moving, not in a straight line, but in a curve. The revolution of the Sun in such an orbit was known to the Author of the Bible when he wrote, " *his circuit* is to the end of heaven." The direction of the circumference of a circle being known, that of its center can be found; for the radius is always a tangent to the circumference, and the intersection of two of these radii will be the center; so that, if we certainly knew the Sun's orbit to be circular, or nearly so, we could calculate the center. But as we do not certainly know its form, we cannot certainly calculate the center: we can only come near it. And as we know that the line which connects the circumference with the center of the Sun's orbit, runs through the group of stars known as the Pleiades, or the Cluster; and as all the stars along that line seem to move in the same direction—a direction different from that of the stars in other regions, just as they must do if they and we were revolving around that group—Argelander and others have concluded, with a high degree of probability, that the grand center around which the Sun and our firmament revolve, is that constellation which the Author of the Bible, more than three thousand years ago, called *kyme—the pivot*.

It would require a greater knowledge of electro-magnetism than most of my readers possess, to explain the connection of the earth's rotation with the Sun's grand movement. I will merely state the facts. Electro-magnetism is induced by friction. The regions of space are not empty, but filled with an ether, whose undulations produce light; and this ether is sufficiently dense to retard the motions of comets. The friction produced by the passage of the Sun and Solar System through this ether, at the rate of 20,000 miles an hour, must be immense, and is one source of electricity, and the principal source of electro-magnetism. This kind of electricity differs from the other kinds, in that *its action is always at right angles to the current, and tends to produce rotation in any wheel, cylinder, or sphere, along whose axis it flows.** The Sun, and all the planets traveling in the direction of their poles, the current is of course in the direction of the axis; and the result is, that while the Sun moves along his grand course, he and all the bodies of the system will rotate, by the influence of the electro-magnetism generated by that motion; and if he stops, his and their rotation stops too. Day and night on earth are produced by the Sun's motion causing the earth's rotation. You can see the principle illustrated by the child, who runs along the street with his windmill, to create a current, which will make it revolve. The Author of the Bible made no mistake when, desiring to lengthen the day, he commanded the Sun to stand still. It is not the Creator, but his correctors, who are ignorant of the mechanism of the universe.

Thus, these long-misunderstood and much-assailed Scriptures are not only vindicated, but far more than vindicated, by the progress of astronomical discovery. It not only proves the language of the Bible to be correct: it assures us that it is divine. The same hand which formed the stars to guide the simple peasant to his dwelling, at the close of day, and to lead the mighty intellects of Newton and of Herschell among the mysteries of the universe, formed those expressions which, to the peasant's eye, describe the apparent reality, and, to the astronomer's reason, demonstrate the reality of the appearance of the heavens, and are thus, alike to peasant and philosopher, the *oracles of God.* Here we have astronomical truth not discovered by astronomers, but revealed by

---

* Connection of the Physical Sciences, 171, 337, 315; Architecture of the Heavens, 286.

prophets—scientific discovery, in advance of science—predictions of the future progress of the human intellect, no less than revelations of the existing motions of the stars. He who wrote these oracles knew that the creatures to whom he gave them would one day unfold their hidden meaning (else he had not so written them), and, in the light of scientific discovery, see them to be as truly divine predictions of the advance of science, as the prophecies of Jeremiah and Ezekiel, read among the ruins of Thebes or Babylon, are seen to be predictions of the ruin of empires. Man's discoveries fade into insignificance in the presence of such unfolding mysteries; and we are led to our Bibles, with the prayer, "open mine eyes, that I may behold wondrous things out of thy law."

4. The ancient charter of the Church was written in the language of one of the most recent astronomical discoveries, thirty-six hundred years before Herschell and Rosse enabled us to understand its full significance: "He brought him forth abroad, and said unto him, '*Look now to heaven, and count the stars, if thou be able to number them.*' And he said unto him, '*So shall thy seed be.*'" *

The scenery was well calculated to impress Abraham's mind with a sense of the ability of Christ to fulfil a very glorious promise, by a very improbable event; but the illustration was as well calculated as the promise to test the character of that faith which takes God's word as sufficient evidence of things not seen; for, if the promise was a trying test of faith, so was the illustration. Before this, God had promised that his seed should be as the dust of the earth; and afterwards he declared it should be as the sand of the sea shore: the well known symbol of a multitude beyond all power of calculation. To couple the stars of heaven with the sand upon the sea shore, in any such connection as to imply that the stars too were innumerable, or that their number came within any degree of comparison with the ocean sands, must have seemed to Abraham in the highest degree mysterious, even as it has appeared to scoffers, in modern times, utterly ridiculous; for, though the first glance at the sky conveys the impression that the stars are really innumerable, the investigations of our imperfect astronomy seem to assure us that this is by no means the case. And, as the patriarch sat, night after night, at his tent door, and, in obedience

---

* Gen. 15: 5.

to the command of Christ, counted the stars, and made such a catalogue of them as his Chaldean preceptors had used, he would very speedily come to the conclusion, that so far as he could see, they were by no means innumerable; for the catalogue of Hipparchus reckons only 1026 as visible to one observer, and the whole number visible in both hemispheres by the naked eye does not exceed 5000.* And even if we suppose, what is very probable, that these old patriarchs had better eyes, as we know they had a clearer sky, than modern western observers, and that Abraham saw the moons of Jupiter and stars as small, still the number would not seem in the least degree comparable with the number of the sands upon the sea-shore—whereof a million are contained in a cubic inch,† a number greater than the population of the globe in a square foot, while the sum total of the human race, from Adam to this hour, would not approach to the aggregate of the sands of a single mile—for, though the stars of a size too small to be visible to our eyes, are much more numerous than the larger stars, yet even up to the range of view possessed by ordinary telescopes, they are by no means innumerable, nor nearly so. In fact, they are counted and registered, and the number of the stars of the 9th magnitude, which are four times as distant as the most distant visible to our eyes—so distant that their light is 586 years in travelling towards us—is declared to be exactly 37,739. Abraham's sense and Abraham's faith must have had many a conflict on this promise, as the faith and the sense of many of his children, especially the scientific portion of them, have since, when reading such portions as this and those other scriptures which represent it as an achievement of Omniscience, that "he counts the number of the stars, and calleth them all by their names." ‡ It is indeed remarkable how God delights to test the faith of his people, and stumble the pride of fools, by presenting this mysterious truth of the innumerable multitude of the stars, in every announcement of the wonderful works of him who is perfect in wisdom. Infant astronomy stretched out her hands to catch the stars, and count them. Many a proud infidel wondered that Moses could be so silly as to suppose he could not count the stars, and the believer often

---

* Nicholl's Architecture of the Heavens, 32.

† Ehrenberg computes that there are are 41,000,000 of the shells of animalculæ in a cubic inch of rotten stone.

‡ Ps. 147: 4.

wondered what these words could mean. But faith rests in the persuasion of two great truths: "God is very wise," and "I am very ignorant."

The increase of knowledge, by widening the boundaries of our ignorance, seemed for a time to render the difficulty even greater. The increased power of Herschell's telescopes, and his discovery of the constitution of the Milky Way, mark an era in the progress of astronomy, and enlarge our views of the extent of the universe, to an extent inconceivable by those who have not studied the science. Where we see only a faint whitish cloud stretching across the sky, Herschell's telescope disclosed a vast bed of stars. At one time he counted 588 stars in the field of his telescope. In a quarter of an hour, 116,000 passed before his eye. In another portion, he found 331,000 stars, in a single cluster.* He found the whole structure of that vast luminous cloud which spans the sky, "to consist entirely of stars, *scattered by millions, like glittering dust*, on the back ground of the general heavens."

Yet still it was not supposed to be at all impossible to estimate their numbers. Even this distinguished astronomer, a few years ago, computed it at eight or ten millions. Schroeter allowed twenty degrees of it to pass before him, and withdrew from the majestic spectacle, exclaiming, "What Omnipotence!" He calculated, however, that the number of the stars visible through one of the best telescopes in Europe, in 1840, was 12,000,000—a number equalled by a single generation of Abraham's descendants—far below the power of computation, and utterly insignificant, as compared with the sands of the sea.

Had our powers of observation stopped here, the great promise must still have seemed as mysterious to the Astronomer, as it once seemed to the Patriarch. But if either the Father of the Faithful, or the Father of Siderial Astronomy, had deluded himself with the notion, that he fully comprehended either the words or the works of him who is wonderful in counsel, and excellent in working, and argued thence that, because the revealed words and the visible works seemed not to correspond, they were really contradictory, he would have committed the blunder of modern infidels, who assume that they know every thing, and that as God's knowledge cannot be any greater than theirs, every scripture which their

---

* Dick's Siderial Heavens, 59; Herschell's Outlines.

science cannot comprehend must be erroneous. The grandest truths, imperfectly perceived in the twilight of incipient science, serve as stumbling-blocks for conceited speculators, as well as landmarks of the boundaries of knowledge to true philosophers, who will ever imbibe the spirit of Newton's celebrated saying: "I seem to myself like a child gathering pebbles on the shore, while the great ocean of knowledge lies unexplored before me;" or the profound remark of Humboldt: "What is seen does not exhaust that which is perceptible."

But the progress of science was not destined merely to coast the shore of this ocean. In 1845, Lord Rosse, and a band of accomplished astronomers, commenced a voyage through the immensities, with a telescope which has enlarged our view of the visible universe to 125,000,000 times the extent before perceived, and displayed far more accurately the real form and nature of objects previously seen. Herschell's researches into the Architecture of the Heavens, which have justly rendered his name immortal as the science he illustrated, had revealed the existence of great numbers of *nebulæ*—clouds of light—faint, yet distinct. He supposed many of these to consist of a luminous fluid, pretty near to us—at least, comparatively so; for to believe that they were stars, so far away as to be severally invisible in his forty feet telescope, while yet several of these clouds are distinctly seen by the naked eye, involved the belief of distance so astounding, and of multitudes so incredible, and of a degree of closeness of the several stars so unparalleled by any thing which even he had observed, that his imagination and reason failed to meet the requirements of such a problem. The supposition was, however, thrown out by this gigantic intellect, that these clouds might be firmaments: that the Bible word *heavens* might be literally plural; and more than that, he labored in the accumulation of facts which tended to confirm it. He disclosed the fact, that several of these apparent clouds, which, to very excellent telescopes, displayed only a larger surface of cloudy matter, did, in the reflector of his largest telescope, display themselves in their true character, as globular clusters, consisting of innumerable multitudes of glorious stars; and, moreover, that, stretching away far beyond star, or Milky Way, or nebulæ, he had seen, in some parts of the heavens, "a stippling," or uniform dotting of the field of view, by points of light too small to admit of any one being steadily or fixedly examined, *and too numerous for counting*, were it possible so to view them! What are these! Millions upon millions of years must have elapsed ere that faint light could reach our globe, from those profundities of space, though it travels like the lightning's flash. If they are stars, the sands of the sea-shore are as inferior in numbers as the surface of earth is inferior in dimensions to the arch of Heaven. But if these faint dots and stipplings are not single stars!—if they are star-clouds—galaxies—firmaments, like our Milky Way—our infinity is multiplied by millions upon millions! Imagination pants, reason grows dizzy, arithmetic fails to fathom, and human eyes fear to look into the abyss. No wonder that this profound astronomer, when a glimpse of infinity flashed on his eye, retired from the telescope, trembing in every nerve, afraid to behold.

And yet this astounding supposition is a literal truth; and the light of those suns, whose twilight thus bowed down that mighty intellect in reverent adoration, now shines before human eyes in all its noon-day refulgence. One of the most remarkable of these nebulæ—one which is visible to a good eye in the belt of Orion—has been disclosed to the observers at Parsontown as a firmament; and minute points, scarce perceptible to common telescopes, blaze forth as magnificent clusters of glorious stars, so close and crowded, that no figure can adequately describe them, save the twin symbol of the promise, "the sand by the sea-shore," or "the dust of the earth." "There is a minute point, near Polaris," says Nicholl, "so minute, that it requires a good telescope to discern its being. I have seen it as represented by a good mirror, blazing like a star of the first magnitude; and though examined by a potent microscope, clear and definite as the distinctest of these our nearest orbs, when beheld through an atmosphere not disturbed. Nay, through distances of an order I shall scarcely name, I have seen a mass of orbs compressed and brilliant, so that each touched on each other, *like the separate grains of a handful of sand*, and yet there seemed no melting or fusion of any one of the points into the surrounding mass. Each sparkled individually its light pure and apart, like that of any constituent of the cluster of the Pleiades." *

"The larger and nearer masses are seen with sufficient distinctness to reveal the grand fact decisive of their character, viz.: that

---

* Architecture of the Heavens, 62.

they consist of multitudes of closely related orbs, forming an independent system. In other cases we find the individual stars by no means so clearly defined. Through effect, in all probability, of distance, the intervals between them appear much less, the shining points themselves being also fainter; while the masses still further off *may be best likened to a handful of golden sand, or, as it is aptly termed, star-dust;* beyond which no stars, or any vestige of them, are seen, but only a patch or streak of milky light, similar to the unresolved portions of our surrounding zone." *

To say, then, that the stars of the sky are actually innumerable, is only a cold statement of the plainest fact. Hear it in the language of one privileged to behold the glories of one out of the thousands of similar firmaments: "The mottled region forming the lighter part of the mass (the nebula in Orion) is a very blaze of stars. But that stellar creation, now that we are freed from all dubiety concerning the significance of those hazes that float numberless in space, how glorious, how endless! Behold, amid that limitless ocean, every speck, however remote or dim: a noble galaxy. Lustrous they are, too: in manifold instances beyond all neighboring reality—beyond the loftiest dream which ever exercised the imagination. The great cluster in Hercules has long dazzled the heart with its splendors, but we have learned now that among circular and compact galaxies, a class to which the nebulous stars belong, there are multitudes which infinitely surpass it —nay, that schemes of being rise above it, sun becoming nearer to sun, until their skies must be one blaze of light—a throng of burning activities! But, far aloft stands Orion, the pre-eminent glory and wonder of the starry universe! Judged by the only criticism yet applicable, it is perhaps so remote that its light does not reach us in less than fifty or sixty thousand years; and as at the same time it occupies so large an apparent portion of the heavens, how stupendous must be the extent of the nebula. It would seem almost as if all the other clusters hitherto gaged were collected and compressed into one, they would not surpass this mighty group, *in which every wisp—every wrinkle—is a sand-heap of stars.* There are cases in which, though Imagination has quailed, Reason may still adventure enquiry, and prolong its speculations; but at times we are brought to a limit across which no human faculty has the

---

* Architecture of the Heavens, 64.

strength to penetrate, and where, as now, at the very footstool of the secret THRONE, we can only bend our heads, and silently *adore*. And from the inner Adyta—the invisible shrine of what alone is and endures—a voice is heard:

"Hast thou an arm like God?
"Canst thou thunder with a voice like him?
"Canst thou bind the sweet influences of the Pleiades,
"Or loosen the bands of Orion?
"Canst thou bring forth Mazzaroth in his seasons?
"Canst thou guide Arcturus and his sons?*
"He telleth the number of the stars:
"He calleth them all by their names.
"Great is our Lord, and of great power;
"His understanding is infinite." †

Thus, nobly does Science vindicate Scripture, and display the wisdom and power of the Lord of Hosts, whose kingdom extends through all space, and endures through all duration. He who called these countless hosts of glorious orbs into being, is abundantly able to multiply to an equally incalculable number, the humble sands which line the oceans of terrestrial grace: the brilliant stars which shall yet adorn the heavens of celestial glory. All, of every nation, who shall partake of Abraham's faith, are Abraham's children. They are Christ's, and so Abraham's seed, and heirs, according to this promise.‡ When the great multitude, which no man can number, out of every nation, and tongue, and people, stand before the throne of God, and cause the many mansions of our Father's house to re-echo the shout, "Salvation to our God which sitteth on the throne, and to the Lamb," the answering hallelujah's of the most distant orbs shall expound the purport of that solemn oath to Abraham and Abraham's seed: "By myself have I sworn, saith the Lord, because thou hast done this thing, and hast not withheld thy son, thine only son, from me; that in blessing I will bless thee, and *in multiplying I will multiply thy seed, as the stars of the heaven, and as the sand which is upon the sea-shore.*" ₰

5. It is not probable that the mysteries of the distant heavens, or of those future glories of the redeemed which the Bible employs

---

* Architecture of the Heavens, 144. ‡ Gen. 22:16.
† Job, 38:31. Ps. 147:4. ₰ Gal. iii, 14:29.

them to symbolize, will ever be fully explored by man, or adequately apprehended in the present state of being. But it is most certain that God would not have employed the mysteries of astronomy so frequently as the symbols of the mysteries of the glory to be revealed, had there not been some correspondence between the things which eye hath not seen, and these patterns shown in the mount. So habitual, indeed, is the scripture use of these visible heavens as the types of all that is exalted, pure, cheering, and glorious, that, to most christians, the word has lost its primary meaning, and the idea first suggested to their minds by the word *heaven* is, that of future glory; yet their views of the locality and physical adornments of the many mansions of their Father's house, are dim and shadowy, just because they do not acquaint themselves sufficiently with the Divine descriptions in the Bible, and the Divine illustrations in the sky. The Bible would be better understood were the heavens better explored. "I go," said Jesus, "to prepare a *place* for you." The bodies of the saints, raised on the resurrection morn, will need a *place* on which to stand. The body of the Lord, which his disciples handled, and "saw that a spirit had not flesh and bones, as they saw him have," is now resident in a place. Where he is, there shall his people be also. Why, then, when the Bible employs all that is beauteous in earth, and glorious in heaven, to describe the adornments of the palace of the King of kings, should we hesitate to believe that the power and wisdom of God are not exhausted in this little earth of ours, but that other worlds may as far transcend ours in glory, as many of them do in magnitude?—or, to allow that the glorious visions of Ezekiel and John were not views of nonentities, or mere visions of clouds, or of some incomprehensible symbols of more incomprehensible spiritualities, but actual views of the existing glories of some portion of the universe, presented to us as vividly as the dullness of our minds and the earthliness of our speech will permit? It is certain that the recent progress of astronomical discovery has revealed celestial scenery which illustrates some of the most mysterious of these visions.

It has long been known, that "one star differeth from another star in glory," and that the orbs of heaven shine with various colors. Sirius is white, Arcturus red, and Procyon yellow. The telescope shows all the smaller stars in various colors. Under the clear skies of Syria their brilliance is vastly greater than in our climate. "*One star shines like a ruby, another as an emerald, and the whole heavens sparkle as with various gems.*" * But the discovery of the double and triple stars has added a new harmony of colors to these coronets of celestial jewels. These stars generally display the complementary colors. If the one star displays a color from the red end of the spectrum, the other is generally of the corresponding shade, from the violet end. For instance, in 0^3 Cygni, the large star is yellow, and the two smaller stars are blue; and so in others, through all the colors of the rainbow. "It may be easier suggested in words," says Sir John Herschell, "than conceived in imagination, what a variety of illumination two stars —a red and a green, or a yellow and blue one—must afford a planet circulating around either, and what cheering contrasts and grateful vicissitudes a red and a green day, for instance, alternating with a white one, and with darkness, must arise from the presence or absence of one, or other, or both, from the horizon." † But suppose one of the globular clusters—for instance, that in the constellation Hercules—thus constituted; its unnumbered thousands of suns, wheeling round central worlds, and exhibiting their glories to their inhabitants: "skies blazing, with grand orbs scattered regularly around, and with a profusion to which our darker heavens are strangers;" the overhead sky, seen from the interior regions of the cluster, *must appear gorgeous beyond description.*" In the strictest literality it might be said to the dwellers in such a cluster, "Thy sun shall no more go down, neither shall thy moon withdraw herself." The surrounding walls of such a celestial palace must seem indeed "garnished with all manner of precious stones." Sapphire, emerald, sardius, chrysolite, and pearl, must seem but dim mirrors of its glorious refulgence. Under its ever rising suns the gates need not be shut at all by day, "for there shall be no night there." That glorious place now exists, though far away.

But the Lord of these Hosts has said, "Behold, I come quickly." He will not tarry. A thousand times faster than the swiftest chariot, our Solar System and the surrounding firmament wing their flight towards that same glorious cluster in Hercules. As our firmament approaches, under the guidance of Omnipotent wisdom, it too must fly to meet our Sun, with a velocity increasing with an incalculable ratio. The celestial city will then be seen to descend

---

* Architecture of the Heavens, 217.   † Architecture of the Heavens, 77, 130.

from heaven. Once within the sphere of its attractions, our Sun and surrounding planets will feel their power. Their ancient orbits and accustomed revolutions must give way to the higher power. Old things must pass away, and all things become new. A new heaven, no less than a new earth, will form the dwelling of righteousness.

These are no longer the visions of prophecy merely, but the sober calculations of mathematical science, based upon a foundation as solid as the attraction of gravitation, and as wide as the existence of that ether whose undulations convey the light of the most distant stars; for, so surely as that attraction is efficient, must all the firmaments of the heavens be drawn more closely together; and as certainly as they revolve not in empty space, but in a medium capable of retarding Encke's comet three days in every revolution, must that retarding medium bring their revolutions to a close. "And so," said Herschell, casting his eye fearlessly towards future infinities, "we may be certain that the stars in the Milky Way will be gradually compressed, through successive stages of accumulation, until they come up to what may be called the ripening period of the globular cluster." Unnumbered ages may be occupied with such a grand evolution of celestial progress, beyond our powers of calculation; but will the changes of created things, even then, have come to an end? Hear again the voice, not of the prophet, but of the astronomer: "Around us lie stabilities of every order; but it is *stability* only that we see, not *permanence*. As the course of our enquiry has already amply illustrated, even majestic systems, that at first appear final and complete, are found to resolve themselves into mere steps or phases of still loftier progress. Verily, it is an astonishing world! Change rising above change—cycle growing out of cycle, in majestic progression—each new one ever widening, like the circles that wreathe from a spark of flame, enlarging as they ascend, finally to become lost in the empyrean! And if all that we see, from earth to sun, and from sun to universal star-work—that wherein we best behold images of Eternity, Immortality, and God—if that is only a state or space of a course of being rolling onward evermore, what must be the Creator, the Preserver, the Guide of all! —He at whose bidding these phantasms came from nothingness,

---

* Architecture of the Heavens, 300.

and shall again disappear;—whose name, amid all things, alone is *Existence*—I AM THAT I AM?

"Of old hast thou laid the foundations of the earth,
"And the heavens are the works of thy hands;
"They shall perish,
"But thou shalt endure;
"Yea, all of them shall wax old, like a garment:
"As a vesture shalt thou change them, and they shall be changed;
"But thou art the same,
"And thy years shall have no end.
"The children of thy servants shall continue,
"And their seed shall be established before thee."

PSALM cii: 25.

"And I saw a new heaven, and a new earth;
"For the first heaven and the first earth were passed away,
"And there was no more sea.
"And I, John, saw the Holy City, New Jerusalem,
"Coming down from God, out of heaven,
"Prepared, as a bride, adorned for her husband.
"And I heard a great voice, out of heaven, saying,
"Behold the tabernacle of God is with men,
"And he will dwell with them,
"And they shall be his people,
"And God himself shall be with them, and be their God."

REVELATIONS, xxi.

Reader, is this glorious heaven your inheritance? Is this Unchangeable Jehovah your God? Are you looking for and hasting unto the coming of the day of God? Is it your daily prayer, Even so, Lord Jesus, come quickly!

No. 34.

SCIENCE, OR FAITH?

'FAITH is destined to be left behind in the onward march of the human intellect. It belongs to an infantile stage of intellectual development, when experience, dependent on testimony, becomes the slave of credulity. Children and childish nations are prone to superstition. Religion belongs properly to such. But as man advances into the knowledge of the physical sciences, and becomes familiarized with mathematical demonstration and scientific experiment, he demands substantial proofs for all kinds of knowledge, and rejects that which is merely matter of faith. Science thus becomes the grave of religion, as religion is vulgarly understood. But science gives a new and better religion to the world. Instead of filling men's minds with the vague terrors of an unknown futurity, it directs us to the best modes of improving this life.'—"This life being the first in certainty, give it the first place in importance; and by giving human duties in reference to men the *precedence*, secure that all interpretations of spiritual duty shall be in harmony with human progress."—"Nature refers us to science for help, and to humanity for sympathy; love to the lovely is our only homage, study our only praise, quiet submission to the inevitable our duty; and truth is our only worship."—"Our *knowledge* is confined to this life; and *testimony*, and *conjecture*, and *probability*, are all that can be set forth in regard to another." "Preach nature and science, morality and art; *nature, the only subject of knowledge;* morality the harmony of action; art the culture of the individual and society."*

Such is the language now used by a large class of half-educated people, who, deriving their philosophy from Comte, and their religion from the Westminster Review, invite us to spend our Sabbaths in the study of nature in the fields and museums, turn our churches into laboratories, exchange our Bibles for encyclopedias, give ourselves no more trouble about religion, but try hard to learn as much science, make as much money, and enjoy as much pleasure in this life as we can; because we

---

* Holyoake *Discussion with Grant*, and, *Discussion with Townley*, passim.

know that we live now, and can only *believe* that we shall live hereafter. I do not propose to take any notice here of the proposal of Secularism—for that is the new name of this old ungodliness—to deliver men from their lusts by scientific lectures, and keep them moral by overturning religion. That experiment has been tried already.* But it is worth while to inquire, Is science really so positive, and religion so uncertain as these persons allege? Is a knowledge of the physical sciences so all-sufficient for our present happiness, so attainable by all mankind, and so certain and infallible, that we should barter our immortality for it? And on the other hand, are the great facts of religious experience, and the foundations of our religious faith, so dim, and vague, and utterly uncertain, that we may safely consign them to oblivion, or that we can so get rid of them if we would?

The object of this tract is to refute both parts of the secularist's statement—to show some of the uncertainties, errors, contradictions, and blunders of the scientific men on whose testimony they receive their science—and to exhibit a few of the facts of religious experience which give a sufficient warrant for the Christian's faith.

I. *The students of the Physical Sciences, have no such certain knowledge of their facts or theories, as Secularists pretend.*

1. To begin with the most positive, *Mathematics*—the science of magnitude and numbers. How very few subjects are capable of a mathematical demonstration. *No fact* whatever which depends on the will of God or man can be so proved. For mathematical demonstration is founded on necessary and eternal relations, and admits of no contingencies in its premises. The mathematician may demonstrate the size and properties of a triangle, but he can not demonstrate the continuance of any actual triangle for one hour, or one minute, after his demonstration. And if he could, how many of my most important affairs can I submit to the multiplication table, or lay off in squares and triangles? It deals with purely ideal figures, which never did or could exist. There is not a mathematical line—length without breadth—in the universe. When we come to the appli-

---

* See Tract No. 25, *Have we any need of the Bible?*

cation of mathematics, we are met at once by the fact that there are no mathematical figures in nature. It is true we speak of the orbits of the planets as elliptical or circular, but it is only in a general way, as we speak of a circular saw, the outline of its teeth being regularity itself compared with the perturbations of the orbits of the planets. We speak of the earth as a spheroid; but it is a spheroid pitted with hollows as deep as the ocean, and crusted with irregular protuberances as vast as the Himmalaya and the Andes, in every conceivable irregularity of form. Its sea coasts and rivers follow no straight lines nor geometrical curves. There is not an acre of absolutely level ground on the face of the earth; and even its waters will pile themselves up in waves, or dash into breakers, rather than remain perfectly level for a single hour. Its minuter formations present the same regular irregularity of form. Even the crystals, which approach the nearest of any natural productions to mathematical figures, break with compound irregular fractures at their bases of attachment. The surface of the pearl is proportionally rougher than the surface of the earth, and the dew-drop is not more spherical than a pear. As nature then gives no mathematical figures, mathematical measurements of such figures can be only approximately applied to natural objects.

The utter absence of any regularity, or assimilation to the spheroidal figure, either in meridional, equatorial, or parallel lines, mountain ranges, sea beaches, or courses of rivers, is fatal to mathematical accuracy in the more extended geographical measurements. It is only by taking the mean of a great many measurements that an approximate accuracy can be obtained. Where this is not possible, as in the case of the measurements of high mountains, the truth remains undetermined by hundreds of feet; or as in the case of the earth's spheroidal axis, Bessel's measurement differs from Newton's, by fully eleven miles.* The smaller measures are proportionably as inaccurate. No field, hill, or lake has an absolute mathematical figure; but its outline is composed of an infinite multitude of irregular curves too minute for man's vision to discover, and too numerous for his intellect to estimate. No natural figure was ever measured with

---

* Humboldt, *Cosmos*, Vol. I, p. 7, 156.

absolute accuracy. In regard then even to the very limited circle of our relations which can be measured by the foot rule, and the small number of our anxieties which may be resolved by an equation—if by mathematical accuracy be meant any thing more than tolerable correctness, or by mathematical demonstration a very high degree of probability—mathematical certainty is all a fable.

2. *Astronomy*, from the comparative simplicity of the forces with which it has to deal, and the approximate regularity of the paths of the heavenly bodies, may be regarded as the science in which the greatest possible certainty is attainable. It opens at once the widest field to the imagination, and the noblest range to the reason, has attracted the most exalted intellects to its pursuit, and has rewarded their toils with the grandest discoveries. These discoveries have been grossly abused by inferior minds, ascribing to the discoverers of the laws of the universe, the glory due to their Creator; and boasting of the power of the human mind, as if it were capable of exploring the infinite in space, and of calculating the movements of the stars through eternity. And persons who could not calculate an eclipse to save their souls, have risked them upon the notion that, because astronomers can do so with considerable accuracy, farmers ought to reject the Bible, unless its predictions can be calculated by algebra. It may do such persons good, or at least prevent them from doing others harm, to take a cursory view of the errors of astronomers.

Sir John Herschell, than whom none has a better right to speak on this subject, and whose devotion to that noble science precludes all supposition of prejudice against it, devotes a chapter to *The Errors of Astronomy*,* which he classifies and enumerates:

"1st. External causes of Error, comprehending such as depend on external uncontrollable cricumstances; such as fluctuations of weather, which disturb the amount of refraction from its tabulated value, and being reducible to no fixed laws, induce uncertainty to the amount of their own possible magnitude.

2d. Errors of observation; such as arise for instance from inexpertness, defective vision, slowness in seizing the exact instant

---

* *Outlines of Astronomy*, III, 213, 140.

of the occurrence of a phenomenon, or precipitancy in anticipating it; from atmospheric indistinctness, insufficient optical power in the instrument, and the like.

3d. The third and by far the most numerous class of errors arise from causes which may be deemed instrumental, and which may be divided into two classes.

The first arises from an instrument not being what it professes to be, which is *error of workmanship*. Thus if an axis or pivot, instead of being as it ought, exactly cylindrical, be slightly flattened or elliptical—if it be not exactly concentric with the circle which it carries—if this circle so called be in reality not exactly circular—or not in one plane—if its divisions, intended to be precisely equi-distant, shall be in reality at unequal intervals—*and a hundred other things of the same sort.*

The other subdivision of instrumental errors comprehends such as arise from an instrument not being placed in the position it ought to have; and from those of its parts which are made purposely movable not being properly disposed, *inter se.* These are *errors of adjustment.* Some are unavoidable, as they arise from a general unsteadiness of the soil or building in which the instruments are placed. Others again are consequences of imperfect workmanship; as when an instrument once well adjusted, will not remain so. But the most important of this class of errors arise from the non-existence of natural indications other than those afforded by astronomical observations themselves, whether an instrument has, or has not, the exact position with respect to the horizon and the cardinal points, etc., which it ought to have, properly to fulfill its object.

Now with regard to the first two classes of error it must be observed, that in so far as they can not be reduced to known laws, and thereby become the subjects of calculation and due allowance, *they actually vitiate to their full extent the results of any observations in which they subsist.* With regard to errors of adjustment, not only the possibility, *but the certainty of their existence in every imaginable form, in all instruments*, must be contemplated. *Human hands or machines never formed a circle, drew a straight line, or executed a perpendicular, nor ever placed an instrument in perfect adjustment, unless accidentally, and then only during an instant of time.*"

The bearing of these important and candid admissions of error in astronomical observations, upon all other kinds of observations made by mortal eyes, and with instruments framed by human hands, in every department of science, is obvious. No philosophical observation or experiment is absolutely accurate, or can possibly be more than tolerably near the truth. The error of a thousandth part of an inch in an instrument will multiply itself into thousands and millions of miles according to the distance of the object, or the profundity of the calculation. Our faith in the absolute infallability of scientific observers, and consequently in the absolute certainty of science, being thus rudely upheaved from its very foundations by Sir John Herschell's crowbar, we are prepared to learn that scientific men have made errors great and numerous.

To begin at home, with our own little globe, where certainty is much more attainable than among distant stars; we have seen that astronomers of the very highest rank are by no means agreed as to its diameter. Its precise form is equally difficult to determine. Newton showed that an ellipsoid of revolution should differ from a sphere by a compression of $\frac{1}{230}$. The mean of a number of varying measurements of arcs, in five different places, would give $\frac{1}{299}$. The pendulum measurement differs very considerably from both, and "no two sets of pendulum experiments give the same result."* The same liability to error, and uncertainty of the actual truth, attends the other modes of ascertaining this fundamental measurement. A very small error here will vitiate all other astronomical calculations; for the earth's radius, and the radius of its orbit, are the foot-rule and surveyors' chain with which the astronomer measures the heavens.— But this last and most used standard, is uncertain by 360,000 miles!†

While such uncertainty prevails regarding the shape, size and distance of our own abode, we need not expect any greater infallibility regarding more distant bodies. Leslie's experiments prove to him that the moon's light is $\frac{1}{150000}$ part that of the sun; Bouguer's experiments make it only half as much; and Wollaston says it is only $\frac{1}{800000}$.‡ Bianchini gives 24 days 8 hours as the period of the rotation of Venus on her axis; Schroeter

---

* Somerville's *Connection of the Physical Sciences*, Section VI.
† Cosmos, Vol. IV, p. 477.
‡ *The Christian Philosopher*, by Thomas Dick, L.L. D., p. 82.

makes it only 23 hours 20 minutes; Sir Wm. Herschell can not tell which is right, or whether both are wrong.* One astronomer fixes the period of the Sun's revolution at 25 days 14 hours 8 minutes; another at 26 days 46 minutes; another still at 24 days 28 minutes.† Svanberg finds the cold of absolute space—the empty places around the stars—to be, —58°; Arago, —70°; Humboldt, —85°; Herschell, —132°; Poullett to be exact to a fraction, —$223\frac{6}{10}°$, though when it gets so cold as that one would hardly be particular about the fraction of a degree; but Poisson thinks he is over 200 degrees too cold, and fixes it accurately, in his own opinion, at $+8\frac{6}{10}°$.‡ Ten or twelve years ago Mercury was believed to be 2.94 times the density of the Earth, and the Developement Theory was founded partly upon the assumed fact; but Hansen finds that, compared with the Earth, it is only 1.22, and that its mass is only $\frac{5}{12}$ of what had been confidently calculated.‖

The omniscience and prescience of the human intellect have been largely glorified by some infidel lecturers, upon the strength of the accuracy with which it is possible to calculate and predict eclipses, and to the disparagement of Bible predictions. And this glorification has been amazingly swollen by Le Verrier's prediction in 1846 of the discovery of the planet Neptune. But the prediction of some unknown motion would form a more correct basis for a comparison of the prophesies of science with those of scripture; such for instance as Immanuell Kant's prediction of the period of Saturn's rotation at 6 hours 23 minutes 53 seconds; "which mathematical calculation of an unknown motion of a heavenly body," he says, "*is the only prediction of that kind in pure Natural Philosophy*, and awaits confirmation at a future period." It is a pity that this unique scientific prediction should not have had better luck, for the encouragement of other guessers; but after waiting long and vainly, for the expected confirmation, it was finally falsified by Herschell's discovery of spots on the surface of the planet, and observation of the true time, 10 hours 16 minutes 44 seconds.§ This, however, was not his only astronomical prediction. He predicted that immense bodies in a transition state between planets and comets, and of very eccentric orbits, would be found beyond the orbit of Saturn,

---

* Kendall's *Uranography*, p. 211.
† *Cosmos*, 4–378.   ‡ Ib., 3–43.   ‖ Ib., 4–474.
§ *Cosmos*, 4, 518.   Dick's *Celestial Scenery*, chap. III, Sec. 7.

and intersecting it, but it is scarcely necessary to say that no such bodies have been discovered. Uranus and Neptune have no cometary character whatever, their orbits are less eccentric than others and do not intersect, nor approach within millions of miles of Saturn's orbit. The verification of Le Verrier's prediction affords even a more satisfactory proof of the necessarily conjectural character of astronomical computations of unknown quantities and distances. The planet Neptune has not one half the mass which he had calculated; his orbit, which was calculated as very elliptical, is nearly circular; and the error of the calculation of his distance, is only three hundred millions of miles!*

"Let us then be candid," says Loomis, "and claim no more for astronomy than is reasonably due. When in 1846 Le Verrier announced the existence of a planet hitherto unseen, and when he assigned it its exact position in the heavens, and declared that it shone like a star of the eighth magnitude, and with a perceptible disc, *not an astronomer of France, and scarce an astronomer in Europe, had sufficient faith in the prediction to prompt him to point his telescope to the heavens.* But when it was announced that the planet had been seen at Berlin, that it was found within one degree of the computed place, that it was indeed a star of the eighth magnitude, and had a sensible disc—then the enthusiasm not only of the public generally, but of astronomers also, was even more wonderful than their former apathy. The sagacity of Le Verrier was felt to be almost superhuman. Language could scarce be found strong enough to express the general admiration. The praise then lavished upon Le Verrier was somewhat extravagant. *The singularly close agreement between the observed and computed places of the planet was accidental.* So exact a coincidence could not reasonably have been anticipated. If the planet had been found even ten degrees from what Le Verrier assigned as its probable place, *this discrepancy would have surprised no astronomer.* The discovery would still have been one of the most remarkable events in the history of astronomy and Le Verrier would have merited the title of First Astronomer of the age."† If we should esti-

---

* *Cosmos*, 1, 75. Loomis' *Progress of Astronomy*, p. 34, 40.
† Loomis' *Progress of Astronomy*, p. 34., etc.

mate the infidel cosmogonies of third and fourth rate astronomers to be only as far from probability, as the sober computation of the First Astronomer of the Age was from truth, we should probably not err much more than three hundred millions of miles.

3. *Geology,* one of the most recent of the sciences, and in the hands of infidel nurses one of the most noisy, has been supposed to be antichristian. The supposition is utterly unfounded. Such of its facts as have been well ascertained have demonstrated the being, wisdom, and goodness of an Almighty Creator, with irresistible evidence. Nor though a wonderful outcry has been raised about the opposition between the records of the rocks and the records of the Bible, regarding the antiquity of the earth, has any one yet succeeded in proving such an opposition; for the plain reason that neither the Bible nor geology says how old it is. They both say it is very old. The Bible says, "In the beginning God created the heavens and the earth;" and by the use which it makes of the word *beginning,* leaves us to infer that it was long before the existence of the human race.† If the geologist could prove that the earth was six thousand millions of years older than Adam, it would contradict no statement of the Bible. The Bible reader, therefore, has no reason to question any well ascertained fact of geology. But when infidels come to us with their geological *theories* about the mode in which God made the earth, or in which the earth made itself, and how long it took to do it, and tell us that they have got scientific demonstration from the rocks that the Bible account is false, and that our old traditions can not stand before the irresistible evidence of science, we are surely bound to look at the foundation of facts, and the logical superstructure, which sustain such startling conclusions.

Now it is remarkable that every infidel argument against the statements of the Bible, or rather against what they suppose to be the statements of the Bible, is based, not on the *facts,* but upon the *theories,* of geology. I do not know one which is based solely on facts and inductions from facts. Every one of them has a wooden leg, and goes hobbling upon an *if.*

Take for example the argument most commonly used—that

---

† See this proved in Tract 32, *Daylight before Sunrise,* p. 228.

which asserts the vast antiquity of the earth—a thing in itself every way likely, and not at all contrary to Scripture, if it could be scientifically proved. But how does our infidel geologist set about his work of proving that the earth is any given age, say six thousand millions of years? A scientific demonstration must rest upon *facts*—well ascertained facts. It admits of *no suppositions.* Now what are the facts given to solve the problem of the earth's age? The geologist finds a great many layers of rocks, one above the other, evidently formed below the water, some of them out of the fragments of former rocks, containing bones, shells, and casts of fishes and tracks of the feet of birds, made when these rocks were in the state of soft mud, and altogether several miles thick. He has a great multitude of such facts before him, but they are all of this character. Not one of them gives him the element of time. They announce to him a succession of events, such as successive generations of fishes and plants; but not one of them tells how long these generations lived. The condition of the world was so utterly different then, from what it is now, that no inference can be drawn from the length of the lives of existing races, which are generally also of different species. The utmost any man can say, in such a case, is, *I suppose*, for there is no determinate element of time in the statement of the problems, and so no certain time can appear in the solution.

Here is a problem exactly similar. A certain house is found to be built with ten courses of hewn stone in the basement, forty courses of brick in the first story, thirty-six courses in the second, thirty-two in the third; with a roof of nine inch rafters covered with inch boards, and an inch and a half layer of coal tar and gravel; how long was it in building? Would not any school-boy laugh at the absurdity of attempting such a problem? He would say, "How can I tell unless I know whence the materials came, how they were conveyed, how many workmen were employed, and how much each could do in a day? If the brick had to be made by hand, the lumber all dressed with the handsaw and jack-plane, the materials all hauled fifty miles in an ox-cart, the brick carried up by an Irishman in a hod, and the work done by an old, slow-going, jobbing contractor who could only afford to pay three or four men at a time,—they would not get through in a year. But if the building stone and sand were found in excavating the cellar, the brick were made by steam and came by railroad, a good master builder, with steam saw and planing mills, steam hoists, and a strong force of workmen, would run it up in three weeks."

So our geologist ought to say; "I do not know either the source of the materials of the earth's strata, nor the means by which they were conveyed to their present positions; therefore I can not tell the time required for their formation. If the crust of the earth was created originally of solid granite, and the materials of the strata were ground down by the slow action of frost and rain, and conveyed to the ocean by the still slower agency of rivers and torrents—hundreds of millions of ages would not effect the work. But if the earth was created in such a shape as would rationally be considered the best adapted for future stratification—if its crust consisted of the various elements of which granite and other rocks are composed; if these materials were ejected in a granular or comminuted form, and in vast quantities by submarine volcanoes generated by the chemical action of these elements upon each other; and if, after being diffused by the currents of the ocean, and consolidated by its vast pressure, the underlying strata were baked and melted and crystallized into granite *—a very few centuries would suffice. Until these indispensible preliminaries are settled, geology can make no calculations of the length of time occupied by the formation of the strata."

But instead of saying so, he *imagines* that God chose to make the earth out of the most impossible materials, by the most unsuitable agencies, and with the most inadequate forces; and that therefore a long time was needed for the work. In short, to revert to our illustration of the house-building, he *supposes* that Almighty God built the earth with the ox-team, and employed only the same force in erecting the building, which he now uses for doing little jobbing repairs. Almost all geological computations of time are made upon the supposition that only the same agents were at work then which we see now, that they only wrought with the same degree of force, and that they produced just the same effects in such a widely different condition of the

---

* See the possibility of such a source of volcanic action, of such a formation of plutonic rocks, proved by Lyell. *Principles*, chs. XXXII & XII.

earth as then prevailed. It takes a year say to deposit mud enough at the bottom of the sea to make an inch of rock now; *and if mud was deposited no faster* when the geological strata were formed, they are as many years old as there are inches in eight or nine miles depth of strata. But this is not the scientific proof we were promised. How does he prove that mud was deposited at just the same rate then as now? The very utmost he can say is that it is a very probable supposition. I can prove it a very improbable supposition. But it is enough for my present purpose to point out that, probable or improbable, it is *only supposition*. No proof is given or can possibly be given for it. Any conclusion drawn from such premises can be only a *supposition* too. And so the whole fabric of geological chronology, upon the stability of which so many infidels are risking the salvation of their souls, and beneath which they are boasting that they will bury the Bible beyond the possibility of a resurrection, vanishes into a mere *unproved notion*, based upon an *if*.

It is truly astonishing, that any sober minded person should allow himself to be shaken in his religious convictions by the alleged results of a science so unformed and imperfect, as geologists themselves acknowledge their favorite science to be. "The dry land upon our globe occupies only *one fourth* of its whole superficies. All the rest is sea. How much of this fourth part have geologists been able to examine? and how small seems to be the area of stratification which they have explored? We venture to say not one *fiftieth part of the whole.*"* "Abstract or speculative geology—were it a perfect science, would present a history of the globe from its origin and formation, through all the changes it has undergone, up to the present time; describing its external appearance, its plants and animals, at each successive period. *As yet, geology is the mere aim to arrive at such knowledge;* and when we consider how difficult it is to trace the history of a nation, even over a few centuries, we can not be surprised at *the small progress geologists have made* in tracing the history of the earth through the lapse of ages. To ascertain the history of a nation possessed of written records is comparatively easy; but when these are wanting, we must examine the

---

* Sir David Brewster, K. H., D. C. L., F. R. S., *More Worlds than One*, p. 56.

ruins of their cities and monuments, and judge of them as a people from the size and structure of their buildings, and from the remains of art found in them. This is often a perplexing, always an arduous task; *much more so is it to decipher the earth's history.*"* "The canoes, for example, and stone hatchets found in our peat bogs afford an insight into the rude arts and manners of the earliest inhabitants of our island; the buried coin fixes the date of some Roman emperor; the ancient encampment indicates the districts once occupied by invading armies, and the former method of constructing military defenses; the Egyptian mummies throw light on the art of embalming, the rites of sepulture, or the average stature of ancient Egypt. This class of memorials yields to no other in authenticity, but it constitutes a small part only of the resources on which the historian relies; whereas in geology it forms the only kind of evidence which is at our command. For this reason *we must not expect to obtain a full and connected account of any series of events beyond the reach of history.*"† "There are no calculations more doubtful than those of the geologist."‡ In fact, no truly scientific geologist pretends that it stands on the same level with any authentic history, much less with the Bible record; inasmuch as the discovery of a single new fact may overturn the whole theory. "It furnishes us with no clue by which to unravel the unapproachable mysteries of creation. These mysteries belong to the wondrous Creator, and to him only. We attempt to theorize upon them, and to reduce them to law, and all nature rises up against us in our presumptuous rebellion. A stray splinter of cone bearing wood—a fish's skull or tooth—the vertebra of a reptile—the humerus of a bird—the jaw of a quadruped—all, any of these things, weak and insignificant as they may seem, become in such a quarrel too strong for us and our theory—the puny fragment in the grasp of truth forms as irresistible a weapon as the dry bone did in that of Sampson of old; and our slaughtered sophisms lie piled up, "heaps upon heaps," before it.§

The history of the progress of geology furnishes abundant proof of the truth of these admissions of weakness and falli-

---

* *Rudiments of Geology,* W. & R. Chambers, p. 10.
† Lyell's *Principles of Geology,* p. 3.   ‡ Miller, *Old Red Sandstone,* p. 25.
§ Hugh Miller, *Footprints of the Creator,* p. 313.

bility. The history of its theories, like that of their framers, begins with their birth and ends with their burial. Each new theory placed the tombstone upon the preceding, and inscribed it with the brief record of the antediluvian, "and he died." A busy, merry time they must have had with their Wernerian, Huttonian, and Diluvian hypotheses; not to mention the Hutchinsonian theory, the animal spirits flowing from the sun, the vegetative power of stones, and other sage and serious facts and theories, theological and philosophical, invented to account for the world's creation. "No theory," says Lyell, "could be so far fetched or fantastical as not to attract some followers, provided it fell in with the popular notion." "Some of the most extravagant systems were invented or controverted by men of acknowledged talent." A more amusing exhibition of philosophical absurdity can not be found than those chapters which he devotes to "The Historical Progress of Geology,"* unless perhaps the scientific discussions of the erudite acquaintances of Lemuel Gulliver.

Let it not be supposed that the progress of inductive science, and the prevalence of the Baconian philosophy have banished absurdities and contradictions from the sphere of Geology. It would require a man of considerable learning to find three geologists agreed either in their facts or in their theories. In a general way, indeed, we have the Catastrophists, with Hugh Miller, overwhelming the earth with dire convulsions in the geological eras, and upheaving the more conservative Lyell and the Progressionists; who affirm that all things continue as they were from the beginning of the world. And there is perhaps a general agreement now that the underlying *primitive* rocks, so called, are not primitive at all, as geologists thought twenty years ago; but like the foundations of a Chicago house, have been put in long after the building was finished and occupied. But then comes the question how they were inserted—whether as Elie de Beaumont thinks, the mountains were upheaved by starts, lever fashion, or as Lyell affirms, very gradually, and imperceptibly, like the elevation of a brick house by screws?† Nor is there the least likelihood of any future agreement among them; inasmuch as they can not agree either as to the thickness of the

---

* *Principles*, Chaps. III and IV. † Ib., Chap. XI.

earth's solid crust which is to be lifted, or the force by which it is to be done? Hopkins proves by astronomical observation that it is 800 miles thick. Lyell affirms that at twenty-four miles deep there can be no solid crust, for the temperature of the earth increases 1° for every 45 feet, and at that depth the heat is great enough to melt iron and almost every known substance. But then there is a difference between philosophers about this last test of solidity—those who believe in Wedgewood's Pyrometer, which was the infallible standard twenty years ago, asserting that the heat of melted iron is 21,000° F; while Professor Daniells demonstrates by another infallible instrument that it is only 2,786° F;* which is rather a difference. In one case the earth's crust would be over two hundred miles thick, in the other twenty-four. But then comes the great question, what is below the granite? and a very important one for any theory of the earth. It evidently underlies the whole foundation of speculative geology, whether we assume with De Beaumont and Humboldt, that "the whole globe, with the exception of a thin envelope, much thinner in proportion than the shell of an egg, is a fused mass, kept fluid by heat—a heat of 450,000° F., at the center, Cordier calculates—but constantly cooling, and contracting its dimensions;" and occasionally cracking and falling in, and "squeezing upward large portions of the mass;" "thus producing those folds or wrinkles which we call mountain chains;" or with Davy and Lyell, that the heat of such a boiling ocean below would melt the solid crust, like ice from the surface of boiling water—and with it the whole theory of the primeval existence of the earth in a state of igneous fusion, its gradual cooling down into continents and mountains of granite, the gradual abrasion of the granite into the mud and sand which formed the stratified rocks, and all the other brilliant hypotheses which have sparked out of this great internal fire. Instead of an original central heat he supposes that "we may *perhaps* refer the heat of the interior to chemical changes constantly going on in the earth's crust."† Now if the very foundations of the science are in such a state of fusion, and floating on a *perhaps*, would it not be wise to allow them to solidify a little before a man risks the salvation of his soul upon them?

---

* *Principles*, p. 530. † Ib., chap. XXXI.

Multitudes of the alleged facts of infidel geologists are as apocryphal as their theories. Thus in a recent ponderous quarto volume, the production of half a dozen philosophers, this identical impossible theory—of the cooling of the earth's crust down to solidity, while an irresistible central heat remains below—is presented to the world as an ascertained fact; we are informed of the discovery of a human skull 57,000 years old, *in good preservation*; asked to believe that two tiers of cypress snags could not be deposited in the delta of the Mississippi in less than 11,400 years; and to calculate that the delta of the Nile must have been a great many ages in growing to its present size, because it is quite certain that for the last 3,000 years *it has never grown at all.**

Nor have even the most respectable geologists failed to establish their fallibility, and to give ample employment to each other in correcting their omissions, mistakes and blunders; as a perusal of our scientific journals will abundantly prove. It were easy to fill a volume with such mistakes of geologists, but my limits restrict me to a single specimen, taken at random from the first scientific magazine which comes to my hand—the last number of Silliman's Journal; in a review of † "*The Geology of North America;* by Julius Marcoe, U. S. Geologist, and Professor of Geology in the Federal Polytechnic School of Switzerland; quarto, with maps and plates."

"The author describes the mountain systems of North America *as he supposes they must be,* according to the theoretical views of Elie de Beaumont." "Thus one single fossil—that one a species of pine, and only very much resembling the *Pinites Fleurotti* of Dr. Monguett, *establishes*—a connection between the New Red of France, and that of America. This is a very strong word for a geologist to use on evidence so small, *and so uncertain,* with the fate of 4,000 or 5,000 feet of rock at stake, and the beds beneath, containing "perhaps Belemnites." The prudent observer would have said, *establishes nothing;* and such is the fact." "*On such evidence* a region over the Rocky Mountains, which is 1,000 miles from North to South, and 800

---

* *Types of Mankind,* 329, 338, 337, 335.

† *The American Journal of Science and Art,* edited by Profs. Silliman & Dana, vol. XXVI, p. 235, 350.

miles from East to West, is for the most part colored in the maps as Triassic. Such a region would take in quite a respectable part of the continent of Europe." "We now know beyond any reasonable doubt, that all the country from the Platte to the British Possessions, and from the Mississippi to the Black Hills, is occupied by Cretaceous and Tertiary rocks. And as regards the region from the Platte southward to the Red River, very far the largest part *is known to be not Triassic*, while it is possible the Trias may occur in some parts of it." "It is unfortunate in its bearing on the progress of geological science to have false views about some 500,000 miles of territory, and much more besides, spread widely abroad through respectable journals, and transactions of distinguished European Societies." So much for the certainties of geology.

If space permitted, it would be easy to go over the whole circle of the sciences, and show similar uncertainties in them all. We have considered the three which are supposed to be the most positive. It is worthy of notice that the uncertainties of science increase just in proportion to our interest in it. It is very uncertain about all my dearest concerns, and very positive about what does not concern me. The greatest certainty is attainable in pure mathematics, which regards only ideal quantities and figures; but biology—the science of life—is utterly obscure. The astronomer can calculate with considerable accuracy the movements of distant planets, with which we have no intercourse; but where is the meteorologist bold enough to predict the wind and weather of next week, on which my crops, my ships, my life may depend? Heat, light and electricity may be pretty accurately measured and registered, but what physician can measure the strength of the malignant virus which is sapping the life of his patient? The chemist can thoroughly analyze any foreign substance, but the disease of his own body which is bringing him to the grave, he can neither weigh, measure nor remove. Science is very positive about distant stars and remote ages, but stammers and hesitates about the very life of its professors.

4. Such, then, are a few of the uncertainties, imperfections, and positive and egregious errors of science at its fountain head. To the actual investigator infallible certainty of any scientific fact is hardly possible, error exceedingly probable, and gross

blunders in fact and theory by no means uncommon. But how greatly diluted must the modified and hesitating conviction, possible to an actual observer, become, when, as is generally the case, a man is not an actual observer himself, but *learns his science at school.* Such a person leaves the ground of demonstrative science, and stands upon faith. The first question then to be proposed to one whose demonstrative certainty of the truths of physical science has disgusted him with a religion received on testimony and faith, is, How have you reached this demonstrative certainty in matters of science? Are you quite sure that your certainty rests not upon the testimony of fallible and erring philosophers, but solely upon your own personal observations and experiments?

To take only the initial standard of astronomical measurements—the earth's distance from the sun. Have you personally measured the earth's radius, observed the transit of Venus in 1769, from Lapland and Tahiti at the same time, calculated the sun's parrallax, and the eccentricity of the earth's orbit? Would you profess yourself competent to take even the preliminary observation for fixing the instruments for such a reckoning? Were you ever within a thousand miles of the proper positions for making such observations? Or have you been necessitated to accept this primary measure, upon the accuracy of which all subsequent astronomical measurers depend, merely upon hearsay and testimony, and subject to all those contingencies of error and prejudice, and mistakes of copyists, which, in your opinion, render the Bible so unreliable in matters of religion?

Or to come down to earth. You are a student of the stone book, with its enduring records graven in the rock forever; and perhaps have satisfied yourself that "under the ponderous strata of geological science the traditionary mythology and cosmogony of the Hebrew poet has found an everlasting tomb." But how many volumes of this stone book have you perused personally? You are quite indignant perhaps that theologians and divines, who have no practical or personal knowledge of geology, should presume to investigate its claims. Have you personally visited the various localities in South America, Siberia, Australia, India, Britain, Italy, and the South Seas, where the various formations are exhibited; and have you personally excavated from their matrices the various fossils which form the hieroglyphics of the science? Have you, in fact, ever seen one in a thousand of these minerals and fossils *in situ?* Or are you dependent on the tales of travelers, the specimens of collectors, the veracity of authors, the accuracy of lecturers, aided by maps of ideal stratifications, in rose-pink, brimstone-yellow, and indigo-blue, for your profound and glowing convictions of the irresistible force of experimental science, and of the shadowy vagueness of a religion dependent upon human testimony?

To come down considerably in our demands and confine ourselves to the narrow limits of the laboratory. You are a chemist perhaps, and proud, as most chemists justly are, of the accuracy attainable in that most palpable and demonstrative science. But how much of it is experimental science *to you?* How many of the 942 substances treated of in Turner's Chemistry have you analyzed? One half? One tenth? Would you face the laughter of a college class to-morrow upon the experiment of taking nine out of the nine hundred, reducing them to their primitive elements, giving an accurate analysis of their component parts, and combining them in the various forms described in that, or any other book, whose statements, because experimentally certain, have filled you with a dislike of Bible truths, which you must receive upon testimony? In fact, do you know any thing worth mention of the facts of science upon your own knowledge, except those of the trade by which you make your living?

Or, after all your boasting about scientific and demonstrative certainty, have you been obliged to receive the certainties of science "upon faith, and at second hand, and upon the word of another;" and to save your life you could not tell half the time who that other is, by naming the discoverers of half the scientific truths you believe? What! are you dependent on hearsay and probability for any little science you possess, having in fact never obtained any personal demonstration or experience of its first principles and measurements, nor being capable of doing so? Then let us hear no more cant from you about the uncertainty of a religion dependent upon testimony, and the certainties of experimental science. Whatever certainty may be attainable by scientific men—and we have seen that is not much—it is very certain you have got none of it. The very best you can have to wrap yourself in is a second hand assurance, grievously torn by rival schools, and needing to be patched every month by later discoveries. Your science, such as it is, *rests solely upon faith* in the testimony of philosophers, often contradictory and improbable, and always fallible and uncertain.

5. Nor would you cease to be dependent upon faith could you personally make all the observations and calculations of demonstrative science. The knowledge of these facts does not constitute science; it is merely the brick pile containing the materials for the building of science. Science is knowledge systematized. But if the parts of nature were not arranged after a plan, the knowledge of them could not be formed into a system.— Chaos is unintelligible. Our minds are so constituted that we look for order and regularity, and can not comprehend confusion. We possess this expectation of order before we begin to learn science, and without it would never begin the search after a system of knowledge. All scientific experiment is but a search after order, and order is only another name for intelligence—for God. Deprive us of this fundamental faith in cause and effect, order and regularity—of reason, in short—and science becomes as impossible to man as to the ourang outang. *All science, even in its first principles, rests upon faith.*

II. We may now proceed to inquire whether or not faith, which we have found so prevalent even among those who repudiate it, is a thing to be ashamed of; or if it be a sufficiently certain and reliable basis for human life and conduct.

1. We are met at the very outset by the great fact that God has so constituted the world and every thing in it, that *in all the great concerns of life we are necessitated to depend on faith;* without any possibility of reaching absolute certainty regarding the result of any ordinary duty. We sow without any certainty of a crop, or that we may live to reap it. We harvest, but our barns may be burned down. We sell our property for bank-bills, but who dare say they will ever be paid in specie? We start on a journey to a distant city, but even though you insure your life, who will insure that fire, or flood, or railroad collision may not send you to the land whence there is no return?

Science is the child of yesterday; but from the beginning of the world men have lived by faith. Before science was born, Cain tilled his ground without any mathematical demonstration that he should reap a crop. Abel fed his flock without any scientific certainty that he should live to enjoy its produce; and Tubal Cain forged axes and swords without any assurance that he should not be plundered of his wages. All the experience of mankind proves that experimental certainty regarding the most important business of this life is impossible. By what process of philosophical induction is religion alone put beyond the sphere of faith and hope? If religious duties are not binding on us, unless religion be scientifically demonstrated, then neither are moral obligations; for these two can not be separated. Is it really so, that none but scientific men are bound to tell truth and pay their debts, and that a person may not fear God and go to heaven unless he has graduated at college? The common sense of mankind declares that we live by faith, not by science.

2. *We demand the knowledge of truths of which science is profoundly ignorant.* Science is but an outlying nook of my farm, which I may neglect and yet have bread to eat. Faith is my house in which all my dearest interests are treasured. Of all the great problems and precious interests which belong to me as a mortal or an immortal, science knows nothing. I ask her whence I came? and she points to her pinions scorched over the abyss of primeval fire, her eyes blinded by its awful glare, and remains silent. I inquire what I am? but the strange and questioning *I* is a mystery which she can neither analyze nor measure. I tell her of the voice of conscience within me—she never heard it, and does not pretend to understand its oracles. I tell her of my anxieties about the future—she is learned only in the past. I inquire how I may be happy hereafter—but happiness is not a scientific term, and she can not tell me how to be happy here! Poor, blind science!

3. *All our dearest interests lie beyond the domains of science, in the regions of faith.* Science treats of things—faith is confidence in persons. Take away the persons, and of what value are the things? The world becomes at once a vast desert, a dreary solitude, and more miserable than any of its former inhabitants the lonely wretch who is left to mourn over the graves of all his former companions—the last man. Solitary science were awful. Could I prosecute the toils of study alone, without companion or friend to share my labors? Would I study eternally with no object, and for no use; none to be benefited, none

to be gratified by my discoveries? Though you hung maps on every tree, made every mountain range a museum, bored mines in every valley, and covered every plain with specimens, made Vesuvius my crucible, and opened the foundations of the earth to my view—yet would the discovery of a single fresh human footprint in the sand fill my heart with more true hope of happiness, than an endless eternity of solitary science. I can live, and love, and be happy without science, *but not without companionship, whose bond is Faith.*

Faith is the condition of all the happiness you can know on earth. Law, order, government, civilization, and family life, depend not upon science, but upon confidence in moral character —upon faith. In its sunshine alone can happiness grow. It is faith sends you out in the morning to your work, nerves your arms through the toils of the day, brings you home in the evening, gathers your wife and your children around your table, inspires the oft repeated efforts of the little prattler to ascend your knee, clasps his chubby arms around your neck, looks with most confiding innocence in your eye, and puts forth his little hand to catch your bread, and share your cup. Undoubting faith is happiness even here below. Need you marvel, then, that you must be converted from your pride of empty, barren science, and casting yourself with all your powers into the arms of faith, become as a little child before you can enter into the kingdom of heaven?

4. But religion is not founded upon faith as distinct from observation and experiment. *It is the most experimental of all the sciences.* There is less of theory, and more of experience in it than in any other science. Its faith is all practical. It is a great mistake to suppose that faith is the opposite pole of experience. On the contrary, experience is just the fruit which ripens from the blossom of faith. We have seen how an underlying conviction of the existence of an intelligent planner and upholder of the laws of nature is the source of all scientific experiment, and systematized knowledge. A similar underlying conviction of the existence of a moral governor of the world is the source of all religious experience. *He that cometh to God must believe that he is, and that he is the rewarder of those that diligently seek him.* But this fundamental axiom believed, long trains of experience follow: of every one of which

you can be, and actually are, infinitely more certain than of any fact of physical science. Your eyes, your ears, your touch, your instruments, your reason, may be deceived—but your consciousness can not. If your soul is filled with joy, that is a *fact.* You know it, and are as sure of it as you are that the sun shines. If you feel miserable, you are so. A sense of neglected duty, a consciousness that you have done wrong and are displeased with yourself for it; a certainty that God is displeased with you for wrong doing, and that he will show his displeasure by suitable punishment; the tenacious grasp of vicious habits on your body and soul, and the fearful thought that by the law of your nature these vipers which you vainly struggle to shake off, will for ever keep involving you more closely in their cursed coils—these are *facts of your experience.* You are as certain that they give you disquiet of mind, when you entertain them, as that the sea rages in a tempest; and that you can no more prevent their entrance, nor compel their departure, nor calm nor drown the anxiety they occasion, than you can prevent the rising of the tempest, dismiss the thunder-storm, or drown Etna in your wineglass. Of these primary facts of moral science, and of others like them, you possess the most absolute and infallible certainty from your own consciousness. They result from the inertia of moral matter, which, when put into a state of disturbance has no power of bringing itself to rest, expressed in the formula, *There is no peace, saith my God, to the wicked.**

Let us now go out of your own experience, as you must do in every other science, into the region of observation, and study a few of the other phenomena of religion. Your comrade, Jones, has taken to drinking of late, and also to going with you to Sunday lectures, and in the evening to other places of amusement. He has, however, been warned that the next time he comes drunk to the workshop he will be discharged; and as he is a clever young fellow, and knows more about the Bible than you, having gone to Sabbath-School when a boy, and is able to use up the saints cleverly, you would be sorry to lose his company. So you set on him to go with you to hear a temperance lecture, hoping he may be induced to take the pledge;

---

* Isaiah 48, 22.

for if he does not you fear he will soon lie in the gutter. He curses you and himself too, if ever he listens to any such stuff; and refuses to go. You can easily gather a hundred other illustrations of the great law of the moral repulsion between vice and truth, expressed in the following formula: *This is the condemnation, that light is come into the world, and men loved darkness rather than light, because their deeds were evil. For every one that doeth evil hateth the light, neither cometh to the light lest his deeds should be reproved.** Your life, however, is but a long illustration of this principle. Have you not willingly remained in ignorance of the contents of the Bible, because you dislike its commands?

There is another fact of the same science—there, in the gutter before you, wallowing in his own vomit, covered with rags, besmeared with mud, smelling worse than a hog, his bruised and bleeding mouth unable to articulate the obscenities and curses he tries to utter. "Is it possible that can be Bill Brown! Why only three years ago we worked at the same bench. It was he who introduced me to the Sunday Institute; as clever a workman and as jovial a comrade as I ever knew, but would get on a spree now and again. He had a good father and mother, got considerable schooling, had good wages, got married to a clever girl and had two fine children. Is it possible he could make such a beast of himself in such a short time?" Yes, quite possible, and more, quite certain. Not only in his case, but in all others, the law of moral gravitation is universal and infallible. *Evil men and seducers wax worse and worse.*† The degradation may not always be in this precise form, nor always as speedy—as all heavy bodies do not fall to the same place, nor with like rapidity. But it is always as certain and always as deep, and will one day be far more public. Fix it firmly in your mind. It concerns you more than all the science you will ever know. You too are in the course of sin and you know it. You have already begun to fall.

Come again into this room. "What, into a prayer meeting? I don't go to such places." But, if you want to study the phenomena of religion scientifically, you should go to such places; just as if you want to study geology you should go to the places

---

* John, 3d chap. † 2 Timothy, 3d ch. Read the whole chapter.

where the strata are exposed to view. I do not ask you to speak and ask people to pray for you, but only to look on and listen. If you are a philosopher I wish you to cease dogmatizing about fanaticism and enthusiasm and the ignorance and credulity of believers, at least until you philosophically examine the evidence upon which they believe. You can set aside, if you please, their unfounded beliefs concerning matters beyond their capacity, and also their confident hopes for futurity. What I wish you to examine is their *actual experience of religion*, as they severally relate it. For as we have seen, the facts of consciousness are just as certain, and as ascertainable, as the facts discovered by our senses; and there is no reason in the world why we should not pursue the study of religion in the same way that we gain a knowledge of science; namely, by collecting and studying the facts accumulated by those who have made experiments, and have obtained a practical knowledge of the matter.

There are here, as you see, a great number of religious experimenters. They are also of very various conditions of life, and of various degrees of education. Many of them are moreover well known to you, so that you are in a favorable position for forming a fair judgment of their discoveries. There is your comrade Smith, Hopkins who does the hauling for your establishment, Lawyer Hammond, Professor Edwards whose chemical lectures you attend, Dr. Lawrence who lectured before the Lyceum last winter, Mr. Heidenberger who wrote a series of articles on Compte's Positive Philosophy for the Investigator, Mrs. Bridgman, your Aunt Polly who nursed you during your typhoid fever, and a great many others whom you know quite well.— Professor Edwards leads in prayer, and gives a brief address. You never dreamt that he was hoaxing you when he told you of his chemical experience; have you any reason to offer for believing that he now solemnly and in the presence of God, lies to you and this assembly, when he tells you of the peace he has found in believing in Christ, and the happiness he experiences in uniting with his brethren in the worship of God? Or is he more liable to error in noting the fact of his mental joy or sorrow, than in observing the effect of the extraordinary ray in double refraction? If not, the fact that he has felt this religious experience, is just as certain as the fact, that he has seen polarized light.

There is your comrade Smith, whom you have known for years, actually got up to speak in meeting. You are surprised; but listen: "Neighbors and friends, most of you know I never cared much about religion, and was often given to take more liquor than was good for me, and then I would fight and curse awful bad. I knew as well as any body that it was n't right, and always felt bad after a spree, and many a time I said I would turn over a new leaf and be good. But it was all no use, for as soon as any of the fellows would come around after me, I always went along with them, till at last I gave it up, and said it was no use to try. Still, whenever any of my acquaintances died, I felt scared like; and I kept away as far as I could from churches and preachers and such like, because I could not bear to think about God and judgment to come. Well, about five weeks ago my little Minnie set on me one Sabbath morning to carry her to church, and to please the little creature—for she is as pert a darling as you could see anywhere—I told my wife to get her ready and we would go. She seemed as if she would cry, and kept talking to herself all the way. When we got into the church the singing almost upset me, for I had not been to a church since I was a little fellow, just before father and mother died. But it seemed as if it was the same tune, and as if the tune brought them all back, and I saw them again and all the family, and heard mother sing as she used to, and I forgot church and every thing, and thought I was a little fellow playing about on the floor just as I used to do when I was a happy child. When they stopped I was so sorry, and wished I could just be as innocent and as happy as I was then. Well, it seemed like the preacher had been reading my thoughts, for he gave out for his text, *Verily, verily I say unto you, unless a man be born again he can not see the kingdom of God.* He began to preach how Jesus can give us new hearts and save us from our sins; that his blood cleanses from all sin; that he is able to save to the uttermost all that come unto God through him. The tears came into my eyes, and I could hardly keep my mouth shut till I got out. When I got home I knelt down and cried to Jesus to save me from my sins; and my wife prayed too, and we cried for mercy. The Lord heard us, and I felt light and happy, and I went to church again, and sung with the rest.— And the best of it is, the Lord delivered me from the drink; as I told a man who asked where I was going to-day, and I told him I was going to prayer-meeting, for I had got religion now. He said there were a great many religions, and most of them wrong, and a great many people said all religion was only a notion, and preaching only nonsense. I says to him, "Look here, stranger, do you see that tavern there?" 'Yes,' says he. 'Well,' says I, 'do you see me?' 'I do, of course,' says he.— 'Well,' says I, 'every little fellow in these parts knows that so long as Tom Smith had a quarter in his pocket he could never pass that tavern without having a drink. All the men in Jefferson could not stop him. Now look here,' says I, 'there is my week's wages, and I can go past, and thank God I do n't feel the least like drinking, for the Lord Jesus has saved me from it. If you call that a notion, it is a mighty powerful notion, and it is a notion that has put clothes on my children's backs, and plenty of good food on my table, and songs of praise to the Lord in my mouth. *That's a fact, stranger.* Glory be to God for it. And I would recommend you to come to prayer meeting with me, and maybe you would get religion too. A great many people are getting religion now.'"

His last remark is certainly very true. There are so many, and of such various characters and grades of life, and in so many places, that every reader can easily find several Tom Smiths of his own acquaintance, whose conversions display all the essential facts of this case, and prove that:

5. The facts of religious experience *are better attested, and more unobjectionable* than those of any other science.

Unless they can be shown to be unreasonable or impossible, we are bound to receive them, when presented by the experimentists who have discovered them, though personally we may not have any such experience; just as we believe the chemists, or the astronomers who relate their discoveries which personally we have not observed. But the facts of religion are *by no means unreasonable*. They can not be shown to contradict any known law of the human mind. It is true they are mysterious. But so are the facts of physical science—heat, light, electricity, gravitation. Of either, we may be quite certain that such phenomena exist, and utterly ignorant of the mode of their operation. It were as utterly unphilosophical to deny that Almighty God could impart nervous energy to the languid limbs of your sick neighbor, because you are ignorant of its origin and means of transmission, as to deny that God could impart spiritual electricity to his paralyzed soul, because you are ignorant of the mode in which he bestows it. And ignorance is all that you can plead in this case. You must just admit that having tried an experiment which you have not, your religious friend has a right to know more than you.

Moreover, the facts of religion are presented for belief upon *the most abundant and reliable testimony*. In physical science you must rely on the testimony of a very few observers—the great bulk even of scientific men having no opportunity of testing the facts themselves, and being well satisfied if any fact is confirmed by the testimony of two or three philosophers—and this testimony often contradictory, and always fallible, as the discordant results of their experiments prove. But here you have a great multitude of experimentists, in every city and village of the land, of every variety of intellect and education, prosecuting the same course of experiments, and all arriving at the same results.—. They do not all confess the *same* sins, but they all felt the power of *some* sin, and felt miserable in their guilt. And however they may differ in their external circumstances, their inward constitution, or in their views of the outward part of religion, there is no difference among them about the great facts of their religious experience. They all believed the faithful saying that Christ Jesus came into the world to save sinners, cried to God for mercy through him, and received peace of mind, grace to live a new life, and to delight in the worship of God. Do you know any science which has been prosecuted by one hundredth part of this number of inquirers? Which has been confirmed by one thousandth part of this number of experimenters? Or any experiment tried with such uniform and unfailing success as this, *Whosoever shall call on the name of the Lord shall be saved?** Why then do you hesitate to admit the correctness of these facts? Is it because you perceive they lead to results which you dislike?

---

* Rom., 10 Ch. Read the chapter.

They do lead to results. They are effects and tell us of a cause. They are powerful effects, and proclaim a powerful cause. They are moral and spiritual effects, and assure us of the existence of a moral and spiritual agent who has caused them. They are holy effects, and convince your sinful soul that they are produced by a holy being. But they are also benevolent, life-giving, blessed effects, and proclaim that God is love. The Lord the Spirit is as plainly declared in the facts of religious experience, as the Creator is in the creation of the universe; and it were as rank Atheism to attribute these orderly and blessed results to chance or to evil passions, as to attribute the Cosmos to blind fate, or to the beasts that perish. He is as much an enemy to his happiness who denies the one, as a foe to his reason who rejects the other. Dear Reader, why should you not believe in,

6. *The only science which can make you happy?* which can bestow peace of mind, nerve you to conquer your evil habits, enable you to live a holy and happy life, and to die with a blessed hope of a glorious resurrection? You know there is no science which makes any such offers, or which you would believe if it did. But the Bible unfolds a science which does, and enables you to believe it too. The facts of religious experience give most convincing evidence of the reality and power of the grace of God. It were as easy to persuade a Christian that he had produced this change of heart and life by the excitement of his own feelings, as that he had kindled the sun with a lucifer match. And the character of the work and the worker assures him that it will not be left unfinished. His faith receives these facts of religious experience as the first installments upon God's bonds, and as pledges for the payment of the remainder of his promises. The joy and peace which God gives him now, prove most satisfactorily his ability and willingness to give him larger measures of these enjoyments when he is capable of receiving them. Just as we have good reason to believe that he who has made the sun to rise out of darkness will guide him onward in his course to perfect day, have we also good reason to believe that he that hath begun the good work of his grace in us will perform it until the day of Jesus Christ. Christ is in us the hope of glory. This eternal life, which is begun in our souls, is so much superior to mere animal vitality, that we can not doubt that he who has given us the greater, will also give us the

lesser, and quicken our mortal bodies also, by his Spirit which dwelleth in us. We know that our Redeemer liveth.

7. And now in conclusion, Dear Reader, we ask you not to take these things on our testimony, nor yet on our experience; *but to try for yourself.* O taste and see that the Lord is good. Come see the Savior who has saved us, and be saved by him too. There is nothing more dangerous, unless resisting the evidence of the truth as it is in Jesus, than acknowledging this to be truth without immediately obeying the gospel. God requires your immediate and cordial acceptance of Christ to save you from your sins. He tells you that the only way of escape from your sins now and from hell hereafter is through him; for there is none other name given under heaven or among men whereby you must be saved. He promises to hear your prayer and give you his Holy Spirit to work in you the work of faith with power, if you will only and earnestly ask. '*Ask, and it shall be given you. Seek and ye shall find. Knock and it shall be opened unto you. What man is there of you whom, if his son ask bread, will he give him a stone? Or if he ask a fish will he give him a serpent? If ye then being evil know how to give good gifts unto your children, how much more shall your Heavenly Father give the Holy Spirit to them that ask him.*' *

Thus you will come to possess an actual experimental knowledge of the most excellent of the sciences. In the present begun enjoyment of eternal life you will, not merely believe in, but positively *know*, its Author, the only true God, and Jesus Christ whom he hath sent. You will rest in no fallible and erring testimony of man's wisdom, but your faith will stand in the power of God. You will be able to say, *Now I believe, not because of thy sayings, for I have seen him myself,* and KNOW *that this is indeed the Christ the Savior of the world.*†

Hear God's own warrant and invitation to your poor, thirsty soul, to forsake your vanities and come and be eternally blessed in Christ. Have the witness in yourself and be a living proof of the blessed reality of religion.

"Ho every one that thirsteth! Come ye to the waters!
And he who hath no money! Come ye buy and eat!

---

* The Sermon on the Mount. Read it all. † John, Chap. IV.

Yea come! Buy wine and milk without money and without
    price.
Wherefore do ye spend money for that which is not bread?
And your labor for that which satisfieth not?
Hearken diligently unto me and eat ye that which is good,
And let your soul delight itself in fatness.
Incline your ear and come unto me:
Hear and your soul shall live:
And I will make an everlasting covenant with you,
Even the sure mercies of David.
Behold! I have given him for a witness to the people,
A leader and a commander to the people:
Behold! thou shalt call nations that thou knowest not,
And nations that knew not thee shall run unto thee,
Because of the Lord thy God,
And for the Holy One of Israel, for he hath glorified thee.

Seek ye the Lord while he may be found,
Call ye upon him while he is near:
Let the wicked forsake his way,
And the unrighteous man his thoughts;
And let him return unto the Lord, and he will have mercy
    upon him,
And to our God for he will abundantly pardon.
For my thoughts are not your thoughts,
Neither are your ways my ways, saith the Lord.
For as the heavens are higher than the earth,
So are my ways higher than your ways,
And my thoughts than your thoughts.
For as the rain cometh down, and the snow from heaven,
And return not thither again,
But water the earth and cause it to bring forth and bud,
That it may give seed to the sower and bread to the eater;
So shall my word be that goeth forth out of my mouth:
It shall not return unto me void,
But it shall accomplish that which I please,
And it shall prosper in the thing whereto I sent it.
For ye shall go out with joy, and be led forth with peace.
The mountains and the hills shall break forth before you into
    singing,

And all the trees of the fields shall clap their hands.
Instead of the thorn shall come up the fir tree,
And instead of the brier shall come up the myrtle tree:
And it shall be to the Lord for a name,
For an everlasting sign that shall not be cut off."

316

www.ingramcontent.com/pod-product-compliance
Lightning Source LLC
Chambersburg PA
CBHW030808230426
43667CB00008B/1114